KT-521-482

THE INTERNET
AND WORKPLACE
TRANSFORMATION

Advances in Management Information Systems

Advisory Board

Eric K. Clemons
University of Pennsylvania

Thomas H. Davenport
Accenture Institute for Strategic Change
and
Babson College

Varun Grover
Clemson University

Robert J. Kauffman
University of Minnesota

Jay F. Nunamaker, Jr.
University of Arizona

Andrew B. Whinston
University of Texas

THE INTERNET AND WORKPLACE TRANSFORMATION

MURUGAN ANANDARAJAN
THOMPSON S.H. TEO
CLAIRE A. SIMMERS
EDITORS

ADVANCES IN MANAGEMENT
INFORMATION SYSTEMS
VLADIMIR ZWASS SERIES EDITOR

M.E.Sharpe
Armonk, New York
London, England

References to the AMIS papers should be as follows:

Caplan, S.E. Problematic Internet use in the workplace. M. Anandarajan, T.S.H. Teo,
and C.A. Simmers, eds., *The Internet and Workplace Transformation: Advances in
Management Information Systems*, Volume 7 (Armonk, NY: M.E. Sharpe, 2006), 63–79.

ISBN-13 978-0-7656-1445-2
ISBN-10 0-7656-1445-6
ISSN 1554-6152

Printed in the United States of America

The paper used in this publication meets the minimum requirements of
American National Standard for Information Sciences
Permanence of Paper for Printed Library Materials,
ANSI Z 39.48-1984.

∞

BM (c) 10 9 8 7 6 5 4 3 2 1

ADVANCES IN MANAGEMENT INFORMATION SYSTEMS

AMIS Vol. 1: Richard Y. Wang,
Elizabeth M. Pierce, Stuart E. Madnick,
and Craig W. Fisher
Information Quality
ISBN-13 978-0-7656-1133-8
ISBN-10 0-7656-1133-3

AMIS Vol. 2: Sergio deCesare,
Mark Lycett, and Robert D. Macredie
*Development of Component-Based
Information System*
ISBN-13 978-0-7656-1248-9
ISBN-10 0-7656-1248-8

AMIS Vol. 3: Jerry Fjermestad and
Nicholas C. Romano, Jr.
*Electronic Customer Relationship
Management*
ISBN-13 978-0-7656-1327-1
ISBN-10 0-7656-1248-1

AMIS Vol. 4: Michael J. Shaw
E-Commerce and the Digital Economy
ISBN-13 978-0-7656-1150-5
ISBN-10 0-7656-1150-3

AMIS Vol. 5: Ping Zhang and
Dennis Galletta
*Human-Computer Interaction and
Management Information Systems:
Foundations*
ISBN-13 978-0-7656-1486-5
ISBN-10 0-7656-1486-3

AMIS Vol. 6: Dennis Galletta and
Ping Zhang
*Human-Computer Interaction and
Management Information Systems:
Applications*
ISBN-13 978-0-7656-1487-2
ISBN-10 0-7656-1487-1

AMIS Vol. 7: Murugan Anandarajan,
Thompson S.H. Teo, and Claire A. Simmers
The Internet and Workplace Transformation
ISBN-13 978-0-7656-1445-2
ISBN-10 0-7656-1445-6

Forthcoming volumes of this series can be found on the series homepage.
www.mesharpe.com/amis.htm

Editor-in-Chief, Vladimir Zwass (zwass@fdu.edu)

CONTENTS

SERIES EDITOR'S INTRODUCTION

Vladimir Zwass

The transformational technologies of the Internet-Web compound have exerted a vast and readily apparent influence on the way we live and work. In the world regions of high Internet penetration, it has been changing the context and the content of work and making porous the boundary between work and private life. It then behooves us to include in the *Advances in Management Information Systems* (AMIS) series this volume that presents the research on the transformation of the workplace by the use of these information technologies. The editors, Murugan Anandarajan, Thompson S.H. Teo, and Claire A. Simmers, skillfully structure the work around the bad, the good, and the ameliorative. Technologies bear opportunities—for use, misuse, and abuse. Taking up this line of thinking, the editors structure the volume by discussing first the deleterious transformations, then the promising ones, and then the ways that the troubling transformations can be redeemed for organizational benefit. The editors and the authors carefully bound the scope of their research work; here, I wish to provide only a measure of the context.

Has the Internet changed the way we work? While editing this volume in my office at home (and disambiguating a few issues in minutes with Google), I needed to consult with the work's lead editor on a matter regarding the contents. I received an almost instantaneous response to my e-mailed query from Murugan, who had access to the volume's electronic text while seated in a lounge of a Sri Lanka airport in transit to Malaysia. Productivity, instantaneous access to people and information, distance as no obstacle, work as not a destination, are all wrapped here in one package. We may conclude that it is now more and more appropriate to talk about work being enacted in a worksphere rather than in a workplace.

The Internet began to bear on the workplace with the invention of the World Wide Web and with its opening by a browser in the early 1990s. Followed closely by the drastically falling costs of telecommunications, these developments have enabled a massive increase and qualitative change in connectivity and, building on it, in human communication and collaboration. The multiple aspects of the Internet-Web compound, which acts as a marketplace, an interactive medium, a store of information, a delivery vehicle for digital products, a forum, a collaboratory, and a universal telecommunications network, fuel its pervasive use and influence (Zwass 2003). The Internet penetration is a global phenomenon, with its role and potential in the national economies best—if not perfectly—reflected by the construct of e-readiness (*Economist Intelligence Unit* 2004). The five countries leading the world in this metric are the Nordics and the United Kingdom, with the United States in sixth place. The digital divide is clearly seen from the score of 8.28 (out of 10) held by Denmark as opposed to 2.43 assigned to Azerbaijan. The penetration of broadband and of mobile commerce has been driving the most recent progress.

Work consists in people performing tasks that will result in products for customers. No place or time inheres in the definition of work. Neither does payment by customers, as well established in charitable pursuits. The availability of the Internet technologies has challenged many notions habitually associated with work. We now know that work is not a place—it is something we do. The separation between work and private life, the balance of work and leisure (or family life), is no longer as crisp as it used to be. In the advanced economies, the climate of work has changed. The ever-faster tempo of events and ever-broader competitive challenges, coming from regions previously separated by distance, call for incessant innovation. Innovation requires work organization that brings forth engagement, commitment, self-efficacy, creativity, and—desirably—a state of flow (Csikszentmihalyi 1996). Compliance is no longer enough. For example, to an ever greater degree the success of organizational information systems depends on their voluntary use, as is the case with many intranet-based knowledge management systems that hold some of the organizational memory. Research shows that the adoption and use of such systems is predicated on affective commitment, that is, the identification with the objectives of the systems, and on peer pressure and recognition (Malhotra and Galletta 2005).

New modes of work emerge. A profoundly new form of work is open-source software development: relying on several layers of the Internet-based technologies, people across the world volunteer their skills to construct and evolve world-class software. Intrinsic motivators, such as altruism and identification with the community, are prominently at play, along with the extrinsic ones of self-marketing, peer recognition, and reputation building (Hars and Ou 2002). Formal organizations are beginning to harness the open-source collaboration methods (Neus and Scherf 2005). As opposed to the induction into formal organizations for business purposes, institutions such as Creative Commons make a variety of work products freely available over the Internet. Indeed, a scholarly volume analyzing the creation of the Internet-based innovation communities that widen the base of personal innovation has itself been made available there (von Hippel 2005). The open mode of innovation is broadened to other products—from Wikipedia to mountain bikes. We see the glimmer of personal fabrication—the ultimate in customization, also freighted with the potential to bring some of the advantages of the Internet to the poorer parts of the world (Gershenfeld 2005). Much of the work and play is done through the same Internet-furnished interface. *Homo faber* and *homo ludens* are becoming an integral person.

The Web-based job marketplaces of global reach have created fluid labor markets in a variety of occupations, creating the opportunities of a close match between a person and a job. Some occupations, particularly those playing a strictly brokering function, are being challenged (e.g., travel agency or real-estate brokerage). New occupations and employment areas emerge to take advantage of the multiple aspects of the Internet-Web compound (a Web site designer, an e-commerce entrepreneur, a blogging journalist are iconic examples). A useful review of some of the other issues attendant on work in the netcentric environment is provided by Wallace (2004).

Entirely new ways of organizing work are becoming effective as decentralization opportunities are increasing and market-oriented structures based on the Internet technologies can be created *within* organizations (Malone 2004). Using these marketlike structures to replace command-based control in organizations, virtual teams distributed around the globe can organize themselves and internally bid for work. Further, some of the organizational decision making can rely on the wisdom of diverse members of a firm with local knowledge, each giving voice independently, with an aggregation system provided over the Internet. The organization of certain work processes is likely to be gradually transformed to fit the Internet-based systems, pooling the collective knowledge of employees, customers, and other volunteers, and thus to accommodate the open-source methods of work (Hof 2005).

Technologies have always showed us their dual, Janus-faced nature. The always-on potential access to people, information, workflows, and the world at large beyond the virtual boundary of the organization challenges that organization, as is well analyzed in several chapters in this volume. The potentialities do not imply desirability from the standpoint of organizational performance. There are also conflicting organizational goals. For example, Web browsing may stimulate innovation, yet may also take away from immediate efficiency. Rapid, instant-messaging-driven decision making is responsive to the needs of the real-time enterprise by delivering the needed volume of decisions. Yet has anyone taken the time to reflect? The availability of the Web as a forum and the blogging tools have empowered individual workers with respect to the employers. On the other hand, employers have acquired an ability to monitor the actions of employees more closely, as ever more of their actions consist in the generation of electronic text. In organizational settings, communication technologies can be used for oppressive purposes (Sproull and Kiesler 1991). This is particularly so as, in a move to ubiquitous computing, the networked computers will disappear into the corporate environment (Russell, Streitz, and Winograd 2005). Extending the pre-Web insight of Zuboff (1988), we now have even greater opportunities to impoverish jobs by computer-assisted routinization or to enrich the jobs by enhancing the user's sense of control.

The world's organizations are a great laboratory of the ongoing Internet-enabled transformation. We are only beginning to research and understand how the Internet has changed the way people work and the lives of working people. A purely instrumental view of transformational technologies will always be too limited. We need, rather, to comprehend the processes of mutual influence between work practices and other human pursuits, and these technologies. The chapters included here should increase current understanding and assist in future research.

REFERENCES

Csikszentmihalyi, M. 1996. *Creativity: Flow and the Psychology of Discovery and Invention.* New York: HarperCollins.

Economist Intelligence Unit Ltd and IBM Corporation. 2005. *The 2005 e-Readiness Rankings.* www.eiv.com/site_info.asp?info_name=eiv_2005_e_readiness_rankings.

Gershenfeld, N. 2005. *Fab: The Coming Revolution on Your Desktop—from Personal Computers to Personal Fabrication.* New York: Basic Books.

Hars, A., and Ou, S. 2002. Working for free? Motivations for participating in open-source projects. *International Journal of Electronic Commerce* 6, 3 (Spring), 25–39.

Hof, R.D. 2005. The power of us: Mass collaboration is shaking up business. *Business Week,* June 20, 74–82.

Malhotra, Y. and Galletta, D. 2005. A multidimensional commitment model of volitional systems adoption and use. *Journal of Management Information Systems* 22, 1 (Summer), 117–151.

Malone, T.W. 2004. *The Future of Work.* Boston: Harvard Business School Press.

Neus, A., and Scherf, P. 2005. Opening minds: Cultural change with the introduction of open-source collaboration methods. *IBM Systems Journal* 44, 2, 215–225.

Russell, D.M., Streitz, N.A., and Winograd, T. 2005. Building disappearing computers. *Communications of the ACM* 48, 3 (March), 42–48.

Sproull, L., and Kiesler, S. 1991. *Connections: New Ways of Working in the Networked Organizations.* Cambridge, MA: MIT Press.

von Hippel, E. 2005. *Democratizing Innovation.* Cambridge, MA: MIT Press. http://web.mit.edu/evhippel/www/democ.htm.

Wallace, P. 2004. *The Internet in the Workplace: How New Technology Is Transforming Work.* Cambridge, UK: Cambridge University Press.

Zuboff, S. 1988. *In the Age of the Smart Machine: The Future of Work and Power.* New York: Basic Books.

Zwass, V. 2003. Electronic commerce and organizational innovation: Aspects and opportunities. *International Journal of Electronic Commerce* 7, 3 (Spring), 7–37.

THE INTERNET AND WORKPLACE TRANSFORMATION

CHAPTER 1

THE INTERNET AND WORKPLACE TRANSFORMATION

An Introduction

MURUGAN ANANDARAJAN, CLAIRE A. SIMMERS,
AND THOMPSON S.H. TEO

The Internet is transforming the workplace, enabling unprecedented access to unlimited information on a twenty-four-hour, seven-day-a-week basis. Robust, two-way communication is available on demand, primarily limited only by the speed of connections; the richness and reach of the Internet have spread into every aspect of our work and personal lives (Evans and Wurster 2000). The physical component of the workplace has not altered significantly; we still have desks, chairs, cubicles, or offices. However, with the growth of Internet usage, the atmosphere of the workplace and of the way we work has been irrevocably altered (Wallace 2004). Now, we are no longer bound to our physical location; through the Internet, we can be anywhere in the world and view countless types of Web sites. The Internet creates a paradox in the workplace unlike any previous technology (Wallace 2004). The obstructing and enabling effects of the Internet are as vast and complicated as the Internet itself. The troubling and promising ways the Internet is transforming our workplaces are due to the enormous amount of information available, the disaggregation of work and location, and the rapid worldwide adoption of this technology. Within this netcentric world, individual and organizational methods of coping that discourage and control the negative usages while fostering the positive usages are not evolving as quickly as the Internet technology. We, as scholars, are called upon to investigate these Internet-induced workplace transformations and the ways to manage this phenomenon.

Individuals and organizations are being transformed in disquieting ways. On the individual level, the ability to be "always on" tends to blend work and personal life: balancing work and private life becomes more difficult because work never seems to end. The potential for deviant and addictive behaviors escalates within an Internet-connected workplace because of the openness and the depth of reach provided by the Internet (Anandarajan 2002). Organizations also face challenges of declining productivity, damaging viruses, security leaks, potential for legal actions, and overloaded networks (Anandarajan et al. 2000).

The Internet-enabled workplace also brings the advantages of greater flexibility to employees and to organizations as work is disconnected from place, time, and information availability constraints. Team members need no longer be located in the same place. Learning can be accomplished without leaving the office, and the Internet becomes a telephone book, reference book, record book, and encyclopedia. Using the Internet can increase productivity; two-thirds of users (65.8 percent) reported that going online at work made them somewhat or much more productive, up from 64.5 percent in 2003 (USC Annenberg School 2004, 89). As scholars, we are called upon to broaden our knowledge about the negative and positive ways that the Internet is transforming workplaces, as well as the ways individuals and organizations can transform and contain negative usage while increasing positive usage (Anandarajan and Simmers 2005).

BACKGROUND

The Internet, designed and developed in the early 1970s, grew slowly and painstakingly as an electronic forum for academic and scientific researchers. Vast quantities of information were scattered about the network; finding this information taxed even those computer-literate devotees. One development that made the Internet a "twenty-five-year overnight success" was the creation of hypertext markup language (HTML) in the beginning of the 1990s. Another was the design of server and browser software to view the interconnected documents that would collectively become the World Wide Web, or the Web. While Internet usage penetration is not as large as that of the radio or television, the rate of adoption for the Internet has outpaced these other information technologies. Worldwide, Internet usage continues to grow; based on 2005 estimated numbers, penetration in world regions (defined as the number of users divided by the total population) varies from 1.5 percent in Africa to 67.4 percent in North America (Internet World Stats 2005). Within ten years, the penetration usage in the United States is expected to match the 80 to 85 percent usage already in existence in Sweden, Finland, and South Korea. In that same time span, other industrialized nations (Japan, Britain, and Germany) will probably reach just below 75 percent usage (Cole 2004). While usage penetration in the rest of the world will be rapid, it is not expected to reach the same levels as in the industrialized nations.

Recognizing the criticality of the Internet, researchers began a longitudinal project in 2000 at the University of Southern California's Annenberg School Center for the Digital Future. The center has been collecting data yearly regarding Internet users and nonusers, the ways people use the Internet, and its effects on their online and offline lives. The panel study, which started with 2,000 Americans, has recently expanded to include participants in more than twenty countries. The trends from the 2004 survey are very clear: (1) the Internet is central to most Americans; (2) for users it is the most significant source of information; (3) use of the Internet increases productivity; but (4) people are working more and the line between work and home is increasingly blurred; and (5) wireless connections will become standard, facilitating increased Internet accessibility as a catalyst for increased usage (USC Annenberg School 2004).

Figure 1.1   **Work/Personal Linkage, Pre- and Post-Internet Diffusion in the Workplace**

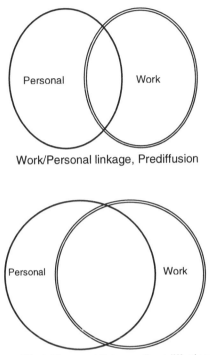

Work/Personal linkage, Prediffusion

Work/Personal linkage, Postdiffusion

It is difficult to recall what life was like before this level of connectivity and instantaneous access to billions of bytes of information was possible. Yet this workplace phenomenon has assumed an important place in corporate America only since 1995 (Websense 2005). Of those who have access to the Internet at work in the United States, visiting Web sites for business purposes increased from 83.7 percent in 2000 to 91.2 percent in 2004. Additionally, reported personal usage at work grew from 50.7 percent in 2000 to 64.7 percent in 2004 (USC Annenberg School 2004).

While some of the transformations in the workplace induced by the Internet are remarkable, others are more understated; some are immediately apparent while others are more long term. What cannot be doubted is that how people work is different from how people worked in the previous century. Before the diffusion of computer-enabled technology in general and the revolution engineered by the Internet, work spheres and personal spheres were largely separated. People went to work, did their job, and went home to their personal lives; companies had defined work shifts in terms of hours and days. People generally left their unfinished work on their desks at the end of their prescribed work time. The diffusion of the Internet into the workplace has dramatically changed this pattern, and the overlap between the two spheres is now considerable (Figure 1.1). People now take their work into their personal time and their personal interests into their work time with fluidity and ease. The rewards are numerous, such as flexibility, autonomy, increased capacity for work, ability to work in a global environment, and access to vast amounts of information. The challenges of the overlapping spheres are also numerous and familiar to individuals and organizations—for example, stress, overwork, loss of organizational control, and proliferation of information and noise.

The Internet has altered the work environment, the business environment, and the competitive environment in a cycle of interdependent relationships. "The Internet became a catalyst for new business models, strategies, and organizational structures. It introduced new factors that affected the competitive landscape, new rivalries, new competitors, and new pressures" (Wallace 2004, 3). The business changes caused by the Internet demanded a recasting of the terms of the employment relationship known as the psychological contract, especially in the United States, but also in the rest of the world (as Internet usage increases). The pre-Internet psychological contract signified the employee's and employer's beliefs or perceptions about the employment association (Robinson and Rousseau 1994). In the pre–Internet-defined psychological contract, the employer was the caretaker and provider; the employee performed the prescribed job and was rewarded for performance; there was job security and certainty. The psychological contract had a transactional component focused primarily on tangible compensation requirements, and a relational component involving socioemotional elements, such as, trust, fairness, and commitment (Robinson et al. 1994).

However, due to changes brought about in large part by the Internet, a new psychological contract has been evolving. This new contract is based on shorter-term employment, employee responsibility for career development, commitment to the work performed rather than the employer, and the diminishing importance of hierarchy (Ehrlich 1994).

In this volume, we present several ways in which the Internet forces attention toward the changing nature of information, business, and management and how best to utilize employees' capabilities and potentials as they operate under the new psychological contract. The role of the Internet is shaping work existence through both promising and troubling transformations. We are seeing promising transformations in knowledge management, in usability of interfaces to promote learning, in virtual teams, and in virtual career support. Simultaneously, we observe troubling transformations such as the increase in deviant Internet behavior, varying in degree of severity from "cyberloafing," defined as the voluntary act of employees using their companies' Internet during office hours to surf non-job-related Web sites for personal purposes (Lim et al. 2002), to diminished capacity for self-control manifested in addictive behavior.

We are also developing insights into how to manage through transformative modes such as human resource management, work commitment, organizational justice, and sensitivity to national culture differences. Thus transformative modes have a containing or diminishing effect on troubling transformations and an encouraging effect on promising transformations.

This volume is divided into three parts: Part I, Troubling Transformations; Part II, Promising Transformations; and Part III, Changing Troubling Transformations Into Prom-

Figure 1.2 **The Internet and Workplace Transformation**

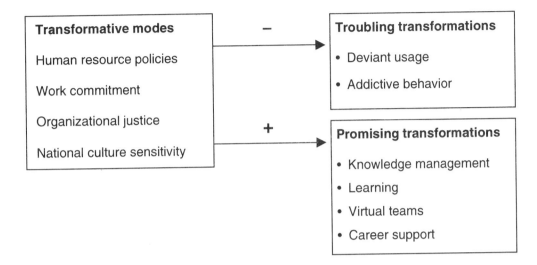

ising Ones. It is a collection of conceptual and empirical work, providing a rich resource as well as an agenda for future scholarly endeavors.

PART I: TROUBLING TRANSFORMATIONS

Part I has four chapters exploring Internet abuse—the troubling side of the Internet in the workplace. Pruthikrai Mahatanankoon in Chapter 2 (Internet Abuse in the Workplace: Extension of Workplace Deviance Model) extends a model of workplace deviance in general to specifically include unproductive Internet usage. Deviant use of Internet technology is defined as usage of Internet technology in the workplace that violates the accepted standards of an organization and in doing so threatens the well-being of the organization and/or its members. Individual, social, and technological factors interact with psychological factors to explain an individual's propensity to commitment deviant Internet behaviors. Mahatanankoon defines four spheres of deviant Internet behaviors: property, production, political, and personal aggression. The consequences of such behaviors negatively impact the individual, others in the organization, and the organizational entity.

The next three chapters examine problematic Internet usage. Problematic Internet usage is distinct from cyberloafing in the degree of severity. While cyberloafing may inhibit productivity, problematic Internet usage is a serious occupational health issue. It is a multidimensional syndrome consisting of cognitive and behavioral symptoms resulting in negative social and professional consequences. All three chapters present strong arguments for psychosocial predispositions as antecedents rather than as consequences of problematic Internet usage. The chapters provide a better understanding of the psychological and interpersonal processes that facilitate the development of problematic Internet usage.

In Chapter 3 (Self-Regulation of Communication Technology in the Workplace), Eastin et al. argue that psychological state and image management relate to self-efficacy perceptions and unregulated Internet use. The transition to problematic usage begins when accessing the Internet acts as an important or exclusive mechanism to heighten one's image and relieve some form of negative affect such as stress, depression, boredom, or anxiety in the presence of a weak self-regulation mechanism.

James Phillips in Chapter 4 (The Psychology of Internet Use and Misuse) and Scott Caplan in Chapter 5 (Problematic Internet Use in the Workplace) continue the discussion on problematic behavior in Internet use. Phillips discusses the role of preexisting tendencies (low self-esteem and procrastinating behaviors) in fostering addictive Internet use. The chapter offers two explanations for inappropriate workplace Internet use: (1) the diminished self-control associated with a strong habit (an addiction) and (2) a deliberate act linked to a tendency to procrastinate with a subsequent tendency to offer diminished self-control as an excuse.

In Chapter 5, Caplan argues that problematic Internet use in the workplace is not analogous to other behavioral addictions. Instead, Caplan views problematic Internet use through a cognitive-behavioral model that proposes that psychosocial problems, such as loneliness or social anxiety, predispose some Internet users to develop cognitions and behaviors involving their online activity that ultimately result in problematic Internet usage.

PART II: PROMISING TRANSFORMATIONS

Part II contains six chapters that characterize promising transformational aspects of the Internet in the workplace. In Chapter 6 (Organizational Intranets and the Transition to Managing Knowledge), Elisabeth Bennett proposes that intranets are different from traditional information systems, signaling a shift from managing information to managing knowledge. This requires greater integration and transparency between technology and the social nature of organizing. She suggests that intranets can facilitate organizational responses to a global environment and continuous change by providing a rich communication milieu. Intranets can foster learning and flexibility and are evolving to represent the social aspects of organizational life.

Chapter 7 (Optimal Flow in Online Interactions: Dimensions, Antecedents, and Consequences) by Manuel Sánchez-Franco delves deeper into understanding the usability of Internet-based applications from an individual's perspective. Specifically, this chapter lays out how the flow constant could be used to identify the factors that influence the experience of employees as they learn and use Internet-based applications. Flow is the holistic awareness that people feel when they act with total involvement. The basic premise is that workers in flow should have higher learning performance and usage levels. This model of flow is a foundation for encouraging increased intranet usage for knowledge management, supplementing Bennett's discussion.

Chapter 8 (Leading Virtual Teams: Modalities of Leadership) by Lille Springall et al. and Chapter 9 (Convergence in Virtual Teams) by Christel Rutte examine another promising transformational potential of the Internet—virtual teams. Springall et al. explore how twenty-nine managers are currently leading thirty-five virtual teams in the Swiss information technology (IT) industry. Their findings suggest that each manager develops a signature "virtual leadership" portfolio. They define four virtual leadership portfolios and conclude that high-"virtuality" teams, led by managers with broad virtual leadership portfolios, probably exhibit higher levels of performance than those led by managers with narrow leadership portfolios. The leadership of the virtual team is critical. Rutte takes a different perspective from that of Springall et al. by focusing on the unique needs of virtual teams and offering interventions to foster successful virtual teams. Adding features such as pictures, names, nicknames, or avatars to messages would personalize the virtual team members or inform team members upon log-in of the work done by other team members. If the patterns of communication are related to status differences in face-to-face team meetings, then it is worthwhile to try to duplicate the status differences by automatically identifying senders and receivers of messages by job titles, seniority, or expertise.

The next two chapters highlight another promising transformation in the workplace shaped by the Internet—the shift toward self-managed career support that has become a prominent component of the new psychological contract. In Chapter 10 (Usage of Internet-Based Career Support), Khapova et al. analyze career self-management and greater individualized career support over the Internet through the usage of an Internet-based career support system within the information technology sector in Europe. Results of a careful monitoring of the actual usage of the system showed that the full potential of the system was not reached. While a substantial number of participants registered, less than half actually used any of the system's functionalities. Khapova et al. offer three recommendations to increase usage and acceptance: (1) strengthen the design to guide users more clearly; (2) consider users' needs and characteristics and their readiness to accept that they are the driving force of their own career development; and (3) accompany e-services with human support.

In Chapter 11 (Mentoring Transformed via the Internet: Effects on Career Management), Veronica Godshalk presents an e-mentoring typology based on computer-mediated communication (CMC) literature. Anecdotal evidence gleaned by Godshalk illustrates many positive outcomes associated with e-mentoring, such as overcoming barriers of locating appropriate mentors, improved matching between those sharing common interests and vocational desires, and enrichment for both the mentor and the protégés.

PART III: CHANGING TROUBLING TRANSFORMATIONS INTO PROMISING ONES

Again, the role of the Internet in transforming the workplace can be both a blessing and a curse.
How do we change the troubling transformations of the workplace into promising

transformations? The five chapters in this section offer ways to manage the transformations, thereby either reducing or preempting the troubling aspects and promoting the promising aspects of Internet usage in the workplace. Managing the transformations involves organizational approaches that singly or in combination proactively minimize risk through organizational policies and procedures, promote work commitment, foster organizational justice, and are sensitive to national cultures.

In Chapter 12 (Controlling Internet Abuse in the Workplace: A Framework for Risk Management) Kimberly Young outlines a framework for controlling Internet abuse employing both the information technology and the human resource departments to proactively manage Internet usage. The framework moves from proactive approaches to reactive approaches and includes: (1) hiring practices incorporating screening for Internet misuse tendencies; (2) prevention through policy development, communication, and reinforcement; (3) enforcement examining the supporting technological infrastructure; and (4) the most reactive approach, rehabilitation or termination.

In Chapter 13 (Work Commitment and Employees' Misuse of the Internet in the Workplace), Abraham Carmeli posits that work commitment may diminish the likelihood of misuse of the Internet at work. Internet misbehavior is defined as behavior that falls outside the reference group set of norms. Carmeli argues that organizational responses that concentrate on disciplinary actions and technical solutions to cope with misbehavior have only limited success. Carmeli proposes that work commitment, which includes work ethic endorsement, job involvement, career commitment, affective commitment, and normative commitment (employees stay because they feel an obligation to the organization), will discourage misuse of the Internet at work.

Both Chapter 14 (Understanding Dysfunctional Cyberbehavior: The Role of Organizational Justice) by Constant Beugré and Chapter 15 (Cyberloafing and Organizational Justice: The Moderating Role of Neutralization Technique) by Vivien Lim and Thompson Teo explore the role of organizational justice in mitigating dysfunctional cyberbehavior. Beugré develops a framework of dysfunctional cyberbehavior that suggests that perceptions of distributive, procedural, and interactional justice would reduce the likelihood of such behavior. Additionally, if employees perceived unfairness, the dysfunctional cyberbehavior would be reduced by organizational policies relating to Internet usage. Lim and Teo collected data from working adults with access to the Internet at the workplace to investigate the relationship between organizational justice and the act of cyberloafing. Specifically, the findings indicate that when organizations are perceived as unjust in their treatment of employees, these employees are likely to invoke the neutralization technique to justify their engagement in cyberloafing. Using the metaphor of the ledger, workers rationalize that they are entitled to indulge in cyberloafing because past good behaviors have led to an accrual of credits in their "ledger." Employers need to be aware of employees' propensity to keep a ledger; this forewarning provides another tool to use in changing troubling transformations into positive transformations.

Mahatanankoon et al. in Chapter 16 (Hofstede's Cultural Dimensions of Personal Web Usage Activities in Thailand and the United States) examine the influence of Hofstede's four dimensions of national culture (collectivism/individualism, power distance, masculinity/femininity, and uncertainty avoidance) on personal Web usage in the workplace. Top-level managers and employees from both Thailand and the United States took part in the study. Results support the existence of cultural differences between the two samples in three of Hofstede's dimensions, with the masculinity/femininity dimension being the exception. Thus sensitivity to national culture differences is important in promoting positive Internet usage and controlling negative usage.

The Internet and Workplace Transformation offers a framework for grouping previous scholarly endeavors; it also provides a workbook for those looking to better understand the Internet-enabled workplace. We have shown that while there are troubling transformations that the Internet has catalyzed, there are also promising transformations. Our challenge is to manage all transformations, to minimize the troubling and maximize the promising ones.

REFERENCES

Anandarajan, M. 2002. Profiling Web usage in the workplace: A behavior-based artificial intelligence approach. *Journal of Management Information Systems* 19, 1 (Summer), 243–266.

Anandarajan, M., and Simmers, C.A. 2005. Developing human capital through personal Web use in the workplace: mapping employee perceptions. *Communication of the AIS* 15, http://cais.isworld.org/contents.aspvol.15article 41june.

Anandarajan, M. Simmers, C.A., and Igbaria, M. 2000. An exploratory investigation of the antecedents and impact of Internet usage: An individual perspective. *Behaviour and Information Technology* 19, 69–85.

Cole, J. 2004. Now is the time to start studying the Internet age. *Chronicle of Higher Education,* 50, 30, B18.

Ehrlich, C.J. 1994. Creating an employer-employee relationship for the future. *Human Resource Management* 33, 491–501.

Evans, P., and Wurster, T.S. 2000. *Blown to Bits.* Boston: Harvard Business School Press.

Internet World Stats. 2005. Internet usage statistics—the big picture. www.internetworldstats.com/stats.htm.

Lim, V.K.G., Teo, T.S.H., and Loo, G.L. 2002. How do I loaf? Let me count the ways: Cyberloafing in an Asian context. *Communications of the Association for Computing Machinery* 45, 66–70.

Robinson, S.L., Kraatz, M.S., and Rousseau, D.M. 1994. Changing obligations and the psychological contract: A longitudinal study. *Academy of Management Journal* 37, 137–152.

Robinson, S.L., and Rousseau, D.M. 1994. Violating the psychological contract: Not the exception but the norm. *Journal of Organizational Behavior* 15, 245–259.

USC Annenberg School Center for the Digital Future. 2004. The digital future report: Surveying the digital future: year four: ten years, ten trends. www.digitalcenter.org/downloads/DigitalFutureReport-Year4-2004.pdf.

Wallace, P. 2004. *The Internet in the Workplace.* Cambridge, UK: Cambridge University Press.

Websense. 2005. Internet usage and the workplace: It's now an HR issue. Anonymous. *Orange County Business Journal* 27, 23 (June 7–13); ABI/INFORM Dateline. www.Websense.com/products/resources/wp/hr_wp.pdf.

PART I

TROUBLING TRANSFORMATIONS

CHAPTER 2

INTERNET ABUSE IN THE WORKPLACE

Extension of Workplace Deviance Model

PRUTHIKRAI MAHATANANKOON

Abstract: *The existence of Internet technologies in today's workplace plays many important roles in supporting and enhancing employees' internal and external communications, including supporting and sustaining organizational business practices. Nevertheless, unproductive Internet usage and abuse in the workplace are progressively becoming a major productivity drain. By extending the workplace deviance model to include unproductive Internet usage behaviors and adopting several important theories and perspectives, this chapter proposes an individual psychological framework that explains the deviant use of Internet technology (DUIT) in the workplace. It is hoped that the conceptual model will stimulate further empirical studies into the topic, with the ultimate goal being to understand, investigate, and prevent Internet abuse in the workplace.*

Keywords: *Internet, Internet Abuse, Workplace Deviance, Theory of Planned Behavior*

INTRODUCTION

Organizations are now at the point at which employees' productivity and knowledge-asset management have become a major workplace concern. Without proper Internet management strategies, employees can misuse the Internet and spend their work time on personal activities. Besides suffering from unproductive wage expenditures, organizations could face legal liabilities from inbound and outbound materials that are not related to their business activities. Outbound activities particularly place companies at risk when sensitive materials or knowledge assets are transmitted through the Internet, and inbound activities can create litigation involving sexual harassment and discrimination, with criminal proceedings against employees and the organization (Scheuermann and Langford 1997).

Management generally refers to unproductive Internet usage in the workplace as "Internet abuse." Companies have tried to reduce the occurrences of Internet abuse by taking necessary precautions through establishing an Internet usage policy or Internet monitoring and filtering tools as preventive policies. However, the root causes of Internet abuse in the workplace have not been fully investigated. For example, why do some employees just read and search for personal information online, while others view pornography or harass fellow employees using e-mail? We need to understand why employees are provoked to abuse the Internet in the workplace, so more effective solutions can be implemented.

This chapter sets as its goal the filling in of this gap by redefining the term *Internet abuse* as deviant use of Internet technology (DUIT) in the workplace to include various types of abusive Internet activities. This goal is accomplished by investigating the issues and using the prominent workplace deviance model defined by Robinson and Bennett (1997). As there are various activities in the workplace that could be classified as Internet abuse, the objectives of the extended workplace deviance model are (1) to categorize different Internet activities according to the workplace deviance model, and (2) to set investigative guidelines that will help researchers focus on finding the determinants and consequences of certain types of deviant Internet behaviors.

DEFINING INTERNET ABUSE IN THE WORKPLACE

Organizations now have to face the dark side of the Internet. Internet abuse in the workplace pushes organizations to implement various strategies to cope with fast-growing concerns regarding productivity, legal liability, and knowledge assets. There are various terms used by researchers to describe Internet abuse in the workplace (Anandarajan 2002). These existing definitions, including such terms as *problematic Internet usage* (David 2001) and *Internet addiction* (Young 1998), have led researchers to investigate the behaviors from various individual psychological perspectives that would be least expected in actual workplace settings. For example, excessive Internet usage may indicate that people use the Internet as a means of escaping from their emotional and physical problems. Psychologists define any extensive usage of the Internet when users have no control over that behavior as "Internet addiction (IA)" (Greenfield 1999; Young 1996, 1998) and "pathological Internet usage (PIU)" (David 2001; Morahan-Martin and Schumacher 2000). IA is currently being viewed as similar to substance abuse or a gambling addiction (Young 1998), while PIU is now defined as Internet usage "which causes a specified number of symptoms, including mood-altering use of the Internet, failure to fulfill major role obligations, guilt and craving" (Morahan-Martin and Schumacher 2000, 14). Brenner (1997) claims that Internet addicts exhibit a higher tolerance of Internet use, withdrawal difficulties, and a craving for the Internet compared to normal Internet users. Nevertheless, Griffiths asserts that although the Internet may be addictive, since it compensates for other problems in a person's social life, such addictive symptoms happen only to an "exceedingly tiny minority" of Internet users, those who are actually obsessive and/or compulsive in their basic nature (Griffiths 2000; Joinson 1998). Thus, it is possible, but unlikely, that an individual's psychological factors, often the core components of addictions, will also lead to unproductive Internet usage behaviors in the workplace, for example, reading Internet news, booking personal travel, or viewing any other legal non-work-related sites on the Internet. The "true" occurrences of Internet-addicted employees are indeed rare. Stanton argues that the profile of employees with high-frequency Internet usage is not similar to that of people who are Internet addicted.

The author finds that "high frequency Internet users may often be otherwise happy and productive workers" (2002, 59).

Definitions such as *cyberloafing* (Lim et al. 2002) or *personal Web usage* (Anandarajan and Simmers 2002) better represent the unproductive patterns that generally occur in the workplace because of the Internet. Cyberloafing is "any voluntary act of employees using their organizations' Internet access during office hours to surf non-work-related Web sites for non-work purposes and access non-work-related email" (Lim 2002, 67). Personal Web usage (PWU) is defined as "voluntary online Web behaviors during working time using any of the organization's resources for activities outside current customary job or work requirements" (Anandarajan and Simmers 2002). There are also several classifications of PWU activities, such as constructive and dysfunctional PWU (Anandarajan and Simmers 2004), disruptive, recreational, personal-learning, and ambiguous PWU (Anandarajan et al. 2004), and e-commerce, information-seeking, and communication PWU (Mahatanankoon et al. 2004). Nevertheless, there are other non-work-related activities that can be categorized not as PWU or cyberloafing but rather simply as unproductive, illegal, or highly deviant. Such activities include the act of moonlighting (using an organization's Internet resources to conduct personal business), harassing people through e-mail, sending confidential data to unauthorized people, sending viruses through a corporate e-mail system, and downloading pirated software at work. The root causes of these activities may come from various organizational and motivational factors that trigger such behaviors. To advance the research in this area, an integrated conceptual model is needed that covers various types of deviant Internet behaviors that potentially may exist in the workplace.

Based on the typology of deviant workplace behavior presented by Robinson and Bennett (1995), this chapter extends the existing model and defines deviant use of internet technology in the workplace as any usage that violates the accepted standards of an organization and in doing so threatens the well-being of the organization and/or its members. Extending from Robinson and Bennett's typology, Table 2.1 summarizes different types of DUIT behaviors, but the behaviors are not limited to this list.

Property-DUIT is the deviant use of Internet technology where employees intentionally acquire intellectual properties or damage or destroy knowledge assets of organizations without authorization. This type of DUIT includes using the Internet illegally to download software at work, send viruses through the corporate intranet, or even to hack organizational databases via the Internet. The most common problems of property-DUIT are the use of unauthorized Internet access to share the connection with friends and family (Siau et al. 2002).

Production-DUIT is the deviant use of Internet technology that violates the formally proscribed norms communicated by an organization delineating the minimal quality and quantity of work to be accomplished. According to organizational behaviorists, these norms can differ from organization to organization. Production-DUIT includes any excessive leisure and/or personal use of the Internet at work—for example, using the Internet to escape from work, spending too much time on the Internet doing personal Web surfing, conducting personal business, playing games, or chatting. With different organizational norms, some employees may argue that these activities are not abusive at all—spending an

Table 2.1

Four Types of DUIT with Examples of Internet Abuse

Types of DUIT	Examples of behavior
Property-DUIT	• Illegally downloading software at work • Stealing and destroying data or essential information • Sending viruses using the corporate e-mail system • Hacking organizational databases via the Internet • Unauthorized using of Internet access and sharing the connection with friends and family • Moonlighting
Production-DUIT	• Excessively using a personal nonwork e-mail account • Any personal Web surfing or cyberloafing to avoid work responsibilities • Using Internet as a way to escape from productive work • Continuously playing online games or chatting online
Political-DUIT	• Transmitting confidential data, intellectual work, or trade secrets to an unauthorized party • Using local or Internet e-mail to gossip, blame, or show favoritism • Defacing intranet, Internet, or extranet Web page
Personal aggression-DUIT	• Spamming and harassing people through e-mail • Making defamatory statements through corporate intranet, e-mail, or Web site • Making racial remarks or playing pranks on people at work

Source: Typology adapted from Robinson and Bennett (1995).

hour a day on the Internet for personal tasks is considered part of a normal and healthy work life. Most employees justify their behavior as appropriate for various reasons (Robinson and Greenberg 1998). Therefore, management should be cautious about implementing deterrent strategies as some personal Web usage activities are subtle, but these activities may lead to or intensify other types of DUIT behaviors if not managed properly.

Political-DUIT is the deviant use of Internet technology as an engagement in social interaction that puts other individuals at a personal or political disadvantage in the workplace—for example, using e-mail to gossip, blame, or show favoritism; defacing companies' Web sites; or spreading rumors about people or organizations. The transmission of confidential data, intellectual work, and trade secrets to outsiders, thus possibly compromising organizational competitive positions, also belongs in this type of DUIT.

Personal aggression-DUIT is the deviant use of Internet technology to express aggression or hostility toward other individuals in the workplace—for example, spamming; using Internet e-mail to send abusive or harassing messages to fellow employees, bosses, or clients; and using the Internet to make fun, make racial remarks, or play pranks on people at work.

RATIONALE FOR THE PROPOSED CONCEPTUAL MODEL

The concept of workplace deviance is multidimensional in nature because it encompasses a very diverse set of behaviors (Bolin and Heatherly 2001), which may also help explain many facets of DUIT in the workplace. For example, an employee harassing another employee by sending sexual messages through e-mail can be considered a serious personal aggression-DUIT, or excessive Internet gaming could be categorized as production-DUIT.

Research in the area of workplace deviance typically investigates problem behaviors based on the work activities of blue-collar and lower-level workers, such as being late for work, absenteeism, drinking or using drugs, or stealing office supplies. Patterns of deviant behaviors stemming from white-collar employees (information and knowledge workers) and upper management levels have not been fully examined. Organizational behaviorists wonder if such patterns can be found in white-collar employees, suggesting that other deviant behaviors are emerging from new workplace technologies, thereby creating new opportunities for employees to be unproductive at work (Bennett and Robinson 2003). From this perspective, two implications follow: (1) Internet technology can be used as a means to achieve an objective of workplace deviant behaviors—those behaviors that otherwise may not be convenient or effective if they were performed physically (e.g., stealing office supplies or harassing others verbally). Papacharissi and Rubin find that "those who were less satisfied and who felt less valued in their face-to-face communication used the Internet as a functional alternative to interpersonal communication or to fill time" (2000, 192). (2) Internet technology can be used as an additional information resource that complements other physical workplace deviance or provides a substitute for other similar workplace deviant behaviors. For example, employees who typically talk excessively on the telephone to avoid work can instead turn to Internet chat rooms or personal e-mail as a substitute in order to escape from their work responsibilities. Also, employees now have an easier channel to satisfy their grievances (Lim et al. 2002).

In order to enhance Robinson and Bennett's conceptual model, the research in the area of computer-mediated communication explains how Internet usage in the workplace can be viewed in the perspective of social networks (Kraut and Kiesler, 2003). The social network perspective states that any computer-mediated communications that have reached their critical mass are considered to resemble a social virtual community (Garton et al. 1997; Haythornthwaite and Wellman 1998). As with organizational social networks, computer-mediated communication usage behavior depends on organizational norms, mandates, structures, and job categories (Haythornthwaite et al. 1998). Clearly, Internet and e-mail usage have reached the level of becoming social networks within organizations; employees exchange resources and knowledge to accomplish their task, as well as to share social support. As Haythornthwaite et al. note, "Their work ties are maintained through many different types of work and social exchange" (1998, 215). These authors also suggest that even in a work group, Internet usage may wander into non-work-related issues that include socioemotional content—the exchange of instrumental, social, and emotional communication—and this activity could be taken as healthy because it enhances group cohesiveness (Haythornthwaite et al. 1998) as a part of an organization. Raghavan (2002) states that the Internet environment is becoming a testing ground for future social theories on virtual communities. In modern organizations, the most effective way that a virtual team can build a social bond among its members is through electronic channels. Papacharissi and Rubin state that "people communicate or use media to gratify needs and wants" (2000, 176). Therefore, in networked and virtual organizations, the Internet can be used socially to coordinate work, build relationships, or even voice to fellow employees opinions about stressful or unsatisfactory situations in the organization. Of course, the usage of the Internet can reach the point where it is beyond organizational norms; management then takes control of the situation to enforce the norms by using various deterrent strategies, such as communicating policy, installing Internet monitoring and filtering software, and training and educating employees to follow proper usage guidelines.

Because employees have "incomplete volitional control" over their Internet usage at work, Ajzen's theory of planned behavior is the theory of choice for predicting information technology usage (Taylor and Todd 1995). Ajzen's theory of reasoned action asserts that attitude and subjective norms are the contributing factors to intentional information technology usage (Davis et al. 1989). These factors incorporate the motivational factors affecting DUIT behaviors. According to the theory of planned behavior, the ability to perform a certain behavior is limited by the actual social and organizational controls over the opportunities and resources to perform that behavior—perceived behavioral control—which in combination with other factors impact intention and action (Ajzen 1988, 1991; Ajzen and Madden 1986). Perceived behavioral control refers to "people's perception of the ease or difficulty of performing the behavior of interest" (Ajzen 1991, 183). This added control over opportunities and resources is appropriate in the workplace situation where aspects of organizational constraint, such as computer resources, organizational policy, and monitoring, can restrict employees' intentions and behaviors regarding their use of the Internet and e-mail.

The extension of Robinson and Bennett's model of workplace deviance is shown in Figure 2.1. This model addresses physical deviant behaviors (stealing office supplies, verbally voicing dissatisfaction, taking long lunch breaks, etc.) as well as the deviant behaviors that may be performed electronically through the Internet and/or e-mail. Provocations—such as workplace pressures and other stressors—cause employees to search for something to channel their dissatisfaction, through instrumental and/or expressive motivations. Some examples of provocations are stress, boredom, role ambiguity, financial pressures, social pressures, unfair treatment, poor quality of work conditions, job dissatisfaction, company contempt, and organizational changes. According to Robinson and Bennett, instrumental motivation is "the attempts to reconcile the disparity by repairing the situation, restoring equity, or improving the current situation." Those with instrumental motivation see deviance as a means that will benefit themselves. Expressive motivation "reflects a need to vent, release, or express one's feelings of outrage, anger, or frustration." However, the two motivations are not mutually exclusive and could work together to resolve a given provocation (Robinson and Bennett 1997, 16). Abusive employees generally seek the least restrictive ways to resolve their problems; therefore, such employees may look for electronic channels to voice their problems or dissatisfactions in the workplace. Evidence supports that Internet usage leads to disinhibited behaviors, which occur in the form of self-disclosure, and seeking personal

Figure 2.1 **Modification of Robinson and Bennett's Workplace Deviance Model with DUIT**

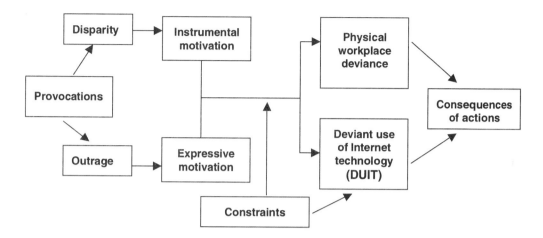

interest information that would generally be avoided physically (Joinson 1998). Cameron and Webster (2005) find that instant messaging (IM) can be used as a "replacement technology" for other physical communication in the workplace (e.g., face-to-face, telephone). Therefore, since the Internet contributes to organizational social networks, there are possibilities that unhappy employees, equipped with personal e-mail and Internet access, may choose to carry out their deviant behavior electronically.

These motivations may not lead to deviant action if the constraints, such as social norms, moral standards, or work ethics, weaken the relationship between provocations and deviant behaviors (Robinson and Bennett 1997). Constraints, once expanded into perceived behavioral controls, differ by the type of behaviors and can include resource availability, organizational policy, Internet usage policy, Internet filtering and monitoring tools, and other resource barriers. In Figure 2.1, the second arrow pointing from constraints to DUIT indicates that performing DUIT behaviors poses another type of constraint that directly influences information technology usage (social norms and perceived behavioral controls). Additional research is needed to examine the mediating and moderating effects of these constraints.

DUIT CONCEPTUAL MODEL

Figure 2.2 shows how the earlier theories and concepts are consolidated to explain DUIT behaviors. The motivation to use the Internet in the workplace leads to both positive and negative consequences. Under normal conditions where employees are motivated to use the Internet productively, the usage of the Internet leads to productive consequences. However, when there are provocations that lead employees to perform negative behaviors, the employees are limited by three mediating and/or moderating constraints—organizational, individual, and technological—that inhibit Internet abuse. These constraints are part of the overall constraints identified in the workplace deviance model, but they also

Figure 2.2   **Deviant Use of Internet Technology Research Framework**

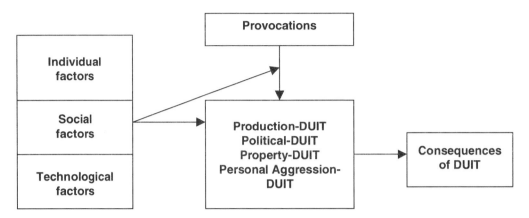

have direct motivational effects on DUIT behaviors—the major determinants of Internet technology usage according to the theory of planned behavior.

Propositions for the Conceptual Model

Proposition 1: Provocations Lead to Potential DUIT Activities

Management generally applies active strategies (e.g., Internet usage policy, employee training) to cope with the situation. However, when these strategies become ineffective, stronger practical solutions are implemented to handle Internet abuse; these include reprimanding employees, terminating employment, or deploying Internet monitoring and filtering software to restrict non-work-related Web site access (Mirchandani and Motwani 2003). Although these are effective deterrent strategies, researchers and practitioners have limited knowledge of the provocation leading to Internet abuse. Organizational behaviorists have suggested a range of provocations, from subtle (e.g., stress, role ambiguity, organizational commitment, job dissatisfaction) to extreme (e.g., injustice, lack of control, frustration, financial or social pressures).

Proposition 2: Individual Factors Can Increase or Decrease Potential
DUIT Activities

- *Individual demographics,* such as gender, education, age, and culture, indicate different Internet usage behaviors, which could assist companies in pointing out potential abuses.
- *Individual personality types,* such as introvert, neurotic, and psychotic, could influence a variety of Internet activities (Amiel and Sargent 2004). Companies are advised to investigate employees' personality types and other such aspects when monitoring and filtering Internet traffic for potentially negative usage patterns.

- *Job descriptions,* such as employees' roles, status, and job responsibilities, generally come with Internet access and e-mail privileges and may sometimes dictate the amount of social interactions employees need to make.
- *Individual work and computer ethics.* Since an individual's productivity and potential abuse behavior are associated with work ethics, companies should hire well-motivated employees. Before hiring, companies may want to test employees' perception of their work and the concept of computer ethics. Employees with a good moral understanding of work and computer ethics are less likely to abuse the Internet. Companies must continuously commit to educating their current employees regarding work and computer ethics by implementing ethical awareness programs.
- *Individual attitude toward unproductive Internet usage* is defined as an individual's positive and negative feelings about using the Internet for purposes other than work. Employees will use Internet technology if they believe they will receive desirable positive or negative outcomes.

*Proposition 3: Social Factors Can Increase or Decrease Potential
DUIT Activities*

- *Characteristics of the organization* help determine how Internet technology and e-mail are used. The more the Internet and e-mail are used in the company's value-adding processes and business, the more likely it is that the employees will potentially abuse them, given certain provocations.
- *Internet usage policy and other formal policies* can deter employees' Internet and e-mail usage behavior. This factor involves planning and drafting the policy, training and educating employees about the policy, and then properly and effectively enforcing it. Companies must take a proactive role in creating a well-written policy to protect themselves against cases of legal liability and to reduce unwarranted Web surfing. When employees sign and acknowledge a policy, they are obligated to follow the content of the policy, which could substantially reduce their intention to commit wrongful actions.
- *Social norms and informal controls* seem to be influential in establishing norms of deviant behaviors (Hollinger and Clark 1982). As the social bond between organizations and employees is severed, employees have a propensity to engage in deviant behaviors. Lewicki et al. emphasize that workplace deviant behaviors are controlled and influenced more by "informal normative mechanisms" than by "formal organizational mechanisms" (1997, 57).

*Proposition 4: Technological Factors Can Increase or Decrease Potential
DUIT Activities*

Internet technologies can specifically be used to cope with and lessen inappropriate site visits and enforce companies' Internet usage policies.

Table 2.2

Consequences of Four Types of DUIT Behaviors

Types of DUIT behaviors	Consequences of DUIT behaviors
Property-DUIT	• Installation of illegal or pirated software • Loss of bandwidth due to unauthorized sharing of Internet access • Loss of essential information and data • Spread of virus-infected software and data • Wasted organizational resources
Production-DUIT	• Increase in employees' work inefficiency • Loss of bandwidth due to non-work-related surfing • Decrease in organizational productivity • Wasted labor hours and wages paid • Increase in possibility of other DUIT behaviors
Political-DUIT	• Publication of defamatory and libelous statements • Loss of organizational trade secrets, intellectual work, or competitive advantage • Conflicts among employees • Negative effects on brand, reputation, and corporate confidence • Possible lawsuits due to information leaks
Personal aggression-DUIT	• Sexual harassment • Defamation and libel • Discrimination and hate speech • Disseminating of pornographic materials • Viewing and sending offensive content • Legal lawsuits due to harassment and racial remarks

- *Preventive technologies,* such as Internet firewalls, proxy servers, and filtering software, block or filter incoming and outgoing Internet traffic.
- *Detecting technologies,* such as spyware, software agents, and Web log mining, are monitoring and tracking software with search capabilities that can locate and detect inappropriate usages.
- *Enforcing technologies* put into effect the Internet usage policy, such as restricting Web site access and/or hours, and integrate with databases to provide comprehensive reports about employees' behaviors to Internet administrators.

Proposition 5: DUIT Activities Lead to Negative Consequences for Organizations

The consequences of DUIT behaviors vary from one type of DUIT behavior to another. These consequences can include the loss of individual and organizational productivity, the increase of unnecessary network bandwidth, and possible legal lawsuits (SurfControl.com 2004; Miller 1997; Scheuermann and Langford 1997; Wen and Lin 1998). Table 2.2 shows possible consequences for each of the DUIT behaviors, although the outcomes are not limited to this list.

Contrary to the workplace deviance model, evidence shows that Internet filtering and monitoring tools have led to employee dissatisfaction and other productivity debates. Employee motivation generally plays a significant role in productivity, performance, and satisfaction in the workplace, but employee dissatisfaction increases with any type of organizational monitoring, including Internet monitoring (Urbaczewski and Jessup 2002). In some cases, organizations should not restrict personal Web browsing but instead take the necessary training steps to "facilitate the transfer of learning from the play domain to work-related tasks" (Belanger and Van Slyke 2002, 65). Thus, the balance between work and play creates an emergent drive to examine the consequences of non-work-related Internet usage.

This chapter takes a negative view of Internet usage in the workplace, but acknowledges that both stringent control and little control generally lead to abuse. Internet management requires a balance of human resource strategies with individual psychological considerations to maintain and improve employee satisfaction. In addition, organizations should act both to empower and educate employees about the balance between work and play (Oravec 2002). However, with limited understanding of provocations and motivational factors behind Internet abuse, practitioners as well as future researchers need to find new ways to implement a workable balance between proper behavioral controls and employee empowerment.

CONCLUSION

By adopting several important theories and perspectives from other disciplines, including the workplace deviance model, social network perspective, and the theory of planned behavior, this chapter proposes an individual psychological conceptual model that explains the deviant use of Internet technology in the workplace. The modified conceptual model of Robinson and Bennett (1997) includes different provocations and motivations that lead an individual to perform deviant behaviors using Internet technology. These occurrences of Internet abuse can be prevented by focusing on several inhibitive factors (individual, organizational, and technological) that may deter or prevent such behaviors. This enhanced model will ultimately bring a new research perspective to the abuse of the Internet technology in the workplace.

REFERENCES

Ajzen, I. 1988. *Attitudes, Personality, and Behavior.* Chicago: Dorsey Press.
———. 1991. The theory of planned behavior. *Organizational Behavior and Human Decision Processes* 50, 2, 179–211.
Ajzen, I., and Madden, T.J. 1986. Prediction of goal-directed behavior: Attitudes, intentions, and perceived behavioral control. *Journal of Experimental Social Psychology* 22, 5, 453–474.
Amiel, T., and Sargent, S.L. 2004. Individual differences in Internet usage motives. *Computers in Human Behavior* 20, 6, 711–726.
Anandarajan, M. 2002. Internet abuse in the workplace. *Communications of the ACM* 45, 1, 53–54.
Anandarajan, M., Devine, P., and Simmers, C.A. 2004. A multidimensional scaling approach to personal Web usage in the workplace. In M. Anandarajan and C.A. Simmers (eds.), *Personal Web Usage in the Workplace: A Guide to Effective Human Resources Management.* Hershey, PA: Idea Group, 61–78.

Anandarajan, M., and Simmers, C.A. 2002. Factors influencing Web access behavior in the workplace: A structural equation approach. In M. Anandarajan (ed.), *Internet Usage in the Workplace: A Social, Ethical and Legal Perspective.* Hershey, PA: Idea Group, 44–66.

———. 2004. Constructive and dyfunctional personal Web usage in the workplace: Mapping employee attitudes. In M. Anandarajan and C.A. Simmers (eds.), *Personal Web Usage in the Workplace: A Guide to Effective Human Resources Management.* Hershey, PA: Idea Group, 1–27.

Belanger, F., and Van Slyke, C. 2002. Abuse or learning? *Communications of the ACM* 45, 1, 64–65.

Bennett, R.J., and Robinson, S.L. 2003. The past, present, and future of workplace deviance research. In J. Greenberg (ed.), *Organizational Behavior,* 2nd ed. Mahwah, NJ: Lawrence Erlbaum Associates, 247–281.

Bolin, A., and Heatherly, L. 2001. Predictors of employee deviance: The relationship between bad attitudes and bad behavior. *Journal of Business and Psychology* 15, 3, 405–418.

Brenner, V. 1997. Psychology of computer use: XLVII. Parameters of Internet use, abuse and addiction: The first 90 days of the Internet Usage Survey. *Psychological Reports* 80, 3, 879–882.

Cameron, A.F., and Webster, J. 2005. Unintended consequences of emerging communication technologies: Instant messaging in the workplace. *Computers in Human Behavior* 21, 1, 85–103.

David, R.A. 2001. A cognitive-behavioral model of pathological Internet use. *Computers in Human Behavior* 17, 2, 187–195.

Davis, F.D., Bagozzi, R.P., and Warshaw, P.R. 1989. User acceptance of computer technology: A comparison of two theoretical models. *Management Science* 35, 8, 982–1003.

Garton, L., Haythornthwaite, C., and Wellman, B. 1997. Studying online social networks. *Journal of Computer-Mediated Communication* 13, 1.

Greenfield, D.N. 1999. *Virtual Addiction: Help for Netheads, Cyberfreaks, and Those Who Love Them.* Oakland, CA: New Harbinger Publications.

Griffiths, M. 2000. Does Internet and computer "addiction" exist? Some case study evidence. *CyberPsychology and Behavior* 3, 2, 211–218.

Haythornthwaite, C., and Wellman, B. 1998. Work, friendship, and media use for information exchange in a networked organization. *Journal of the American Society for Information Science* 49, 12, 1101–1114.

Haythornthwaite, C., Wellman, B., and Garton, L. 1998. Work and community via computer-mediated communication. In J. Gackenbach (ed.), *Psychology and the Internet: Intrapersonal, Interpersonal, and Transpersonal Implications.* San Diego: Academic Press, 199–225.

Hollinger, R.C., and Clark, J.P. 1982. Formal and informal social controls of employee deviance. *Sociological Quarterly* 23, 3, 333–343.

Joinson, A. 1998. Causes and implications of disinhibited behavior on the Internet. In J. Gackenbach (ed.), *Psychology and the Internet: Intrapersonal, Interpersonal, and Transpersonal Implications.* San Diego: Academic Press, 43–59.

Kraut, R., and Kiesler, S. 2003. The social impact of Internet use. *Psychological Science Agenda* 16, 3, 8–10.

Lewicki, R.J., Poland, T., Minton, J.W., and Sheppard, B.H. 1997. Dishonesty as deviance: A typology of workplace dishonesty and contributing factors. In R.J. Lewicki, R.J. Bies, and B.H. Sheppard (eds.), *Research on Negotiation in Organizations.* Greenwich, CT: Jai Press, 53–86.

Lim, V.K.G. 2002. The IT way of loafing on the job: Cyberloafing, neutralizing, and organizational justice. *Journal of Organizational Behavior* 23, 675–694.

Lim, V.K.G., Teo, T.S.H., and Loo, G.L. 2002. How do I loaf here? Let me count the ways. *Communications of the ACM* 45, 1, 66–70.

Mahatanankoon, P., Anandarajan, M., and Igbaria, M. 2004. Development of a measure of personal Web usage in the workplace. *CyberPsychology and Behavior* 7, 1, 93–104.

Miller, N. 1997. Employees on the Net. *Computers and Law* 8, 4, 3–4.

Mirchandani, D., and Motwani, J. 2003. Reducing Internet abuse in the workplace. *S.A.M.® Advanced Management Journal,* 68, 1 (2003), 22–26.

Morahan-Martin, J., and Schumacher, P. 2000. Incidence and correlates of pathological Internet use among college students. *Computers in Human Behavior* 16, 1, 13–29.

Oravec, J.A. 2002. Constructive approach to Internet recreation in the workplace. *Communications of the ACM* 45, 1, 60–63.

Papacharissi, Z., and Rubin, A.M. 2000. Predictors of Internet use. *Journal of Broadcasting and Electronic Media* 44, 2, 175–196.

Raghavan, P. 2002. Social networks. *Internet Computing* 6, 1, 91.

Robinson, S.L., and Bennett, R.J. 1995. A typology of deviant workplace behaviors: A multidimensional scaling study. *Academy of Management Journal* 38, 2, 555–572.

———. 1997. Workplace deviance: Its definition, its manifestations, and its causes. In R.J. Lewicki, R.J. Bies, and B.H. Sheppard (eds.), *Research on Negotiation in Organizations*. Greenwich, CT: Jai Press, 3–27.

Robinson, S.L., and Greenberg, J. 1998. Employees behaving badly: dimensions, determinants and dilemmas in the study of workplace deviance. In C.L. Cooper and D.M. Rousseau (eds.), *Trends in Organizational Behavior*. New York: John Wiley, 1–30.

Scheuermann, L.E., and Langford, H.P. 1997. Perceptions of Internet abuse, liability, and fair use. *Perceptual and Motor Skills* 85, 3, 847–850.

Siau, K., Fui-Hoon Nah, F., and Teng, L. 2002. Acceptable Internet use policy. *Communications of the ACM* 45, 1, 75–79.

Stanton, J.M. 2002. Company profile of the frequent Internet user. *Communications of the ACM* 45, 1, 55–59.

SurfControl.com. 2004. The cost of non-business browsing. www.surfcontrol.com/products/web/.

Taylor, S., and Todd, P.A. 1995. Understanding information technology usage: A test of competing models. *Information Systems Research* 6, 2, 144–176.

Urbaczewski, A., and Jessup, L.M. 2002. Does electronic monitoring of employee Internet usage work? *Communications of the ACM* 45, 1, 80–83.

Wen, H.J., and Lin, B. 1998. Internet and employee productivity. *Management Decision* 36, 6, 395–398.

Young, K.S. 1996. Psychology of computer use: XL. Addictive use of the Internet: A case that breaks the stereotype. *Psychological Reports* 79, 3, 899–902.

———. 1998. Internet addiction: The emergence of a new clinical disorder. *CyberPsychology and Behavior* 1, 3, 237–244.

CHAPTER 3

SELF-REGULATION OF COMMUNICATION TECHNOLOGY IN THE WORKPLACE

MATTHEW S. EASTIN, CARROLL J. GLYNN, AND ROBERT P. GRIFFITHS

Abstract: Prior research regarding employee technology use has produced varied findings. The purpose of this chapter is to discuss how and why technology in the workplace can have both positive and negative effects on employee productivity. The discussion will center on a model outlining the relationships between an individual's psychological state, self-efficacy, deficient self-regulation, habitual use, and general use of computer technologies. A new component to the model is proposed with the addition of image management. The model attempts to explain how psychological state and image management relate both directly and indirectly to self-efficacy perceptions and unregulated Internet use and how, in turn, these variables influence use.

Keywords: Communication Technology, Internet Use, Self-efficacy, Social Cognitive Theory, Self-regulation, Internet Addiction, Habit, Employee Productivity, Job Satisfaction

TECHNOLOGY USE IN ORGANIZATIONS

Employees are the critical driving force in acquiring and distributing information within and between organizations. Individuals rarely work alone; instead, they now tend to work in mediated groups (Cohen and Bailey 1997; Hollenbeck et al. 1998; Mason and Griffin 2002; Prasad and Akhilesh 2002; Schilder 1992; Stewart and Barrick 2000; Stough et al. 2000). The tendency for group work to be conducted through the use of computer technologies increases the need for understanding the dynamic relationship between technology, employee use, and employer needs.

In order to understand how and why employees adopt various computer-mediated technologies in the workplace, it is important to understand the technologies available to employees. Not surprisingly, nearly 70 percent of companies provide Internet access to at least half of their employees (Young and Case 2004), this occurring after the Internet boom in the early 1990s (Hannemyr 2003). Many employees have access to e-mail, instant messaging (IM), and Web browsing, for example. Simply because communication technologies are available does not mean that they are automatically put to use. In fact, studies have found that nearly 24 percent of Americans prefer not to use the World

Wide Web (Powell 2003). Nonetheless, the availability of these technologies and their use by a majority of employees at some level indicates a need to study the impact of computer-mediated technologies on employees and employee interactions.

Using Bandura's (1986) social cognitive theory (SCT), we examine two behavioral incentives as motivations for technology use—self-reactive and image or status management. We also explore how activities such as IM and electronic mail (e-mail), while seen as methods for increasing productivity in the workplace, can also contribute to non-work-related problematic Internet use, resulting in a decrease in overall productivity.

Electronic communication, like other forms of organizational communication, is classified into genres that help organize community structures and shape communicative actions (Yates et al. 1999). The most prominent communication technology in the workplace is e-mail. E-mail has been available at some level for public use for more than thirty-five years (Myers 2003; see also Pankoke-Babatz and Jeffrey 2002) and has been in the mainstream of technology use for nearly fifteen years (Hannemyr 2003). In fact, the use of e-mail has increased dramatically over the past seven years (Pankoke-Babatz and Jeffrey 2002). Use is estimated to range from fifty to ninety minutes per day (Conrad and Poole 2002; Dawley and Anthony 2003; Hymans 2002; Lantz 1998; Van Waes 2003) to nearly a quarter of the day (Frazee 1996). Most of this time is spent solely on managing e-mail, clearly establishing that this type of technology is firmly rooted in organizational culture.

Another computer-mediated communication (CMC) technology seeing increased use is instant messaging. IM is a program that allows direct and virtually synchronous communication. The technology permits "users to set up a list of partners who will be able to receive notes that pop up on their screens the moment one of them writes and hits the send button" (Castelluccio 1999, 35). Research has shown that nearly 45 percent of Internet users at work currently have access to consumer IM services (Varchaver and Bonamici 2003), and IM technology use is drastically rising (Powell 2003). Additionally, Bellman found that companies have reduced their phone use by 81 percent and e-mail by 67 percent when using IM software (2003). IM has a multitude of benefits: it is virtually spam-free (does not receive unsolicited messages), users are capable of participating in multiple conversations, and use of IM saves time and money. IM use may be on a steep incline because "U.S. citizens have much more information-handling capacity now than a half-century ago" (Bimber 1998, 140). This access potentially results in increased multitasking and media use, especially since IM often runs in the computer's background concurrently with other programs.

MOTIVATIONS FOR TECHNOLOGY USE: EXAMINATION OF TWO MODELS

In order to better understand the use of computer technology by workers, two models will be examined: Fishbein and Ajzen's theory of reasoned action and Bandura's social cognitive theory.

The first model, the theory of reasoned action, often was applied in early research for understanding the use of computer technology (Fishbein and Ajzen 1975). This model specifies the relationship between beliefs, attitudes, and behaviors. The theory is based on the assumption that humans are rational. Because they are rational, they calculate the costs and benefits of engaging in particular actions, taking into account the perceptions that significant others (like coworkers) might have concerning their actions. While this approach had success predicting the use of computing technologies (Thompson et al. 1991; Triandis 1980), later studies indicated that modifications to the model were needed. For example, by linking beliefs to emotion, future consequences increase the predictive power and understanding of information system uses and individual behaviors. Compeau and Higgins (1995) and Ajzen (1985) suggest that an individual's perceived ability to perform a behavior also could play an important role in the adoption process. These scholars suggest that the level of complexity each behavior presents could influence the role that internal perceptions play in adoption. According to Eastin and LaRose (2000), the complex nature of using the Internet, as well as information systems in general, requires researchers to include self-regulating mechanisms, such as self-efficacy, outcome expectancies, and self-regulation in their studies.

The second model, SCT, posits a complex causal structure that establishes the development of competency and the regulation of action (Bandura 1986). Through the development of knowledge structures, cognitive models of effective action that guide behavior are created. These cognitive models afford individuals the ability to produce skills as well as internal standards needed to execute proficiently a behavior. Cognitive guidance toward behavior is essential to the developmental stages of a behavior. Scholars identified cognitive components such as perceived abilities and outcomes and self-regulation as important determinants to online behavior. Specifically, in an attempt to theoretically position problematic Internet use, LaRose et al. (2003) developed a model of Internet use that includes variables such as perceived information complexity, Internet self-efficacy, outcome expectancies, deficient self-regulation, and habit, all of which directly and indirectly influence use.

In this model, self-efficacy, defined as the belief in one's capability to organize and execute a particular course of action (as it pertains to Internet use), is treated as an exogenous variable influencing behavioral incentives, self-regulation, and use (Bandura 1986). Self-efficacy is particularly relevant as it pertains to novice users. These individuals have not yet acquired the skills needed to obtain information and deal with the many problems of life online, ranging from viruses to balky home Internet connections. Here, scholars found that prior experience with the Internet in turn causally preceded Internet self-efficacy (Eastin and LaRose 2000), probably through the process of enactive mastery (Bandura 1986) in which users gradually master complex tasks. Researchers found not only a direct relationship between self-efficacy and Internet usage (Eastin and LaRose 2000; LaRose and Eastin 2004; LaRose et al. 2001) but also an indirect relationship through expected outcomes. Simply, when Internet users become more self-efficacious, their usage expectations also increase, encouraging more usage.

According to SCT, outcome expectancies are organized around six theoretically constructed types of incentives for human behavior: activity, social, novel sensory, monetary, self-reactive, and status incentives (Bandura 1986). Activity incentives stem from the desire to take part in enjoyable activities, while social incentives arise from rewarding interactions with others. Novel sensory incentives include the search for new and novel information, and monetary incentives are simply expectancies to achieve some sort of financial gain. Particular to organizations and technology use is the concept of self-reactive (or self-evaluative) incentives, which involve the attempt to regulate dysphoric moods such as depression and boredom, and status or image management (improving oneself in the eyes of others).

Self-reactive incentives provide behavioral or psychological rewards. These rewards can include self-evaluative ones, such as self-satisfaction derived from engaging in an activity that meets desired outcomes. Reactive incentives allow users to regulate moods such as boredom and stress. That said, self-reactive incentives (LaRose and Eastin 2004; LaRose et al. 2003) recently have been identified as playing a key role in new media consumption. Psychological states such as boredom are positively related to self-reactive incentives that in turn result in problematic Internet use (LaRose et al. 2003). In the workplace, boredom is costly and detrimental to the organization. It is "an unpleasant, transient affective state in which the individual feels a pervasive lack of interest in and difficulty concentrating on the current activity . . . [and] feels that it takes conscious effort to maintain or return attention to that activity" (Fisher 1993, 396; cf. Fisher 1998, 503). Such a negative and dissatisfying emotional state moves the employees away from the work at hand, requiring more time and effort to get the job accomplished—a state of being opposite to the concept of "flow" as defined by Csikszentmihalyi (1975). Bored employees are dissatisfied with the work itself and their pay, lack of promotion, supervisor, and coworkers. Additionally, boredom has been associated with a decrease in performance (Kass et al. 2001).

Boredom may result from job tasks that are monotonous and provide little variety. At work, boredom motivates individuals to find activities that provide stimulation and excitement. To this end, networked technologies provide a ready source of diversion in the workplace. It is a quick shift from monotonous tasks to opening a new browser window and playing online games while communicating with family and friends, activities that subsequently reduce the effect of dysphoric moods such as boredom. This type of behavioral or affective management can be interpreted through SCT as a self-reactive incentive. A summary of these important concepts and significant research is in Table 3.1.

MODELS OF ONLINE ADDICTION

Research has focused on three primary models of addiction—the addictive personality model, the disease model, and the operant conditioning model. Media addictions are a type of behavioral addiction in which there is no chemical substance involved (Marks 1990). Media addicts feel compelled to consume media despite potentially negative consequences that make continued use appear irrational or out of control. Operant conditioning formulations of the general problem of addiction (e.g., Marks 1990; Marlatt et al.

Table 3.1

Summary of Important Concepts and Significant Research

Authors	Behavioral and psychological control	Psychological state	Behavioral incentive
Landis, Triandis, and Adamopoulos (1978)	Habit		
Arkin (1981)			Image management
Bandura (1986)	Self-efficacy	Psychological well-being	Self-reactive incentives Status incentives
Marlatt, Baer, Donovan, and Kivlahan (1988)	Addiction		
Marks (1990)	Addiction		
Stone and Stone (1990)	Habit		
Ajzen (1985)	Self-efficacy		
Compeau and Higgins (1995)	Self-efficacy		
Eastin and LaRose (2000)	Self-efficacy	Psychological well-being	
LaRose, Mastro, and Eastin (2001)	Self-efficacy Addiction		Activity incentives
Crane and Crane (2002)			Image management
Gardner (2002)			Image management
LaRose, Lin, and Eastin (2003)	Self-efficacy Deficient self-regulation habit	Psychological well-being	Self-reactive incentives
Eastin and LaRose (2004)	Self-efficacy Deficient self-regulation habit		Self-reactive incentives
Glynn (2004)			Image management

Note: This is not an exhaustive list of important research in the field or projects conducted. It merely represents significant research and key concepts used to develop the conceptual model presented in this chapter.

1988) have been commonly cited by media addiction researchers (e.g., Brenner 1997; Davis 2001; Griffiths 1995, 1999; Young 1999). This model posits that consumption behavior progresses in four phases: initiation, transition to ongoing use, addiction, and behavior change (Marlatt et al. 1988).

Addictive behaviors are experienced and can be perceived as inherently pleasurable and rewarding. Thus, the perceived outcomes of media behavior (LaRose et al. 2001; Lin 2001) could explain ongoing media behavior. Further, it is possible for media behavior to become habitual, automatic (Stone and Stone 1990), or ritualistic (Lin 1993; Rubin 1984) while remaining consistent with conscious self-interest during the early phase of addiction.

As explained by LaRose et al. (2003), the transition to problematic usage begins when the behavior acts as an important or exclusive mechanism to relieve some form of negative affect—stress, loneliness, depression, boredom, or anxiety. When this problematic media use becomes excessive, it in turn causes life problems including confrontations with employers or an inability to stop media consumption once started. Negative life events may further heighten dysphoric moods, leading to further reliance on media consumption, thus creating a cyclical relationship. Transitioning from acceptable to unacceptable use is marked by diminished response to the addictive behavior and withdrawal symptoms in its absence. Also, there is a narrowing of addictive behaviors; for example, an individual may spend more time chatting or gaming online and less time with other online activities. This response can increase the importance of the behavior, resulting in a neglect of work responsibilities. Finally, awareness of the compulsion and relapse following periods of abstinence complete the addictive cycle (Marlatt et al. 1988).

It is important to understand that media usage need only be excessive relative to the individual's prior consumption patterns rather than in absolute terms. Individuals with consumption levels far above average are not necessarily considered "addicts" if their media usage does not result in a cyclical pattern. Thus, behaviors, including media usage, are not considered inherently harmful by nature but can be considered harmful habits when they turn into conditioned responses.

Reliance on the Internet to overcome loneliness (Eastin and LaRose 2004; Morahan-Martin and Schumacher 2000; Scherer 1997; Young and Rogers 1998), to develop a feeling of mastery, or to provide a means of escape (Morahan-Martin and Schumacher 2000) also can indicate a state in which the consumption of the medium, as opposed to content in the medium, becomes rewarding in itself. Researchers who conducted an initial exploration of unpleasant mood levels and Internet consumption found that unpleasant levels of excitation affected online behavioral search patterns; online behavior (search pace), but not content, was used to alleviate heightened levels of stress and boredom (Mastro et al. 2002). In the present context, employees who are bored or depressed while at work and view the Internet or applications available online as a means of reducing these states could in fact turn to the Internet as a conditioned response.

To review, addictive media consumption may be prompted by internal cues (such as boredom) or external cues (such as the sight of a computer or computer mouse) that activate the same affective response as the media stimuli themselves did initially. Media addictions can eventually cause users to experience some form of life crisis and a need for professional help (Marks 1990). That said, unregulated Internet use or Internet addiction becomes a problem only when self-regulation fails. In this case, increased media consumption may be expected (LaRose et al. 2003). From this perspective, unregulated Internet use has been conceptualized in terms of habit and deficient self-regulation (LaRose et al. 2003).

Simply put, a habit is a recurring behavior pattern and is a well-established predictor of behavior (Ouellette and Wood 1998; Triandis 1980). Research (Aarts et al. 1998; LaRose and Eastin 2004; LaRose et al. 2003) suggests that habit is a form of automaticity —a pattern of behavior (e.g., checking one's e-mail) that follows a fixed cognitive schema, triggered by an environmental stimulus (e.g., seeing the computer in the morning) or by recalling a goal (e.g., keeping up with family or friends) and performed without self-instruction. Automatic media consumption is initially framed by active considerations that are eventually forgotten (Stone and Stone 1990). For example, a person checking the news online when arriving at work may consider all the communication options during the first hundred times but during the 101st time may not (LaRose and Eastin 2004). Repeated media consumption increases habit strength and subsequently future usage (Landis et al. 1978). Here, the processing and learning of information takes place even when persons are not attending to the behavior in question (LaBerge and Samuels 1974), so habit strength may increase with habitual use. Within SCT, habit is a failure of the self-monitoring subfunction of self-regulation. Through repetition Internet users become inattentive to the reasoning behind their media behavior; the mind no longer devotes attention resources to evaluating the behavior, freeing itself for more important decisions. To this end, habit strength influences ongoing behavior independent of current active thinking about behavioral incentives. Habit is causally determined by outcome expectations, which precede habit in time.

Deficient self-regulation, a state in which conscious self-control is diminished, has been proposed as an explanatory mechanism for problematic Internet use (LaRose et al. 2003). LaRose et al. found that deficient self-regulation was directly related to Internet usage and that deficient self-regulation also contributed to usage indirectly, through habit strength. As deficient self-regulation initiates, media behavior becomes an end unto itself and is no longer subject to active consideration of its expected outcomes. One important exception to this finding occurs when users counteract the negative effects that result from personal problems. These problems intensify with excessive media usage as part of a self-reinforcing "downward spiral" into problematic usage (for details, see LaRose et al. 2003).

It appears that when employees grow bored or stressed at work they may turn to Internet applications to counter their negative feelings. This use will eventually cause employees' self-regulation mechanisms to fail and habitual use to increase, which could potentially have a negative effect on job productivity (see Figure 3.1).

IMAGE MANAGEMENT AND TECHNOLOGY USE

Another factor to be considered when evaluating individual incentives for engaging in various forms of technology use is the psychological need to monitor others' perceptions of one's abilities and skills in the use of information technology. Similar to Bandura's "status" incentive, organizational literature defines this need as "impression management," which will be the term used in this chapter. Impression management theory establishes how people present an image to others in order to achieve a particular goal. Most studies of impression management assume that the primary goal is to attain social approval (Arkin 1981). According to organizational scholars, impression management (also called "dramaturgy") can explain much about the behavior that occurs in organizational settings (Crane and Crane 2002; Gardner 1992). Impression management theorists assume that people want to convey, given social constraints, as positive and consistent a public image as possible in order to obtain social rewards—regardless of whether that image is consistent with internalized attitudes (Glynn 2004). As Nelson and Quick note, "Impression management is the process by which individuals try to control (influence) the impressions others have of them" (2003, 102).

Figure 3.1 **Structural Model to Internet Use**

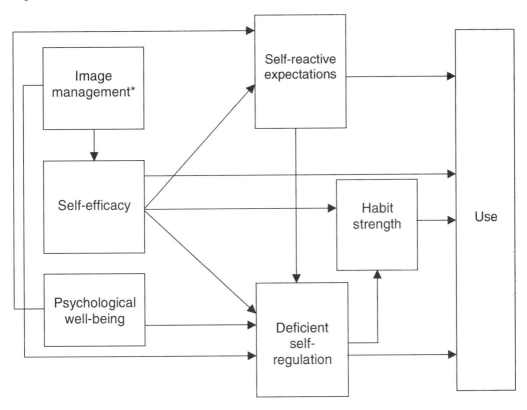

Source: Adapted from LaRose et al. (2003).
*Not part of the original proposed by LaRose et al. (2003).

The impressions individuals make on others have implications for how others perceive, evaluate, and treat them. Individuals tend to behave in ways that will create the intended or desired impressions (Crane and Crane 2002; Leary and Kowalski 1990), regardless of the dissonance this facade may create internally. Gardner (1992) states that impression management is pervasive throughout an organization in many formal and informal workplace contexts.

Certainly the management of perceptions and one's image also should apply to the use of communication technologies. From a social cognitive perspective, image management through technology use measures the extent to which people believe using a technology will enhance their image. For example, at work it may be important to be perceived as having exceptional skills in maneuvering through various informational spaces or using complicated applications such as communication technology to seek information on the Web. In this case, the use of technology for these purposes could increase, subsequently increasing productivity. However, from a social context, using technology to communicate with others through IM or e-mail or being able to show complex interactions through the use of online multiuser environments may be the desirable impression. Here, skills could be viewed as negative within an organization because engagement in such activities would have a negative impact on productivity in the workplace. Further, even if skills are developed for positive organization purposes, the skills could later be used for noncompany outcomes like using the Internet when bored.

In terms of impression management, the inherent efficiency of sending messages out to many individuals by e-mail is an easy way to promote authority, not to mention the myriad of subtle clues included in e-mails that regularly reinforce status (e.g., signature blocks that include organizational title). To this end, impression management should have a positive effect on an individual's self-efficacy and deficient self-regulation, an effect that then theoretically leads to an increase in usage through habit. Thus, the effect of image management on overall productivity could be positive or negative, depending on the individual activity and reasons for engagement.

Researchers have provided several taxonomies of impression management strategies used by individuals—both to acquire and promote favorable impressions (e.g., ingratiation, exemplification) and to protect or repair one's image (apologies) and accounts (explanations) (Crane and Crane 2002; Ellis et al. 2002). Regardless of the reasons for engaging in impression management behaviors, it is clear such management permeates an entire organization and includes the use (or abuse) of communication technologies.

The issues concerning self-regulation can be problematic and potentially very costly in traditional workplace environments. The potential exists for even more negative consequences from deficient self-regulation as companies look toward the future and begin implementing teleworkers and virtual organizations. Additionally, the more difficult and diverse jobs (requiring consistency in output) are increasingly automated by machines, leaving employees with less strenuous tasks and promoting the potential for boredom in the workplace. Practically all business communication is electronic, consisting of a hybrid of technologies to accomplish work. Face-to-face interaction is still a communication medium option (often of choice); however, that medium is often supplemented with a myriad of other options, including e-mail and IM.

DEFINING MODELS OF TECHNOLOGY ABUSE IN ORGANIZATIONS

Another deficient self-regulation issue concerns bandwidth. Bandwidth often is currency in the business world. The terminals and networks that employees use are the company's, not the employees'. Problematic and addictive new media use abuses company property and inherently involves the employee not performing at peak level. On the other hand, businesses set up employees for failure by not addressing workplace environments that could cause boredom, stress, or the need to improve one's status through technology. Clearly, this problem will only become more complex as technologies are improved and new ones are created.

This chapter defines and adapts a model of problematic communication technology use within an organization. Within this model, as workers employ image management strategies through communication technology, self-efficacy perceptions regarding technology use increase, subsequently influencing use, directly and indirectly, through self-reactive behavioral incentives, deficient self-regulation, and habit. Here, self-efficacy increases habit strength since users are inattentive to behaviors they are still mastering (LaRose et al. 2003; LaRose and Eastin 2004). Employee psychological state also increases use indirectly through self-reactive incentives and deficient self-regulation. As workers become bored, they seek self-reactive incentives as a means to counter the boredom. At the same time, boredom acts as a diminished psychological state in which self-regulation is inherently diminished. Finally, deficient self-regulation positively influences habit through repetition; both deficient self-regulation and self-reactive incentives positively impact overall use.

FUTURE RESEARCH

While this chapter has posited that employee perceptions and psychological states can influence addictive behavior and productivity, little empirical evidence exists within the organizational context to support these relationships. Future research should begin to question the relationships between workplace-induced psychological states, socially constructed image, technology use, and productivity. In doing so, employee satisfaction, job boredom, and stress at work could all be considered psychological triggers to self-reactive incentives. This type of project would require an organization that has an open Internet use policy, as download and site restrictions would influence use.

Another logical avenue for future research would be to examine employees' perceptions of other employees. Investigations could include the study of how employees perceive others' technology use and whether employees believe that use of applications (such as IM or gaming) decreases job productivity. While it is well known that not all technology use in the workplace is for the organization, how actual use and perceived use influence actual productivity and perceived productivity is still relatively unknown. These perceptions could help explain negative attitudes that employees harbor toward others and the workplace. This information would help organizations better understand how to implement technology use by employees most effectively.

CONCLUSION

As researchers it is our responsibility to continually challenge old ideas with new ones. This chapter moves away from several commonly held beliefs about general technology use in organizations. For example, while past research has focused on the positive impact of technology on productivity, this chapter suggests that use itself could be detrimental to both productivity and employee well-being. Additionally, the reconstruction of Internet addiction through the social cognitive constructs of deficient self-regulation and habit is not part of the mainstream logic driving online addiction research. The authors believe that within a social cognitive framework, research on technology use within an organization can be further understood outside the generic conceptualization of media addiction. We believe that the concepts outlined in this chapter, although framed within an organizational context, can be used to investigate the use of communication technology not only at work, but also at home, at school, and in various other settings and for a variety of different audiences (e.g., teenagers, the elderly, and families).

REFERENCES

Aarts, H., Verplanken, B., and van Knippenberg, A. 1998. Predicting behavior from actions in the past: Repeated decision making or a matter of habit? *Journal of Applied Social Psychology* 28, 1355–1374.

Ajzen, I. 1985. From intentions to actions: A theory of planned behavior. In J. Kuhl and J. Beckman (eds.), *Action-Control: From Cognition to Behavior.* Heidelberg: Springer, 11–39.

Arkin, R.M. 1981. Self-presentation styles. In J.T. Tedeschi (ed.), *Impression Management Theory and Social Psychological Theory.* London: Academic Press, 311–333.

Bandura, A. 1986. *Social Foundations of Thought and Action: A Social Cognitive Theory.* Englewood Cliffs, NJ: Prentice-Hall, xiii.

Bimber, B. 1998. The Internet and political transformation: Populism, community, and accelerated pluralism. *Journal of the Northeastern Political Science Association* 31, 1, 133–160.

Brenner, V. 1997. Psychology of computer use: XLVII. Parameters of Internet use, abuse and addiction: The first 90 days of the Internet usage survey. *Psychological Reports* 80, 879–882.

Castelluccio, M. 1999. E-mail in real time. *Strategic Finance* 81, 3, 34–37.

Cohen, S.G., and Bailey, D.E. 1997. What makes teams work: Group effectiveness research from the shop floor to the executive suite. *Journal of Management* 23, 3, 239–290.

Compeau, D., and Higgins, C. 1995. Computer self-efficacy: Development of a measure and initial test. *MIS Quarterly* 1, 189–211.

Conrad, C., and Poole, M.S. 2002. *Strategic Organizational Communication in a Global Economy.* 5th ed. Philadelphia: Harcourt College Publishers.

Crane, E., and Crane, F.G. 2002. Usage and effectiveness of impression management strategies in organizational settings. *Journal of Group Psychotherapy, Psychodrama, and Sociometry* 25, 25–34.

Csikszentmihalyi, M. 1975. *Beyond Boredom and Anxiety.* San Francisco: Jossey-Bass.

Davis, R.A. 2001. A cognitive-behavioral model of pathological Internet use. *Computers in Human Behavior* 17, 187–195.

Dawley, D.D., and Anthony, W.P. 2003. User perceptions of e-mail at work. *Journal of Business and Technical Communication* 17, 2, 170–200.

Eastin, M.S., and LaRose, R. 2000. Internet self-efficacy and the psychology of the digital divide. *Journal of Computer Mediated Communication* 6, 1. www.ascusc.org/jcmc/v016/issue1/eastin.html.

———. 2004. Alt.support: Modeling social support on-line. *Computers in Human Behavior,* 21, 6, 977–992.

Ellis, A.P., West, B.J., Ryan, A.M, and Deshon, R.P. 2002. The use of impression management tactics in structured interviews: A function of question type? *Journal of Applied Psychology* 87, 1200–1208.

Fishbein, M., and Ajzen, I. 1975. *Belief, Attitude, Intentions and Behavior: An Introductory to Theory and Research.* Boston: Addison-Wesley.

Fisher, C.D. 1993. Boredom at work: A neglected concept. *Human Relations* 46, 395–417.

———. 1998. Effects of external and internal interruptions on boredom at work: Two studies. *Journal of Organizational Behavior* 19, 503–522.

Frazee, V. 1996. Is e-mail doing more harm than good? *Personnel Journal* 75, 5, 23.

Gardner, W.L. 1992. Lessons in organizational dramaturgy: The art of impression management. *Organizational Dynamics* 21, 33–47.

Glynn, C.J. 2004. *Public Opinion.* Boulder, CO: Westview/Harper Collins Press.

Griffiths, M. 1995. Technological addictions. *Clinical Psychology Forum* 71, 14–19.

———. 1999. Internet addiction: Fact or fiction? *Psychologist* 12, 246–250.

Hannemyr, G. 2003. The Internet as hyperbole: A critical examination of adoption rates. *Information Society* 19, 111–121.

Hollenbeck, J.R., Ilgen, D.R., LePine, J.A., Colquitt, J.A., and Hedlund, J. 1998. Extending the multi-level theory of team decision making: Effects of feedback and experience in hierarchical teams. *Academy of Management Journal* 41, 3, 269–282.

Hymans, N. 2002. Is e-mail your black hole of productivity? *NZ Business* 16, 5, 11.

Jackson, T., Dawson, R., and Wilson, D. 2003. Reducing the effect of e-mail interruptions on employees. *International Journal of Information Management* 23, 55–65.

Kass, S.J., Vodanovich, S.J., and Callender, A. 2001. State-trait boredom: Relationship to absenteeism, tenure, and job satisfaction. *Journal of Business and Psychology* 16, 2, 317–327.

LaBerge, D., and Samuels, S.J. 1974. Toward a theory of automatic information processing in reading. *Cognitive Psychology* 6, 293–323.

Landis D., Triandis, H.C., and Adamopoulos, J. 1978. Habit and behavioral intentions as predictors of social behavior. *Journal of Social Psychology* 106, 227–237.

Lantz, A. 1998. Heavy users of electronic mail. *International Journal of Human-Computer Interaction* 10, 4, 361–379.

LaRose, R., and Eastin, M.S. 2004. A social cognitive explanation of Internet usage: Toward a new theory of media attendance. *Journal of Broadcasting and Electronic Media* 48, 3, 358–377.

LaRose, R., Lin, C., and Eastin, M.S. 2003. Unregulated Internet usage: Addiction, habits, or deficient self-regulation? *Media Psychology* 5, 3, 225–253.

LaRose, R., Mastro, D., and Eastin, M.S. 2001. Understanding Internet usage. *Social Science and Computer Review* 19, 395–413.

Leary, M.R., and Kowalski, R.M. 1990. Impression management: A literature review and two-component model. *Psychological Bulletin* 107, 34–47.

Lim, V.K.G., Teo, T.S.H., and Loo, G.L. 2002. How do I loaf here? Let me count the ways. *Journal of the ACM* 45, 1, 66–70.

Lin, C.A. 1993. Adolescents' viewing activity and gratifications in a new media environment. *Mass Communication Review* 20, 39–50.

———. 2001. Audience attributes, media supplementation and likely online service adoption. *Mass Communication and Society* 4, 19–38.

Marks, I. 1990. Behavioral (non-chemical) addictions. *British Journal of Addiction* 85, 1389–1394.

Marlatt, G.A., Baer, J.S., Donovan, D.M., and Kivlahan, D.R. 1988. Addictive behaviors: Etiology and treatment. *Annual Review of Psychology* 39, 223–252.

Mason, C.M., and Griffin, M.A. 2002. Group task satisfaction: Applying the construct of job satisfaction to groups. *Small Group Research* 33, 3, 271–312.

Mastro, D., Eastin, M.S., and Tamborini, R. 2002. Internet search behavior and mood alteration: Replication and expansion of selective exposure theory. *Media Psychology* 4, 157–172.

McCune, J.C. 1998. Technology: The productivity paradox. *HR Focus* 75, 4, 3–5.

Morahan-Martin, J., and Schumacher, P. 2000. Incidence and correlates of pathological Internet use among college students. *Computers in Human Behavior* 16, 13–29.

Myers, G. 2003. Indispensable Internet. *Columbus Dispatch,* April 14.

Nelson, D.L., and Quick, J.C. 2003. *Organizational Behavior.* Mason, OH: Southwestern.

Oravec, J.A. 2002. Constructive approaches to Internet recreation in the workplace. *Communications of the ACM* 45, 1, 60–63.

Ouellette, J.A., and Wood, W. 1998. Habit and intention in everyday life: The multiple processes by which past behavior predicts future behavior. *Psychological Bulletin* 124, 54–74.

Pankoke-Babatz, U., and Jeffrey, P. 2002. Documented norms and conventions on the Internet. *International Journal of Human-Computer Interaction* 14, 2, 219–235.

Powell, W. 2003. Web = Waste of time? *T+D* 57, 3, 28.

Prasad, K., and Akhilesh, K.B. 2002. Global virtual teams: What impacts their design and performance? *Team Performance Management* 8, 5, 102–112.

Rubin, A.M. 1984. Ritualized and instrumental television viewing. *Journal of Communication* 34, 67–77.

Scherer, K. 1997. College life on-line: Healthy and unhealthy Internet use. *Journal of College Student Development* 38, 655–664.

Schilder, J. 1992. Work teams boost productivity. *Personnel Journal* 71, 2, 67–71.

Stewart, G.L., and Barrick, M.R. 2000. Team structure and performance: Assessing the mediating role of intrateam process and the moderating role of task type. *Academy of Management Journal* 43, 2, 135–148.

Stone, G., and Stone, D. 1990. Lurking in the literature: Another look at media use habits. *Mass Communication Review* 17, 25–33.

Stough, S., Eom, S., and Buckenmyer, J. 2000. Virtual teaming: A strategy for moving your organization into the new millennium. *Industrial Management and Data Systems* 100, 8, 370–378.

Thompson, R.L., Higgins, C.A., and Howell, J. 1991. Personal computing: Towards a conceptual model of utilization. *MIS Quarterly* 14, 125–143.

Triandis, H.C. 1980. Values, attitudes, and interpersonal behavior. *Nebraska Symposium on Motivation: Beliefs, Attitude, and Values.* Lincoln: University of Nebraska Press, 195–259.

Van Waes, L. 2003. Use and misuse of e-mail. *Document Design* 4, 3, 279–280.

Varchaver, N., and Bonamici, K. 2003. The perils of e-mail. *Fortune (Europe)* 147, 3, 66–71.

Yates, J., Orlikowski, W.J., and Okamura, K. 1999. Explicit and implicit structuring of genres in electronic communication: Reinforcement and change of social interaction. *Organization Science* 10, 1, 83–117.

Young, K.S. 1999. Evaluation and treatment of Internet addiction. In L. VandeCreek and T. Jackson (eds.), *Innovations in Clinical Practice: A Sourcebook.* Sarasota, FL: Professional Resource Press 17, 19–31.

Young, K.S., and Case, C.J. 2004. Internet abuse in the workplace: New trends in risk management. *CyberPsychology and Behavior* 7, 1, 105–111.

Young, K.S., and Rogers, R.C. 1998. The relationship between depression and Internet addiction. *CyberPsychology and Behavior* 1, 1, 25–36.

CHAPTER 4

THE PSYCHOLOGY OF INTERNET
USE AND MISUSE

JAMES G. PHILLIPS

Abstract: *Psychologists use questionnaires to assess personality traits that are correlated with self-reported Internet use and misuse. Usage reflects technological predispositions, such as, gender, education, computer anxiety, accessibility, and preexisting tendencies (for example, lonely people appear to engage in solitary activities). Indeed, it is a measure of the degree of acceptance of the Internet that this technology has been described as addictive. For some individuals, Internet use has assumed problematic levels, occupying an inappropriate proportion of their time. The misuse of the Internet is liable to arise from problems of self-control and potentially can be explained by the behavioral addictions. Problematic Internet use is associated with low self-esteem, and within the workplace it is linked to tendencies to procrastinate. From this viewpoint, when considering workplace Internet misuse, the technology tends to be an offence facilitator or documenter. While there is debate about the nature of addiction and also about the addictive nature of the Internet, the literature on the behavioral addictions serves as a useful starting point for considering problematic Internet use.*

Keywords: *Internet, Addiction, Internet Use, Internet Misuse*

INTRODUCTION

Factors promoting Internet use are of interest within a variety of paradigms but for different reasons. For instance, the realization is just dawning that what could be good for e-commerce could be bad for workplace productivity. Considerable effort has been devoted to the usability of interfaces (e.g., W3C); nevertheless, additional factors are also likely to influence people's use of computer-mediated interactions, such as the potential for applications to reward the user (Newhagen and Rafaeli 1996) and the dispositions of individual users (Amichai-Hamburger 2002). Hence, this chapter will explore the personality traits of people who use the Internet. By identifying factors that predispose people to use and misuse the Internet, this chapter will provide insights that may assist systems designers in the provision and maintenance of this technology.

Researchers have only just begun to address the behavior of Internet users. Research is still limited in its amount and depth, and findings have so far been mixed (Riva and

Galimberti 2001). Indeed, researchers are still searching for suitable paradigms upon which to base research (Riva and Galimberti 2001). Theoretical explanations of employees' Internet misuse are only just appearing (Charney and Greenberg 2002; Davis 2001; LaRose, Mastro, and Eastin 2001; Lim 2002), being drawn from other domains, and probably require more testing within the context of Internet behavior (Riva and Galimberti 2001).

WHERE TO START?

Timothy Leary gave a lecture series in 1987 on the mind-expanding potential of personal computers and the Internet (see Leary 1994; Prensky 2001a, 2001b), and while this concept may be relevant, it is not particularly helpful for researchers attempting to understand people's use of technology (Griffiths 1996, 1998) as it does not afford a clear starting point for research. Instead, usability should be one of the starting points for understanding Internet habits. Technology, such as the Internet, is part of a designed environment and does not afford the same sorts of opportunities that exist within the environment humans evolved in. Adoption of the Internet is only possible to the extent that preexisting tendencies and abilities can be used to access its interface (Baber 1997; Nielsen 2000). In fact, it can be illegal to overlook this point (Australian Human Rights and Equal Opportunity Commission 1999; Rehabilitation Act 1998). Indeed, even when humans have been directly connected to the Internet (see Warwick 2002, 2003), the connection itself still makes use of the capacities of the nervous system.

To clarify, consider the potential determinants of Internet use and abuse in the light of behavioral addictions. Theorists considering behavioral addictions (e.g., gambling) have drawn parallels between the behavioral addictions and drugs of abuse (e.g., heroin, amphetamine). Most drugs of abuse utilize a preexisting neurotransmitter system—for example, heroin accesses endorphin receptors, while amphetamines potentiate the effects of noradrenaline. While users revel in the "magical" properties of the substance, these drugs work only because they are skeleton keys to a preexisting lock (or locks). From this viewpoint, it is obvious that people did not evolve in the context of the Internet, and any Internet use or abuse must in some way make use of preexisting mechanisms (Griffiths 1996, 1998). The success of any interaction, to some extent, is liable to depend upon the efficiency of the interface (Baber 1997; Nielsen 2000; Stevenson et al. 2004). Regardless, preexisting tendencies and existing explanations of behavior serve as useful starting points when attempting to understand Internet usage.

In the early development stage the Internet was difficult to use due to its code-based interfaces. Thus usage was concentrated among specially qualified people, most likely educated males with military or engineering backgrounds (Young 1996). However, the improving usability of this medium means that this pattern is liable to change as new cohorts of individuals access the Internet. Indeed, as usability improves, other factors are liable to predict use of this technology.

This chapter will consider some factors contributing to the increasing uptake and use of the Internet before considering factors contributing to misuse. In so doing, this chapter will identify some necessary precursors and risk factors, before addressing traits associated with problem behaviors.

USABILITY PLUS?

While considerable effort has been devoted to usability of the Web (Nielsen 2000), other factors can influence people's use of the Web (Amichai-Hamburger 2002). Researchers have suggested that Internet use may be influenced by the Internet's capacity to reward (Davis 2001). It is unclear whether it is the medium itself (Shaffer 1996) or its capacity to assist access to desired objects (Griffiths 1996, 1998) that is rewarding. However, it is clear that use of technology may also be influenced by other factors.

For instance, designers are increasingly aware of a potential interplay between aesthetics and usability. For example, Tractinsky et al. (2000) found that aesthetic issues could be related to usability. The researchers asked industrial engineering students to rate the perceived aesthetics and usability of simulated Automatic Teller Machine (ATM) layouts. The researchers observed a correlation of 0.66 between the perceived attractiveness and usability of the ATM. More importantly, after the engineering students used the ATM, aesthetics affected perceptions of usability more than actual usability. Considering aesthetics within the context of Web sites, Lindgaard and Dudek (2003) reported that usability and aesthetics are potentially independent dimensions, but both can contribute to user satisfaction.

Techniques such as Osgood's semantic-differential have also been used to address the affective dimensions of the Internet. King (2001) used the semantic-differential to rate Internet behaviors and settings on the three dimensions of potency, activity, and evaluation. The survey was viewed by 28,388 people in a six-month period and completed by 2,431 users of Yahoo (a response rate of around 10 percent). King found that most aspects of Internet behavior and settings were rated very strongly, indicating that the Internet is not a bland or neutral environment to its users and implying that usability alone will not predict Internet use.

INTERNET USE

While some researchers have addressed the usability of the Internet (e.g., Nielsen 2000), others have considered the reasons why people use the Internet. According to use-gratification theory, people use the Internet to fulfill some need (Newhagen and Rafaelli 1996). A number of researchers have used this framework to address Internet use. For instance, Papacharissi and Rubin (2000) considered the motives underlying the Internet use of 279 students. Their factor analysis revealed five factors underlying Internet use: interpersonal utility, passing time, seeking information, convenience, and entertainment. Charney and Greenberg (2002) identified eight factors underlying Internet use in their study, namely keeping informed, diversion and entertainment, peer identity, good feelings, communication, sights and sounds, career, and coolness. Song et al. (2004) reported seven factors underlying Internet use: virtual community, information seeking, aesthetic experience, monetary compensation, diversion, personal status, and relationship maintenance. Similarly, Korgaonkar and Wolin (1999) considered the motives underlying the Internet use of 420 consumers and found that Internet use could be explained by seven factors: social escapism, transactional security and privacy, information motivation, interactive control, socialization, nontransactional security and privacy, and economics. From these previous studies, common uses such as communication, information searching, entertainment, and commerce are identified.

Even though particular types of Internet usage can be identified, unanswered is why some people are more predisposed to certain applications than others (LaRose et al. 2003; Song et al. 2004). The use of the Internet may in part be directed by individual predispositions and tendencies (Amichai-Hamburger 2002).

There has been some discussion of whether the Internet is used by lonely people to pursue solitary activities. Kraut et al. (1998) suggests that time spent on the Internet means less time spent on interactions with other people and therefore promotes loneliness. Other researchers observe that people who are already lonely spend more time on the Internet than in other activities (Amichai-Hamburger and Ben-Artzi 2003) and use the Internet to modulate their moods (Morahan-Martin and Schumacher 2003).

These observations can be qualified by a further study by Kraut et al. (2002). In a replication of previous work, Kraut et al. performed a longitudinal study of 406 participants from 216 households. Those individuals who were outgoing and sociable in their outlook (extroverts) exhibited increased community involvement with high levels of Internet use. Those individuals who were less outgoing and sociable in their outlook (introverts) reported greater levels of loneliness with higher levels of Internet use. In each case the Internet appears to support preexisting interests.

A series of studies at Monash University in Australia investigated Internet usage (Matanda et al. 2004; Reddie and Phillips 2005; Scealy et al. 2002). In each study, the self-reported usage patterns of Internet users were considered for the extent to which self-reported use of specific applications could be predicted from personality traits and demographic variables.

POTENTIAL BARRIERS TO ACCESS

Although legislation and guidelines exist intending to make the Internet universally accessible (Rehabilitation Act 1998; World Wide Web Consortium 2000), some people still experience barriers to access to this technology. Indeed, some people have reported a sense of being cut off or disconnected from the emerging information society (Katsikides 1998). This impression has led to concerns about technological disenfranchisement or what has been termed the "digital divide" between those who do and do not use the Internet (World Wide Web Consortium 2000).

There are segments of the population that are reluctant to use computers for some reason. This aversion may be because they lack the necessary education, or perhaps computers make them nervous (Howard 1986). Certainly, age can be a major influence in the uptake and use of technology. Indeed, several studies have found that increasing age is negatively correlated with Internet use (Kubeck et al. 1999; Kraut et al. 1996). Even in studies where Internet access and help services were readily available, older adults have been found to use the Internet less frequently (Kraut et al. 1998). In addition, some groups may be less disposed to interacting with computers than with people. For instance, Shotton (1989) observed that heavy computer users were less socially oriented as children. As content analysis has revealed that most software addresses male interests (Morahan-Martin 1998), Matanda et al. (2004) also considered whether gender posed obstacles to Internet access.

Matanda et al. (2004) considered potential psychological barriers to Internet access that could lead to technological disenfranchisement. Poor education, high levels of computer anxiety, and older age are all potential obstacles to Internet usage. Interests may also pose barriers to Internet use. Females might find less to interest them on the Internet than males do, and a sociable individual might be less likely to engage in a solitary activity such as Internet use.

Matanda et al. (2004) considered a convenience sample of 158 adult computer users from the community (71 male, 87 female) ranging in age from 19 to 76 years old (mean = 38.78, standard deviation = 16.11 years). The participants were recruited through posters at university campuses, local libraries, Internet cafés, and seniors' community groups. Computer anxiety was measured using the computer anxiety rating scale (form C) (Rosen and Weil 1992), and sociability was addressed using the UCLA loneliness scale (version 3). This standard is a self-reported one-dimensional measure of subjective feelings of global or general loneliness (Russell 1996). Participants were asked to estimate their overall Internet use and specific uses such as communication, information searching, entertainment, and commerce as suggested by researchers Korgaonkar and Wolin (1999).

It was difficult to predict overall levels of Internet use, presumably because of the wide range of possibilities offered by the Internet (Matanda et al. 2004). Nevertheless, when considering specific applications, the data suggest a potential for technological disenfranchisement. Any technological disenfranchisement would appear to be driven by education rather than age. Matanda et al. found that people with high levels of educational attainment were likely to use the Internet for communication (e.g., e-mail). Conversely, the more computer-anxious people were, the less likely they were to use the Internet to search for information. In addition, it was observed that prior interests might influence Internet usage. Young, lonely men were apparently more likely to use the Internet for entertainment purposes. However, this assimilation could be easily interpreted as an effect of cohort, since young generations of males are far more familiar with computer games. Men were more likely than women to use the Internet for commercial activities, but it was unclear whether this finding reflects user interests or privilege and status.

ROLE OF SPECIFIC INTERESTS

Although it can be difficult to predict overall Internet use, it might be possible to predict specific forms of Internet use. Scealy et al. (2002) subdivided four categories of use (i.e., information searches, commerce, entertainment, and communication) suggested by Korgaonkar and Wolin's (1999) work into more specific categories. Scealy et al. considered the extent to which the use of specific applications could be predicted by factors such as gender and education, but this study also considered whether social anxieties would predispose people to greater use of the Internet, as has been implied by Shotton (1989). To assess these personality traits, the researchers administered personality inventories addressing shyness-social reticence scale (Jones and Briggs 1986) and anxiety–trait anxiety inventory (Spielberger et al. 1983). Scealy et al. used a convenience sample of 177 individuals (105 females and 72 males) who participated in the study (mean age = 30.27, standard deviation = 12.30 years). Since Matanda et al. (2004) had experienced difficulties predicting overall use, Scealy et al. asked participants to estimate the periods of time they spent in eight specific categories: e-mail, chat room, work or study searches, recreation and leisure searches, interactive entertainment, downloading, banking and paying bills, and buying products.

Scealy et al. also experienced difficulty predicting overall levels of Internet use, but by using personality traits, they found it possible to predict the use of specific applications. Shy males were more likely to use the Internet for recreation and leisure searches. This result suggests that Internet usage occurs along the lines of preexisting interests. The use of e-mail and chat rooms was not related to shyness or anxiety, suggesting that shyness or anxiety does not pose an obstacle to these Internet applications. Nevertheless, it was not clear whether the socially isolated would seek these mediums out. Men were using the Internet more for downloading of material, and there was a trend suggesting that downloads were more often engaged in by the less educated individuals. In contrast, highly educated males were more likely to use the Internet for banking and paying bills, but it was not possible to predict work or study searches.

These studies of self-reported Internet use from Australia indicate that Internet use is governed by preexisting interests (Matanda et al. 2004; Scealy et al. 2002). Such data are consistent with the observations of other researchers that solitary individuals are more likely to use the Internet for solitary purposes (Amichai-Hamburger and Ben-Artzi 2003; Morahan-Martin and Schumacher 2003). The use of the Internet for business purposes was influenced by gender and education. To further address such issues, the use of the Internet within the workplace for communication purposes was examined.

Reddie and Phillips (2005) considered workplace e-mail use. Participants were asked how many hours per week they spent using e-mail for personal purposes and for work-related purposes. Additional questionnaires that were administered to assess decisional style and self-esteem will be discussed later.

Reddie and Phillips's study had 90 participants (64 females and 26 males) with a mean age of 36.7 years (standard deviation = 19.3 years). Ages ranged from 18 to 75. Participants were to have access to e-mail at their place of work. Participants were recruited from a number of private organizations and from Monash University. Previous studies (Matanda et al. 2004; Scealy et al. 2002) had difficulty predicting total Internet use, although it was feasible to predict use of specific applications. Reddie and Phillips could predict total e-mail use. The more educated the individuals, the more likely they were to use e-mail. Such specific uses of workplace technologies such as e-mail can be predicted on the basis of age and education. Older educated individuals were more likely to use e-mail for work-related purposes. Younger educated individuals were more likely to use e-mail for personal purposes. Another study (Bianchi and Phillips 2005) observed similar trends in mobile phone use, with older individuals using the mobile phone for business purposes, while younger individuals used mobile phones for social purposes.

These were strong results; however, it remains to be seen whether these effects are developmental in nature or reflect a specific cohort of individuals. Indeed, some researchers have likened heavy use of the Internet to a fad like citizens band radios (Grohol 1999). If links between Internet use and age are developmental in origin, then the use of this technology for social purposes in the young will shift to business use as individuals age and acquire new roles in society. Alternatively, if these effects are a function of cohort, then an increasing use of these technologies would be expected for social purposes as this cohort ages. If this technology is being used during work time, then there is the potential for a greater misuse of this technology in the future.

In the previous paragraphs, factors predisposing people to the uptake and heavy use of the Internet have been considered. To some extent, such data also indicate factors predisposing people to use the Internet for commercial purposes. The data imply that the Internet is used by males for commercial purposes. It also supports the importance of the discipline of human factors in assisting accessibility to this technology because factors such as computer anxiety and education influence Internet usage. Preexisting interests would also seem to influence the use of this medium, and factors such as aesthetics and affiliative tendencies are not irrelevant. Indeed, the previous paragraphs, while of relevance to e-commerce applications, also point to necessary conditions or risk factors leading to Internet misuse that are potentially of interest to management and accounting from the point of view of productivity.

INTERNET MISUSE

Internet misuse has been likened to a behavioral addiction (Griffiths 1995, 1996, 1998, 1999; Young 1996, 1998). The concept of any behavioral addiction is a vexed one (Walker 1992). It seeks validation by drawing similarities with the pharmacological addictions, and yet even the pharmacological addictions are not uniform. Drugs such as morphine clearly elicit symptoms such as cravings, tolerance, and withdrawal, but it is debatable whether the same symptoms are present for other drugs such as marijuana or cocaine (Craig and Stitzel 1990). As with a number of diagnostic categories, there is perhaps a pattern or a constellation of symptoms rather than a 100 percent concordance. Perhaps the degree of association is less than perfect, but the extent to which self-reported symptoms co-occur is sufficient to generate usable psychometric instruments. For example, Armstrong et al. (2000) obtained a reliability coefficient of 0.8776 for a scale addressing symptoms such as craving, tolerance, and withdrawal associated with Internet use. Such observations indicate that even if researchers find that craving, tolerance, and withdrawal are not strongly associated with behavioral addictions (see Blaszczynski and McConaghy 1989), they may be strongly associated by self-report, suggesting that people at the very least have a coherent concept of what constitutes addiction.

In opposition, Shaffer et al. (2000) suggest that broadening the concept of addiction to include behaviors such as heavy Internet use might be deleterious because it distracts from the primary cause of such problems. Indeed, Walker (1992) notes that on that basis a number of other behavioral excesses, such as golf, football, and other sports, could also be considered as addictions. Hence there is an argument to consider the behavioral addictions as instances of problem behaviors instead.

Indeed, the term *Internet addiction* was proposed by psychiatrist Ivan Goldberg more for discussion purposes than for diagnostic reasons (Griffiths 1996). Nevertheless, the term has been used because there has been a need to focus not just upon Internet use but also upon misuse. The change has occurred because of the growth in adoption and use of this technology. In the early 1970s, there were a number of reasons why computer misuse was not an issue: (1) access—it was difficult to have unconstrained access to a computer; (2) interest—computers were limited in what they were capable of doing; (3) legislation—there were fewer ways of breaking the law using a computer; and (4) monitoring—there were fewer ways of detecting violations of the law using a computer.

With the growth in access and the wealth of material available, there is now a need to discuss computer misuse. The Internet allows a range of offences that challenge existing legislative controls (see Gasaway 1998). For example, many forms of gambling are illegal in parts of the Americas and Southeast Asia; however, the Internet now enables people to engage in gambling in their own homes or the workplace. The Internet thus has the potential to embarrass legislators' attempts to prevent or limit the availability of opportunities to gamble (Toneguzzo 1995, 1997). To this extent then, the Internet can serve as an offense facilitator. However, computers also create logs of the dates and the forms of Internet activity. This is not a trivial point. Many new office technologies have previously been abused. The office photocopier was regularly used to disseminate inappropriate or humorous material. However, the photocopier took no record of whether it was an invoice or a buttock that was photocopied. In contrast, the history of the browser can indicate sites visited although, perhaps, not the intent of the user (Burke et al. 2002).

Problem Behaviors

Attempts to understand Internet addiction have borrowed from behavioral addiction literature. Studies deliberately used questions with parallels in the Diagnostic and Statistical Manual of Mental Disorders, Fourth Edition (DSM-IV) criteria for pathological gambling (Brenner 1997). It should be noted that the most influential instrument for assessing pathological gambling has been the South Oaks Gambling Screen (Lesieur and Blume 1987). As scored, the South Oaks Gambling Screen focuses upon the self-reported problems caused by gambling rather than the gambler's reported symptoms. Although this instrument tends to sidestep symptoms, it does have the potential to address social or occupational dysfunction or degree of harm. Indeed, it is important to consider inappropriate Internet use, because management can potentially monitor and document aspects of Internet misuse in the workplace.

A general conceptualization of inappropriate Internet use can be drawn from emerging community standards, particularly those involving legislation and the workplace. Within this context, a problem behavior can be inferred when a person who is engaging in activity X should be performing activity Y and when activity X prevents the person from engaging in other obligations (whether intrapersonal, interpersonal, or organizational). The entity affected by the problem behavior has an expectation that these obligations are consensual or previously agreed upon, but the problem person either does not feel bound by this expectation or does not have the necessary self-control over resources to comply with this obligation. Within the context of Internet usage, a problem could be inferred if Internet usage prevents a person from attaining self-imposed goals or meeting workplace deadlines, contravenes the workplace's fair-use guidelines, or violates legislative guidelines. Indeed, the same conceptualization could also be applied to inappropriate mobile phone use (see Bianchi and Phillips 2005).

As with some other behavioral guidelines within the workplace (e.g., sexual harassment), there is an element of subjectivity in the definition. Other people may perceive an element of deviance in the problem behaviors of the individual, but this deviance may not be experienced as such by the individual. Indeed, this divergence can be put in the context of the fundamental errors made by individuals when attributing causes to their behaviors (Chau and Phillips 1995; Snyder et al. 1976). Researchers have observed that winners tend to ascribe their success to skill and ability, while losers tend to ascribe their failure to luck and circumstance. This observation can be rephrased as "perpetrators tend to attribute their behaviors to circumstances, while an observer tends to attribute the behavior of perpetrators to their personality." Nevertheless, the nature of such self-serving attributions may vary when applied to the domain of Internet misuse. Burke et al. (2002) observed that individuals caught accessing inappropriate Web sites dissemble as to their motives, claiming that they are engaging in "research."

To some extent, computers can be used as an excuse for individual problems. Under some circumstances computers are certainly used as scapegoats (Moon and Nass 1998). But there are clearly contributing factors such as usability and the unpredictability of download times. For the user, the accessibility of an Internet site can be a source of problems (Nielsen 2000). In addition, there are a number of aggressive instances of Web usage (home page hijacking, spam, etc.) that contribute to the problem of workplace computer misuse. Nevertheless, can this kernel of truth associated with computer usability be extended to factors such as time wasting and inappropriate use?

Within the context of Internet misuse, this chapter has outlined some factors associated with Internet uptake and use. Necessary precursors and risk factors have been identified and Internet-related problem behaviors have been defined. The notion of Internet misuse has been delineated, but it has arisen within the context of increasing Internet use. Personality traits predisposing individuals to misuse of the Internet will now be considered.

Heavier Use

The Internet can be considered a thief of time, and some have described the Internet as addictive (Young 1996, 1998). To understand any addictive tendencies associated with the Internet, researchers have drawn from psychiatric criteria for substance abuse and from the behavioral addictions (e.g., gambling) to produce Internet-related problem scales (Armstrong et al. 2000; Brenner 1997).

Armstrong et al. (2000) created a questionnaire considering the extent to which Internet users reported cravings, withdrawal symptoms, tolerance, and a number of other Internet-related problems. To validate this scale, the Minnesota Multiphase Personality Inventory-2 (MMPI-2) addiction potential scale (Hathaway and McKinley 1989) was administered. As behavioral addictions are associated with low self-esteem (Marlatt et al. 1988) and impulsivity (Zuckerman 1979), the study considered the extent to which scales assessing self-esteem and impulsivity could predict Internet usage or Internet-related problems.

Armstrong et al. (2000) solicited participants from the Internet Addiction Support Group site and from the general community. Most members of this sample were employed and highly educated. Participants completed an Internet use questionnaire, an Internet-related problem scale, the Coopersmith self-esteem inventory (Coopersmith 1991), the sensation-seeking scale (form IV) (Zuckerman 1979), and the MMPI-2 addiction potential scale.

The Internet-related problem scale had good internal consistency. Validity was indicated by significant correlations between the Internet-related problem scale and both the amounts of time spent on the Internet and the addiction potential scale.

Self-reported Internet problems were linked to poor self-esteem rather than impulsivity and disinhibition (Armstrong et al. 2000). Although disinhibition did not appear to lead to Internet-related problem use in this study, the anonymity currently associated with some forms of Internet use may still lead to disinhibited behavior (see Griffiths 1998; Morahan-Martin and Schumacher 2000; Roberts et al. 2000). While disinhibited behavior has the potential to get employees into trouble within the workplace (Posen 2003), the anonymity causing disinhibition is less likely to occur within the workplace.

Additionally, Armstrong et al. (2000) observed that self-reported Internet problems were associated with poor self-esteem rather than sensation seeking. This observation contradicts beliefs that the Internet is used to excess because it is exciting (Shaffer 1996). Indeed, the prolonged periods spent struggling through search engines and waiting for downloads argue against this promise. Even the physical postures adopted by people suggest that surfing the Net can be a casual waiting activity (English and Andre 1999). Instead, these data imply that the Internet serves in another way, perhaps as a form of escape from other activities. Hills and Argyle (2003) have also suggested that the Internet is used as a means of escape from other activities.

Decisional Style in the Workplace

Researchers have observed that the Internet is used as a means of avoidance (Hills and Argyle 2003). For instance, Lim (2002), examining personal Internet use during work hours (cyberloafing), noted that employees justified using the Internet to avoid work by citing organizational injustices in their treatment within the workplace. Similarly, Lavoie and Pychyl (2001) observed that high levels of Internet use could be linked to negative moods and behaviors such as procrastination. Reddie and Phillips (2005) considered the extent to which a specific Internet use such as e-mail might constitute avoidance behavior.

Avoidance behavior is well delineated in Janis and Mann's (1977) established model of decision making. This model has the potential to be applied to an understanding of e-mail use and productivity because it incorporates issues such as resourcing, is relevant to the workplace, and also makes predictions about the success of decision making. In their conflict model of decision making, Janis and Mann suggested that the specific response to conflict depends upon time pressure, resources, and perceptions of likely outcomes. A considered (vigilant) response is adaptive, but there are a variety of forms of defensive avoidance (procrastination, buck-passing) that are less adaptive.

Janis and Mann's model suggests that coping patterns are determined by the presence or absence of three conditions: awareness of serious risks about preferred alternatives, hope of finding a better alternative, and belief that there is adequate time to search and deliberate before a decision is required (Mann et al. 1997). Procrastination and buck-passing are forms of defensive avoidance associated with pessimism about the ability to find a good solution to a dilemma. Such behaviors are ultimately maladaptive when a problem becomes serious. When resources are scarce or time is short, hypervigilance (panic) may be the outcome.

As described previously, Reddie and Phillips (2005) considered workplace e-mail use. Participants were asked the extent to which they used e-mail within the workplace for work-related or personal use. The Melbourne decision-making scale (Mann et al. 1997) was used to assess decisional styles such as vigilance, procrastination, buck-passing, and hypervigilance. The Coopersmith self-esteem inventory (Coopersmith 1991) was again used to evaluate self-esteem (Armstrong et al. 2000).

The use of e-mail within the workplace for personal reasons could be regarded as inappropriate or unproductive depending upon workplace Internet use guidelines (Scheuermann and Langford 1997). As indicated previously, young, highly educated individuals were likely to send e-mails for personal use, whereas older educated individuals were likely to use e-mails for work-related purposes. The amount of time reportedly spent on work-related e-mails (3.9 hours per week) was about three times the amount of time spent on personal e-mails (1.4 hours per week). Therefore, it was of interest as to whether decisional style could predict e-mail use.

Of the defensive avoidance scales Reddie and Phillips (2005) used, the buck-passing scale proved disappointing and did not predict work-related use of e-mails. This result implied that higher levels of e-mail use within the workplace were not due to avoidance behavior in the form of buck-passing. Additionally, the adaptive, vigilance scale did not predict e-mail use. However, the procrastination scale predicted both the total number of e-mails sent and the number of work-related e-mails sent. High levels of self-reported procrastination were associated with high levels of work-related e-mails. As these findings are correlational in nature, it is unclear whether procrastination was causing high levels of e-mails or whether high levels of e-mails were interfering with work requirements. There are indications supporting both interpretations. Work-related e-mails may be interfering with productivity. Indeed, to overcome this problem, technology has been developed to prioritize e-mails (Lee et al. 2002) and filter spam. On the other hand, researchers have also observed that workers use the Internet to fill time or to avoid doing something less rewarding (Hills and Argyle 2003; Lavoie and Pychyl 2001).

Personality and the Workplace

In an attempt to relate Internet misuse to established psychological constructs, Wyatt and Phillips (2005) employed the five-factor model of personality. The NEO PI-R (Costa and McRae 1992) is a commercially published 240-item questionnaire that measures five dimensions of personality: neuroticism, extraversion, openness to experience, agreeableness, and conscientiousness. Within each dimension, the NEO PI-R also measures six facets of personality. This well-documented account of personality (Anastasi and Urbina 1997) has the potential to account for Internet misuse along several dimensions. For instance, the degree of sociability as measured by variables such as extraversion has the potential to predict Internet use (Hamburger and Ben-Artzi 2000). Openness to experience also has the potential to predict Internet use, since heavy Internet users have been reported to have a greater need for stimulation (Young 1996, 1998). Agreeableness could predict Internet use: Lim (2002) suggested that cyberslacking reflects disagreements with organizational policies and treatments. The factor of conscientiousness has intuitive appeal when considering appropriate workplace Internet use, and neuroticism has been linked previously to addictive behaviors (see Hamburger and Ben-Artzi 2000).

Wyatt and Phillips (2005) solicited eight workplaces via electronic appeal, and eighty-eight individuals submitted questionnaires. Participants reported on their use of the Internet at work, specifically reporting the amounts of time spent on work-related and non-work-related e-mail, Internet searches, banking, interactive game playing, and non-work-related downloads. Participants also completed the NEO-FFI (Costa and McCrae 1992). Wyatt and Phillips obtained a number of significant correlations, but due to the large number of correlations examined, the results should be viewed with caution as there was a somewhat heightened experiment error rate. For the first time, a correlation was observed between personality and total self-reported Internet use. Less agreeable participants reported spending more time overall on the Internet than agreeable participants. Such an observation is consistent with suggestions that the Internet may be a suitable medium for the socially unskilled (Amichai-Hamburger and Ben-Artzi 2003; Morahan-Martin and Schumacher 2003). The Internet, in some way, provides a means of overcoming a deficit and otherwise allows access to services (see Papacharissi and Rubin 2000).

When considering work-appropriate behaviors, Wyatt and Phillips (2005) observed that extraverted individuals sent more work-related e-mails than introvert individuals. In addition, those individuals who were open to experience were likely to engage in work-related information searches. Wyatt and Phillips had difficulty predicting the use of the Internet for non-work-related purposes. The only significant correlation indicated that extraverted people were more likely than introverts to engage in non-work-related e-mails as well as the previously observed work-related e-mails. This observation is consistent with Kraut et al. (2002) that the Internet supported preexisting tendencies, with the extraverted using it to enhance their contacts regardless of whether they are work-related or social in nature. Unfortunately, it was difficult to predict the use of the Internet for commercial purposes. Nor could Wyatt and Phillips predict game playing and downloads from personality variables, although the directions of relationships were in keeping with what might be expected from previous studies.

Wyatt and Phillips (2005) had difficulty using personality to predict other forms of non-work-related Internet use (e.g., searches, e-commerce, games, downloads) because employed individuals spend less time in these behaviors. In fact, the best predictors of non-work-related activities were the self-reported amounts of time spent on the Internet. Wyatt and Phillips found that the more time participants reported they spent on the Internet in the workplace, the more likely it was that they were engaging in non-work-related activities. In particular, the more time spent on non-work-related e-mails, the more likely it was for a person to be engaging in other non-work-related activities. Conversely, the more self-reported time spent in work-related Internet use, particularly e-mail, the less time participants reported spent in non-work-related applications.

The studies by Reddie and Phillips (2005) and Wyatt and Phillips (2005) imply that the misuse of workplace Internet privileges will follow people's previous patterns of interests (Kraut et al. 2002), with the solitary and socially unskilled pursuing isolated activities and the extraverted using this medium to enhance their social contacts. It would appear that less agreeable staff members report that they use the Internet more overall, and there were indications that extraverts were potentially using the Internet to waste time at work.

Summary of Findings on Use and Misuse

Although accessibility is the law, factors such as computer anxiety and education still influence Internet usage, implying that usability remains important. Inappropriate use is liable to be linked to high rates of use overall. Heavy and inappropriate Internet use appears to follow preexisting dispositions and interests. For example, shy individuals use the Internet for recreation and leisure searches, and extraverts use the Internet for communication purposes within the workplace. Inappropriate workplace Internet use appears to be linked to problems of self-control associated with factors such as poor self-esteem or procrastination, rather than other workplace practices such as buck-passing. Findings from Monash University are summarized in Table 4.1. Even though there are parallels to the addictions, the concept of Internet addiction deserves further consideration and will be dealt with in the following section.

INTERNET ADDICTION

Davis (2001) attempted an overarching account of pathological Internet use, distinguishing individuals who engage in generalized Internet use from individuals who use

Table 4.1

Personality Traits Associated with Internet Use or Potential Misuse

	Personality trait	Behavior	Reference
Internet use	Low computer anxiety	Searches	Matanda et al. (2004)
	Openness to experience	Searches	Wyatt and Phillips (submitted)
	Educated	E-mail	Matanda et al. (2004)
			Reddie and Phillips (submitted)
	Extraversion	E-mail	Wyatt and Phillips (submitted)
Internet misuse	Poor self-esteem	General problems	Armstrong et al. (2000)
	Lonely	Entertainment[a]	Matanda et al. (2004)
	Shy	Recreation and leisure searches[a]	Scealy et al. (2002)
	Procrastination	E-mail	Reddie and Phillips (submitted)
	Extraversion	E-mail[a]	Wyatt and Phillips (submitted)
	Uneducated	Downloads[a]	Scealy et al. (2002)

[a]A potential problem if inappropriate use occurrs in the workplace.

the Internet to access information that is relevant to a specific interest. At the very least, there can be a difficulty predicting generalized Internet overuse but a greater potential for success in predicting specific interests (Matanda et al. 2004; Scealy et al. 2002).

Is the Internet addictive? At the very least, the correlations between items on questionnaires (Armstrong et al. 2000; Brenner 1997) confirm that by self-report people understand the concept of addiction. In addition, variables linked to other addictive behaviors can assist in the prediction of inappropriate Internet behaviors. For instance, Internet use can be linked to avoidance behaviors. Nevertheless, Shaffer (1996) and Davis (2001) make much of the role of excitement and arousal in generating behavioral addictions. Heavy Internet use has not been consistently linked to sensation seeking and extraversion in these studies, as would be expected if excitement were the sole motivating factor. Indeed, it is unclear which elements would be exciting (Griffiths 1998). Using the Internet is hardly as exciting as gambling or game playing. Using the Internet can be more like a vigilance task in which time is wasted by downloads and inappropriate hits (English and Andre 1999). Indeed, at times the Internet has more in common with a learning schedule such as Differential Low Rate of Responding, with too fast a response rate impairing receipt of reinforcement. Instead, heavy problem Internet use is probably better seen as a product of a strong habit—a habit so strong that it could get in the way of other more appropriate behaviors.

Instead of an exciting new addiction, it would appear that Internet use follows the lines of previous interests (Griffiths 1996, 1998) and, according to longitudinal studies (Kraut et al. 2002), may reinforce these tendencies, such that sociable people become more sociable and the introverted become more socially isolated. Therefore, some other mechanism should probably be invoked to explain heavy or problem Internet usage.

Problem Use as Conflicting Tendencies

Welford (1976, 1987) likened social interaction between two individuals to the interplay between two communication channels. The form of interaction is, to some extent, influenced by factors such as the information-processing capacities of the individuals, the bandwidth of the communication channels, and sources of noise that might influence communications. The continuation of interaction is considered to be linked to the type of feedback received. If feedback is judged positively by the individual, then attempts at interaction continue. Such an approach to social interaction is well suited to an explanation of Internet behavior. In the context of Internet usage, the initial choice of interaction and the response to feedback certainly appears to be governed by individual differences. Problem Internet use could thus be considered to involve conflicting tendencies toward: (1) workplace-appropriate behaviors and (2) workplace-inappropriate behaviors. There are two mechanisms that could explain this conflict: the automaticity associated with learned behaviors and the tendency to maximize rewards.

Workplace Internet Misuse as Automaticity

With repeated use of the Internet, use of applications can develop into strong habits (LaRose et al. 2001) that are potentially automatized. Under such circumstances, there are two tendencies: conscious controlled actions and automatic tendencies. Conscious controlled actions should be those actions in the workplace that are potentially governed by personal commitments, workplace deadlines, and legislation. In contrast, automatic tendencies, such as checking e-mail or the tendency to start surfing the Net, have the potential to get in the way of work requirements. In effect, "Internet addiction" could be seen as a Stroop-like interference between two responses, where the highly learned and automatized response tends to interfere with the appropriate response (Kornblum 1994). The cost of automatization is potential conflict with required activities (Reason 1979) as the automatic behavior captures the person's activity at inappropriate times. From this point of view, the self-reported symptoms of reduced control associated with heavy Internet use (Armstrong et al. 2000; LaRose et al. 2001) reflect a phenomenological description of the automatic, obligatory aspects of Internet use.

It is likely that those individuals who are self-directed with high self-esteem will overcome automatic tendencies (Bargh and Chartrand 1999), but other individuals will yield to such habits. The experience of these strong habits resembles that of an addiction and indeed is reported as such, but ongoing research implies that it more likely resembles a learned tendency.

Workplace Internet Misuse as Automaticity: Possible Interventions

If inappropriate workplace Internet use is an automatic tendency associated with prolonged exposure to the Internet, then it can be addressed using the understanding of automatic behaviors. Factors contributing to the development of automatic tendencies are well documented—namely repetition under consistent conditions (Schneider and Shiffrin 1977). This observation implies that the workplace might benefit by occasional alteration in work practices (e.g., "Net free days" [free to use the Net]). In addition, as automatic behaviors tend to be stimulus-driven rather than consciously controlled, interventions could seek to reduce the attention-capturing elements of interfaces (Choi and Kim 2004; Wood et al. 2004), although such a recommendation may potentially conflict with the marketing of these browsers and search engines.

Workplace Internet Misuse as the Maximization of Rewards

When supervision is lacking within the workplace, employees potentially have a choice between work-related activities and non-work-related activities (Billington and DiTommaso 2003). The reward for work-related activities can involve extrinsic factors like money, but it can also involve intrinsic, intangible things like satisfaction. When presented with two courses of action, it is known that over time organisms will choose the combination that maximizes their rewards (Hernstein 1961). Most employed individuals concentrate on work-related activities, but there are likely to be others who do not (Lim 2002). Whether due to perceived organizational injustices (Lim 2002) or depressed mood (Armstrong et al. 2000; Morahan-Martin and Schumacher 2003), the perceived value of work-related activity diminishes, and the value of non-work-related activity is enhanced. When non-work-related activity generates a problem for employees, they may then make self-serving attributions to diminish their responsibility for the behavior (Snyder et al. 1976). In this case, employees may claim that they are addicted to the Internet (Hall and Pritchard 1996).

Workplace Internet Misuse as Maximization of Rewards: Possible Interventions

If Internet misuse is a product of poor employee priorities associated with perceived organizational injustices (Lim 2002) or depressed mood (Armstrong et al. 2000; Morahan-Martin and Schumacher 2003), then possible interventions might address supervisory practices or workplace satisfaction. For instance, Billington and DiTommaso (2003) suggest that tendencies toward appropriate and inappropriate activities can be manipulated by varying the rate and immediacy of reinforcement. For example, employers who are competing with the Internet for their workers' attention might consider reducing the size of tasks (but not necessarily the number of tasks) to assist task completions and the reinforcement of work-related activities (Billington and DiTommaso 2003). In this regard, techniques such as Gantt charts (Stibic 1982) could be adopted to draw attention to completion of work-related activities.

There are some indications that the Internet has had an effect upon workplace satisfaction (Hills and Argyle 2003) by adding to workloads or altering working patterns. For instance, the relative immediacy of the Internet, with its capacity to time stamp communications, has dramatically added to perceived workloads (Posen 2003). To ameliorate such problems, technology already exists to prioritize (Lee et al. 2002) or summarize or digest e-mails (Murray et al. 1999).

Implications

There are implications for the workplace when considering a concept such as Internet addiction (Warden et al. 2004). If Internet-related problems result from an inability to overcome conflict arising from a strong habit, then medicalizing and diminishing the role of self-control will only make the problem worse (Shaffer et al. 2000). Medicalizing heavy or problem Internet usage implies diminished responsibility of the user and tends to place the burden of treatment upon the employer, while potentially overlooking underlying causes of the problem (Shaffer et al. 2000).

In light of the earlier definition of problem behavior, fair use and appropriate workplace Internet use need to be clear (Scheuermann and Langford 1997); otherwise, the employer and the legislator cannot claim inappropriate use. By the same token, realistic goal setting and work patterns should be set by the individual. To the extent that the employer positively encourages the use of technology, such as e-mail, then research is required (Kraut et al. 2004) to monitor workplace use (Mahatanankoon et al. 2004; Stanton and Julian 2002) and to encourage appropriate use with the workplace (Young and Case 2004).

FUTURE RESEARCH DIRECTIONS

Given the increasing interest in inappropriate Internet use within the workplace (Anandarajan 2002), it is likely that future scales addressing Internet misuse may address the number of problems generated by users' inappropriate Internet behavior rather than focusing upon symptoms (see Mahatanankoon et al. 2004). Studies of behavioral addictions such as gambling have previously taken this approach (Lesieur and Blume 1987), which has the merits of addressing potential harm rather than symptomatology.

The present chapter offered two explanations for inappropriate workplace Internet use. Inappropriate workplace Internet use could involve the diminished self-control associated with a strong habit (an addiction). Alternatively, inappropriate workplace Internet use could be a deliberate act linked to a tendency to procrastinate with a subsequent tendency to offer diminished self-control as an excuse. Future research should compare and contrast recreational Internet use with Internet use within the workplace, along with a specific emphasis upon the extent to which these behaviors are influenced by factors such as social desirability. If high levels of Internet-related problems are linked to low responses on social desirability scales, it would lend support to claims of the addictive nature of Internet use.

Future research should also go beyond an examination of Internet use to address other technologies (Griffiths 1995) with a view to understanding the factors contributing to their use and misuse (Bianchi and Phillips 2005). There are emerging similarities in the capabilities of the Internet and mobile phone networks. Both networks now support messaging e-mail, short message service (SMS), voice, and face-to-face communication, but the diminished immediacy, context, and interpersonal cues in some modes of communication may have implications for successful communication (Welford 1976) that will interact with users' predispositions. For instance, extraverts are predisposed to use mobile phone technology (Bianchi and Phillips 2005). It would be interesting to consider how personality influences the use of these new technologies, particularly as mobile phone use can be illegal under certain circumstances and jurisdictions (e.g., driving), even though the technology has the potential to date and time stamp the inappropriate behavior.

CONCLUSION

Internet use and misuse arise from preexisting tendencies. Internet use is a function not just of factors such as education but also of affiliative tendencies. Hence, usability is important, but other factors deserve consideration as well. Internet misuse has elements in keeping with addictions. But since heavy use is not necessarily linked to sensation seeking, then heavy use is perhaps better seen as a problem behavior. Problem Internet behavior seems likely to reflect conflict between controlled intentional behaviors and previously developed habits and potentially has implications for productivity within the workplace.

REFERENCES

Amichai-Hamburger, Y. 2002. Internet and personality. *Computers in Human Behavior* 18, 1–10.
Amichai-Hamburger, Y., and Ben-Artzi, E. 2003. Loneliness and Internet use. *Computers in Human Behavior* 19, 71–80.
Anandarajan, M. 2002. Internet abuse in the workplace. *Communications of the ACM* 45, 53–54.
Anastasi, A., and Urbina, S. 1997. *Psychological Testing,* 7th ed. Englewood Cliffs, NJ: Prentice Hall.
Armstrong, L., Phillips, J.G., and Saling, L.L. 2000. Potential determinants of heavier Internet usage. *International Journal of Human Computer Studies* 53, 537–550.
Australian Human Rights and Equal Opportunity Commission. 1999. *World Wide Web access: Disability Discrimination Act advisory notes.* www.hreoc.gov.au/disabilty_rights/standards/standards.html.
Baber, C. 1997. *Beyond the Desktop: Designing and Using Interaction Devices.* San Diego: Academic Press.
Bargh, J.A., and Chartrand, T.L. 1999. The unbearable automaticity of being. *American Psychologist* 54, 462–479.
Bianchi, A., and Phillips, J.G. 2005. Psychological predictors of problem mobile phone use. *CyberPsychology and Behavior* 8, 39–51.
Billington, E., and DiTommaso, N.M. 2003. Demonstrations and applications of the matching law in education. *Journal of Behavioral Education* 12, 91–104.
Blaszczynski, A.P., and McConaghy, N. 1989. The medical model of pathological gambling: Current shortcomings. *Journal of Gambling Behavior* 5, 42–52.
Brenner, V. 1997. Psychology of computer use: XLVII. Parameters of Internet use, abuse and addiction: The first 90 days of the Internet usage survey. *Psychological Reports* 80, 879–882.
Burke, A., Sowerbutts, S., Blundell, B., and Sherry, M. 2002. Child pornography and the Internet: Policing and treatment issues. *Psychiatry, Psychology and Law* 9, 79–84.

Charney T., and Greenberg, B.S. 2002. Uses and gratification of the Internet. Communication, technology and science. In C. Lin and D. Atkin (eds.), *Communication, Technology and Society: New Media Adoption and Use.* Cresskill, NJ: Hampton Press, 379–407.

Chau, A.W., and Phillips, J.G. 1995. Effects of perceived control upon wagering and attributions in computer blackjack. *Journal of General Psychology* 122, 253–269.

Choi, D., and Kim, J. 2004. Why people continue to play online games: In search of critical design factors to increase customer loyalty to online contents. *CyberPsychology and Behavior* 7, 11–24.

Coopersmith, S. 1991. *Self-Esteem Inventories.* Palo Alto, CA: Consulting Psychologists Press.

Costa, P., and McCrae, R.R. 1992. *Revised NEO Personality Inventory: Professional Manual.* Odessa, FL: Psychological Assessment Resources.

Craig, C.R., and Stitzel, R.E. 1990. *Modern Pharmacology.* Boston: Little, Brown.

Davis, R.A. 2001. A cognitive-behavioral model of pathological Internet use. *Computers in Human Behavior* 17, 187–195.

English, J.D., and Andre, A.D. 1999. Posture and Internet navigation: An observational study. In Proceedings of the Silicon Valley Ergonomics Conference and Exposition. San Jose, CA: San Jose State University, 126–135.

Gasaway, L.N. 1998. Copyright, the Internet, and other legal issues. *Journal of the American Society for Information Science* 49, 1003–1009.

Gottschalk, J. 2005. The risks associated with the business use of email. *Intellectual Property and Technology Law Journal* 17, 7, 16–18.

Griffiths, M. 1995. Technological addictions. *Clinical Psychology Forum* 76, 14–19.

———. 1996. Gambling on the Internet: A brief note. *Journal of Gambling Studies* 12, 471–473.

———. 1998. Internet addiction: Does it really exist? In J. Gackenbach (ed.), *Psychology and the Internet: Interpersonal and Transpersonal Applications.* New York: Academic Press, 61–75.

———. 1999. Internet addiction: Fact or fiction? *The Psychologist* 12, 246–250.

Grohol, J.M. 1999. *Internet Addiction Guide.* www.psychcentral.com/netaddiction/.

Hall, H.V., and Pritchard, D.A. 1996. *Detecting Malingering and Deception.* Boca Raton, FL: St. Lucie Press.

Hamburger, Y., and Ben-Artzi, E. 2000. The relationship between extraversion and neuroticism and the different uses of the Internet. *Computers in Human Behavior* 16, 441–449.

Hathaway S.R., and McKinley, J.C. 1989. *Minnesota Multiphasic Personality Inventory–2.* Minneapolis: University of Minnesota Press.

Hernstein, R.J. 1961. Relative and absolute strength of response as a function of frequency of reinforcement. *Journal of the Experimental Analysis of Behavior* 4, 267–272.

Hills, P., and Argyle M. 2003. Uses of the Internet and their relationships with individual differences in personality. *Computers in Human Behavior* 19, 59–70.

Howard, G. 1986. *Computer Anxiety and the Use of Microcomputers in Management.* Ann Arbor, Michigan: University Microfilms International.

Janis, I.L., and Mann L. 1977. *Decision Making: A Psychological Analysis of Conflict, Choice and Commitment.* New York: Free Press.

Jones, W.H., and Briggs, S.R. 1986. *Social Reticence Scale Manual.* Redwood City, CA: Mind Garden.

Katsikides, S. 1998. *The Societal Impact of Technology.* Aldershot, UK: Ashgate.

King, A.B. 2001. Affective dimensions of Internet culture. *Social Science Computer Review* 19, 414–430.

Korgaonkar, P., and Wolin, L. 1999. A multivariate analysis of Web usage. *Journal of Advertising Research* 2, 3–20.

Kornblum, S. 1994. The way irrelevant dimensions are processed depends on what they overlap with: The case of Stroop- and Simon-like stimuli. *Psychological Research* 56, 130–135.

Kraut, R., Kiesler, A., Boneva, B., Cummings, J., Helgeson, V., and Crawford, A. 2002. Internet paradox revisited. *Journal of Social Issues* 58, 49–74.

Kraut, R., Olson, J., Banaji, M., Bruckman, A., Cohen, J., and Couper, M. 2004. Psychological research online: Report of Board of Scientific Affairs' Advisory Group on the conduct of research on the Internet. *American Psychologist* 59, 105–117.

Kraut, R., Patterson, M., Lundmark, V., Kiesler, S., Mukopadhyay, T., and Scherlis, W. 1998. Internet paradox: A social technology that reduces social involvement and psychological well-being? *American Psychologist* 53, 1017–1031.

Kraut, R., Scherlis, W., Mukopadhyay, T., Manning, J., and Kiesler, S. 1996. Homenet field trial of residential Internet services. *Communications of the ACM* 39, 55–63.

Kubeck, J., Miller-Albercht, S., and Murphy, M. 1999. Finding information on the World Wide Web: Exploring older adults' exploration. *Educational Gerontology* 25, 167–188.

LaRose, R., Lin, C.A., and Eastin, M.S. 2003. Unregulated Internet usage: Addiction, habit, or deficient self-regulation. *Media Psychology* 5, 225–253.

LaRose, R.L., Mastro, D., and Eastin, M.S. 2001. Understanding Internet usage: A social cognitive approach to uses and gratifications. *Social Science Computer Review* 19, 395–413.

Lavoie, J.A.A., and Pychyl, T.A. 2001. Cyberslacking and the procrastination superhighway: A Web-based survey of online procrastination, attitudes, and emotion. *Social Science Computer Review* 19, 431–444.

Leary, T.F. 1994. *Chaos and Cyberculture*. Berkeley, CA: Ronin Publications.

Lee M.D., Chandrasena, L.H., and Navarro, D.J. 2002. Using cognitive decision models to prioritize E-mails. In I.W.G. Gray and C.D. Schunn (eds.), *Proceedings of the 24th Annual Conference of the Cognitive Science Society*. Mahwah, NJ: Erlbaum Associates, 478–483.

Lesieur, H.R., and Blume, S.B. 1987. The South Oaks Gambling Screen (SOGS): A new instrument for the identification of pathological gamblers. *American Journal of Psychiatry* 144, 1184–1188.

Lim, V.K.G. 2002. The IT way of loafing on the job: Cyberloafing, neutralizing and organizational justice. *Journal of Organizational Behavior* 23, 675–694.

Lindgaard, G., and Dudek, C. 2003. What is this evasive beast we call user satisfaction. *Interacting with Computers* 15, 429–452.

Mahatanankoon, P., Anandarajan, M., and Igbaria, M. 2004. Development of a measure of personal Web usage in the workplace. *CyberPsychology and Behavior* 7, 93–104.

Mann, L., Burnett, P., Radford, M., and Ford, S. 1997. The Melbourne decision making questionnaire: An instrument for measuring patterns of coping with decisional conflict. *Journal of Behavioral Decision Making* 10, 1–19.

Marlatt, A.G., Baer, J.S., Donovan, D.M., and Kivlahan, D.R. 1988. Addictive behaviors: Etiology and treatment. *Annual Review of Psychology* 39, 223–252.

Matanda, M., Jenvey, V.B., and Phillips, J.G. 2004. Internet usage in adulthood: Loneliness, computer anxiety and education. *Behavior Change* 21, 103–114.

Moon, Y., and Nass, C. 1998. Are computers scapegoats? Attributions of responsibility in human-computer interaction. *International Journal of Human-Computer Studies* 49, 79–94.

Morahan-Martin, J. 1998. The gender gap in Internet use: Why men use the Internet more. In J. Morahan-Martin (ed.). *Cyber Psychology and Behavior: The Impact of the Internet, Multimedia and Virtual Reality on Behavior and Society*. Amsterdam: Mary Ann Liebert Publishers, 3–10.

Morahan-Martin, J., and Schumacher, P. 2000. Incidence and correlates of pathological Internet use among college students. *Computers in Human Behavior* 16, 13–29.

———. 2003. Loneliness and social uses of the Internet. *Computers in Human Behavior* 19, 659–671.

Murray, J., Gross, M.M., and Ayres, T.J. 1999. Human error in power plants: A search for pattern and context. In Proceedings of the Silicon Valley Ergonomics Conference and Exposition. San Jose, CA: San Jose State University, 187–191.

Newhagen, J.E., and Rafaeli S. 1996. Why communication researchers should study the Internet: A dialogue. *Journal of Communication* 46, 4–13.

Nielsen, J. 2000. *Designing Web Usability: The Practice of Simplicity*. Indianapolis: New Riders Publishing.

Papacharissi, Z., and Rubin, A.M. 2000. Predictors of Internet use. *Journal of Broadcasting and Electronic Media* 44, 175–197.

Phillips, J.G., and Reddie, L. (in press). Decisional style and self-reported e-mail use in the workplace. *Computers in Human Behavior.*

Prensky, M. 2001a. Digital natives, digital immigrants. *On the Horizon* 9, 1–6.

———. 2001b. Digital natives, digital immigrants, Part II: Do they really *think* differently? *On the Horizon* 9, 1–10.

Reason, J. 1979. Actions not as planned: The price of automatization. In G. Underwood (ed.), *Aspects of Consciousness.* London: Academic Press, 67–90.

Rehabilitation Act. 1998. 29 U.S.C. 794d, Section 508.

Riva, G., and Galimberti, C. 2001. The mind in the Web: Psychology in the Internet age. *CyberPsychology and Behavior* 4, 1–5.

Roberts, L.D., Smith, L.M., and Pollock, C.M. 2000. "u r a lot bolder on the net": Shyness and Internet use. In W.R. Crozier (ed.), *Shyness: Development, Consolidation and Change.* London: Routledge, 121–138.

Rosen, L., and Weil, M. 1992. *A Manual for the Administration and the Scoring of the Computer Anxiety Rating Scale (Form C).* www.technostress.com.

Russell, D. 1996. UCLA loneliness scale (Version 3): Reliability, validity and factor structure. *Journal of Personality Assessment* 66, 20–40.

Scealy, M., Phillips, J.G., and Stevenson, R. 2002. Shyness and anxiety as predictors of patterns of Internet usage. *CyberPsychology and Behavior* 6, 507–515.

Scheuermann, L.E., and Langford, H.P. 1997. Perceptions of Internet abuse, liability, and fair use. *Perceptual and Motor Skills* 85, 847–850.

Schneider, D., and Shiffrin, R.M. 1977. Controlled and automatic human information processing: I. Detection, search, and attention. *Psychological Review* 84, 1–66.

Shaffer, H.J. 1996. Understanding the means and objects of addiction: Technology, the Internet and gambling, *Journal of Gambling Studies* 12, 461–469.

Shaffer, H.J., Hall, M.N., and Vanderbilt, J. 2000. Computer addiction: A critical consideration. *American Journal of Orthopsychiatry* 70, 2, 162–168.

Shotton, M. 1989. *Computer Addiction? A study of Computer Dependency.* New York: Taylor and Francis.

Snyder, M.L., Stephan, W.G., and Rosenfeld, D. 1976. Egotism and attribution. *Journal of Personality and Social Psychology* 33, 435–441.

Song, I., LaRose, R., Eastin, M.S., and Lin, C.A. 2004. Internet gratifications and Internet addiction: On the uses and abuses of new media. *CyberPsychology and Behavior* 7, 384–394.

Spielberger, C.D., Gorsuch, R.L., Vagg, P.R., and Jacobs, G.A. 1983. *Manual for the State-Trait Anxiety Inventory (Form Y).* Palo Alto, CA: Consulting Psychologists Press.

Stanton, J.M., and Julian, A.L. 2002. The impact of electronic monitoring on quality and quantity of performance. *Computers in Human Behavior* 18, 85–101.

Stevenson, R., Phillips, J.G., and Triggs, T.J. 2004. Mouse and display tablets as cursor control devices. *International Journal of Pattern Recognition and Artificial Intelligence* 18, 1–12.

Stibic, V. 1982. *Tools of the Mind.* Amsterdam: North-Holland.

Toneguzzo, S.J. 1995. The Internet: Entrepreneur's dream or regulator's nightmare? In J. O'Connor (ed.), *High Stakes in the Nineties.* Perth, Australia: Curtin University, 73–86.

———. 1997. Internet gaming—evidence for parliament of South Australia, Social Development Committee. In G. Coman, B. Evans, and R. Wootton (eds.), *Responsible Gambling: A Future Winner.* Adelaide, Australia: National Association for Gambling Studies, 369–389.

Tractinsky, N., Katz, A.S., and Ikar, D. 2000. What is beautiful is usable. *Interacting with Computers* 13, 127–145.

Walker, M.B. 1992. *The Psychology of Gambling.* Oxford, UK: Pergamon Press, 1992.

Warden, N., Phillips, J.G., and Ogloff, J.R.P. 2004. Internet addiction. *Psychiatry, Psychology and Law* 11, 280–295.

Warwick, K. 2002. *I, Cyborg*. London: Century Books.

———. 2003. Control of a robot hand and other applications using neural signals through an implant. In H.L. Teulings and A.W.A. van Gemmert (eds.), Proceedings of the 11th Conference of the International Graphonomics Society. Scottsdale, Arizona, 1–4.

Welford, A.T. 1976. *Skilled Performance*. Glenview, IL: Scott Foresman.

———. 1987. Ergonomics of human relations. *Ergonomics* 30, 3–8.

Wood, T.A., Griffiths, M.D., Chappell, D., and Davies, M.N.O. 2004. The structural characteristics of video games: A psycho-structural analysis. *CyberPsychology and Behavior* 7, 1–10.

World Wide Web Consortium. 2000. Bridging the digital divide. www.w3c.org.

Wyatt, K., and Phillips, J.G. 2005. Personality as a predictor of workplace Internet use. Proceedings of OZCHI2005 (OZCHI is Australia and New Zealand's forum for work in all areas of human-computer interaction. November 21–25. Canberra, Australia. http://portal.acm.org/dl.cfm.

Young, K. 1996. Psychology of computer use: Addictive use of the Internet: A case that breaks the stereotype. *Psychological Reports* 79, 899–902.

———. 1998. Internet addiction: The emergence of a new clinical disorder. *CyberPsychology and Behavior* 1, 237–244.

Young, K.S., and Case, C.J. 2004. Internet abuse in the workplace: New trends in risk management. *CyberPsychology and Behavior* 7, 105–111.

Zuckerman, M. 1979. *Sensation Seeking: Beyond the Optimal Level of Arousal*. Mahwah, NJ: Lawrence Erlbaum Associates.

CHAPTER 5

PROBLEMATIC INTERNET USE
IN THE WORKPLACE

SCOTT E. CAPLAN

Abstract: *A growing body of literature has raised concerns over employees' online activities in the workplace. Regardless of the terminology used to describe the problem, today's employers, managers, and human resources professionals face the challenge of understanding and handling employees' problematic Internet use (PIU). The current chapter attempts to shed light on the issue of PIU in the workplace by offering a theoretical account of the cognitive and behavioral processes that give rise to Internet use that results in negative personal and professional outcomes. The chapter presents the cognitive behavioral model of PIU and reviews literature supporting some of its major claims.*

Keywords: *Problematic Internet Use, Internet Addiction, Computer-mediated Communication, Online Social Interaction, Social Anxiety, Social Skill, Loneliness*

INTRODUCTION

In recent years, Internet use in the workplace has become more than commonplace—it has become an essential tool for many organizations. Young and Case (2004) review several different surveys suggesting that Internet use in the workplace is widespread and, for some, potentially problematic. Indeed, a growing body of literature has raised concerns over employees' online activities in the workplace. In fact, *Communications of the ACM* devoted an entire special issue to Internet abuse and misuse in the workplace (see Anandarajan 2002).

Thus far, scholars have employed a number of terms to describe nonproductive and potentially problematic Internet use (PIU) in the workplace: problematic Internet use (Davis et al. 2002), personal Web use (Mahatanankoon et al. 2004), cyberloafing (Lim 2002; Lim et al. 2002), Internet abuse (Young and Case 2004), and Internet addiction (Griffiths 2003). Regardless of the terminology used to describe the problem, today's employers, managers, and human resources professionals face the challenge of understanding and handling employees' non-work-related Internet use. In fact, Young and Case argue that "the issue has become critical as organizations attempt to minimize productivity losses that result from such employee Internet abuse, which can represent billions in lost revenue" (2004, 105). The purpose of this chapter is to shed further light on the issue and present a theoretical account of the cognitive and behavioral processes that give rise to Internet use that results in negative personal and professional outcomes.

First, however, it is necessary to clarify an important distinction in degree of severity between "cyberloafing" or personal Web use on one hand and PIU or Internet addiction disorder on the other. While cyberloafing and personal Web use may inhibit productivity, they involve relatively mundane activities that alleviate boredom or allow an employee to take care of personal business at work. Lim et al. (2002) define cyberloafing as "any voluntary act of employees using their companies' Internet access during office hours to surf non-work-related Web sites for nonwork purposes and to access (including receiving and sending) non-work-related email" (67). Mahatanankoon et al.'s personal Web use construct refers to "voluntary online Web behaviors during working time using any of the organization's resources for activities outside current customary job/work requirements" (2004, 93).

On the other hand, Internet addiction and PIU are relatively more serious issues. Beyond the growing concern that PIU may negatively affect employee productivity (Griffiths 2003; Young and Case 2004), research also indicates a significant relationship between PIU and workers' psychosocial well-being. In fact, Griffiths (2002) argues that PIU may be a serious occupational health issue. The current chapter focuses primarily on PIU because it involves employees' psychosocial health, which, in the long run, may significantly influence organizational stability, productivity, and liability.

Previous research indicates that there is a significant association among people's Internet use, psychosocial health, and negative outcomes at home and work (e.g., Beard and Wolf 2001; Caplan 2002, 2003; Davis 2001; Morahan-Martin and Schumacher 2000, 2003; Pratarelli et al. 1999; Sanders et al. 2000; Shotton 1991; Young 1996, 1998a, 1998b). For the purposes of this chapter, PIU is defined as a multidimensional syndrome consisting of cognitive and behavioral symptoms that result in negative social, academic, and professional consequences (Caplan 2002; Davis 2001; Davis et al. 2002; Morahan-Martin and Schumacher 2003).

Despite the growing concern with PIU and its effects on productivity as well as on employees' health, the current social scientific literature is limited in its understanding of PIU. For example, Caplan (2002) reports that there is little agreement about how to define or measure PIU. Moreover, much of the current literature lacks an empirically testable theory that explains, in detail, *how* PIU is associated with mental health and social well-being. Unfortunately, these limitations hinder both the development of PIU research and employers' attempts to understand and manage PIU in the workplace.

Thus, the purpose of this chapter is to offer a detailed theoretical account of PIU that will shed light on some of the factors that predict PIU, explain the cognitive and behavioral processes that constitute PIU, and review results of recent research designed to test the theory. The first section of the chapter contextualizes research on PIU and reviews the challenges facing researchers in this area. Next, the chapter presents the cognitive behavioral model of PIU, a promising theory that is both conceptually detailed and empirically testable. Additionally, the chapter will review emerging lines of social scientific research that have sought to test aspects of the cognitive behavioral model of PIU.

Conceptualizing PIU: Problematic Use or Addiction?

One factor that hinders the development of testable theories of PIU is the debate about how to theoretically and operationally define PIU (Beard and Wolf 2001; Caplan 2002). Scholars from a variety of disciplines have employed different labels to describe people who engage in online behaviors that result in negative outcomes, including "Internet addicts, computer-mediated communication addicts, and computer junkies" (Beard and Wolf 2001, 378).

One of the first, and most popular, approaches is the Internet addiction perspective (see Beard and Wolf 2001; Caplan 2002; Giffiths 1996, 1997, 1998; Pratarelli et al. 1999; Shaffer et al. 2000; Shotton 1991; Surratt 1999; Young 1996, 1998a, 1988b). According to Kandell, Internet addiction entails a "psychological dependence on the Internet and is characterized by (a) an increasing investment of resources on Internet-related activities, (b) unpleasant feelings (e.g., anxiety, depression, emptiness) when offline, (c) an increasing tolerance to the effects of being online, and (d) denial of the problematic behaviors" (1998, 11). The Internet addiction perspective characterizes PIU as a behavioral addiction similar in character to other impulse control disorders, such as gambling (for a recent review, see Beard and Wolf 2001; see also Brenner 1997; Griffiths 1996, 1997, 1998, 2000; Shotton 1991; Surratt 1999; Young 1996, 1998a; 1998b; Young and Rogers 1998). Moreover, individuals who meet these diagnostic criteria are held to experience "social, psychological, and occupational impairment" resulting from their Internet use, including "poor grade performance among students, discord among couples, and reduced work performance among employees" (Young and Rogers 1998, 25).

Despite its popularity, scholars have criticized the Internet addiction framework (e.g., Beard and Wolf 2001; Caplan 2002; Davis 2001; Shaffer et al. 2000; Surratt 1999). As Wallace (1999) notes, "many researchers find the disease label of Internet Addiction Disorder to be premature or wrong-headed" (188). The addiction framework suffers from at least three serious limitations. First, critics note that it lacks sufficient theoretical detail. For instance, Davis argues that the current addiction perspective is "loosely described" (2001, 187), and others have voiced similar concerns over "conceptual confusion surrounding the construct of 'Internet addiction'" (Shaffer et al. 2000, 163). Second, critics note a paucity of empirical research within the addiction paradigm. In fact, according to one review of the Internet addiction literature, "many published articles contain information that has not been empirically researched . . . [or] . . . review findings in the current literature but provide no independent empirical support" (Beard and Wolf 2001, 377). Additionally, Shaffer et al. argue that "empirical support for the construct validity has yet to emerge that defines [addiction] construct as a unique psychiatric disorder . . . and that, in most cases, excessive computer use may be symptomatic of other more primary disorders" (2000, 162). Finally, a third criticism of the addiction concept is that it fails to account for what people are actually *doing* online. Beard and Wolf argue that future research needs to "focus on what it actually is that people are addicted to. Is it the computer? Is it the typing? Is it the information gained? Is it the anonymity? Is it the types of activities in which the individual is engaged?" (2001, 381).

Overall, the criticisms presented above identify several serious limitations in the addiction perspective that reduce its usefulness for building detailed theories and developing empirical research programs. In order to move forward, researchers need a theory of PIU and well-being with clearly defined constructs and well-detailed descriptions of key causal processes involved in PIU. Toward this end, the next section presents the cognitive behavioral theory of PIU introduced by Davis (2001) and further developed by Caplan (2002, 2003, 2005) as a candidate theory for developing a program of research on PIU and health.

THE COGNITIVE BEHAVIORAL THEORY OF PIU

Overview

Davis introduced a cognitive behavioral theory of PIU that attempts to model the etiology, development, and outcomes associated with PIU. (Although Davis uses the term *pathological* Internet, the current paper adopts the term *problematic* Internet use to maintain consistency.) The cognitive behavioral model proposes that psychosocial problems, such as loneliness or social anxiety, predispose some Internet users to develop cognitions and behaviors involving their online activity that ultimately result in negative outcomes (Davis 2001). Although Davis's model is relatively new, recent work by Caplan (2002, 2003, 2004, 2005) supports some of its major claims. Beyond its appeal as a detailed explanatory account of the processes involved in PIU, Davis's theory also offers a clear conceptualization of PIU, as a construct that lends itself to empirical operationalization. The following paragraphs outline the general principles of the cognitive behavioral theory.

Conceptual Definition of PIU

Davis (2001) characterizes PIU as much more than a mere behavioral addiction; instead, he conceptualizes PIU as a distinct pattern of Internet-related *cognitions* and *behaviors* that result in negative life outcomes. Moreover, he makes an important theoretical distinction between two types of PIU: *specific* and *generalized*.

Specific PIU involves negative outcomes resulting from one's use of content-specific Internet functions, involving stimuli that can be accessed both on- and offline (e.g., viewing sexually explicit materials, gambling, and playing games online). Thus, Davis casts specific PIU as one of many possible manifestations of a broader behavioral disorder. He asserts that "specific PIU is related to only one aspect of the Internet and exists entirely independent of multiple Internet functions" (188). In other words, specific PIU involves a behavioral disorder that is not entirely dependent on the Internet; the desired stimuli can also be obtained offline. From an organizational standpoint, specific PIU may be addressed with the same policies and procedures that are used for other addictions or behavioral disorders. However, beyond these stimuli-specific problems, there is another form of PIU that would not exist without the Internet: generalized PIU.

Figure 5.1   **The Cognitive Behavioral Model of Problematic Internet Use**

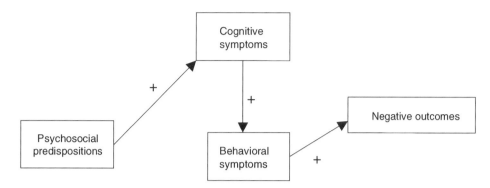

Whereas specific PIU is cast as one of many possible manifestations of a broader behavioral disorder, generalized PIU refers to a problem associated with the unique social context available on the Internet. In cases of generalized PIU, the Internet represents a vital "life line to the outer world" that "acts as a means of communication to the most extreme degree" (Davis 2001, 193). For individuals experiencing generalized PIU, the cost of increased allocation of resources to their Internet use accompanies a growing neglect of offline professional, social, and personal responsibilities, resulting in negative consequences. Generalized PIU in the workplace presents a unique challenge to organizations. Here, a stimuli-specific behavioral addiction model does not necessarily apply.

Given that generalized PIU is relatively new compared with other behavioral disorders, it is likely that many organizations do not have policies that address it. Moreover, the literature examining generalized PIU is relatively sparse and can offer some, but not much, guidance to organizations. To date, most literature on PIU lacks a theoretical perspective that conceptually distinguishes different types of PIU. Much of the literature has either focused solely on stimuli-specific PIU (e.g., online gambling) or been more concerned with how much time people spend online instead of why they are online. The remainder of this chapter will focus primarily on explaining generalized PIU.

Psychosocial Predispositions

An especially useful feature of the cognitive behavioral model is its explanatory account of why some individuals are more likely to develop generalized PIU than others (i.e., individual differences). The cognitive behavioral theory of PIU proposes that generalized PIU cognitions and behaviors are *consequences*, rather than *causes*, of broader psychosocial problems such as depression, social anxiety, and loneliness (Davis 2001). In turn, the cognitive and behavioral symptoms of generalized PIU lead to negative personal and professional outcomes. Figure 5.1 illustrates the general causal relations hypothesized by the cognitive behavioral model.

The model presented in Figure 5.1 represents a major step forward from previous scholarship, which often produced ambiguous results because they were not sufficiently grounded in theory. For example, one well-known early study reported results indicating that the amount of time one spends on the Internet leads to depression and loneliness (Kraut et al. 1998). Kraut and colleagues conducted a longitudinal study examining how new Internet users would respond to having a Internet connection in their home. The results indicated that people who spent more time online were more likely to exhibit increases in depression and social separation than those who spent less time online. The researchers were so surprised by their findings that they titled their report with a question: "Internet paradox: A social technology that reduces social involvement and psychological well-being?"

One important contribution of the Internet paradox study was that it drew widespread attention to the question of whether there might be negative outcomes associated with Internet use. However, the validity of Kraut et al.'s findings was called into question by subsequent studies that failed to replicate the earlier findings. For example, in a follow-up to their original 1998 study, Kraut and colleagues failed to find evidence to support the earlier conclusion that frequent Internet use leads to psychosocial health problems (Kraut et al. 2002). One reason that such results are considered ambiguous is the research lacked a sufficiently detailed theoretical account of *how* Internet use facilitates the development of psychosocial problems. Moreover, the only aspect of Internet use that the earlier study examined was frequency of Internet use, without examining what people were actually doing online.

In a departure from previous literature that focused solely on the effects of the amount of Internet use and its correlation with negative outcomes, the cognitive behavioral model provides a significantly more detailed and testable model of the etiology of PIU (Caplan 2002). The following paragraphs describe, in greater detail, each part of the model (see Figure 5.1) and review new lines of empirical investigation, which have begun to test parts of the model.

Davis (2001) hypothesizes that, rather than Internet use causing psychosocial problems, existing psychosocial difficulties predispose individuals to develop maladaptive cognitions associated with their Internet use and maladaptive online behavior that results in negative outcomes (see Figure 5.1). Preexisting problems such as loneliness or social anxiety, from this perspective, are necessary but not sufficient distal factors that predispose one to generalized PIU. Together with one's experiences with the Internet, these psychosocial problems may spur the development of problematic cognitions and behaviors involving the Internet that lead to negative outcomes.

The available research has yielded results consistent with the cognitive behavioral model's description of the role of psychosocial predictors of the negative outcomes of PIU. A number of studies on loneliness (one example of a psychosocial problem) and negative outcomes due to Internet use suggest a significant positive correlation between the two (e.g., Amichai-Hamburger and Ben-Artzi 2003; Caplan 2002; Kubey et al. 2001; Morahan-Martin and Schumacher 2003). For example, in one recent study, Caplan (2002) found that participants' level of loneliness predicted the extent to which they reported negative outcomes resulting from their Internet use.

In another study, Morahan-Martin and Schumacher (2003) found that compared to nonlonely individuals, lonely people were significantly more likely to report that their online behavior was causing disruptions in their lives. Lonely individuals also reported feeling more guilt about the amount of time they spend online, were more likely to have been told they spend too much time online, were more likely to routinely cut short sleep to be online, were more likely to have missed social engagements, work, or school to be online, and were more likely to have tried to hide how much time they had spent online than their nonlonely counterparts.

To explain the empirical association between loneliness and the negative outcomes of PIU reviewed above, some researchers (e.g., Morahan-Martin 1999; Morahan-Martin and Schumacher 2000, 2003) have advanced the "lonely-drawn-to-the-Internet hypothesis," proposing that compared to nonlonely people who prefer face-to-face (FtF) interaction, the lonely are particularly drawn to interpersonal processes in synchronous online social interaction. Similarly, La Rose, Eastin, and Gregg (2001) argue that for people who are isolated or lack mobility, the Internet is a social technology that is vital for maintaining relationships and obtaining social support (also see La Rose et al. 2001). The next section explains, in more detail, the nature of proximal cognitive variables that mediate the relationship between psychosocial well-being variables such as loneliness and negative outcomes of Internet use.

Proximal Cognitive Predictors of the Negative Outcomes of PIU

The cognitive behavioral model of PIU proposes that the presence of maladaptive cognitions that accompany most psychopathologies is critical to the development of generalized PIU behaviors. With regard to the model, the presence of these maladaptive cognitions is a proximal sufficient cause of PIU. In other words, preexisting psychosocial problems, along with associated maladaptive cognitions about self, predispose an individual to exhibit PIU cognitions and behaviors. Examples of maladaptive cognitions provided by Davis (2001) include self-focused rumination, self-doubt, low self-efficacy, and negative self-appraisals. More recently, Caplan (2003, 2004, 2005) proposed and tested the hypothesis that a preference for online social interaction (POSI) over FtF conversation is a key cognitive symptom of generalized PIU and a significant positive predictor of negative outcomes resulting from Internet use. Caplan's research offers some initial empirical support for relationships hypothesized by the cognitive behavioral model.

Caplan (2003) argues that loneliness, along with exposure to online social activity, may predispose an individual to develop a POSI, which predicts negative outcomes. POSI is a cognitive individual difference characterized by beliefs that one is safer, more efficacious, more confident, and more comfortable with online interpersonal interactions and relationships than with traditional FtF communication (Caplan 2003; see also Morahan-Martin 1999).

Whereas the cognitive behavioral model identifies psychosocial predisposition (i.e., loneliness) as a distal cause of generalized PIU, POSI is an example of a proximal maladaptive cognitive predictor of negative outcomes due to Internet use. In terms of the cognitive behavioral model, people with psychosocial problems should be more likely than those without such problems to develop a POSI, which then leads to patterns of behaviors resulting in negative outcomes.

Why might an individual prefer to communicate with others online rather than face to face? A growing literature suggests that FtF interaction and synchronous computer-mediated communication (CMC) differ from each other in important ways (see Hancock and Dunham 2001; Walther and Parks 2002; Ramirez et al. 2002). Some of the features of online social interaction that may be especially appealing to lonely individuals are greater anonymity (see Bargh et al. 2002; McKenna and Bargh 1999, 2000; McKenna et al. 2002), greater control over self-presentation (Cornwell and Lundgren 2001; Noonan 1998), and less perceived social risk (i.e., diminished personal cost if interactions or relationships fail) than in traditional FtF communication (Morahan-Martin and Schumacher 2000; Turkle 1995; Wallace 1999; Walther 1996).

Walther proposes that online social interaction can be hyperpersonal in the sense that it "goes beyond the interpersonal levels typically achieved in FtF associations" (Walther and Parks 2002, 540; Walther 1996). Hyperpersonal communication may be more advantageous than traditional FtF behavior for some interpersonal endeavors. For example, Walther maintains that online interactants can be more selective and strategic in their self-presentation, form more idealized impressions of their partners, and, consequently, engage in more intimate exchanges than people in FtF situations (Tidwell and Walther 2002; Walther 1993, 1996; Walther and Burgoon 1992).

Ramirez et al. propose that "although most [computer-mediated communication] environments eliminate or severely reduce nonverbal and contextual information available to address uncertainty, form impressions, and develop relationships, such environments offer alternative mechanisms for acquiring social information about others" (2002, 213). Indeed, researchers have noted differences in impression formation processes in online versus FtF interaction (Lea and Spears 1992; Reicher et al. 1995; Spears and Lea 1992, 1994; Spears et al. 2002).

Morahan-Martin and Schumacher propose that the communicative features of CMC identified above "may be particularly attractive to those who are lonely" and may lead to Internet use that results in negative outcomes (2003, 661). Along the same line, McKenna et al. argue that lonely individuals are "somewhat more likely to feel that they can better express their real selves with others on the Internet than they can with those they know offline" (2002, 28). Recent research supports Caplan's hypothesis that POSI mediates the influence of loneliness on negative outcomes of PIU. For example, one study (Caplan 2003) found that participants' self-reported level of POSI mediated the association between their level of loneliness and the extent to which they reported experiencing negative outcomes due to their Internet use.

Caplan (2004) argues, however, that one important implication of the mediated association between loneliness and negative outcomes of one's Internet use is that, contrary to the lonely-drawn-to-the-Internet hypothesis, not all lonely people will necessarily engage in problematic Internet use. Rather, Caplan's earlier findings (2003) raise the question of what distinguishes lonely Internet users who exhibit a substantial preference for online social interaction from lonely Internet users who do not have this preference.

Caplan (2004) argues that some people are lonely for reasons that have nothing to do with their attitudes about interpersonal behavior, such as job relocation, frequent traveling for work, or insufficient time for social activities. He asks why people who are lonely for these reasons would prefer the altered communicative characteristics of online social interaction over regular FtF communication. To answer this question, Caplan recently advanced and tested an alternative to the lonely-drawn-to-the-Internet hypothesis, the socially-anxious-drawn-to-the-Internet hypothesis.

This hypothesis proposes that the previously observed association between loneliness and POSI is spurious and is a manifestation of the association of social anxiety with both variables (Caplan 2004). Moreover, Caplan suggests that social anxiety represents a more useful theoretical predictor of PIU than loneliness. Specifically, he proposes that one important theoretical benefit of focusing on social anxiety rather than loneliness is that social anxiety involves a motivation to seek less risky interpersonal encounters whereas loneliness may, but does not necessarily, involve such a motivation.

Caplan (2004) employs the self-presentational theory of social anxiety (Leary 1983; Leary and Kowalski 1995; Schlenker and Leary 1982, 1985) to explain the motivating dynamic that leads the socially anxious to prefer online social interaction. The self-presentational theory maintains that social anxiety arises when a person desires to make a good impression on others but lacks the confidence to do so. Most importantly, the theory posits that, in order to increase their perceived self-presentational efficacy, socially anxious individuals are highly motivated to seek low-risk communicative encounters.

Thus, according to Caplan (2004), the socially anxious should be more likely than those who are not socially anxious to prefer online social interaction because they perceive their self-presentational efficacy online to be greater than in FtF interaction. In other words, a POSI should arise from a perceived increase in self-presentational efficacy and reduction in social anxiety that socially anxious people experience when engaged in online social interaction.

In his recent study, Caplan (2004) tested the relative value of both loneliness and social anxiety as predictors of POSI and negative outcomes of Internet use. In the study, 343 undergraduate research participants completed measures of POSI, negative outcomes associated with their Internet use, loneliness, and social anxiety. In addition to variables in the hypothesized model, the study also included measures of several key exogenous variables, including the participants' gender and their self-reported frequency of three stimuli-specific PIU behaviors thought to influence negative outcomes (gambling, playing interactive games, and viewing sexually explicit materials).

Caplan performed a path analysis technique recommended by Cohen and Cohen (1983) to test the hypothesis that the relationship between loneliness and POSI is spurious and that social anxiety confounds that association. The path analysis employed two hierarchical multiple regression equations in which the order of entry of the predictors of POSI (i.e., loneliness and social anxiety) was reversed in the second analysis. The analysis revealed that, after social anxiety had been taken into account, loneliness added no significant predictive value to the model. The results supported the claim that the relationship between loneliness and POSI is spurious and that this relationship is confounded by

Figure 5.2   **Social Anxiety and Preference for Online Social Interaction**

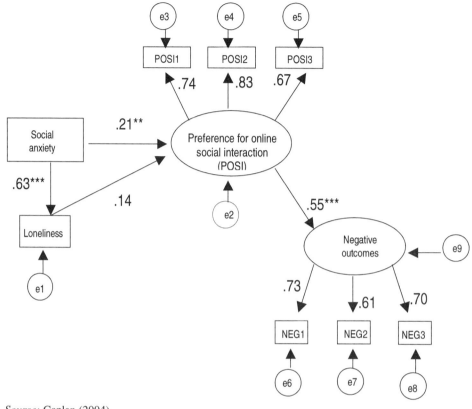

Source: Caplan (2004).
** $p < .01$; *** $p < .001$.

both variables' association with social anxiety. Caplan's results indicated that social anxiety is a significant positive predictor of POSI, accounting for approximately 18 percent of the explained variance in POSI scores.

In addition to the path analysis, Caplan (2004) also performed a structural equation modeling (SEM) analysis to test the hypotheses that social anxiety would have a direct effect on POSI, that POSI would have a direct positive influence on negative outcome scores, and that social anxiety would have an indirect effect on negative outcomes of Internet use mediated by POSI (see Figure 5.2). The SEM analysis employed several exogenous variables thought to influence social anxiety and negative outcomes. Gender was included as an exogenous predictor of social anxiety. Additionally, stimuli-specific Internet uses (gambling, viewing sexually explicit materials, and playing interactive games) were included as direct predictors of negative outcomes. Overall, the hypothesized model fit the data well, accounting for 24 percent of the variance in POSI scores and 31 percent of the variance in negative outcomes of Internet use. The results also indicated that social anxiety was a significant direct predictor of POSI, and POSI was a direct predictor of negative outcomes. In fact, POSI was the strongest direct predictor of negative outcomes, with a path estimate more than twice the size of any of the stimuli-specific exogenous predictors. Finally, the analysis revealed an indirect effect of social anxiety on negative outcomes, mediated by preference for online social interaction.

Proximal Behavioral Predictors of Negative Outcomes of Internet Use

To date, the available research on the cognitive behavioral model has focused mainly on the association between distal psychosocial predictors and proximal cognitive predictors of PIU (e.g., preference for online social interaction). Yet little is known about the maladaptive behavioral predictors specified in the model.

In terms of specifying particular online behaviors that give rise to generalized PIU, Davis deviates from the Internet addiction literature by suggesting that "there is not a specific time limit or behavioral benchmark" for identifying Internet use as problematic; instead, the cognitive behavioral model of PIU "posits a continuum of functioning" (2001, 193). From the cognitive behavioral approach, examples of dysfunctional behaviors that arise along with cognitive predictors of PIU include compulsive Internet use, denying or lying about Internet use, and using the Internet to escape from one's problems (depression, loneliness, etc.). Davis (2001) maintains that, over time, maladaptive cognitions and behaviors intensify and continue to produce negative outcomes.

When specifying the nature of maladaptive Internet behaviors, it is imperative to distinguish between compulsive Internet use and excessive use. Caplan (2003) maintains that *excessive* Internet use involves a quantity or degree of online activity that exceeds what a person thinks of as normal, usual, or planned, whereas *compulsive* use involves difficulty with impulse control.

Compulsive and excessive Internet use are closely related but have conceptually distinct behavioral patterns. Although many people consider the amount of time they spend online excessive, their excessive use may have more to do with their reliance on the Internet to do their work (i.e., functional rather than dysfunctional purposes) than with their psychosocial well-being. People who rely on the Internet to manage various aspects of their lives (finances, travel plans, research, etc.) may find themselves spending excessive time online in order to attain positive outcomes at work and at home. For example, a student who is working late into the night on a research paper may consider his time online to be excessive, but his assignment may require excessive time online. Similarly, a computer network administrator probably spends most of her time online, but her behavior is motivated by the functional demands of the job, rather than by an impulse control disorder. Indeed, many people would probably report that they use the Internet excessively but out of practical necessity for doing their work, which would then result in positive, rather than negative, outcomes.

Thus, the argument advanced in this chapter is that the quantity or amount of time online is not necessarily indicative of a problem—many functional Internet behaviors require excessive time online. Instead, it is probably more accurate to specify that compulsive use plays a key role in the development of negative outcomes from Internet use.

Recent empirical studies support the claim that compulsive behavior, rather than excessive use, is closely associated with negative outcomes. Caplan (2003) compared the relative power of excessive Internet use and compulsive Internet use as predictors of negative outcomes associated with PIU. He found that both excessive and compulsive Internet use predicted negative personal outcomes associated with Internet use. However, comparatively speaking, the extent to which compulsive behavior predicted the negative outcomes of PIU was stronger than that of excessive use. In fact, Caplan reported that "excessive use was one of the weakest predictors of negative outcomes, whereas preference for online social interaction, compulsive use, and withdrawal [another cognitive predictor] were among the strongest" (637–638). In another study, Shapira et al. interviewed people suffering from PIU (defined as engaging in Internet use that was uncontrollable, distressing, time-consuming, or resulting in negative outcomes) and found that all subjects' "problematic Internet use met the [Diagnostic and Statistical Manual of Mental Disorders, Fourth Edition (DSM-IV)] [American Psychiatric Association 1994] criteria for an impulse control disorder" (267).

In a review of research on PIU, Shapira and colleagues concluded that, "based on the current limited empirical evidence, problematic Internet use may best be classified as an impulse control disorder" (2003, 207). Indeed, many scholars make a similar argument that PIU entails a problem with behavioral impulse control (for a review see Beard and Wolf 2001; see also Brenner 1997; Davis 2001; Griffiths 2000; Shapira et al. 2000; Young 1998a, 1998b; Young and Rogers 1998). For instance, according to Davis, PIU involves "diminished impulse control [and an] inability to cease Internet usage" (2001, 193).

Wallace (1999) argues that, for some, online social interaction involves a conditioned-response reward structure (the reward being positive reactions from others) that increases use and leads to compulsive Internet use. The impulse control problems may begin with the adaptive, social-anxiety-reducing effect of online social interaction. However, over time, when an individual suffering from social anxiety becomes increasingly dependent on the anxiety-reducing qualities of online social interaction, that person may begin to replace potential FtF interactions with computer-mediated communication. Although online social interaction may be more comfortable for socially anxious individuals, it may not be a functional alternative to FtF communication.

Currently, the available literature is unclear about whether online social interaction is a valid functional alternative to FtF conversation. In one study, Flaherty et al. concluded that "the use of the Internet as a communication channel was not perceived as a functional alternative for face-to-face communication" (1998, 250). However, in another study, Papacharissi and Rubin reported that "the relationships between Internet motives and the social and psychological antecedents support the use of the Internet as a functional alternative for Internet users for whom other channels are not as available or rewarding" (2000, 191). Although a person suffering from PIU might perceive online social interaction as a functional alternative to FtF relationships, this preference does not necessarily mean that both have equally beneficial consequences.

On the surface, there may be nothing inherently problematic about engaging in online social interaction or preferring it. Indeed, for the socially anxious, online interaction may help them develop intimate social ties that function to alleviate loneliness. How-

Figure 5.3 **Preference for Online Social Interaction and Compulsive Use**

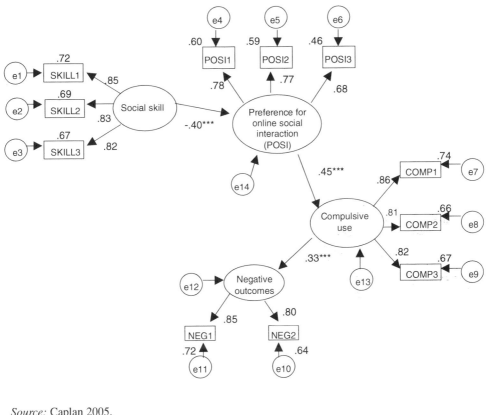

Source: Caplan 2005.
*** *p* < .001.

ever, one cannot forgo the world of FtF communication entirely without suffering negative personal and professional consequences. As people who increasingly prefer online
social interaction devote more of their resources (e.g., time, money, and attention) to
their online social lives, their careers and FtF relationships are likely to become secondary priorities.

A recent study conducted by Caplan (2005) sought to test the validity of the hypothesis that compulsive online behavior plays a key role in the development of PIU. The
study tested an indirect effect hypothesis that people who develop a preference for online
social interaction engage in compulsive Internet use that results in negative outcomes. In
the study, 251 undergraduate participants completed measures of social skill, preference
for online social interaction, compulsive Internet use, and negative outcomes associated
with Internet use. The study found that social skill predicted one's degree of preference
for online social interaction. Additionally, the results indicated that preference for online
social interaction predicted compulsive Internet use, which predicted negative outcomes
associated with Internet use (see Figure 5.3).

In sum, the available research supports the cognitive behavioral model's prediction that maladaptive patterns of online behavior, such as compulsive use, predict negative outcomes due to one's Internet use. The last section of this chapter summarizes the research presented thus far and offers recommendations for future research on PIU.

CONCLUSION

If nothing else, the literature reviewed throughout this chapter illustrates that researchers from a variety of disciplines are engaged in a thorough and active program designed to better understand PIU, its causes, and its effects. As the first section of the chapter pointed out, PIU in the workplace may represent a new occupational health concern for organizational managers. Moreover, the debate about whether to consider PIU as a behavioral addiction similar to others, such as gambling, raises the question of whether existing policies designed to deal with addiction in the workplace can also be applied to PIU. The position advanced in the current chapter is that PIU, and generalized PIU in particular, is *not* analogous to other behavioral addictions.

For the reasons presented earlier, the Internet addiction perspective fails to acknowledge or consider ways in which PIU is more than simply a stimuli-specific addiction. Rather, as Caplan (2002), Davis (2001), and others point out, many people have a problematic relationship with the social world available only online. In fact, evidence reported by Caplan (2004) suggests that when stimuli-specific uses and POSI are compared in terms of their ability to predict negative outcomes, POSI accounts for a greater percentage of variance. In other words, relatively speaking, POSI is a stronger predictor of negative outcomes of Internet use than behaviors such as gambling or playing interactive games online.

Although stimuli-specific PIU exists, generalized PIU represents a new and unfamiliar challenge to researchers and organizational managers. The cognitive behavioral model of PIU is one promising theory that has already begun to help researchers better understand PIU in a more detailed manner. Davis's model (2001) offers a focused explication of the psychosocial, cognitive, and behavioral aspects of PIU. Caplan's research suggests that generalized PIU is strongly associated with one's thoughts and feelings about interpersonal communication (Caplan 2003, 2004, 2005).

Although research on the cognitive behavioral model is only just beginning, the results obtained thus far are promising. Of course, future researchers of the cognitive behavioral model have much work to do. For example, one question researchers now need to address is this: besides through compulsive behavior, how else might a preference for online social interaction lead to negative outcomes?

Currently, the available literature on PIU and on PIU in the workplace raises more questions than it provides answers. Although scholars of management information systems and organizational behavior may be more interested in how PIU affects members of an organization, how it affects an organization's productivity, and how to manage PIU in the workplace, a detailed understanding of the issue must begin with an understanding of the etiology of PIU. In other words, a better understanding of the psychological and interpersonal processes that facilitate the development of PIU is necessary in order to understand exactly what PIU is, how it develops, and how we might be able to help individuals whose Internet use is creating problems for them in the workplace.

REFERENCES

American Psychiatric Association. 1994. *Diagnostic and Statistical Manual of Mental Disorders.* 4th ed. Washington, DC: American Psychological Association.

Amichai-Hamburger, Y., and Ben-Artzi, E. 2003. Loneliness and Internet use. *Computers in Human Behavior* 19, 71–80.

Anandarajan, M. 2002. Introduction to special section on Internet abuse in the workplace. *Communications of the ACM* 45, 53–54.

Bargh, J.A., McKenna, K.Y.A., and Fitzsimmons, G.M. 2002. Can you see the real me? Activation and expression of the "true self" on the Internet. *Journal of Social Issues* 58, 33–48.

Beard, K.W., and Wolf, E.M. 2001. Modification in the proposed diagnostic criteria for Internet addiction. *CyberPsychology and Behavior* 4, 377–383.

Brenner, V. 1997. Psychology of computer use: XLVII. Parameters of Internet use, abuse and addiction: The first 90 days of the Internet Usage Survey. *Psychological Reports* 80, 879–882.

Caplan, S.E. 2002. Problematic Internet use and psychosocial well-being: Development of a theory-based cognitive-behavioral measure. *Computers in Human Behavior* 18, 533–575.

———. 2003. Preference for online social interaction: A theory of problematic Internet use and psychosocial well-being. *Communication Research* 30, 625–648.

———. 2004. Relations among loneliness, social anxiety, and problematic Internet use. Paper presented at the National Communication Association Convention in Chicago.

———. 2005. A social skill account of problematic Internet use. *Journal of Communication* 55, 4, 721–736.

Cohen, J., and Cohen, P. 1983. *Applied Multiple Regression/Correlation Analysis for the Behavioral Sciences.* 2nd ed. New York: Wiley.

Cornwell, B., and Lundgren, D. 2001. Love on the Internet: Involvement and misrepresentation in romantic relationships in cyberspace vs. realspace. *Computers in Human Behavior* 17, 197–211.

Davis, R.A. 2001. A cognitive-behavioral model of pathological Internet use. *Computers in Human Behavior* 17, 187–195.

Davis, R.A., Flett, G.L., and Besser, A. 2002. Validation of a new measure of problematic Internet use: Implications for pre-employment screening. *CyberPsychology and Behavior* 5, 331–346.

Flaherty, L.M., Pearce, K.J., and Rubin, R.B. 1998. Internet and face-to-face communication: Not functional alternatives. *Communication Quarterly* 46, 250–268.

Griffiths, M. 1996. Internet "addiction": An issue for clinical psychology? *Clinical Psychology Forum* 97, 32–36.

———. 1997. Psychology of computer use: XLIII. Some comments on "Addictive use of the Internet" by Young. *Psychological Reports* 80, 81–82.

———. 1998. Internet addiction: Does it really exist? In J.E. Gackenbach (ed.), *Psychology and the Internet: Intrapersonal, Interpersonal, and Transpersonal Implications.* New York: Academic Press, 61–75.

———. 2000. Does Internet and computer "addiction" exist? Some case study evidence. *CyberPsychology and Behavior* 3, 211–218.

———. 2002. Occupational health issues concerning Internet use in the workplace. *Work and Stress* 6, 283–286.

———. 2003. Internet abuse in the workplace: Issues and concerns for employers and employment counselors. *Journal of Employment Counseling* 40, 87–96.

Hancock, J.T., and Dunham, P.J. 2001. Impression formation in computer-mediated communication revisited: An analysis of the breadth and intensity of impressions. *Communication Research* 28, 325–347.

Kandell, J.J. 1998. Internet addiction on campus: The vulnerability of college students. *CyberPsychology and Behavior* 1, 11–17.

Kraut, R., Kiesler, S., Boneva, B., Cummings, J., Helgeson, V., and Crawford, A. 2002. Internet paradox revisited. *Journal of Social Issues* 58, 49–74.

Kraut, R., Patterson, M., Lundmark, V., Kiesler, S., Mukopadhyay, T., and Scherlis, W. 1998. Internet paradox: A social technology that reduces social involvement and psychological well-being? *American Psychologist* 53, 1017–1031.

Kubey, R.W., Lavin, M.J., and Barrows, J.R. 2001. Internet use and collegiate academic performance decrements: Early findings. *Journal of Communication* 51, 366–382.

LaRose, R., Eastin, M.S., Gregg, J. 2001. Reformulating the Internet paradox: Social cognitive explanations of Internet use and depression. *Journal of Online Behavior* 1. www.behavior.net/JOB/v1n2/paradox.html.

La Rose, R., Mastro, D., and Eastin, M.S. 2001. Understanding Internet usage: A social-cognitive approach to uses and gratifications. *Social Science Computer Review* 19, 395–413.

Lea, M., and Spears, R. 1992. Paralanguage and social perception in computer-mediated communication. *Journal of Organizational Computing* 2, 321–341.

Leary, M.L. 1983. *Understanding Social Anxiety: Social, Personality, and Clinical Perspective.* Newbury Park, CA: Sage.

Leary, M.R., and Kowalski, R.M. 1995. *Social Anxiety.* New York: Guilford Press.

Lim, V.K.G. 2002. The IT way of loafing on the job: Cyberloafing, neutralizing and organizational justice. *Journal of Organizational Behavior* 23, 5, 675–694.

Lim, V.K.G., Teo, T.S.H., and Loo, G.L. 2002. How do I loaf here? Let me count the ways. *Communications of the ACM* 45, 66–70.

Mahatanankoon, P., Anandarajan, M., and Igbaria, M. 2004. Development of a measure of personal Web usage in the workplace. *CyberPsychology and Behavior* 7, 93–104.

McKenna, K.Y.A., and Bargh, J.A. 1999. Causes and consequences of social interaction on the Internet: A conceptual framework. *Media Psychology* 1, 249–269.

———. 2000. Plan 9 from cyberspace: The implications of the Internet for personality and social psychology. *Journal of Personality and Social Psychology* 75, 681–694.

McKenna, K.Y.A., Greene, A.S., and Gleason, M.E.J. 2002. Relationship formation on the Internet: What's the big attraction? *Journal of Social Issues* 58, 9–31.

Morahan-Martin, J. 1999. The relationship between loneliness and Internet use and abuse. *CyberPsychology and Behavior* 2, 431–440.

Morahan-Martin, J., and Schumacher, P. 2000. Incidence and correlates of pathological Internet use among college students. *Computers in Human Behavior* 16, 13–29.

———. 2003. Loneliness and social uses of the Internet. *Computers in Human Behavior* 19, 659–671.

Noonan, R.J. 1998. The psychology of sex: A mirror from the Internet. In J. Gackenbach (ed). *Psychology and the Internet: Intrapersonal, Interpersonal, and Transpersonal Implications.* San Diego, CA: Academic Press, 143–168.

Papacharissi, Z., and Rubin, A.M. 2000. Predictors of Internet use. *Journal of Broadcasting and Electronic Media* 44, 175–196.

Pratarelli, M.E., Browne, B.L., and Johnson, K. 1999. The bits and bytes of computer/Internet addiction: A factor analytic approach. *Behavior Research Methods, Instruments, and Computers* 31, 305–314.

Ramirez, A., Jr., Walther, J.B., Burgoon, J.K., and Sunnafrank, M. 2002. Information-seeking strategies, uncertainty, and computer-mediated communication: Toward a conceptual model. *Human Communication Research* 28, 213–228.

Reicher, S.D., Spears, R., and Postmes, T. 1995. Effects of public and private self-awareness on deindividuation and aggression. *Journal of Personality and Social Psychology* 43, 503–513.

Sanders, C.E., Field, T.M., Diego, M., and Kaplan, M. 2000. The relationship of Internet use to depression and social isolation among adolescents. *Adolescence* 35, 237– 242.

Schlenker, B.R., and Leary, M.R. 1982. Social anxiety and self-preservation: A conceptualization and model. *Psychological Bulletin* 92, 641–669.

———. 1985. Social anxiety and communication about the self. *Journal of Language and Psychology* 4, 171–193. (Invited paper for a special issue.)

Shaffer, H.J., Hall, M.N., Vanderbilt, J. 2000. "Computer addiction": A critical consideration. *American Journal of Orthopsychiatry* 70, 162–168.

Shapira N.A., Goldsmith T.D., Keck, P.E., Jr., Khosla, U.M., and McElroy S.L. 2000. Psychiatric features of individuals with problematic Internet use. *Journal of Affective Disorders* 57, 267–272.

Shapira, N.A., Lessing, M.C., Goldsmith, T.D., Szabo, S.T., Lazortiz, M., Gold, M.S., and Stein, D.J. 2003. Problematic Internet use: Proposed classification and diagnostic criteria. *Depression and Anxiety* 17, 207–216.

Shotton, M.A. 1991. The costs and benefits of computer addiction. *Behaviour and Information Technology* 10, 219–230.

Spears, R., and Lea, M. 1992. Social influence and the influence of the "social" in computer-mediated communication. In M. Lea (ed.), *Contexts of Computer-Mediated Communication*. London: Harvester-Wheatsheaf, 30–65.

———. 1994. Panacea or panopticon? The hidden power in computer-mediated communication. *Communication Research* 21, 427–459.

Spears, R., Postmes, T., and Lea, M. 2002. The power of influence and the influence of power in virtual groups: A SIDE look at CMC and the Internet. *Journal of Social Issues* 58, 91–108.

Surratt, C.G. 1999. *Netaholics? The Creation of a Pathology*. Commack, NY: Nova Science Publishers.

Tidwell, L.C., and Walther, J.B. 2002. Computer-mediated communication effects on disclosure, impressions, and interpersonal evaluations: Getting to know one another a bit at a time. *Human Communication Research* 28, 317–348.

Turkle, S. 1995. *Life on the Screen*. New York: Simon and Schuster.

Wallace, P.M. 1999. *The Psychology of the Internet*. New York: Cambridge University Press.

Walther, J.B. 1993. Impression development in computer-mediated interaction. *Western Journal of Communication* 57, 381–398.

———. 1996. Computer-mediated communication: Impersonal, interpersonal, and hyperpersonal interaction. *Communication Research* 23, 3–43.

Walther, J.B., and Burgoon, J.K. 1992. Relational communication in computer-mediated interaction. *Human Communication Research* 19, 50–88.

Walther, J.B., and Parks, M.R. 2002. Cues filtered out, cues filtered in: Computer-mediated communication relationships. In M.L. Knapp, J.A. Daly, and G.R. Miller (eds.), *The Handbook of Interpersonal Communication*. 3rd ed. Thousand Oaks, CA: Sage.

Young, K.S. 1996. Psychology of computer use: XI. Addictive use of the Internet: A case study that breaks the stereotype. *Psychological Reports* 79, 899–902.

———. 1998a. *Caught in the Net: How to Recognize the Signs of Internet Addiction and a Winning Strategy for Recovery*. New York: John Wiley.

———. 1998b. Internet addiction: The emergence of a new clinical disorder. *CyberPsychology and Behavior* 1, 237–244.

Young, K.S., and Case, C.J. 2004. Internet abuse in the workplace: New trends in risk management. *CyberPsychology and Behavior* 7, 105–111.

Young, K.S, and Rogers, R.C. 1998. The relationship between depression and Internet addiction. *CyberPsychology and Behavior* 1, 25–28.

PART II

PROMISING TRANSFORMATIONS

CHAPTER 6

ORGANIZATIONAL INTRANETS AND THE TRANSITION TO MANAGING KNOWLEDGE

ELISABETH E. BENNETT

Abstract: Globalization, the Internet, and the transition to a knowledge and service economy have dramatically altered the workplace, creating fresh challenges and opportunities for organizations using technology for competitive advantage. Internet technology created new capabilities in the form of organizational intranets to create, store, and disseminate organizational knowledge. This chapter advances two propositions. First, intranets are fundamentally different from traditional information systems, epitomizing a shift from managing information to managing knowledge. Second, managing knowledge requires greater integration and transparency between technology and the social nature of organizing. Examination of organizational culture and knowledge management theories suggests two critical connections between the theories: first, organizational culture, particularly organizational assumptions and values, can facilitate or hinder interpretation of information, and, second, management of cultural content can maintain or change organizational culture. The chapter concludes with organizational strategies for using intranets in the knowledge economy and a discussion of qualitative methods for researching organizational use of technology.

Keywords: Knowledge Management, Organizational Culture, Information Technology, Intranets, Qualitative Research

INTRODUCTION

The very landscape of the workplace has changed with the rapid rise of Web technology at the end of the twentieth century and the transition into a global knowledge and service economy. The Internet is the backbone of the global economy (Cummings and Worley 2005) that continues to open up markets and make information available that had been nonexistent or inaccessible in the past; however, this access is not uniform among international populations. At the forefront of the digital side of the growing divide are the United States, Canada, and Scandinavian countries (Schemmann 2003). The divide may be seen at the organizational level as groups use Internet technology in diverse ways, ranging from simple to intricate and highly integrated systems. Organizational intranets use Internet technology to link documents and databases that are accessible and relevant to a defined audience. This distinction makes intranets a fascinating focus for research into organizations because they are capable of reflecting organizational dynamics and may lead to organizational change in ways that have yet to be uncovered through empirical research.

Various bodies of literature touch upon intranets but often focus on technology or its functionality. Little attention has been given to how intranets shape and are shaped by organizations as social systems and how this relationship affects the production and management of knowledge. Knowledge, or everything that is "known," is an encompassing term that creates new problems for a world used to handling discrete, rationale, and bounded forms of information, and these problems are at the crux of the present economy. This chapter entertains two propositions. First, intranets are fundamentally different from traditional information systems, signaling a shift from managing information to managing knowledge. Second, managing knowledge requires greater integration and transparency between technology and the social nature of organizing. To further understanding of intranets on a theoretical level, this chapter examines two critical connections between organizational culture and knowledge management theory. On a practical level, intranet design may allow organizations flexibility for reshaping work structures in response to external changes. This chapter discusses (1) the changing climate of the 1990s that gave rise to intranets and the knowledge economy, (2) the move from centralized to decentralized information management, (3) the definition and characteristics of intranets, (4) knowledge management theory, (5)·organizational culture theory with connections to knowledge management, (6) organizational strategies for using intranets in the knowledge economy, and (7) implications for future research and the potential of qualitative methods for organizational research.

To provide a historical perspective, we look to Diebold (1985), who predicted that word processing software would change the way that organizations function by promoting individual workstations to communication centers. He saw centralized data processing shifting to a decentralized approach that involved primarily white-collar employees. We have far exceeded these predictions. Network infrastructure is now the norm in countries on the digital side of the divide. An increasing number of organizations are requiring network identities and computer skills at all job levels, including traditionally blue-collar jobs, so that critical announcements can be disseminated quickly and employees have access to policies and procedures that would have once been printed in handbooks. When access is opened to the majority of organizational members, it reflects a real and lasting change in the professional environment. This change, briefly reviewed in the next section, underpins how intranets have evolved to solve new organizational problems and needs.

A DECADE OF CHANGE

The 1990s ushered in a fundamental shift in paradigms for the working world. The development of the knowledge economy was founded on the concept that growth and innovation depend more on ideas, information, and forms of knowledge than on production and distribution; and more jobs, therefore, stem from services surrounding production—research and development, logistics, marketing—than from actual production (Bron and Schemmann 2003). Factors that led to intranet development occurred as a three-pronged change in the use of organizational technology. The change essentially followed Diebold's (1985) prediction of movement to information management strategies that are less centralized and more dispersed throughout the organization.

First, with the development of the microchip and subsequent increase in processing speed and drop in price for computer components, it became feasible to place desktop computers in homes and offices across the United States and internationally. The increasing availability and affordability of desktops moved portions of data processing out of central locations and into the hands of a growing number of knowledge workers. Second, hypertext markup language (HTML) created a standard language by which Web browsers could display media downloaded from remote Web servers. Although the Internet has been in existence in one form or another since the 1950s, the popularization of the Internet in the 1990s truly made it a Web of worldwide computers. Thus, a powerful communication channel opened to businesses of all sizes and to individuals, facilitating connections to diverse groups of people and providing new marketing opportunities. The Internet has grown so dramatically that the technically savvy public has come to *expect* corporate and governmental Web sites. Third, the network infrastructure that information technology (IT) professionals installed over the last decade has connected the workplace so well that electronic documents and other forms of digital information can be disseminated quite easily. More businesses than ever are networked, requiring fewer face-to-face points of communication and greater capability for Internet technology to mediate human interaction.

With these changes afoot, the average employee must now acquire new competencies with software applications to manipulate and route data. For example, creating, saving, and attaching files in correct formats are necessary technical tasks that affect the dissemination of information. Judgment, expertise, and sensitivity to context accompany technical tasks because organization members must determine if, when, and how to share what they know. Simply managing e-mail is a challenge given how much communication occurs through the medium, including junk mail and spam that draw energy away from critical work. The ease with which digital information can be distributed opens new vulnerabilities for companies. Organizations have responded by developing and expanding information policies for all organizational members, not just IT professionals and leaders. Digital instincts have become necessary for working within information policies and exploiting information networks to fulfill organizational mission.

In the current knowledge and service economy, *how* an organization consumes information rivals *what* information is available as a critical factor for organizational success. Denison (1990) suggests that unused knowledge and skill are competitive disadvantages while shared understandings promote consistency needed for organizations to function. Shared understandings often have been outside traditional information systems yet are important for successfully applying information within a specific context. Choo (1995) believes that complex organizations are able to balance order and chaos through the ability to process information. Further, failure can occur in an information-poor environment and also in an information-laden environment where there is too much information. Neither extreme is healthy. Simply anticipating the future can have a tremendous impact on organizational systems. For example, the rumor of a production material shortage can have profound effects even if an actual shortage does not materialize; belief is a strong motivator to act (Choo 1995). The challenge for managing information is intimately connected with managing knowledge, which means dealing with interdependencies of process and people in an often chaotic environment.

DECENTRALIZED INFORMATION MANAGEMENT

As information management has become increasingly decentralized, there has been a corresponding change in organizations. Members of networked organizations are able to communicate more directly with other members, and direct communication tends to lead to flatter organizations (Dyson 1998). Flat or horizontal organizational structures are not only possible; they are often preferable in a fast-changing environment because they allow greater speed and flexibility to respond to problems. Communication, even in the traditional hierarchical structures, is less top-down and more Web-like. Information tends to be filtered through fewer layers of middle management and instead flows directly from those closest to the source of information. Intranets are instrumental in this respect because they are naturally expanding and able to overcome organizational hierarchies (Begbie and Chudry 2002).

Although intranets vary tremendously in sophistication and strategic integration of applications, many have capitalized on the features of Internet technology to link content and multimedia from diverse sources. This distinction supports the first proposition that intranets are fundamentally different from traditional information systems because they allow the central, seamless display of decentralized knowledge in more forms than discrete data or information. The ability to link video, graphics, symbols, colors, and sounds suggests that organizations are managing broader knowledge resources than just what is formal and explicit.

During the shift to decentralization, other organizational movements affected the need to transform the workplace through technology. Reengineering of the late twentieth century brought mixed results to organizations, often focusing too much on the technical side of structure and missing the human equation (Cummings and Worley 2005). Hall (2002) suggests that reengineering violated unspoken agreements and destroyed the myth of the long-term career with one organization, giving rise to a new career "contract." This contract places responsibility for career development on the individual and emphasizes acquiring skills and experiences that are transportable. Organization-jumping presents fresh challenges for capturing and utilizing knowledge and for socializing new employees. Here, intranets can be used to retain knowledge within an organization when an employee leaves (Begbie and Chudry 2002) and to orient employees when new ones arrive. Succession planning for leadership roles is also more difficult since executives-in-training in middle management have largely disappeared. Organizations are more prone to filling positions by enticing officers away from other organizations. Turnover may bring new ideas and fresh perspectives, but there is also potential for conflicting values and ideology that can demoralize members.

Decentralization requires technology to keep information clusters organized, integrated when possible, and useful to the organization. This requires knowledge of all types, including knowledge of the context and needs of the organization. One definition of technology is helpful for understanding how it is connected to knowledge. Hendricks and Sterry define technology broadly as "knowhow that extends human potential" (1986, 2). Although one could equate technology with knowledge, they believe that "knowhow" refers to more than knowing—rather, putting knowledge into action. The focus on action demonstrates why managing knowledge is so critical for organizations in the knowledge economy; knowledge should work to solve organizational problems and to generate new knowledge. Organizations can no longer depend upon static stores of information but must extend organizational potential by putting into action knowledge that is dynamic and evolving.

INTRANETS DEFINED

To understand how intranets put knowledge to work, this section discusses definitions and characteristics that make intranets responsive to organizational needs. Koehler et al. (1998) describe intranets as the internal application of technologies developed for the Internet. A more advanced definition comes from Marcus and Watters, who state that an intranet is "a private knowledge network that provides secure collective access to integrated information, services, business applications, and communication" (2002, 26). Extranets allow external agents access to intranets through authentication processes based on a person's role or network identity within an organization. Organizations that have strategic partnerships with other businesses may extend membership of some internal information clusters so that partners can find critical information such as part specifications or work order confirmations and participate in online planning through e-conferencing. The dividing line between who is and who is not an organizational member becomes blurred as work structures overlap.

An intranet is a place, a virtual space, where knowledge is stored and retrieved and where essential work and learning occur. When members of an organization post material, they are leaving messages for the rest of the community in a space not unlike a physical bulletin board but with much greater capability. While an intranet requires users to "pull" information rather than pushing it to them (Gilbert 1998) as with face-to-face or e-mail communication, the emphasis still must be on providing timely and relevant information. To determine relevancy one must have knowledge of the community for which the information is intended. Understanding the concerns and needs of the audience is critical for building intranets (Koehler et al. 1998; Marcus and Watters 2002). Intranet users are typically internal customers that are charged with creating the products and accomplishing the mission of the organization, which necessitates different design than public Web sites (Evans 1996). Appropriate presentation, language, and graphical organization help deliver information that can be readily applied within the context.

Organizations that do not yet see the strategic potential of intranets may view them as an electronic form of employee handbook. Simply repackaging paper-based content will not use IT to the fullest potential. Rather, intranets provide organizations with "an information channel that is richer, more efficient, more interactive, and more dynamic than such traditional channels as newsletters and memos" (Cummings and Worley 2005, 621). More sophisticated intranets, or "next-generation" intranets, are portals that integrate business processes and disparate databases (Marcus and Watters 2002). As previously mentioned, handling proprietary information is a serious consideration for information managers, given how easy it is to copy and transmit digital documents. Although intranets are internal and private, Evans (1996) suggests viewing all intranet documents as potentially public.

Evans (1996) delineates three different approaches for building corporate intranets with different implications for organizations. The *centralized model* is top-down, requiring content coming from diverse groups to flow through a person or team for approval. This process creates a restrictive but consistent environment. It is also easy to administer. The *decentralized model* allows individual users and departments to develop their own Web pages and, in some cases, set up department Web servers. This model increases the relevance and timeliness of content dissemination to specific users and requires more people in the organization to understand how to build and publish Web pages. The decentralized model increases the risk of accidental deletions and complicates security structures when ad hoc committees and cross-functional team members ask to post material outside their authorized spaces, if such exist. The third approach is the *mixed model,* which combines the features of the two prior models at whatever point on the spectrum the organization desires. A broad policy on use and abuse of intranet space would cover many potential problems but still allow for flexibility.

Begbie and Chudry (2000) researched the growth of knowledge through intranet sites based on levels of control or chaos. Their findings suggest that intranets should not be too tightly controlled because some chaos is important for problem solving and generating innovative knowledge. Given the need for prediction and control in management, allowing chaos or seeming disorganization may appear counterintuitive, yet it is upon this paradox that the knowledge economy is built.

Clearly, the reduction of physical space and time constraints has changed the workplace. Professionals are able to access knowledge from many more sources within and outside the organization to produce surprising results. The networks of relationships that develop from the present business environment create a challenge for information managers to build consistent yet flexible systems to manage the access and alteration of collective data. Although some technologists might favor concentrating on technical capability in terms of hardware and software, organizational information systems will increasingly mirror the dynamics of the social context or human side of organizing. The webbed design of an intranet represents a more realistic, and more complicated, pattern of organizational interaction that better supports a trend toward managing knowledge.

KNOWLEDGE MANAGEMENT

The people-centered approach to IT found in decentralized information management hinted at what we now call knowledge management. Knowledge management is a new line of inquiry that developed rapidly in the late 1990s. Perspectives on knowledge management are coming out of human resources, information technology, management, and other disciplines (Bahra 2001), which illustrates that the emphasis on knowledge has permeated many areas. Knowledge management focuses on how knowledge is acquired, created, and distributed within organizations (Alvesson and Karreman 2001; Lengnick-Hall and Lengnick-Hall 2003). Blending IT with knowledge tasks, it has been critiqued for having an overly technical focus (Easterby-Smith and Lyles 2003). According to Alavi and Tiwana (2003), knowledge management has sociocultural, organizational, and behavioral dimensions.

Knowledge management overlaps with organizational learning theory around the creation, retention, and transfer of knowledge (Vera and Crossan 2003). An organization is said to learn when the products of learning are embedded into organizational structures (Watkins and Marsick 1996). This structural embedding should involve IT and, therefore, knowledge management in many instances. Knowledge can be viewed as the kind or degree of understanding, while learning is the process by which knowledge is obtained (Chakravarthy et al. 2003). Vera and Crossan (2003) agree with this distinction, adding that knowledge affects future learning. This idea is supported by Lee and Strong (2003), who found that data collectors who had knowledge of why data processes were needed contributed the most to producing quality data. Data collectors in organizations were more likely to question bad data and solve data quality problems than data custodians —typically IT professionals—and data consumers. The questioning and learning that occurred to solve data problems were predicated on different types of knowledge based on roles within the organization. This example also shows how different types of knowledge and experience can affect knowledge management process.

Although knowledge and information are often used as interchangeable terms in practice, knowledge management literature makes a distinction between data, information, and knowledge (Bhatt 2001; Drucker 1998). Data are the smallest pieces or discrete units used to build information. Information becomes knowledge when a person makes meaning or interprets the information toward some end. Drucker describes the interaction among the three levels: "Information is data endowed with relevance and purpose. Converting data into information thus requires knowledge. And knowledge, by definition, is specialized" (1998, 5) or context-specific. Knowledge can function in the background as a type of filter through which data passes, but it can also stand on its own as a product. A practical example that emphasizes this interplay is how data are used to build an information report on finances or sales. Facts alone are not the only significant factor in using the information in the report. The user must have many different types of knowledge to "read" the report, including understanding the language, symbols, calculations, and format. To successfully apply the information, the user must have knowledge of what changes within the organization need to be made, how to judge consequences, and who will be affected. A fourth level of knowledge, wisdom, is advanced by some scholars. Harris (1998) suggests that there is an evolutionary development that advances data through a value-adding process that has the creation of wisdom as the last step. Very little makes it all the way to wisdom.

Knowledge management literature also distinguishes between tacit and explicit knowledge (Nonaka 1998). Tacit knowledge is difficult to uncover and is second nature. Explicit knowledge is more visible and often more technical in nature. Similarly, Choo (1995) describes three types of knowledge that are important to organizations. The first is tacit knowledge rooted in action and intuition; tacit knowledge is hard to articulate. The second is rule-based knowledge, which includes knowledge of how to match actions to situations to ensure consistent organizational responses for efficiency and control. The third is background knowledge, which is part of the organizational culture communicated through oral and verbal texts. Here, background knowledge provides a frame of reference or context for knowledge management.

Nonaka (1998) believes that Western managers have too narrow a view of knowledge and how to exploit it. Knowledge creation depends on tapping tacit and highly subjective insights, intuition, and ideals and embodying them into technologies, particularly through the use of images and symbols. Tacit knowledge is difficult to codify and not easily managed. To change tacit knowledge to explicit, organizations must learn how to "express the inexpressible" (Nonaka 1998, 31) by using figurative language and symbols. Technologies that allow symbols, pictures, metaphors, and other expressionistic methods may facilitate use of tacit knowledge.

Even when newly created knowledge is explicit enough to be captured and communicated, there are social factors that affect whether people will disclose information. The level of trust employees have in the organization significantly impacts their willingness to share information (Ipe 2003). Trust, which is forged through daily work experiences and interactions, brings in the dimension of values and politics present in human systems. Organizational behavior and structures can encourage or discourage the trust needed for effective knowledge sharing. Information systems, including intranets, depend on knowledge communities supporting and managing their information and suffer when information is hoarded (Chin 2004). Organizations, then, must evaluate whether interactions are conducive to critical knowledge sharing or whether there may be hidden messages, social factors, or technical obstructions that inhibit knowledge management.

Knowledge as a term can represent both concrete and abstract information that is learned and managed through the daily experience of work. According to Myers (1996), knowledge can be managed only to the extent that it has been captured in organizational process, systems, products, rules, and culture. Intellectual capital of this sort represents the difference between the liquidation value and stock market value of a company; this gap represents the organizational knowledge and structures that allow the organization to produce value beyond physical assets (Stewart 1997). It also is the primary advantage organizations have to compete in today's marketplace (Choo 1995).

Intense competition requires new ways of interacting with information to create knowledge. Wikstrom and Normann write, "the supply of knowledge itself is not the only important factor. At least as significant is the ability to absorb, apply and exploit knowledge in new production processes, products and services, new forms of organization and hitherto untried forms of co-operation with customers and suppliers" (1994, 2). They further state that knowledge is accumulated in organizations through research efforts and through daily problem solving, which may be creative in nature if existing collective knowledge is recombined in new ways. Organizations that collectively discover that no one person has all the answers are more liberated and open because answers are never final and can be continually improved upon (Senge 1990). This dynamic process affects information technologies that must continuously evolve to fit organizational needs that are also evolving and unpredictable. Hayes and Walshum (2003) indicate that it is important to understand technology in relation to the social context. A large part of the social context of organizing is organizational culture.

ORGANIZATIONAL CULTURE

Management of information and knowledge is affected by the social structure and organizational culture. Organizations generally have a predominant outlook on knowledge that is part of the culture (Wikstrom and Normann 1994). This outlook shapes what information is valued and how it is distributed. For example, organizational structure and hierarchy specify who has the authority to make decisions about organizational process, functions, and finances. These structures tie into IT security rights and intranet design. Knowledge is required to make decisions, but knowledge, especially specific, local knowledge, can be costly to transfer. Organizations must decide whether to move knowledge to central leadership or move decision authority to local agents (Jensen and Meckling 1996). How this exchange occurs depends on organizational assumptions and values that are integral to organizational culture.

Definitions of organizational culture can be as simple as "the way things are done here" (Drennan 1992) or extremely complex, including almost all structures, behaviors, artifacts, and knowledge bits that create ideological practice in organizations (Sentell 1998). Kotter and Heskett (1992) rely on a broad, dictionary definition of culture but they add that organizations have two levels of culture. The first is invisible and made up of goals and concerns that persist over time and, therefore, are difficult to change. The second, which is more visible, is made up of group behavior norms that affect how group members act and how new members are socialized. Organizational culture is not static; it arises through interaction over time and is connected to a firm's success. Learning is central to the development of organizational culture because "solutions that repeatedly appear to solve the problems they encounter tend to become a part of their culture" (Kotter and Heskett 1992, 6). The connection between learning and knowledge previously discussed is also intertwined with organizational culture, which carries implications for intranet design and use. Intranets communicate more than facts when they tap into user needs and desires (Jackson 2000).

Schein's organizational culture model (1991) delineates three levels of organizational culture. The first level, artifacts, is easily observable. It consists of the physical surroundings, the presentation of the company, and daily behavior and processes. These facets of culture are on the surface but can only hint at meaning. The second level, espoused values, is fairly easily elicited by asking employees about corporate values. Examples include mission statements and the vision of the organization that articulates what the firm portrays as important. Two companies could have the same espoused values but have very different artifacts reflecting the values. I would add that technical artifacts, like intranet pages, might reflect organizational culture in both observable and hidden ways. The third level, shared tacit assumptions, reflects the very deep beliefs, values, and assumptions that are historically linked to the founding of the firm and collective learning over time. This level is the deepest layer that provides the plumb line by which events are interpreted and decisions made.

Connections Between Organizational Culture and Knowledge Management Theory

Figure 6.1 models two critical connections between organizational culture and knowledge management. At the center of the model are organizational intranets whose chief tasks include the creation, storage, and dissemination of knowledge. Knowledge creation is a very active part of the intranet, occurring as members internalize information from repositories or interact with other members through bulletin boards, chat rooms, and e-conferences. This interaction is important for supporting a relationship between knowledge management and organizational culture. Organizational culture and knowledge management both have tacit and explicit types of knowledge that are listed under the respective headings. The tasks and activities in knowledge management and organizational culture spring from the knowledge types and can occur through the intranet or outside the intranet in other applications or materials.

The first connection is at the top of Figure 6.1. It shows how organizational culture and values are used to interpret information and determine relevance and action. It is a meaning-making activity that affects what people do with new information. This facet can facilitate or hinder information from becoming incorporated into the knowledge base. For example, values, the building blocks for behavior and choice, are fundamental to organizational culture (Starkman et al. 2000). People make choices based on values as they decide how to handle information, including ignoring it because it does not seem to fit the context. Although technology can handle tasks such as storing, sorting, displaying, disseminating, and calculating information, people must interpret and evaluate information (Olstedt 2003). Knowledge, then, depends upon human interpretation, and one factor in interpreting information is organizational culture; it is a lens through which members determine relevancy. Additionally, whether information is determined to be relevant will affect how it is incorporated into collective organizational knowledge.

The second connection is illustrated at the bottom of Figure 6.1. Organizational culture has content, which can be communicated and managed (Sackman 1991; Schein 1999) through knowledge management processes. Cultural knowledge may be inferred through shared sayings, doings, and feelings of members (Sathe 1985). Many interven-

Figure 6.1 **Intranets and the Connections Between Organizational Culture and Knowledge Management Theory**

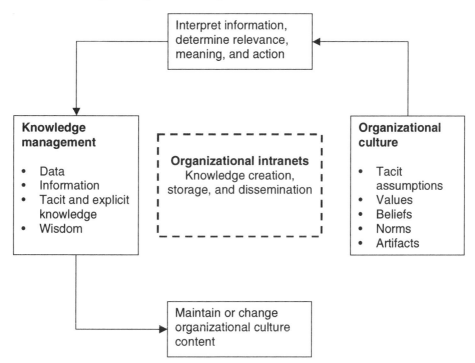

tions, procedures, and policies found on intranets may in fact be there in order to reinforce or to reshape organizational culture. Organizations cognizant of cultural content may purposely use the intranets to maintain or change the culture. The difficulty level of cultural change will probably depend on how deeply the change runs and the strength of the need for change. Change may occur even if an organization does not purposely choose to change. For example, displaying new policies or symbols that reflect different values can spark change. Because of the graphic nature of Internet and intranet technology, symbols are especially important features that can send powerful messages conveying cultural and contextual meaning. Symbols have four basic functions: (1) they reflect basic, shared assumptions, (2) they influence behavior by eliciting internalized values and norms, (3) they facilitate member communication about organizational life, and (4) they capture systems of meaning that intertwine emotion, cognition, and behavior in shared codes (Rafaeli and Worline 2000). Nonaka (1998) believes that symbols are an important method for tapping into tacit knowledge, which would include tacit assumptions in the organizational culture.

The dynamic relationship between organizational culture and knowledge management represented in Figure 6.1 suggests that an intranet can be both a tool for knowledge management and a cultural artifact. Intranets mirror social aspects of the organization. It stands to reason that the more sophisticated and integrated an intranet is, the more transparent and taken for granted might be the reflection. IT implementation teams sometimes experience these connections when they run into problems and the project scope begins to creep. Chin (2004) likens going against the force of organizational culture while developing intranets to attempting to paddle a canoe upstream against the current. It can leave the designer fatigued and off-track. Simply put, knowledge managed through intranets must intersect with organizational culture to be relevant. This statement supports the second proposition that managing knowledge requires greater integration and transparency between technology and the social nature of organization. The role of information management, now, is further entwined and complicated by the need for information specialists to understand the cultural context so that products and services meet collective needs. The very content and display of information, or organizational power structures, could send cultural messages that have unintended consequences for the organization and consumption of knowledge. These unintended consequences could lead to culture change in unproductive or unhealthy directions that affect new learning and knowledge.

ORGANIZATIONAL STRATEGIES FOR INTRANETS IN THE KNOWLEDGE ECONOMY

This section outlines some of the challenges in the knowledge economy and how organizational strategies are responding to these challenges. Intranets are increasingly used to respond to the highly competitive and changeable economic environment. These strategies support the propositions outlined in the beginning of the chapter because they detail how intranets can be used to promote new knowledge and new ways of organizing and, thus, become more fully integrated and transparent within the organization than traditional IT systems.

Globalization and Virtual Supply Chains

Globalization, facilitated by Internet technology, drives the need for flexibility and adaptability of intranets and of the organizations that host intranets. Marquardt (2003) outlines four characteristics of the global economy. First, the global economy is defined by a single marketplace with expanding free trade. Second, there is an increasing flow and sharing of information internationally. Third, people around the world are connected or linked, and, fourth, both organizations and individuals are no longer constrained by national boundaries but have the ability to shop around the world.

While some criticize globalization because it may lead to inequity and marginalization of some international communities, Marquardt (2003) believes that improvements in South Korea illustrate how countries that engage in free markets can lower poverty and increase literacy rates. Higher levels of education and more people engaging in free markets affect the competitive environment. Local knowledge becomes even more important to manage through intranets or through organizational decision-making structures. Because globalization increases consumers' choices for both products and producers, customers can demand goods that suit their lives and require increased customization. Competition to attract and retain customers requires continual product improvement or differentiation and effective use of technology. The shelf life of information, then, is shortened so that rapid updating is necessary.

Organization design is changing with the times. In the heyday of U.S. manufacturing, companies focused on owning the entire production process, creating the vertically integrated firm and tying up vast amounts of capital. Reddy and Reddy (2001) believe that we are moving from vertical integration to virtual integration. The difference is using information technology, including intranets and extranets, to coordinate outsourcing and strategic alliances so organizations can concentrate on specific points within the production cycle. Integration and communication are obviously critical. Organizations are better able to customize products in a cost-effective manner. The effect is to give customers more say in the production process as a type of partner, which requires their input earlier or at the beginning of the production cycle.

Globalization emphasizes the need for intercultural communication skills and knowledge of the sociopolitical environments for effective work and learning (Ziegahn 2000). As organizations and individuals interact with diverse populations and cultures, opportunities arise to build new knowledge and capacity. Gleerup and Horsdal (2003) suggest that interactions among diverse cultures produce radical or innovative knowledge that allows organizations to offer new products and services for already saturated marketplaces. Strategic intranets can be used at the intersection of cultures for knowledge generation and renewal. Global competition and demands for innovation, however, imply a "risk of marginalization and social exclusion, probably the biggest threat in a knowledge society, mainly affecting groups who are unable to reconstruct and reconfigure their biographical narrative in an ongoing process of renegotiation of meaning" (Gleerup and Horsdal 2003, 125). The construction and reconstruction of meaning are necessary for individuals, as well as for organizations. Dynamics between knowledge management and organizational culture may help explain how organizations successfully or unsuccessfully deal with the new work paradigm.

Organizational Change

Globalization, evolving technology, and new knowledge make change omnipresent for organizations. Bridges (2003) suggests that an important aspect of transition is the transformative process by which an organization becomes more complex and better adapted to the wider environment. He suggests that organizations go through a life cycle that often ends in death, but renewal may occur if an organization successfully returns to the beginning of the cycle where innovation represents a "new dream." Change is not often easy even when organizations face a choice between innovation or extinction. Even change that is accepted by organizational members can produce an assimilation cost when unanticipated consequences occur (Conner 1992).

A desire for stability, fear of change, or even different applications of knowledge can cause resistance to change. Argyris's (1990) research is helpful for understanding that resistance to change can occur as part of an organizationally sanctioned defensive routine. A defensive organization can have strong morale, satisfaction, and loyalty because members are able to distance themselves from the responsibility to work toward excellence. Organizational defensive routines are actions or policies that prevent individuals and groups of people from experiencing embarrassment or threat at sensitive or undiscussable topics. They also prevent the accurate diagnosis of problems, and organizations cannot solve a problem that cannot be subjected to analysis. Defensive reasoning that affects how knowledge is managed on the intranet or faulty information can make organizational change difficult. In Agyris's perspective, knowledge management processes could illuminate and change taboo or tacit understandings.

Good communication channels and the ability to discuss problems openly give change initiatives a better chance of success. Internet and intranet technology offers interactive communication capability that allows the gathering of feedback through bulletin boards, chat rooms, online surveys, e-conferencing, and the like. Online media allow an organization to get real-time information and interact with it, although it is important not to request employee feedback if employers have no real expectation of acting on the information (Koehler et al. 1998). Information managers collecting and analyzing data for interventions may have trouble with information quality or even with response rate if employees perceive that their opinions will make no difference.

Technology contributes to information overload because of the abundance of information to which members must attend. The ability to find good information at the point that it is needed is an important feature for intranets. Search engines allow users to sort data and pick the best for their specific applications (Koehler et al. 1998). Because so much communication has been moved to e-mail, intranets are considered a good way to off-load the details of internal communiqués. Sometimes a simple e-mail announcing that details are available online helps to integrate the use of e-mail and intranets. Information managers must find ways to motivate colleagues to go and retrieve information. In some cases, this may require a change in the organizations cultural norms and values.

Training and Telecommuting

Training is not just a way for an organization's members to acquire critical knowledge and skills; it may be used to change organizational culture. In fact, Williams et al. (1989) found that most organizations they studied used training as a mechanism for culture change. Training delivered through intranets has the advantages of being easily distributed, easily accessed, and using existing network infrastructure, but it brings up the question of what needs to be learned and, just as importantly, what does not need to be learned (Gilbert 1998). Kasworm and Londoner caution organizations to focus not solely on discrete learning steps, but also on how adults make meaning when learning about technology. They state, "There is a challenge to be innovative with and through new technology delivery, to be a change agent, and to provide adult learners with new strategies for gaining and applying knowledge" (2000, 230). Thus, the technical side, or technique of training through technology, should not be allowed to overshadow the even more important act of building and applying knowledge.

Two primary implications exist for training and adult learning in connection with intranets. First, organizational members, including strategic partners in some instances, must know how to use intranet technology. Navigation, file retrieval, and saving skills are critical but also critical is understanding cultural content and contextually bound terms on intranet pages and linked applications. These skills cannot be assumed for all levels of an organization nor for clients and strategic partners that may access parts of an intranet. Second, intranets can accomplish training tasks through e-learning systems, synchronous and asynchronous instructional programs, electronic conferencing, self-directed materials, and electronic "handouts." Training modules, especially in relation to human resources applications, are often found on intranets.

The concept of collaborative learning found on the Internet that breaks the barrier of space and time (Roth 1995) can be extended to intranets. The same technologies that support instruction can support online cooperation, which is important for involving telecommuting or traveling colleagues. Social bonds can be built by using chat rooms, discussion groups, and bulletin boards as an avenue for people to interact about common topics of interest. Dyson (1998) is not a fan of telecommuting because she believes it lacks the high-intensity communication that can only be done face to face; however, she sees the Internet as a way for people to stay in contact when off-site.

There is evidence that telecommuting may reduce work-family conflict in some situations, which is important for the overall health of an organizational system (Madsen 2003). A downside is the extension of the workplace into people's homes and the problem of defining appropriate employee behavior occurring off-site. Intranets may help telecommuting employees feel a greater affinity with the organization than a traditional phone and fax setup. They may also promote organizational culture. Logos, symbols, and statements convey organizational characteristics in virtual space. The look and feel of intranet pages provide visual cues that reflect the culture and mission of the organization (Marcus and Watters 2002). There should be no doubt when employees authenticate through a company server that they are signing on to corporate property. In creating a virtual environment, organizations are touching knowledge of all types.

RESEARCH IMPLICATIONS AND QUALITATIVE METHODS

If organizational structure is superimposed on extant human interactions (Weick 1979), then intranets may be seen as superimposed on organizational knowledge and communication dynamics. When striving for community through technology, technology both shapes and is shaped by human interaction (Palloff and Pratt 1999). At the organizational level there are implications for future research to uncover how social dynamics affect intranet development and use how organizational cultural knowledge is managed through intranets. Because intranets are tailored to organizations, they represent an intersection between knowledge capabilities and values as a potent resource for renewal and growth. Marcus and Watters (2002) suggest that the qualitative return on investment in intranet technology may far surpass what can be measured in dollars because intranets may lead top-line growth and new business models. Growth does not necessarily have to be measured by money but could be evaluated by new services offered or people contacted for nonprofit, academic, and government organizations.

Sentell (1998) believes that capability to change can be characteristic of organizational culture and is necessary for survival given the unpredictable and sometimes chaotic nature of change in the present economy. Individuals and organizations change and mature over time, sometimes in very unpredictable and cataclysmic ways. Organizational culture and knowledge, as outlined in this chapter, are critical for the new work paradigm but also present new complexities for researchers, especially when knowledge is difficult to explicate. Polanyi (1967) believes that tacit knowledge is found in problems, hunches, tools, skills, and knowledge from the senses. The problem, then, is how to understand what is happening to organizations and organizational members as technology becomes further integrated into organizing structures and involves deeply embedded, tacit knowledge. There is no denying the power of quantitative research in organizations for analyzing marketing trends, quality standards, and so on. However, qualitative research methods offer tools for eliciting deep, rich data needed to study the social side of organizing.

Qualitative methods, which attempt to understand the complex meaning-making of people as they interact in social settings, therefore can delve deeply into the values and meanings that affect interpretation and generation of knowledge. This research perspective is founded on the underlying assumption of multiple realities dependent on how individuals construct meaning (Merriam and Simpson 2000), and research questions are focused on the nature or essence of the phenomena of study (Merriam 1998). Sutton (2000) states that the value of good qualitative research is in gaining new insights rather than testing insights. Additionally, ethnographic methods may be appropriate for organizational research when social dynamics and cultural issues affect knowledge management and the generation of new knowledge. Schwartzman (1993) believes that the emic or internal perspective is a defining characteristic of ethnographic research. Myers connects ethnographic methods with information systems research. He states:

> Ethnographic research is one of the most in-depth research methods possible. Because the researcher is at a research site for a long time—and sees what people are doing as well as what they say they are doing—an ethnographer obtains a deep understanding of the people, the organization, and the broader context within which they work. Ethnographic research is, thus, well suited to providing information systems researchers with rich insights into the human, social, and organizational aspects of information systems. (1999, 1)

Denison (1990) views qualitative case study, which can be ethnographic, as an important means for exploring the nuances of organizational culture. His own research found that organizational culture can be both an asset to an organization and also a constraint, depending on the environment and fluctuations in market conditions.

Despite the benefits of doing organizational ethnography, there is a lack of development in this arena. Ouroussoff (2001) suggests that researchers may lack interest in organizational ethnography because of the assumption that rationality explains group behavior, yet rationality does not wholly explain the discrepancy between explicit structure and day-to-day practice. Qualitative research can be powerful for exploring manifestations of culture, such as symbols and rituals, and deeper levels that may be found on intranet documents and other knowledge systems.

SUMMARY AND CONCLUSION

Clearly, globalization and the advance of technology continue to have a tremendous impact on the modern workplace. The virtual boundaries of nations, communities, and companies are changing radically as market shifts ripple through even isolated regions connected by the Internet. This chapter entertained two propositions. First, intranets are fundamentally different from traditional information systems, signaling a shift from managing information to managing knowledge. Second, managing knowledge requires greater integration and transparency between technology and the social nature of organizing. These propositions were supported by detailing the capabilities of intranets to integrate multimedia, including sounds, graphics, colors, symbols, and video, that may tap into tacit knowledge, including tacit assumptions in the organizational culture. Additionally, intranets are capable of supporting new knowledge, interaction among organizational members, and strategies for responding to market changes in the global economy.

Another contribution this chapter makes is through modeling connections between organizational culture and knowledge management. These connections suggest that (1) organizational culture, like a lens through which information is interpreted, is necessary for managing knowledge and (2) knowledge management can potentially change organizational culture if it maintains or alters cultural content. Intranets are integrated with the social nature of organizing because they handle broad organizational knowledge rather than just discrete data.

Further, this chapter discussed how working with diverse knowledge types is necessary for organizational survival in the knowledge economy. A greater understanding of the social side of organizing and the need for continual innovation require organizations to recognize and utilize different forms of knowledge or risk being behind the competitive curve. The diversity of knowledge types bears tremendous importance for growth, innovation, and communication. Of particular importance is tacit knowledge, which is highly embedded and contextual and may have emotional or intuitive facets outside traditional information systems that were built around formal and codifiable data.

The value of Internet technology is in assisting the fulfillment of organizational mission, which means putting knowledge into action. The nature of developing intranet content and applications requires cooperation among diverse groups of people within an organization. A great deal of development work must be done initially in order to publish an accurate and approved intranet document. Quite often this document is created cooperatively by human resources, management, and technical groups, but members from every level can participate, especially if intranet management is decentralized. A number of interests must be balanced in order to deliver relevant and useful information, but the worth of the intranet increases when it is integrated with the organizational context. The ease with which electronic documents can be assembled and published belies the complexity of developing the content. Questions of authority, relevance, usefulness, ethics, policy, politics, and culture are intrinsically part of organizational communication and management.

Knowledge is so central to global competition that it must occupy an important place on the agenda for information managers. Organizations, too, must value knowledge and the people who produce knowledge in order to use information technologies effectively for innovation. As intranets become more sophisticated, integrated, and representative of social aspects of organizational life, they become an important site for research. Ambiguity and change are the norm for the workplace when organizations are caught between the old and the new. Internet technology has transformed the workplace by opening new knowledge networks and creating new possibilities for organizational design. The true challenge for future knowledge management and leadership is learning how to foster wisdom in a world where information overload and constant change fracture past understandings. Intranets can rebuild understandings not only through the capability to manage knowledge but by promoting organizational learning and community through human interaction.

REFERENCES

Alavi, M., and Tiwana, A. 2003. Knowledge management: The information technology dimensions. In M. Easterby-Smith and M.A. Lyles (eds.), *The Blackwell Handbook of Organizational Learning and Knowledge Management*. Malden, MA: Blackwell Publishing, 104–121.

Alvesson, M., and Karreman, J.D. 2001. Odd couple: Making sense of the curious concept of knowledge management. *Journal of Management Studies* 38, 7, 995–1018.

Argyris, C. 1990. *Overcoming Organizational Defenses: Facilitating Organizational Learning*. Boston: Allyn and Bacon.

Bahra, N. 2001. *Competitive Knowledge Management*. New York: Palgrave.

Begbie, R., and Chudry, F. 2002. The intranet chaos matrix: A conceptual framework for designing an effective knowledge management intranet. *Journal of Database Marketing* 9, 4, 325–338.

Bhatt, G.D. 2001. Knowledge management in organizations. *Journal of Knowledge Management* 5, 1, 68–75.

Bridges, W. 2003. *Managing Transitions: Making the Most of Change*. 2nd ed. Cambridge, MA: De Capo Press.

Bron, A., and Schemmann, M. (eds.). 2003. *Knowledge Society, Information Society and Adult Education: Trends, Issues, Challenges*. Hamburg: Lit Verlag Münster.

Chakravarthy, B., McEvily, S., Doz, Y., and Rau, D. 2003. Knowledge management and competitive advantage. In M. Easterby-Smith and M.A. Lyles (eds.), *The Blackwell Handbook of Organizational Learning and Knowledge Management*. Malden, MA: Blackwell Publishing, 305–323.

Chin, P. 2004. The river wild: The influence of corporate culture on intranets. *Intranet Journal*. www.intranetjournal.com/articles/200401/pij_01_15_04a.html.

Choo, C.W. 1995. *Information Management for the Intelligent Organization: The Art of Scanning the Environment*. Medford, NJ: Information Today.

Conner, D.R. 1992. *Managing at the Speed of Change: How Resilient Managers Succeed and Prosper Where Others Fail*. New York: Villard.

Cummings, T.G., and Worley, C.G. 2005. *Organization Development and Change*. 8th ed. Cincinnati: South-Western.

Denison, D.R. 1990. *Corporate Culture and Organizational Effectiveness*. New York: John Wiley.

Diebold, J. 1985. *Managing Information: The Challenge and the Opportunity.* New York: American Management Association.

Drennan, D. 1992. *Transforming Company Culture: Getting Your Company from Where You Are Now to Where You Want to Be.* London: McGraw-Hill.

Drucker, P. 1998. The coming of the new organization. In *Harvard Business Review on Knowledge Management.* Boston: Harvard Business School Press, 1–19.

Dyson, E. 1998. *Release 2.1: A Design for Living in the Digital Age.* New York: Broadway Books.

Easterby-Smith, M., and Lyles, M.A. (eds.). 2003. *The Blackwell Handbook of Organizational Learning and Knowledge Management.* Malden, MA: Blackwell Publishing.

Evans, T. 1996. Building an intranet: A hands-on guide to setting up an internal Web. Indianapolis: am.net.

Gilbert, L. 1998. Intranets for learning and performance support. In B. Cahoon (ed.), *Adult Learning and the Internet.* New Directions for Adult and Continuing Education, no. 78. San Francisco: Jossey-Bass Publishers, 15–23.

Gleerup, J., and Horsdal, M. 2003. Changes in politics, self-politics, and learning. In A. Bron and M. Schemmann (eds.), *Knowledge Society, Information Society and Adult Education: Trends, Issues, Challenges.* Hamburg: Lit Verlag Münster, 111–128.

Hall, D.T. 2002. *Careers In and Out of Organizations.* Thousand Oaks, CA: Sage.

Harris, M.C. 1998. *Value Leadership: Winning Competitive Advantage in the Information Age.* Milwaukee: Quality Press.

Hayes, N., and Walshum, G. 2003. Knowledge sharing and ICTs: A relational perspective. In M. Easterby-Smith and M.A. Lyles (eds.), *The Blackwell Handbook of Organizational Learning and Knowledge Management.* Malden, MA: Blackwell Publishing, 54–76.

Hendricks, R.W. and Sterry, L.F. 1986. *Communication Technology.* 2nd ed. Menomonie, WI: T & E Publications.

Ipe, M. 2003. Knowledge sharing in organizations: A conceptual framework. *Human Resource Development Review* 2, 4, 337–359.

Jackson, L.A. 2000. The rhetoric of design: Implications for corporate intranets. *Technical Communication* 47, 2, 212–220.

Jensen, M.C., and Meckling, W.H. 1996. Specific and general knowledge, and organizational structure. In P. Myers (ed.), *Knowledge Management and Organizational Design.* Newton, MA: Butterworth-Heinemann, 17–38.

Kasworm, C.E., and Londoner, C.A. 2000. Adult learning and technology. In A.L. Wilson and E.R. Hayes (eds.), *Handbook of Adult and Continuing Education.* San Francisco: Jossey-Bass, 224–241.

Koehler, J.W., Dupper, T., Scaff, M.D., Reitberger, F., and Paxon, P. 1998. *The Human Side of Intranets: Content, Style and Politics.* Boca Raton, FL: St. Lucie Press.

Kotter, J.P., and Heskett, J.L. 1992. *Corporate Culture and Performance.* New York: Free Press.

Lee, Y.W., and Strong, D.M. 2003. Knowing—why about data processes and data quality. *Journal of Management Information Systems* 20, 3, 13–39.

Lengnick-Hall, M.L., and Lengnick-Hall, C.A. 2003. *Human Resource Management in the Knowledge Economy: New Challenges, New Roles, and New Capabilities.* San Francisco: Barrett-Koehler Publishers.

Madsen, S.R. 2003. The effects of home-based teleworking on work-family conflict. *Human Resource Development Quarterly* 14, 1, 35–58.

Marcus, R., and Watters, B. 2002. *Collective Knowledge: Intranets, Productivity, and the Promise of the Knowledge Workplace.* Redmond, WA: Microsoft Press.

Marquardt, M.J. 2003. Globalization and human resource development. In A.M. Gilley, J.L. Callahan, and L.L. Bierema (eds.), *Critical Issues in HRD.* Cambridge, MA: Perseus, 69–86.

Merriam, S.B. 1998. *Qualitative Research and Case Study Applications in Education.* Rev. ed. San Francisco: John Wiley.

Merriam, S.B., and Simpson, E.L. 2002. *A Guide to Research for Educators and Trainers of Adults.* 2nd ed. Malabar, FL: Krieger Publishing.

Myers, M.D. 1999. Investigating information systems with ethnographic research. *Communications of the Association for Information Systems* 2, 23 1–20.

Myers, P. 1996. *Knowledge Management and Organizational Design.* Newton, MA: Butterworth-Heinemann.

Neuhauser, P., Bender, R., and Stromberg, K. 2000. *Culture.com: Building Corporate Culture in the Connected Workplace.* Toronto: John Wiley.

Nonaka, I. 1998. The knowledge-creating company. In *Harvard Business Review on Knowledge Management.* Boston: Harvard Business School Press, 21–45.

Olstedt, E. 2003. ICT—burden or benefit for education? In A. Bron and M. Schemmann (eds.), *Knowledge Society, Information Society and Adult Education: Trends, Issues, Challenges.* Hamburg: Lit Verlag Münster, 222–239.

Ouroussoff, A. 2001. What is an ethnographic study? In D.D. Gellner and E. Hirsch (eds.), *Inside Organizations: Anthropologists at Work.* Oxford, UK: Berg, 35–58.

Palloff, R.M., and Pratt, K. 1999. *Building Learning Communities in Cyberspace: Effective Strategies for the Online Classroom.* San Francisco: Jossey-Bass.

Polanyi, M.C. 1967. *The Tacit Dimension.* Garden City, NY: Anchor Books.

Rafaeli, A., and Worline, M. 2000. Symbols in organizational culture. In N.M. Ashkanasy, P.M. Wilderom, and M.F. Peterson (eds.), *Handbook of Organizational Culture and Climate.* Thousand Oaks, CA: Sage, 71–84.

Reddy, R., and Reddy, S. 2001. *Supply Chains to Virtual Organization.* New York: McGraw-Hill.

Roth, G.R. 1995. Information technologies and workplace learning. In W.F. Spikes (ed.) *Workplace learning.* New directions for Adult and Continuing Education, no. 68. San Francisco: Jossey-Bass, 75–85.

Sackman, S.A. 1991. *Cultural Knowledge in Organizations: Exploring the Collective Mind.* Newbury Park, CA: Sage.

Sathe, V. 1985. How to decipher and change culture. In R.H. Kilman, M.J. Saxton, R. Serpa, and Associates, *Gaining Control of Corporate Culture.* San Francisco: Jossey-Bass, 230–261.

Schein, E.H. 1991. *Organizational Culture and Leadership.* 2nd ed. San Francisco, CA: Jossey-Bass.

Schein, E.H. 1999. *The Corporate Culture Survival Guide.* San Francisco: Jossey-Bass.

Schemmann, M. 2003. International policies for a global information society: An analysis of the policy approach of the G8 states. In A. Bron and M. Schemmann (eds.), *Knowledge Society, Information Society and Adult Education: Trends, Issues, Challenges.* Hamburg: Lit Verlag Münster, 95–110.

Schwartzman, H.B. 1993. *Ethnography in Organizations.* Newbury Park, CA: Sage.

Senge, P.M. 1960. *The Fifth Discipline: The Art and Practice of the Learning Organization.* New York: Currency Doubleday.

Sentell, G. 1998. *Creating Change-Capable Cultures.* Alcoa, TN: Pressmark International.

Starkman, R.W., Pinder, C.C., and Connor, P.E. 2000. Values lost: Redirecting research on values in the workplace. In N.M. Ashkanasy, P.M. Wilderom, and M.F. Peterson (eds.), *Handbook of Organizational Culture and Climate.* Thousand Oaks, CA: Sage, 37–54.

Stewart, T. 1997. *Intellectual Capital: The New Wealth of Organizations.* New York: Doubleday.

Sutton, R.I. 2000. The virtues of closet qualitative research. In P.J. Frost, A.Y. Lewin, and R.L. Daft (eds.), *Talking About Organization Science: Debates and Dialogue from Crossroads.* Thousand Oaks, CA: Sage, 245–260.

Vera, D., and Crossan, M. 2003. Organizational learning and knowledge management: Toward an integrative framework. In M. Easterby-Smith and M.A. Lyles (eds.), *The Blackwell Handbook of Organizational Learning and Knowledge Management.* Malden, MA: Blackwell Publishing, 122–141.

Watkins, K.E. 1996. Of course organizations learn! In R.W. Rowden (ed.), *Workplace Learning: Questions of Theory and Practice.* New Directions for Adult and Continuing Education, no. 72. San Francisco: Jossey-Bass, 879–896.

Watkins, K.E., and Marsick, V.J. 1996. In action: Creating the learning organization. Alexandria, VA: American Society for Training and Development.

Weick, K.E. 1979. *The Social Psychology of Organizing.* 2nd ed. Reading, MA: Addison-Wesley.

Wikstrom, S., and Normann, R. 1994. *Knowledge and Value.* London: Routledge.

Williams, A., Dobson, P., and Walters, M. 1989. *Changing Culture: New Organizational Approaches.* London: Institute of Personnel Management.

Ziegahn, L. 2000. Adult education, communication, and the global context. In A.L. Wilson and E.R. Hayes, *Handbook of Adult and Continuing Education.* San Francisco: Jossey-Bass, 312–326.

Chapter 7

OPTIMAL FLOW IN ONLINE INTERACTIONS

Dimensions, Antecedents, and Consequences

Manuel J. Sánchez-Franco

Abstract: The study theoretically examines Web interaction using the flow concept as a useful construct for describing general human-computer interactions (HCI) during working activities. Flow could be used to identify the factors that influence the experience of individuals as they learn and use the Web-based applications and, in turn, as a way of defining the nature of compelling online experiences. Going beyond flow, this study takes a holistic approach to understanding the experiences of Web users, exploring concepts such as involvement, concentration, ability, challenge, arousal, perceived control, playfulness, and personal innovativeness.

Users will tend to use the Web when they are completely immersed and intrinsically enjoy the online experience. Increasing intrinsic enjoyment through navigation oriented to exploration and control is an essential tool for successful management of Web-based applications. Specifically, this theoretical review proposes that the experience of flow is a highly desirable goal to increase the effectiveness of Web experiences and users' satisfaction.

Flow can have significant consequences for organizations: it may result in playful and exploratory behaviors but also in high-quality results. Individuals in flow will have a higher learning performance and usage levels compared to individuals "in boredom."

Keywords: Flow, Web, Web Behavior, User Involvement, Playfulness, Internet Behaviors

INTRODUCTION

Academics and professionals are beginning to gain an understanding of the strategies that will attract visitors to Web sites. However, very little is known about how to entertain and retain users once they arrive. Few studies actually focus directly on Web usage, on its primary and secondary antecedents and consequences, and on the mediating and moderating personal factors that (1) affect usage in online environments and (2) ensure that users return (see Sánchez-Franco and Rodríguez 2004).

In this context and according to the results of human-computer interaction (HCI) research in management information systems (MIS) (Zhang et al. 2001), individuals have a full range of opportunities to interact with technologies for different purposes in nonrational or bounded rational ways. The holistic view of HCI includes not only cognitive but affective aspects in all possible interactions humans have with technologies (e.g., the Web). In fact, there is a significant and growing body of subsequent research regarding the importance of the role of intrinsic motives in technology acceptance and use (Childers et al. 2001; Davis et al. 1992; Malone 1981; Moon and Kim 2001; Sánchez-Franco and Rondán 2004; Teo et al. 1999; Van der Heijden 2003; Venkatesh and Davis 2000; Venkatesh and Speier 1999; Webster and Martocchio 1992). There is thus a need for incorporating intrinsic motives and integrating other theories.

Academics suggest that intrinsic motives can partly explain how to attract and retain users once they arrive. For instance, users may use the Web because they genuinely enjoy it (Chung and Tan 2004). Specifically, flow—as an intrinsically enjoyable state—has been particularly studied in the context of information technologies (IT) and computer-mediated environments (CMEs) and has been recommended as a possible metric of the user experience (see Agarwal and Karahanna 2000; Ghani et al. 1991; Ghani and Deshpande 1994; Hoffman and Novak 1996b; Novak et al. 2000; Trevino and Webster 1992; Webster et al. 1993). Flow theory predicts that experience will be most positive when a person perceives that the environment contains high enough opportunities for action (or challenges) that are matched with the person's own capacities to act (or skills). When both challenges and skills are high, the person not only enjoys the moment but "is also stretching his or her capabilities with the likelihood of learning new skills and increasing self-esteem and personal complexity" (Csikszentmihalyi and LeFevre 1989). Although ease of use and usefulness are clearly important in work settings, the flow-based experiences could be even more important and should not be overlooked.

In contrast with previous research that suggests that flow would be more likely to occur during recreational than task-oriented activities (related to work environment), flow has been introduced for the latter. Workers who enjoy an information system-related activity will probably want to maintain or increase their positive responses and, in turn, their usage of Web applications. Flow can have a substantial effect on users's level of satisfaction with their CMEs. The degree of use of a technology has been shown to increase when a user experiences flow (Trevino and Webster 1992). In addition, individuals in flow state are more creative, more helpful, better negotiators, and more persistent in uncertain tasks (George and Brief 1992; Isen and Baron 1991). Csikszentmihalyi and LeFevre (1989), as mentioned above, assumed that flow strengthens personal capabilities with the likelihood of learning new skills. Several studies collected evidence that optimal states can predict employee performance (Konradt and Sulz 2001). In short, individuals in flow are supposed to have a higher learning performance and usage levels compared to individuals who are feeling apathy, fear, anxiety, or boredom. Workers in flow reduce their boredom and anxiety and increase positive work outcomes. The growing research concerning theory of optimal flow is thus proposed as a useful framework (1) for studying the experience of individuals as they learn and use Web-based applications; (2) for identifying the factors that influence this experience; and (3) as a way of defining the nature of compelling online experiences and valuable outcomes.

In this situation of theoretical development, the role of flow is evaluated as it affects Web-based behavior as a highly subjective variable among individuals, and, in turn, as a way of explaining and improving the users' experience of being on and returning to the Web. The main objectives of this chapter are to (1) integrate literature on the concept of flow; (2) propose a flow-based model; and (3) develop user profiles that may assign higher values to certain dimensions of a Web site. Given that intrinsic individual factors have been directly linked with behaviors, perhaps understanding the fundamental underpinnings of how individual differences can arise would be of value for developing Web design more effectively. "It is expected that our understanding of the flow phenomenon would guide information and communication technology (ICT) designers to be able to design a product that will lead users to flow experiences" (Finneran and Zhang 2005, 83). Web-based technologies would be designed to be stimulating to use, evoking compelling user experiences to increase profitable usage. The online environment would promote a long-term perspective with a worker retention focus and involvement based on intrinsic motives (i.e., stimulating, controllable, and enjoyable experiences), leading to flow-states and valuable behaviors. An increase in flow-related experience among workers allows interaction and enhancement of the relationships among them, while they also perform their activities. As Yi and Hwang suggest, "given that the Web is a relatively new technology and is a richer environment than any other traditional information technology in meeting various personal needs, we expect that these motivational variables will play critical roles in influencing individuals' decision to use a Web-based technology" (2003, 1080).

THEORETICAL FOUNDATIONS

Flow

Over the years, there has been a growing significant body of theoretical and empirical research regarding the importance of the role of intrinsic motivation in understanding facets of behavior (Bagozzi et al. 1999; Eastlick and Feinberg 1999; Holt 1995; Hopkinson and Pujari 1999; Sherman and Mathur 1997). Specifically, there is a significant body of theoretical and empirical evidence emphasizing the role of intrinsic motives in technology use (Davis et al. 1992; Malone 1981; Venkatesh and Speier 1999; Webster and Martocchio 1992). Researchers have become increasingly aware of the relevance of the noncognitive aspects of use motives, such as intrinsically enjoyable experiences, in understanding online behaviors. In fact, the original goal of the activity, or extrinsic reward, could be partly replaced by an intrinsic motivation to use the Web that, in turn, requires the capability of accumulating enough knowledge and competence (i.e., skills and perceived control) to adjust to the new modes of working, learning, creating, and focusing on the process. In this context, one of the positive psychological states related to prior factors is flow.

Definition

The founder of flow research, Csikszentmihalyi (1975, 36), defined it as "the holistic sensation that people feel when they act with total involvement." Such sensation may occur not only in the pursuit of physical activities but also in interactions with symbolic systems such as mathematics and computer languages. The state is so satisfying that time seems to stand still; individuals lose their sense of self and want to repeat the activity continually. Therefore, flow is an optimal, intense, and intrinsically enjoyable experience when an individual engages in an activity with total involvement and concentration. The person experiences an intrinsic interest and the sense of time distortion during the engagement (Privette and Bundrick 1987).

The flow construct has been expanded and refined by researchers concerned with increasing our understanding of HCI. For instance, in Trevino and Webster's study of workers' perceptions of flow during e-mail and voice mail interactions, flow represents the users' perception of interaction with the medium as playful and exploratory (1992). Involvement in a playful and exploratory experience is self-motivating, pleasurable, and encourages repetition. Trevino and Webster described four dimensions of the flow in the HCI experience: (1) the user perceives a sense of control over the computer interaction, (2) the user perceives that his or her attention is focused on the interaction, (3) the user's curiosity is aroused during the interaction, and (4) the user finds the interaction intrinsically interesting, implying that the user's interaction with the technology extends beyond mere instrumentality, becoming a pleasure and an enjoyable experience as an end in itself (see Table 7.1).

In a later experiment, Webster et al. (1993) refined the model to just three dimensions: control, focused attention, and curiosity and intrinsic interest coalescing to become cognitive enjoyment (a construct comprised of curiosity and intrinsic interest that were highly interdependent). Flow was also associated with specific characteristics of the software (specifically, perceptions of flexibility and modifiability) and with certain technology-use behaviors (experimentation and future voluntary computer interactions).

Ghani et al. (1991) argued that two key characteristics of flow are total concentration in an activity and the enjoyment one derives from an activity. Perceived control and challenge predict flow. In a later study exploring flow occurring among individuals using computers in the workplace, Ghani and Deshpande also analyzed control as well as challenge. These authors agreed that there is an optimal level of challenge relative to a certain skill level. "If the challenges are too high, the individual feels a lack of control over the environment and becomes anxious and frustrated. If the challenges are too low, the individual loses interest" (1994, 382). They also found that a sense of being in control is a key determinant of flow. Also, flow is linked to exploratory behavior, which in turn influences the extent of computer use. As Novak et al. (2000) noted, the model provided empirical support for definitions that specify that flow occurs when challenges and skill are both high, since skill and challenges independently contribute to flow. The precondition for flow is, therefore, a balance between the challenges perceived in a given situation and the skills a person brings to it.

In his 1995 study, Ghani develops a model of flow. His model places fitness of task (difference between challenges and skills), perceived control, and cognitive spontaneity (playfulness) as the antecedents of flow. Flow itself is measured through the constructs of enjoyment and concentration. The consequences of flow are increased learning, in-

Table 7.1

Summary of Empirical Research

Authors	Dimensions	Antecedents	Consequences
Ghani, Supnick, and Rooney (1991)	Concentration Enjoyment	Individual skills Control Challenge	
Trevino and Webster (1992)	Control Attention focus Curiosity Intrinsic interest	Computer skill Technology type Ease of use	Attitudes Effectiveness Quantity Barrier reduction
Webster, Trevino, and Ryan (1993)	Control Attention focus Cognitive enjoyment	Perceived flexibility Perceived modifiability Experimentation Future voluntary use Actual use Perceived communication quantity Perceived communication affectiveness	
Ghani and Deshpande (1994)	Concentration Enjoyment	Control Challenge	Exploratory use
Ghani (1995)	Enjoyment Concentration	Fitness of task (difference between challenges and skills) Perceived control Cognitive spontaneity (playfulness)	Learning Increased creativity Focus on the process
Hoffman and Novak (1996b)	Not specified	*Primary antecedents:* Skills/challenges Focused attention *Secondary antecedents:* Telepresence Interactivity	Learning Perceived behavioral control Positive subjective experience Exploratory mind-set
Webster and Ho (1997)	Attention focus Curiosity Intrinsic interest	Technology characteristics Instructor attitudes Teaching style Instructor control Number of student locations Student comfort with having image displayed Classmates' attitudes	
Novak, Hoffman, and Yung (2000)	Not specified	*Primary antecedents:* Control Arousal Focused attention Concentration *Secondary antecedents:* Challenge Skill Interaction speed Involvement	Positive affects Exploratory behavior

(continued)

Authors	Dimensions	Antecedents	Consequences

Chen (2000)	Concentration
	Telepresence
	Time distortion
	Loss of self-
	  consciousness
		Clear goals
		Immediate feedback
		Potential control
		
		Merger of action and
		  awareness
			Positive affect
			Autotelic experience

Agarwal and Karahanna (2000)	Temporal dissociation Focused immersion Heightened enjoyment Control Curiosity	Cognitive playfulness Personal innovativeness	

Koufaris (2002)	Instrinsic enjoyment
	Perceived control
	Concentration and
	  attention
		Product involvement
		Web skills
		Value-added search
		  mechanisms
		Challenges
			Unplanned purchase
			Intention to return

Koufaris, Kambil, and LaBarbera (2001–2)	Perceived control Shopping enjoyment	Search mechanism Positive challenge	Unplanned purchase Intention to return

Skadberg and
Kimmel (2004)
	Enjoyment
	
	Time distortion
		Skill: visitor's knowledge
		  of the Web site topic
		Challenge: Web page
		  content
		Telepresence
		Attractiveness
		Experience with Web site's
		  interactivity
		Speed
		Ease of use
			Increased learning
			
			Changes of attitude
			  and behavior (indirect,
			  through learning)

creased creativity, and a focus on the process. After testing the model, Ghani noted that the construct of fit influences flow indirectly, mediated through perceived control. As Finneran and Zhang (2002) summarize, Ghani's work illustrates the complexity of the balance of a user's skills and challenges. With an excess of skills, the user feels more in control, which can lead to flow. However, when the skills greatly exceed challenges, boredom is likely to result, providing a negative influence on flow.

A significantly more complex version of flow was described by Hoffman and Novak, who suggest that, when in the flow state, "irrelevant thoughts and perceptions are screened out and the consumer's attention is focused entirely on the interaction. Flow, thus, involves a merging of actions and awareness, with concentration so intense there is little attention left over to consider anything else" (1996b, 58).

Hoffman and Novak (1996b) developed a conceptual model that attempted to explain the relationship between flow and the behavior of online users. These authors indicated that the primary antecedents to flow are challenges, skills, and focused attention. From the literature on communication media, they added secondary antecedents: telepresence and interactivity. Specifically, telepresence is the extent to which one feels present in the mediated environment, rather than in the immediate physical environment (Steuer 1992). Telepresence is, therefore, the experience of presence in an environment by means of a communication medium, an experience induced by vividness and interactivity (Sheridan 1992). Hoffman and Novak (1996b) incorporated these two dimensions into their model as content characteristics. They also added the construct of involvement, which encompasses intrinsic motivation and self-reliance and is influenced by whether the activity is goal-directed or experiential. Finally, they theorized that flow would result in several outcomes such as a positive subjective experience, increased learning, exploratory mindset, and perceived behavioral control.

More recently, Novak et al. took the definition of flow to the operational level (in a CME), stating that flow is "determined by: a) high levels of skill and control; b) high levels of challenge and arousal; c) focused attention; and . . . d) enhanced by interactivity and telepresence" (2000, 24). Thus, flow occurs when an activity challenges and interests individuals enough to encourage greater expected Web use and playful, exploratory behavior without the activity being beyond the individuals' reach. In the revised model, the primary antecedents are control, arousal, and focused attention. The secondary antecedents are challenge, skill, interactive speed, and involvement. The consequences are positive affect and exploratory behavior.

In Chen's dissertation (2000), a correlation was found between a Web user's flow experience and ten flow dimensions. These ten dimensions are broken down with factor analysis into three factors labeled: flow antecedents, flow experience, and flow consequences. The flow antecedents are clear goals, immediate feedback, potential control, and merging of action and awareness. The flow experience dimensions are concentration, telepresence, time distortion, and loss of self-consciousness. Consequences of flow are positive affects and autotelic experiences. The merging of action and awareness is the only dimension that does not clearly fall into one factor. Its highest loading was in the flow experience factor, so Chen placed it there.

Skadberg and Kimmel (2004) proposed a flow model to predict the level of flow for a tourism Web site. The user's domain knowledge represents his or her skill and the content of the Web sites represents the challenge. The third direct antecedent of flow is telepresence, which is influenced by site attractiveness and interactivity; the latter is further influenced by speed and ease of use. Flow is measured by time distortion and enjoyment. Also, flow experience while browsing a Web site influences a number of important outcomes that are typically expected by Web site developers. First, when people are in a state of flow they tend to learn more about the content presented in the Web site. Second, the increased learning leads to changes of attitude and behavior, including taking positive actions.

Finally, other studies use the flow concept in studying other related constructs such as playfulness, enjoyment, fun, engagement, and cognitive absorption (see, for example, Agarwal and Karahanna 2000; Webster and Ho 1997). On the one hand, Webster and Ho (1997) defined a construct labeled cognitive engagement, which encompasses the dimensions of intrinsic interest, curiosity, and attention focus. Cognitive engagement is concerned with users' subjective experiences of pleasure and involvement due to their intrinsic interest. Arguing that cognitive engagement relates to the state of playfulness and that the state of playfulness could be identical to the flow experience, these authors presented engagement as flow without the notion of control and, as Agarwal and Karahanna (2000) summarize, noted that there is a need for future work investigating whether flow and engagement are the same constructs or whether they are conceptually and empirically distinct. On the other hand, Agarwal and Karahanna (2000) defined a construct called cognitive absorption. Cognitive absorption is one of the important factors in the study of technology use behavior because it serves as a key antecedent to salient beliefs about IT. The authors defined cognitive absorption as a state of deep attention and engagement with software and identified its five dimensions: temporal dissociation, focused immersion, heightened enjoyment, control, and curiosity. Agarwal and Karahanna also argued that cognitive absorption, as a state of perceived playfulness, would be influenced by the personal trial of playfulness and personal innovativeness as important antecedents. Individuals who perceive cognitive spontaneity (i.e., playfulness) during their computer interactions or who are willing to try out new information technology (i.e., personal innovativeness) to support their activities are likely to experience cognitive absorption.

To summarize, flow is a positive, highly enjoyable state of consciousness that occurs when perceived skills match the perceived challenges undertaken. When individuals' goals are clear, when their abilities are up to the challenge, and when feedback is immediate, they become involved in the activity and experience flow-based states. Researchers have found that stable individual differences as well as dynamic situation-specific individual differences influence how individuals perceive and use information technology and experience episodes of flow. The Web users' situational versus enduring involvement and extrinsic versus intrinsic motivation, as flow-related constructs, underlie the entire flow-based Web usage process. Web users' involvement types, ability as a personal factor, and challenge as users' opportunities for action on the Web could help explain how today's users approach and process information and, consequently, evoke emotional responses (i.e., pleasure, arousal, and perceived control) affecting flow-related experience and flow consequence (i.e., positive affects, playfulness as a short-lived cognitive experience, and exploratory behaviors). However, as Finneran and Zhang (2002) note, discrepancies exist about which constructs are important within the flow model; in fact, some models place the constructs in different stages of the flow model. As displayed in Table 7.1, Ghani et al. (1991) and Ghani and Deshpande (1994) consider concentration as the flow experience itself, while others (Novak et al. 2000) place concentration as an antecedent to flow. Therefore, as stated by Hoffman and Novak, "if we can determine the variables that relate to a consumer's propensity to enter the flow state and how these variables interact with each other, we can then develop a strategy to maximize the chances of the consumer entering the flow state on the Web pages" (1996b, 66).

Once the flow construct is defined, outlining how responses to a Web site could affect users' behaviors, the next logical step is figuring out how to elicit the right responses: involvement (submodel 1, see Figure 7.1 on page 114), ability and challenge (submodel 2, see Figure 7.2 on page 118), and consequences (playfulness, exploratory behaviors, and positive affects, see Figure 7.3 on page 119).

Submodel 1: Involvement and Attention

Flow has also been defined as "the holistic sensation that people feel when they act with total involvement" (Csikszentimihalyi 1975) or "a state of mind sometimes experienced by people who are deeply involved in some event, object or activity" (Lutz and Guiry 1994). In the flow state, individuals are absorbed (involved) in an activity (e.g., Web browsing), their focus of awareness is narrowed, they lose self-consciousness, and they feel in control of their environment. Accordingly, the MIS research community has recently recognized the importance of involvement with an information system for user acceptance (Hess et al. 2003) and its related activities.

Prior researchers have maintained that involvement is a major sociopsychological variable that explains individual differences (Festinger 1957; Petty et al. 1981) impacting on behavior (e.g., information seeking or experiential browsing and a range of other Web activities). Following a review of the construct of involvement in psychology, organizational behavior, and marketing, Barki and Hartwick conclude that these disciplines have converged in a definition of involvement "as a subjective psychological state, reflecting the importance and personal relevance of an object or event" (Barki and Hartwick 1994, 62). A common feature of the cognitively based definitions of involvement is that they view involvement as the perceived personal importance and relevance of an object or event.

This chapter adopts the position that involvement is a continuum that may vary between a specific decision and a product class or an activity. In other words, involvement can be understood further not only by considering the levels of involvement or personal relevance (high versus low) but also by distinguishing the types of involvement according to the motives underlying involvement (Park and Young 1986). For example, when individuals are intrinsically motivated, they engage in an activity because they are interested in it and enjoy it. When extrinsically motivated, individuals engage in activities for instrumental or other reasons, such as receiving a reward.

- The internal motive is related to effective involvement and creates intrinsic self-relevance leading to experiential Web behaviors. Internal motives (1) apply to activities performed "for no apparent reinforcement other than the process of performing the activity" (i.e., autotelic activities) (Davis et al. 1992) and (2) relate to perceptions of pleasure and satisfaction from performing the behavior (Vallerand 1997). Users specifically focus their attention on symbolic or experiential cues (Park and Young 1986) and evoke emotional responses (e.g., enjoyment—similar to the emotional response of pleasure from environmental psychology). In short, an essential contributor toward a person's capacity to experience flow is his or her "autotelic nature" or intrinsic motivation.
- The external motive is related to cognitive involvement leading to a goal-directed behavior and creates situational self-relevance (Bloch and Richins 1983; Celsi and

Olson 1988). External motives apply to activities performed because they are instrumental in achieving a valued outcome that is distinct from the activity itself (Davis et al. 1992).

With regard to these points, two types of involvement have been identified (see Houston and Rothschild 1978): (1) enduring and (2) situational involvement. A third type of involvement has been proposed by Rothschild (1984): response involvement. Situational and enduring involvement together influence response involvement. In this sense, response involvement has since been demonstrated to be a combination of enduring and situational involvement (Richins et al. 1992). Thus, this type of involvement is not examined further in this section.

- Enduring involvement is an intrinsically motivated individual difference variable that is relatively long-lasting. The focus may be either on a product class or an activity that endures beyond a specific choice task. Involvement increases with familiarity with the product class or the user's prior knowledge or ability (Houston and Rothschild 1978). In turn, the ability increases with involvement. In addition, enduring involvement varies by the degree to which the stimulus is related to the individual's self-image or pleasure received from thought about, or the utility of, the product class or practice of the activity (Higie and Feick 1989).
- Situational involvement arises from several transitory factors that affect the relationship between the individual and the stimulus (Celsi and Olson 1988). As opposed to the cognitively based definition, this type of involvement does not require personal relevance for its existence. In other words, the individual-state definitions of involvement focus on the mental state of an individual evoked by a stimulus when determining involvement. Rothschild (1984) defines this type of involvement as the ability of a situation to elicit individuals' concern for their behavior in that situation. Situational involvement is externally motivated. According to Hoffman and Novak (1996b), it is more likely to result in a goal-directed behavior. It is related to the degree to which users believe that using the Web would enhance their task performance.

Finally, involvement is a key driver of user response, and higher levels of involvement stimulate users to be more attentive to the information presented to them (Andrews and Shimp 1990; Petty et al. 1983). In turn, the users' state, or how much they are able to concentrate or how absorbed they can become, makes a difference in the ability to reach an optimal state. According to Csikszentmihalyi and Csikszentmihalyi (1988), a user who is in flow simply does not have enough attention left to think about anything else. Webster et al. (1993) found significant positive correlations between intrinsic factors (i.e., cognitive enjoyment) and concentration. Moreover, as Ghani and Deshpande (1994) pointed out, the total concentration on an activity and the enjoyment derived from it are the key characteristics of flow; users in a flow state focus their attention on a limited stimulus field, filtering out irrelevant thoughts and perceptions. Also, Hoffman and Novak (1996b) proposed that centering of attention is a necessary condition for achieving flow.

Figure 7.1   **Summary of Basic Relationships of Related Constructs. Antecedents (I) Submodel 1**

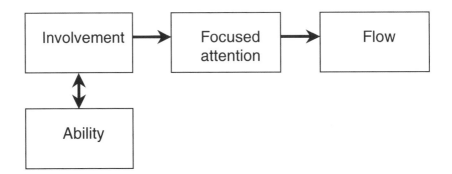

In short, when individuals are completely involved with an activity and totally absorbed in it, they could experience a state of flow, which Csikszentmihalyi (1990) has characterized as "optimal experience." However, an important prerequisite for this rewarding experience is ability to accomplish the task. But it is equally important for the experience to be a challenge; the individual gets stimulation (i.e., arousal) and unambiguous feedback (i.e., perceived control) inherent in the performance of the activity. To complete the global model, a second submodel is introduced based on users' ability, challenge, arousal, and perceived control.

Submodel 2: Challenges and Abilities

Csikszentmihalyi (1990) cited the balance of skills and challenges as the most important factor in flow experience. On the one hand, one of the primary antecedents of flow is the individual's level of ability. As the users gain skill, they strive to gain further expertise and develop advanced experience. The increasing perceived control and ease of use offer the opportunity to explore different skills. On the other hand, users must perceive a balance between their abilities and the challenges of the activity, defined as their opportunities for action on the Web (Novak et al. 2000). As Koufaris (2002) noted, along with individual skills, the challenges presented by an activity are the main important predictors of flow (Csikszentmihalyi 1975; Ghani et al. 1991; Ghani and Deshpande 1994; Hoffman and Novak 1996b; Novak et al. 2000; Trevino and Webster 1992; Webster et al. 1993). Both abilities and challenges must be above a critical threshold; i.e., both the challenges and skills must be relatively high before a flow experience becomes possible (Massimini and Carli 1988).

Furthermore, situations in which challenges and skills are perceived to be equivalent are thought to facilitate the emergence of such indicators of flow as high levels of arousal, intrinsic motivation, and perceived freedom (Ellis et al. 1994). Also, the balance between challenges and skills facilitates the experiences of enjoyment, learning, and personal growth. Otherwise, users may become bored or anxious. Too much stimulation could lead users to make errors and feel out of control (i.e., anxiety as a negative reaction toward use), while too little could leave them feeling bored, with their attention wandering. Finally, apathy ensues if both challenges and skills are below the user's average. In this sense, as Novak et al. (2000) note, flow channel segmentation models provide a simpler alternative to structural modeling. These segmentation models attempt to account for all possible combinations of high, moderate, and low skills and challenges, thus defining flow solely on the basis of the constructs of skill and challenge.

- If the challenges of an activity, defined as those barriers that hinder users from navigating Web sites or those opportunities that provoke users to further explore Web sites, demand more than the individual can handle, a state of stimulation ensues (anxiety: high challenge/low skill versus arousal: high challenge/moderate skill). For instance, users become aroused until they are familiarized with the system through more frequent use, such as practice or training (Gardner et al. 1989).
- On the contrary, when the challenges are lower than the individual's skill level (or capacity for action), boredom (low challenge/high skill) or perceived control (moderate challenge/high skill) may be the result. If the challenges are *too* low, users lose interest and tend to use the Web sporadically.

In other words, as the skills increase, so must the challenges in order to maintain interest. Hence, the model shows time progression as a user continues to learn a new skill and progresses up the flow channel. However, if the challenges increase too fast, then there is danger of anxiety at not being able to control the situation, which could result in exiting the CME (Hoffman and Novak 1996b). On the contrary, if skills develop too fast, or challenges are not increased sufficiently, then there is a danger of boredom.

This congruence requirement (skills to challenge) for presence of the flow state is also consistent with the optimal stimulation level (OSL) theory, which holds that "the relationship between stimulation and a person's affective reaction to stimulation follows an inverted U curve, with intermediate levels of stimulation creating the most satisfaction" (Steenkamp and Baumgartner 1992). In a time- and space-specific Web session, the skills of the user are fixed. As noted above, if the amount of stimulation the person is experiencing exceeds a certain subjective limit, the user will become anxious and the level of enjoyment of the experience will start to fall off dramatically. This loss of the OSL will cause the user to end the session (Lewis 1997).

Accordingly, Trevino and Webster (1992) suggest that CMC-based (computer-mediated communication) technologies can encourage sensory curiosity through such technological characteristics as color and sound. They can also stimulate cognitive curiosity and the desire to attain competence with the technology by providing options, such as menus, that encourage exploration (Malone and Lepper 1987) and competence attainment. CMC can encourage sensory curiosity through aesthetic qualities or through hyperlinks that provide options that encourage experiential behaviors (Rayport and Jaworski 2000).

In this context and given the growing evidence that extrinsic incentives and pressures could undermine motivation to perform even inherently interesting activities, Deci and Ryan (1985) proposed a self-determination theory in which they integrated two perspectives on human motivation: (1) individuals are motivated to maintain an optimal level of stimulation (Hebb 1955), and (2) individuals have basic needs for competence (White 1959) and personal causation or self-determination (deCharms 1968). Eccles and Wigfield (2002) argued that people seek out optimal stimulation and challenging activities and find these activities intrinsically motivating because they have a basic need for competence.

Specifically, computer playfulness refers to an individual's tendency to interact spontaneously with a computer. As Hackbarth et al. (2003) argue, playfulness can be considered either a state of mind or an individual trait. A state of mind is a short-lived cognitive experience felt by the individual. A trait represents a characteristic of the individual, which tends to be stable but also slowly changes over time. Playfulness is defined as (1) a system-specific trait that could change because the experience in using the Web increases over time; and (2) a short-lived cognitive experience caused by the need to generate interactions with the environment or self that maintain an optimal experience (i.e., flow).

Yager et al. (1997) note that those individuals higher in playfulness, as a trait, are expected to exercise and develop skills through exploratory behaviors, resulting in improved performance or increased learning. For instance, employees with higher cognitive playfulness demonstrated (1) higher test performance and (2) more positive affective outcomes than those with lower cognitive playfulness (Webster and Martocchio 1992). Those people would be less likely to experience anxiety in new interactive activities on the Web. In other words, they would be more likely to seek out high challenges to maintain consistency with their increasing abilities. In this sense, Webster and Martocchio (1995) argued that the individual trait of cognitive playfulness would be a relevant antecedent of the state of flow.

Particularly relevant to the congruence of skills with challenges is also personal innovativeness in the domain of information technology (PIIT). Individuals high in technology innovativeness (as an individual trait) have a strong intrinsic motivation to use new technologies and *enjoy* the stimulation of trying new technologies. Compared with less innovative individuals, they would not be greatly concerned about whether the new technologies are easy to use and would still intend to try them despite the possible difficulties (Dabholkar and Bagozzi 2002). Specifically, Agarwal and Prasad (1998a) differentiate between global innovativeness and domain-specific innovativeness in the domain of IT and conceptualize PIIT as a relatively stable descriptor of individuals that is invariant beyond situational considerations, such as the willingness of an individual to try out any new IT. The construct PIIT is, therefore, hypothesized to exhibit effects on the antecedents as well as the consequences of individual perceptions about ITs. Research suggests that individuals with higher PIIT require fewer positive perceptions to accept a new technology than individuals who are less innovative, that higher levels of PIIT result in increased levels of technology use and experimentation, and that higher PIIT is positively related to the computer self-efficacy of the individuals. The results indicate that personal innovativeness is, thus, fully related to the cognitive absorption response elicited from using the Web. In short, an individual's inherent playfulness and PIIT traits will influence his or her ability to reach an optimal flow state.

Finally, Csikszentmihalyi (1975) argued that activities that allow for control facilitate perceptions of flow. Control can be defined as the level of one's self-efficacy over the environment and one's actions. Ghani et al. (1991) found flow to significantly correlate with perceived control and to be facilitated by the medium adapting to feedback from the individual and by providing explicit choices among alternatives. Webster et al. (1993) defined control as one of three dimensions of flow and found it significantly correlated with one of the other two dimensions (cognitive enjoyment). On the other hand, as Trevino and Webster (1992) suggest, objective technology characteristics (e.g., programmability, malleability, customizability) may be related to flow through their impact on the user's perception of control in the CMC technology interaction. For example, a control belief in the usage of the Internet might be "I have easy access to a high-speed connection" with a corresponding perceived facilitation of "A high-speed connection is important to using the Internet."

Perceived control is similar to the emotional response of dominance in environmental psychology (Koufaris 2002), where it is defined as feeling "unrestricted or free to act in a variety of ways in a specific situation and environment" (Mehrabian and Russel 1974). Perceived control is also similar to Bandura's self-efficacy (1986), since it is specific to an action and it can be different according to situations or actions. Particularly, computer self-efficacy "represents an individual's perceptions of his or her ability to use computers in the accomplishment of a task" and "refers to a judgment of one's capability to use a computer" (Compeau and Higgins 1995). Self-efficacy refers to the sense that a person has an effect on the environment. In addition, social learning theory (SLT) research has found that efficacy beliefs are the primary influence on how individuals make decisions about their ability to perform tasks or interpretations of experiences (Bandura 1997).

To summarize, perceived control comes from users' perception of their ability to adjust the CME and their perception of how the CME responds to their input. Users believe that their actions and abilities determine their successes or failures (internal locus control). Moreover, the notion of a sense of control is related to perceived behavioral control (Ajzen 1991) in that it reflects the extent to which an individual feels that he or she has the power to influence and control the events occurring in their lives (adapted from Baronas and Louis 1988).

Accordingly, existing studies of computer self-efficacy have emphasized its importance during technology acceptance and training (Compeau and Higgins 1995; Marakas et al. 1998). Users with a high level of perceived control are likely to feel able to perform the activity, showing a high comfort level with the activity. They would be inclined, on the one hand, to feel intrinsic enjoyment while engaged in the activity and, on the other hand, to use the Web frequently. Users experience comfort levels with the activity after a certain level of competence in it has been achieved (Ghani and Deshpande 1994), positively affecting the length of Web exposure.

Figure 7.2 **Summary of Basic Relationships of Related Constructs. Antecedents (II) Submodel 2**

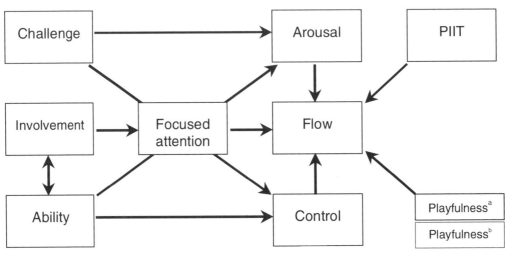

ªIndividual trait.
ᵇShort-lived cognitive experience.

Submodel 3: Consequences

Prior research suggests that individuals in positive affective states are more creative, more helpful, better negotiators, and more persistent in uncertain tasks (George and Brief 1992; Isen and Baron 1991). Higher behavioral efficiency and creativity have been commonly attributed to the influence of the flow state (Canter et al. 1985). In fact, several studies collected evidence that affective states can predict employee performance (Konradt and Sulz 2001). Webster et al. stated, "employees who interact more playfully with computers should view computer interactions more positively than those who interact less playfully" (1993, 413). These drawbacks pose a concern (in the work environment) for managers who are responsible for organizational productivity (Lewis 1997).

As Finneran and Zhang (2002) summarize, flow theory explains positive user experiences within a CME (Ghani 1995; Ghani and Deshpande 1994; Ghani et al. 1991; Trevino and Webster 1992; Webster et al. 1993), and, more recently and specifically, the Web (Chen 2000; Chen et al. 1999; Hoffman and Novak 1996b; Nel et al. 1999; Novak et al. 2000). In particular, the experience of flow has been shown to lead to increased exploratory behavior (Ghani 1995; Ghani and Deshpande 1994; Webster et al. 1993), communication (Trevino and Webster 1992), learning (Ghani 1995), positive affect (Chen 2000; Trevino and Webster 1992), and computer use (Ghani and Deshpande 1994; Trevino and Webster 1992; Webster et al. 1993). Moreover, previous research on HCI (Sandelands and Buckner 1989; Starbuck and Webster 1991; Webster and Martocchio 1992) has shown that higher degrees of pleasure and involvement during computer interactions

Figure 7.3   **Summary of Basic Relationships of Related Constructs. Consequences Submodel 3**

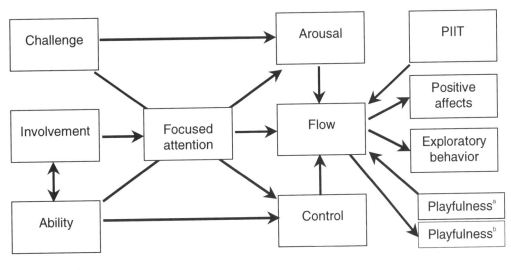

[a]Individual trait.
[b]Short-lived cognitive experience.

lead to concurrent subjective perceptions of positive affect and mood (Hoffman and Novak 1996b).

According to Hoffman and Novak (1996b), when customers experience the flow while browsing, they gain optimal experience, which results in increased participatory behaviors and positive subjective experiences from their visit. Flow is positively related to more fun, recreational, and exploratory behavior. Amabile noted that "only the intrinsically motivated person . . . who is motivated by the interest, challenge, and the enjoyment of being in the maze . . . will explore, and take the risk of running into a dead-end here and there" (1988, 79–80). Also, Ghani and Deshpande (1994) found that flow had a significant impact on exploratory use of the computer, which, in turn, had a significant effect on the extent of computer use. Flow could affect these outputs and the experience on the Web could be translated into increased exploratory behavior, longer duration of time spent, and repeated visits.

People with optimal stimulation levels will exhibit increased playfulness. In his flow experiment, Ghani (1991) found a significant correlation between flow and his cognitive spontaneity scale, adapted from Webster's (1989) scale to measure an individual's inventiveness and flexibility when using computing technologies. Also, Katz (1987) and Ghani (1991) found that higher levels of playfulness correlated with higher experimentation. In short, playfulness and exploratory behavior are considered two important consequences (and feedbacks) of the optimal experience (i.e., flow) and are caused by the need to generate interactions with the environment or self that maintain (or enhance) an optimal experience. On the one hand, people with high optimal stimulation levels will exhibit playfulness (as a short-lived cognitive experience: "I feel creative, original, imaginative when I visit a time- and space-specific Web site") and exploratory behavior to maintain (or enhance) flow and avoid boredom. Individuals engage in playfulness and experiential behavior in an attempt to adjust their perceived stimulation level to their desired optimal level, and they participate in more optimal experiences than persons with low optimal stimulation levels. Hence it is expected that more skillful people would be engaged in more playful and exploratory activities in which their abilities can be tested. On the other hand, as I commented above, playfulness as an individual trait will influence the user's ability to reach a flow state.

IMPLICATIONS FOR WEB USE

We have theoretically explored important flow constructs and described Web users' flow experiences using the model as a lens to verify the existence of flow on the Web. In this Web usage-based context, users' online browsing modes can be categorized. Users not only search the Web for specific information, they also surf it for entertainment, stimulation, and socializing. The search for specific information is the result of goal-directed need, whereas surfing the Web for other purposes is the result of the experiential need of users (see Huang 2003). In other words, as Pedersen and Nysveen (2003) suggest, categorizing users according to their objectives when visiting a Web site seems to be a useful strategy. Hoffman and Novak (1996b) divided online users' search processes into goal-directed and experiential. Based on the customers' mind-sets, Dholakia and Bagozzi (2001) suggested a differentiation between goal-oriented and experiential mind-sets. The two mind-sets are furthermore divided into sub-mind-sets. Moe (2003) divided online users into four categories based on users' search behaviors (directed versus exploratory) and customers' purchasing horizon (immediate versus future).

Based on the above personal factors, theoretical foundations, and the situation and goals of the user, two pure Web user-types are proposed. The distinction is a continuum rather than a dichotomy. Individual motives drive a person's information and entertainment consumption processes. Individuals shift from one mode to the other. If these theories apply to the Web, users may start surfing a Web site, then shift to see if the information interests them, or the reverse situation may occur. For example, Chen et al. (1999) discovered that subjects experienced flow in different types of Web activities: 61 percent from information seeking and 18 percent from correspondence via e-mail and newsgroups. As Novak et al. (2000) suggest, because the Web mixes experiential and goal-directed behaviors, the model can be used as a first step in evaluating Web sites in terms of the extent to which they deliver these two types of experience.

- Pure browsers (experiential browsers) are those users with highly enduring involvement related to intrinsic motives and perceived control levels induced by critical ability levels. Likewise, the perceived challenge (e.g., searching for the latest interesting sites) is one of the key determinants of the experiential behavior that an individual experiences while browsing.

- Pure seekers (goal-directed seekers) are users who browse with high ability levels, pursuing a well-defined goal (high situational involvement) with utilitarian risk perception and without intrinsic motivation.

In the first case, the users *flow*. They are mainly moved by an intrinsic motive: "to feel pleasure and enjoyment from the activity itself" (Bloch et al. 1986). Users show ritualized orientations, exploring the Web in their daily quest for the latest interesting sites. When users are in the flow state, they find the interaction intrinsically interesting (Csikszentmihalyi 1975), meaning that they are involved in the activity for the responses it provides (i.e., perceived enjoyment) rather than for utilitarian purposes (i.e., perceived usefulness). Pure browsers value the Web not because it lets them achieve set goals but because it allows them to browse, oriented toward enjoyable navigational choices. It is an autotelic experience: the experience itself acts as a primary intrinsic reward, even if extensive external rewards are present. This positive subjective experience becomes an important reason for performing an activity (Csikszentmihalyi 1975). This result suggests that people could adopt the Web because its use is enjoyable. If an activity *"feels good,"* it is intrinsically motivating (Deci 1976); and pure browsers are more likely to engage in the activity for its own sake.

In the second case, pure seekers search for contents adapted to their needs and goals and leave the Web after an active and efficient search. Pure seekers (versus experiential users) are generally involved in tasks that already have a high motivating potential (i.e., external rewards). Such individuals are less likely to seek challenges and arousal in Web use. In other words, users show an instrumental orientation to the Web. Pure seekers use the Web less for experiential activities and more for goal-directed activities. Browsing appears to involve more cognitive processing than emotional evaluation. If users do not find the Web site utilitarian, they will immediately terminate the visit at that point by clicking out (Raman and Leckenby 1998). Pure seekers tend to use the Web to the extent they believe it will help them perform their job better. Moreover, they wish to find the contents and services in the shortest possible time and judge them according to valuable decision criteria. As users become more experienced, their information search shifts from an extensive manner to a simplified one (Howard and Sheth 1969; Johnson et al. 2003). A navigation scheme that can be apprehended by visitors and various forms of customization, including personalization, recommendations, or easy checkout, can decrease session lengths. Likewise, Web users can appreciate the opportunity cost of time and confront a variety of time constraints. An idea advanced in some early empirical research on the Web holds that Web users will continue to browse as long as the expected benefit or value of an additional page view exceeds the cost (Huberman et al. 1998). However, a longer Web session does not necessarily mean that the Web is not useful. In a marketing context, when Web users engage in prepurchase deliberation (extrinsically motivating), they may engage in a longer Web site visit when the advertised brand is in the consideration set or has close competition (Raman and Leckenby 1998). In this context, the study by Clarke and Belk (1978) also points out the relevance of the different products or differentiation among alternatives in investigating the dependent measures of search time and cost. The amount of differentiation may interact with personal factors, leading to the greatest search effort under high personal importance and high differentiation of alternatives and high situational importance (Zaichkowsky 1986). Therefore, no discernible relationship is expected between goal-directed behaviors and lengths of Web sessions (Sánchez-Franco and Rodríguez 2004).

DISCUSSION AND RECOMMENDATIONS

The purpose of this study was to theoretically examine the optimal states in Web interaction using the flow concept. Specifically, two questions have been analyzed: what are the different dimensions, antecedents, and consequences of flow, and what makes flow happen. Rather than focus solely on flow concept, this study has taken a more holistic approach to understanding the experiences of Web users, exploring concepts such as involvement, concentration, ability, challenge, arousal, perceived control, playfulness, and personal innovativeness. The flow experience is difficult to isolate and analyze because of its dynamic and holistic nature. In this sense, I have analyzed theoretically that flow is a complex construct that can be defined as a set of directed relationships among constructs. Our research thus has relevance to both academic scientists and industry practitioners interested in the usage of the Web.

Accordingly, rather than just evaluating the theoretical aspects, this study can also be used to assess motivational design aspects during the working process. As noted in the introduction, "it is expected that our understanding of the flow phenomenon would guide information and communication technology (ICT) designers to be able to design a product that will lead users to flow experiences" (Finneran and Zhang 2005). Flow is situated in a particular time and task (Chen et al. 1999). In addition to individual characteristics, the characteristics of the particular task and the tool being used impact the potential for flow. Although this study has essentially focused on the motivational aspects of the user, research might extend the model by incorporating various Web site usability and other design factors (Palmer 2002) and delineating their effects on technology acceptance model variables (i.e., perceived ease of use and usefulness). In fact, the layout and content can be an important strategic tool for online Web sites.

Exploring flow antecedents and consequences for predicting and explaining Web use has practical value both for Web site owners that would like to assess user demand for new design ideas to facilitate flow and users who would like to find a Web site leading to an enduring relationship and a reduction in boredom and anxiety. Flow experience could thus increase positive work outcome. Flow strengthens personal capabilities with the likelihood of learning new skills. Therefore, individuals in flow are supposed to have a higher learning performance compared with individuals who feel apathy, fear, anxiety, and boredom.

However, if users return to the same Web site over time, it is reasonable to expect learning to occur and session lengths to decline (Johnson et al. 2003, on "the power law of practice"). In this sense, usefulness and ease of use should not be the only key criteria for Web site design, as Web site usage would decrease with time. On the contrary, the main determinant must be stimulating use of the Web so that it evokes compelling experiences and, therefore, increases profitable Web site use. In other words, the Web will need to be not only useful but also enjoyable relative to its competing alternatives. This substantiates the importance of the Web's being intrinsically enjoyable in order to promote a strong positive intention to usage. For instance, design scripts should focus on the following user-interface and design elements; on the one hand, work tasks, roles, and mastery, with quick results for limited tasks (aspects traditionally related to instrumental activities); and, on the other hand, navigation oriented to exploration and control (aspects traditionally related to flow-based activities) and attention gained through cognitive competitions. Although Pace's (2004) theory suggests that the flow experiences of Web users depend on a complex network of factors, most of which are beyond the influence of Web designers, through the inclusion of attributes that cause users to perceive a site as stimulating, interactive, and dynamic, or innovative and playful, a Web site provides users with opportunities to experience flow and meets both their extrinsic and intrinsic motives. Users who interact more playfully with a Web site will view the interaction more positively than those who interact less playfully, and consequently they may be more motivated to engage in enduring interactions in the future (Webster et al. 1993) and enhance their skills. The desirable relationships between the extrinsic and intrinsic aspects of Web design mean that a Web site that satisfies one aspect will bring out the other aspect, increasing the overall satisfaction.

By adding options that encourage flow, the Web professional could enhance users' perception of interaction with the Web as enjoyable and increase enduring exposures to the site facilitating the likelihood of reaping the rewards of increased repeat visits and longer times at each visit. The experience of flow is thus a highly desirable goal to increase the effectiveness of Web experiences. As we stated above, pure seekers who enjoy an activity will probably want to maintain or increase their emotional responses. More specifically, an increase in flow-related experience among pure seekers users favors the acceptance and usage of the Web.

To sum up, in this theoretical study, individual differences include both traits and states, each having an influence when interacting with the Web. Individual differences, which are shown to be important in early non-computer-mediated flow studies, are probably even more important on the Web. For instance, an individual's inherent playfulness and PIIT traits will influence the probability of reaching an optimal flow state while browsing. However, as Finneran and Zhang (2003) suggest, empirical research is much needed to validate or clarify which individual factors influence the flow experience and where they occur in the process.

Web sites need to provide for flow by motivating users to participate, promoting user stimulation, and including interesting features to attract and retain users and facilitate their learning and creativity and focus on process. Web academics and professionals seek to capture users' interest so that their minds might reflect profoundly on the job matter and stimulate deep concentration, creativity, and learning. Flow can yield positive user experiences within the Web, increased exploratory behavior and learning, improved attitudes and positive affects, increased computer use, and, overall, optimal experiences within the Web. The benefits of flow experiences are thus clear. Creating a compelling Web site depends on the facilitation of a state of flow for its users and suggests that an important objective is to provide these flow opportunities. Kraut et al. comment: "The evolution of the Internet and the domestication process is only just starting. Perhaps the principal lesson of our study is that we must expend the effort to understand actual usage experience, to evaluate social impacts, and to use this understanding to make better informed design decisions" (1998, 22).

REFERENCES

Agarwal, R., and Karahanna, E. 2000. Time flies when you're having fun: Cognitive absorption and beliefs about information technology usage. *MIS Quarterly* 24, 4, 665–694.

Agarwal, R., and Prasad, J. 1998a. A conceptual and operational definition of personal innovativeness in the domain of information technology. *Information Systems Research* 9, 2, 204–215.

———. 1998b. The antecedents and consequences of user perceptions in information technology adoption. *Decision Support Systems* 22, 15–29.

Ajzen, I. 1991. The theory of planned behavior. *Organizational Behavior and Human Decision Processes* 50, 179–211.

Amabile, T.M. 1988. A model of creativity and innovations in organizations. In B.M. Straw and L.L. Cummings (eds.), *Research in Organizational Behavior.* Greenwich, CT: JAI Press, 123–167.

Andrews, J.C., and Shimp, T.A. 1990. Effects of involvement, argument strength, and source characteristics on central and peripheral processing in advertising. *Psychology and Marketing* 7 (Fall), 195–214.

Bagozzi, R.P., Gopinath, M., and Nyer, P.U. 1999. The role of emotions in marketing. *Journal of Academy of Marketing Sciences* 27, 2, 184–206.

Bandura, A. 1986. *Social Foundations of Thought and Action: A Social Cognitive Theory.* Englewood Cliffs, NJ: Prentice Hall, 1986.

———. 1997. *Self-efficacy: The Exercise of Control.* New York: W.H. Freeman.

Barki, H., and Hartwick, J. 1989. Rethinking the concept of user involvement. *MIS Quarterly* 13, 1, 53–63.

———. 1994. Measuring user participation, user involvement, and user attitude. *MIS Quarterly* 18, 1, 59–82.

Baronas, A., and Louis, M. 1988. Restoring a sense of control during implementation: How user involvement leads to system acceptance. *MIS Quarterly* 12, 1, 111–124.

Bloch, P., and Richins, M. 1983. A theoretical model for the study of product importance perceptions. *Journal of Marketing* 47, 69–81.

Bloch, P., Sherrell, D.L, and Ridgway, N.M. 1986. Consumer search: An extended framework. *Journal of Consumer Research* 13, 119–126.

Canter, D., Rivers, R., and Storrs, G. 1985. Characterizing user navigation through complex data structures. *Behavior and Information Technology* 4, 2, 93–102.

Celsi, R.L., and Olson, J.C. 1988. The role of involvement in attention and comprehension processes. *Journal of Consumer Research* 5 (September), 210–224.

Chen, H. 2000. Exploring Web users' on-line optimal flow experiences. PhD diss., Syracuse University.

Chen, H., Wigand, R., and Nilan, M.S. 1999. Optimal experience of Web activities. *Computers in Human Behavior* 15, 5, 585–608.

Childers, T.L., Carr, C., Peek, J., and Carson, S. 2001. Hedonic and utilitarian motivations for online retail shopping behavior. *Journal of Retailing* 77, 511–535.

Chung, J., and Tan, F.B. 2004. Antecedents of perceived playfulness: An exploratory study on user acceptance of general information-searching Web sites. *Information & Management* 41, 7, 869–881.

Clarke, K., and Belk, R. 1978. The effects of product involvement and task definition on anticipated consumer effort. *Advances in Consumer Research* 5, 313–318.

Compeau, D., and Higgins, C. 1995. Application of social cognitive theory to training for computer skills. *Information Systems Research* 6, 2, 118–143.

Csikszentmihalyi, M. 1975. *Beyond Boredom and Anxiety: Experiencing Flow in Work and Play.* San Francisco: Jossey-Bass.

———. 1988. The flow experience and its significance for human psychology. In M. Csikszentmihalyi and I.S. Csikszentmihalyi (eds.), *Optimal Experience: Psychological Studies of Flow in Consciousness.* Cambridge, UK: Cambridge University Press, 15–35.

———. 1990. *Flow: The Psychology of Optimal Experience.* New York: Harper & Row.

Csikszentmihalyi, M., and Csikszentmihalyi, I.S. 1988. *Optimal Experience: Psychological Studies of Flow in Consciousness.* Cambridge, UK: Cambridge University Press.

Csikszentmihalyi, M., and LeFevre, J. 1989. Optimal experience in work and leisure. *Journal of Personality and Social Psychology* 56, 5, 815–822.

Dabholkar, P.A., and Bagozzi, R.P. 2002. An attitudinal model of technology-based self-service: Moderating effects of consumer traits and situational factors. *Journal of the Academy of Marketing Science* 30, 3, 184–201.

Davis, F.D., Bagozzi, R.P., and Warshaw, P.R. 1992. Extrinsic and intrinsic motivation to use computers in the workplace. *Journal of Applied Social Psychology* 22, 14, 1111–1132.

deCharms R. 1968. *Personal Causation: The Internal Affective Determinants of Behavior.* New York: Academia.

Deci, E.L. 1976. Notes on the theory and metatheory of intrinsic motivation. *Organizational Behavior and Human Performance* 15, 130–145.

Deci, E.L., and Ryan, R. 1985. *Intrinsic Motivation and Self-determination in Human Behavior.* New York: Plenum Press.

Dholakia, U., and Bagozzi, R.P. 2001. Consumer behavior in digital environments. *Digital Marketing* (2001), 163–200.

Eastlick, M.A., and Feinberg, R.A. 1999. Shopping motives for mail catalog shopping. *Journal of Business Research* 45, 3, 281–290.

Eccles, J.S., and Wigfield, A. 2002. Motivational beliefs, values, and goals. *Annual Review of Psychology* 53, 109–132.

Ellis, G.D., Voelkl, J.E., and Morris, C. 1994. Measurement and analysis issues with explanation of variance in daily experience using the flow model. *Journal of Leisure Research* 26, 4, 337–356.

Festinger, L. 1957. *A Theory of Cognitive Dissonance.* New York: Harper & Row.

Finneran, C.M., and Zhang, P. 2002. The challenges of studying flow within a computer-mediated environment. In *Proceedings of the Americas Conference on Information Systems.* Dallas: ACIS, 1047–1054.

———. 2003. A Person-artefact-task (PAT) model of flow antecedents in computer-mediated environments. *International Journal of Human-Computer Studies* 59, 4, 475–496.

———. 2005. Flow in computer-mediated environments: Promises and challenges. *Communications of the Association for Information Systems* 15, 82–101.

Gardner, E.P., Young, P., and Ruth, S.R. 1989. Evolution of attitudes toward computers: A retrospective view. *Behavior and Information Technology* 8, 89–98.

George, J.M., and Brief, A.P. 1992. Feeling good—doing good: A conceptual analysis of the mood at work—organizational spontaneity relationship. *Psychological Bulletin* 112, 310–329.

Ghani, J.A. 1995. Flow in human-computer interactions: Test of a model. In J. Carey (ed.), *Factors in Management Information Systems: An Organizational Perspective.* Norwood, NJ: Ablex, 229–237.

———. 1995. Flow in human-computer interactions: Test of a model. In J. Carey (ed.), *Human Factors in Information Systems: Emerging Theoretical Base.* Norwood, NJ: Ablex, 291–311.

Ghani, J.A., and Deshpande, S.P. 1994. Task characteristics and the experience of optimal flow in human-computer interaction. *Journal of Psychology* 128, 4, 383–391.

Ghani, J.A., Supnick, R., and Rooney, P. 1991. The experience of flow in computer-mediated and in face-to-face groups. In J.I. DeGross, I. Benbasat, G. DeSanctis, and C.M. Beath (eds.), *Proceedings of the 12th International Conference on Information Systems*. Minneapolis: University of Minnesota (in press): 16–18.

Hackbarth, G., Grover, V., and Yi, M.Y. 2003. Computer playfulness and anxiety: Positive and negative mediators of the system experience effect on perceived ease of use. *Information and Management* 40, 3, 221–232.

Haworth, J., Jarman, M., and Lee, S. 1997. Positive psychological states in the daily life of a sample of working women. *Journal of Applied Social Psychology* 27, 4, 345–370.

Hebb, D.O. 1955. Drives and the C.N.S. (conceptual nervous system). *Psychological Review* 62, 243–245.

Hess, T.J., Fuller, M.A., and Mathew, J. 2003. Gender and personality in media rich interfaces: Do birds of a feather flock together? In *Proceedings of the Second Annual Workshop on HCI Research in MIS*. Seattle: University of Washington, 12–13, 192.

Higie, R.A., and Feick, L.F. 1989. Enduring involvement: Conceptual and measurement issues. *Advances in Consumer Research* 16, 690–696.

Hoffman, D.L., and Novak, T.P. 1996a. *A New Marketing Paradigm for Electronic Commerce. Project 2000.* Nashville, TN: Vanderbilt University, Owen Graduate School of Management.

———. 1996b. Marketing in hypermedia computer-mediated environments: Conceptual foundations. *Journal of Marketing* 60 (July), 50–68.

Holbrook, M.B., and Hirschman, E.C. 1982. The experiential aspects of consumer behavior: Consumer fantasies, feelings, and fun. *Journal of Consumer Research* 9 (September), 132–140.

Holt, D.B. 1995. How consumers consume: A typology of consumption practices. *Journal of Consumer Research* 22 (June), 1–16

Hopkinson, G.C., and Pujari, D. 1999. A factor analytic study of the sources of meaning in hedonic consumption. *European Journal of Marketing* 33, 3–4, 273–289.

Houston, M.J., and Rothschild, M.L. 1978. Conceptual and methodological perspectives in involvement. In S. Jain (ed.), *Research Frontiers in Marketing: Dialogues and Directions*. Chicago: American Marketing Association, 184–187.

Howard, J., and Sheth, J. 1969. *The Theory of Buyer Behavior*. New York: Wiley.

Huang, M.H. 2003. Designing Web site attributes to induce experiential encounters. *Computers in Human Behavior* 19, 4, 425–442.

Huberman, B.A., Pirolli, P.L.T., Pitkow, J.E., and Lukose, R.M. 1998. Strong regularities in World Wide Web surfing. *Science* 280, 95–97.

Isen, A.M., and Baron, R.A. 1991. Positive affect as a factor in organizational behavior. In B.M. Staw and L.L. Cummings (eds.), *Research in Organizational Behavior*. Greenwich: JAI Press, 1–54.

Johnson, E.J., Bellman, S., and Lohse, G.L. 2003. Cognitive lock-in and the power law of practice. *Journal of Marketing* 67 (April), 62–75.

Katz, J. 1987. Playing at innovation in the computer revolution. In M. Frese, E. Ulich, and W. Dzida (eds.), *Psychological Issues of Human Computer Interaction in the Work Place*. Amsterdam: North-Holland, 97–112.

Konradt, U., and Sulz, K. 2001. The experience of flow in interacting with a hypermedia learning environment. *Journal of Educational Multimedia and Hypermedia* 10, 1, 69–84.

Koufaris, M. 2002. Applying the technology acceptance model and flow theory to online consumer behavior. *Information Systems Research* 13, 2, 205–223.

Koufaris, M., Kambil, A., and LaBarbera, P.A. 2001–2. Consumer behavior in Web-based commerce: An empirical study. *International Journal of Electronic Commerce* 6, 2, 115–138.

Kraut, R., Lundmark, V., Patterson, M., Kiesler, S., Mukopadhyay, T., and Scherlis, W. 1998. Social impact of the Internet: What does it mean?" *Communications of the ACM* 41, 12, 21–22.

Lewis, W. 1997. Flow in computer-mediated environments: Strategies for electronic commerce on the World Wide Web. In *Proceedings of the Third Americas Conference on Information Systems*. India-

napolis: ACIS. http://aisel.isworld.org/password.asp?Vpath=AMCIS/1997&HTMLpath=
Publications/AMCIS/1997/lewis.htm.

Lutz, R.J., and Guiry, M. 1994. Intense consumption experiences: Peaks, performances, and flows.
Paper presented at the Winter Marketing Educators' Conference, St. Petersburg, Florida, February.

Malone, T.W. 1981. Toward a theory of intrinsically motivating instructions. *Cognitive Science* 4, 333–
369.

Malone, T., and Lepper, M.R. 1987. Making learning fun. In R. Snow and M. Farr. (eds.), *Aptitude,
Learning and Instruction: Cognative and Affective Process Analyses*. Hillsdale, NJ: Lawrence Erlbaum
Associates, 223–253.

Marakas, G.M., Yi, M.Y., and Johnson, R.D. 1998. The multilevel and multifaceted character of computer self-efficacy: Toward clarification of the construct and an integrative framework for research.
Information Systems Research 9, 2, 126–163.

Massimini, F., and Carli, M. 1988. The systematic assessment of flow in daily experience. In M.
Csikszentmihalyi and I. Csikszentmihalyi (eds.), *Optimal Experience: Psychological Studies of Flow
in Consciousness*. New York: Cambridge University Press, 288–306.

Mehrabian, A., and Russel, J. 1974. *An Approach to Environmental Psychology*. Cambridge, MA: MIT
Press.

Miller, S. 1973. Ends, means, and galumphing: Some leitmotifs of play. *American Anthropologist* 75,
87–98.

Mittal, B. 1994. Public assessment of TV advertising: Faint praise and harsh criticism. *Journal of
Advertising Research* 34, 1, 35–53.

Moe, W.W. 2003. Buying, searching, or browsing: Differentiating between online shoppers using in-
store navigational clickstream. *Journal of Consumer Psychology* 13, 1–2, 29–39.

Moon, J.-W., and Kim, Y.-G. 2001. Extending the TAM for a World-Wide-Web context. *Information
and Management* 38, 4, 217–230.

Nel, D., van Niekerk, R., Berthon, J.P., and Davies, T. 1999. Going with the flow: Web sites and
customer involvement. *Internet Research: Electronic Networking Applications and Policy* 9, 2,
109–116.

Novak T.P., Hoffman, D.L., and Yung, Y. 2000. Measuring the customer experience in online environments: A structural modeling approach. *Marketing Science* 19, 1, 22–42.

Pace, S. 2004. A grounded theory of the flow experiences of Web users. *International Journal of Human-
Computer Studies* 60, 3, 327–363.

Palmer, J.W. 2002. Web site usability, design, and performance metrics. *Information Systems Research*
13, 2, 151–167.

Park, C.W., and Young, S.M. 1986. Consumer response to television commercials: The impact of involvement and background music on brand attitude formation. *Journal of Marketing Research* 22
(February), 11–24.

Pedersen, P.E., and Nysveen, H. 2003. Search mode and purchase intention in online shopping behavior. Working Paper, Agder University College and Norwegian School of Economics and Business
Administration.

Petty, R.E., Cacioppo, J.T., and Goldman, R. 1981. Personal involvement as a determinant of argument-
based prescription. *Journal of Personality and Social Psychology* 37, 1915–1926.

Petty, R.E., Cacioppo, J.T., and Schumann, D. 1983. Central and peripheral routes to advertising effectiveness: The moderating role of involvement. *Journal of Consumer Research* 10 (September), 135–146.

Privette, G., and Bundrick, C.M. 1987. Measurement of experience: Construct and content validity of
the experience questionnaire. *Perceptual and Motor Skills* 65, 315–332.

Raman, N.V., and Leckenby, J.D. 1998. Factors affecting consumers' "webad" visits. *European Journal of Marketing* 32, 7/8, 737–748.

Rayport, J.F., and Jaworski, B.J. 2000. *e-Commerce*. New York: McGraw-Hill.

Richins, M.L, Bloch, P.H., and McQuarrie, E. 1992. How enduring and situational involvement com-
bine to create involvement responses. *Journal of Consumer Psychology* 1, 2, 143–153.

Rothschild, M.L. 1984. Perspectives on involvement: Current problems and future directions. *Advances in Consumer Research* 11, 216–217.

Sánchez-Franco, M.J., and Rodríguez, J. 2004. Personal factors affecting users' Web session lengths. *Internet Research: Electronic Networking Applications and Policy* 14, 1, 62–80.

Sánchez-Franco, J.M., and F.J. Rondan-Cataluña. 2004. Aceptación y uso de la Web por los usuarios dirigidos por un objetivo (Web acceptance and usage by task-oriented users.) In XVI Encuentro de Profesores Universitarios de Marketing. Alicante, Spain: 779–794.

Sandelands, L.E., and Buckner, G.C. 1989. Of art and work: Aesthetic experience and the psychology of work feelings. In L.L. Cummings and B.M. Staw (eds.), *Research in Organizational Behavior.* Greenwich, CT: JAI Press, 105–131.

Sheridan, T.B. 1992. Musings on telepresence and virtual presence. *Teleoperators and Virtual Environments* 1, 1, 120–126.

Sherman, E., and Mathur, A. 1997. Store environment and consumer purchase behavior: Mediating role of consumer emotions. *Psychology and Marketing* 14, 4, 361–378.

Singletary, L.A., Akbulut, A.Y., and Houston, A.L. 2002. Innovative uses of software after mandatory adoption. In R. Ramsower and J. Windsor (eds.), *Proceedings of the Eighth Americas Conference on Information Systems,* Dallas: ACIS, 1135–1138.

Skadberg, Y.X., and Kimmel, J.R. 2004. Visitors' flow experience while browsing a Web site: Its measurement, contributing factors and consequences. *Computers in Human Behavior* 20, 403–422.

Starbuck, W.J., and Webster, J. 1991. When is play productive? *Accounting, Management, and Information Technology* 1, 71–90.

Steenkamp, J.B., and Baumgartner, H. 1992. Development and cross-cultural validation of a short form of CSI as a measure of optimum stimulation level. *International Journal of Research in Marketing* 12, 97–104.

Steuer, J. 1992. Defining virtual reality: Dimensions determining telepresence. *Journal of Communication* 42, 4, 73–93.

Teo, T.S.H., Tan, M., and Buk, W.K. 1999. Intrinsic and extrinsic motivation in Internet usage. *Omega* 27, 25–37.

Trevino, L.K., and Webster, J. 1992. Flow in computer-mediated communication. *Communication Research* 19, 5, 539–573.

Vallerand, R.J. 1997. Toward a hierarchical model of intrinsic and extrinsic motivation. In M.P. Zanna (ed.), *Advances in Experimental Social Psychology* 29. San Diego: Academic Press, 271–360.

Van der Heijden, H., Verhagen, T., and Creemers, M. 2003. Understanding online purchase intentions: Contributions from technology and trust perspectives. *European Journal of Information Systems* 12, 41–48.

Venkatesh, V. 2000. Determinants of perceived ease of use: Integration control, intrinsic motivation, and emotion into the Technology Acceptance Model. *Information Systems Research* 11, 4, 342–365.

Venkatesh, V., and Davis, F.D. 2000. Theoretical extension of the technology acceptance model: Four longitudinal field studies. *Management Science* 46, 2, 186–204.

Venkatesh, V., and Speier, C. 1999. Computer technology training in the workplace: A longitudinal investigation of the effect of mood. *Organizational Behavior and Human Decision Processes* 79, 1–28.

Webster, J. 1989. Playfulness and computers at work. PhD diss., New York University.

Webster, J., and Ho, H. 1997. Audience engagement in multi-media presentations. *Data Base for the Advances in Information Systems* 29, 2, 63–77.

Webster, J., and Martocchio, J.J. 1992. Microcomputer playfulness: Development of a measure with workplace implications. *MIS Quarterly* 16, 2, 201–226.

Webster, J., and Martocchio, J.J. 1995. The differential effects of software training previews on training outcomes. *Journal of Management* 21, 757–787.

Webster, L., Trevino, K., and Ryan, L. 1993. The dimensionality and correlates of flow in human computer interactions. *Computers in Human Behavior* 9, 4, 411–426.

White, R.H. 1959. Motivation reconsidered: The concept of competence. *Psychological Review* 66, 297–333.

Yager, S.E., Kappelman, L.A., Maples, G.A., and Prybutok V. 1997. Microcomputer playfulness: Stable or dynamic trait? *Data Base for the Advances in Information Systems* 28, 2, 43–52.

Yi, M.Y., and Hwang, J. 2003. Predicting the use of Web-based information systems: Self-efficacy, enjoyment, learning goal orientation, and the technology acceptance model. *International Journal of Human-Computer Studies* 59, 431–449.

Zaichkowsky, J. 1986. Conceptualizing involvement. *Journal of Advertising* 15, 2, 4–14.

Zhang, P., Benbasat, I., Carey, J., Davis, F., Galletta, D., and Strong, D. 2001. Human-computer interaction research in the MIS discipline. *Communications of the Association for Information Systems* 9, 334–355.

CHAPTER 8

LEADING VIRTUAL TEAMS

Modalities of Leadership

LILLE SPRINGALL, SYLVIA MANCHEN-SPÖRRI, AND GUDELA GROTE

Abstract: Based on a broader, inductive study of twenty-nine managers leading thirty-five virtual teams in the Swiss Information Technology (IT) industry, the aim of this chapter is to explore how managers are currently leading virtual teams, what types of communication technologies they use in order to manage their teams, and what constitutes effective virtual team management. Findings suggest that each manager develops a signature "virtual leadership portfolio" comprised of idiosyncratic combinations of managerial practices and implicit theories of virtual leadership (ITVLs). Findings further show that managers can be categorized into one of four virtual leadership portfolios based on the number of ITVLs that they develop and that these virtual leadership portfolios may be related to managers' use of communication technology. Lastly, the study suggests that high virtuality teams led by managers with broad virtual leadership portfolios may have higher levels of performance than high virtuality teams led by managers with narrow portfolios.

Keywords: Virtual Teams, Leadership, Implicit Leadership Theories, Team Performance, Virtual Communication, e-Leadership

INTRODUCTION

Globalization, increasing competition, growing economic pressures, the introduction of the World Wide Web, and the explosion and widespread availability of new communication technologies continue to revolutionize the modern workplace. Organizations increasingly face the need to innovate continuously, to minimize costs, and to work across geographical, temporal, cultural, and organizational boundaries. In order to cope with the challenges of the new business environment, organizations are taking advantage of the World Wide Web and of new communication technologies and structuring work using virtual teams. In essence, as Lipnack and Stamps explain, virtual teams are simply groups of "people who interact through interdependent tasks guided by a common purpose . . . [and which] unlike conventional teams, work across space, time and organizational boundaries with links strengthened by webs of communication technologies" (1997, 7).

By leveraging the specific know-how and skills of workers located in different locations for a specific project or task at low cost, virtual teams help organizations to work across boundaries quickly, easily, and cheaply. Thus, virtual teams allow modern organizations to overcome many of the challenges of the new business environment. For this reason they are becoming increasingly popular as well as ubiquitous. Yet in spite of their obvious organizational advantages, virtual teams are not without significant potential pitfalls and challenges.

From a managerial perspective, leading a virtual team is not an easy proposition. Although a manager's core leadership task of influencing, motivating, and enabling others to contribute toward the effectiveness and success of the organization (House et al. 1999) remains the same in a virtual team as in a traditional, nonvirtual environment, the parameters that delineate the leadership task in a virtual team are completely different. Managers leading virtual teams cannot see their subordinates; they cannot drop by informally to build rapport, assess situations, gather valuable information, provide support and mentorship, or resolve conflicts. Moreover, because team members do not have the opportunity to engage in casual, frequent, face-to-face interaction, managers are faced with the challenge of planning, structuring, and even managing the team's communication and social interaction, as well as building team cohesion and trust and resolving interpersonal conflicts mostly via technologically mediated communication.

Furthermore, although communicating technologies have evolved at an explosive rate, human beings' natural form of interaction is face-to-face communication. This standard means that in addition to fulfilling normal leadership tasks, managers leading virtual teams face another challenge: learning to manage themselves and other human beings primarily through technologically mediated means.

Clearly, virtual team leadership is an interesting, current, and highly relevant issue. Yet from a scholarly standpoint, empirical research on virtual leadership lags behind the developments in the workplace to a significant extent and the literature is extremely scant. With a few exceptions (e.g., Hertel et al. 2004), the vast majority of literature on virtual leadership has tended to be nonempirical and descriptive or prescriptive in nature. As a result of the dearth of empirical research on virtual leadership thus far, very little is known about how real managers are actually leading virtual teams, how they are solving the communication challenges of leading a virtual team, or what makes a virtual team manager effective.

In order to begin to address these important gaps in the leadership literature, a two-year, inductive, exploratory study of virtual leadership was carried out in the Swiss information technology (IT) industry. This chapter describes and summarize key findings of the investigation, providing answers to the following research questions: (1) How do managers conceptualize virtual team leadership? (2) What managerial practices do managers currently leading virtual teams employ? (3) What is the relationship, if any, between managers' conceptualizations of virtual leadership, their managerial practices, and the communication channels and technologies they use? (4) What constitutes effective virtual leadership?

Following standard methodological guidelines for research in the social sciences (e.g.,

Creswell 1998), given the dearth of literature on virtual team leadership, an inductive approach was selected to address the research questions. In contrast to the more commonly used positivistic, deductive approach, in which existing theory is used to generate a series of testable hypotheses, which are then tested statistically using a given research sample, the objective of inductive research is to increase understanding about a research question that is not well understood. This research is done by gathering data, identifying patterns, and deriving a series of generalizations from those patterns. The analyses used in an inductive study are therefore interpretive, often qualitative (complemented in some cases with quantitative analysis), and geared toward the identification of patterns that the researchers can use to derive a series of generalizations. In order to address the core research questions in this chapter, an inductive interpretive approach was used; as explained in detail in the methods section, a few statistical analyses were executed to support the inductive exploration.

THEORETICAL BACKGROUND

Although the literature on virtual leadership to date is scant and mostly nonempirical, it nevertheless served as an important backdrop for this study. Similarly, the conventional, nonvirtual leadership literature provided important background information. In particular, matching our first two research questions geared toward understanding how managers think about virtual leadership and what managerial practices they use, we found implicit leadership theories and behavioral theories of leadership especially useful.

Implicit leadership theories (ILTs), which focus on how managers "see" and "think" about leadership, provided a good match for our first research question, while behavioral theories of leadership, which focus on managers' actual behaviors, matched the second research question very well. More recent leadership research on behavioral complexity leadership theory (BCLT) additionally helped frame and interpret some of the findings.

In addition to leadership research, research on technology-mediated communication also provided an important reference point for the investigation. In particular, media richness theory proved to be especially helpful for exploring the relationship between virtual leadership and use of communication technology.

After briefly reviewing the virtual leadership literature, this chapter provides short reviews of implicit theories, behavioral theories, and behavioral complexity theories of leadership. Lastly, media richness theory, which helped to structure the analyses, is also briefly described.

Virtual Leadership

Developed in the context of conventional teams, traditional research on leadership is largely built on the following assumptions: leadership is essentially a top-down influence process, a leader's core tasks are to influence and to control team members, and communication is mostly face to face. In the context of a virtual team, however, since team members have to work alone, away from the leader most of the time in a largely autonomous fashion, and since communication is mostly carried out using technology, the traditional top-down assumptions of leadership are called into question.

Furthermore, since virtual team managers cannot control and influence subordinates they cannot see and with whom they cannot spontaneously interact face to face as easily as in a conventional team, the team leader, at first blush, no longer seems to be as powerful and central a figure as in a traditional team. On the contrary, in a virtual team, where team members appear to enjoy a great deal of de facto autonomy and the team manager's role appears to be less salient, it is the team's dynamics and processes that appear to come to the foreground.

Reflecting this perceptual shift, the literature on virtual teams has tended to focus on team processes. For instance, in a recent review of the virtual team literature (Axtell et al. 2004), virtual team processes rather than leadership were the focus of the vast majority of studies on virtual teams.

Further reflecting the conceptual difficulty of understanding leadership and the leader's role(s) in a virtual context, existing research highlights some disagreement among researchers about how to conceptualize virtual leadership. On the one hand, some researchers argue that although virtual leadership is somewhat different from conventional leadership because managers have to influence subordinates virtually (e.g., Avolio and Kahai 2002; Cascio and Shurygailo 2002), in essence it is still very similar to conventional leadership in purpose, content, and style. According to this view, virtual leadership is different from conventional leadership only in how it is manifested. The implicit assumption underlying this view is that virtual leadership remains for the most part a top-down influence process centered on a manager controlling and influencing a team of subordinates.

On the other hand, other researchers (e.g., Zigurs 2002) argue that virtual leadership is significantly different from conventional leadership. These researchers claim that virtual leadership does not consist of a manager influencing and controlling a team of subordinates in the conventional sense, but rather is a dynamic, shared influence process residing in the interplay of team members and technology. According to this view, different team members adopt specific leadership behaviors at given times, and technology mediates or even replaces certain leadership tasks, such as facilitating participation.

While a general consensus concerning how to conceptualize virtual leadership does not yet exist, the aim of the vast majority of research studies on virtual leadership, whether purely descriptive (Avolio and Kahai 2002; Cascio 2000; Cascio and Shurygailo 2002; Duarte and Snyder 1999; Jarvenpaa and Tanriverdi 2002; Lipnack and Stamps 1997; Staples et al. 1998; Zaccaro and Baider 2002; Zigurs 2002), empirical (Kayworth and Leidner 2002), or theoretical (Bell and Kozlowski 2002), is to pinpoint prescriptions and strategies to help managers lead virtual teams effectively.

For example, managers are exhorted to lead virtual teams by focusing on building and maintaining team trust (Jarvenpaa and Tanriverdi 2002; Zaccaro and Baider 2002), structuring work processes (Cascio and Shurygailo 2002; Zigurs 2002), managing relationships (Avolio and Kahai 2002; Jarvenpaa and Tanriverdi 2002; Zaccaro and Baider 2002; Zigurs 2002), motivating and rewarding team members (Cascio and Shurygailo 2002; Jarvenpaa and Tanriverdi 2002; Zaccaro and Baider 2002; Zigurs 2002), and managing conflict (Zaccaro and Baider 2002). While affording important insights, the main limitations of much of this work are that the insights are for the most part not empirically based and that comprehensive theories of virtual leadership have not yet been developed.

Taking these limitations into account, a few researchers have started to carry out empirical, field-based studies of virtual team leadership (Hertel et al. 2003; Kayworth and Leidner 2002). For example, in one of the few real-life, empirical studies of leadership that have been carried out, Hertel et al. (2003) investigated how management practices influence motivational processes in virtual teams. They found that in effective virtual teams, the quality of goal-setting processes as well as task interdependence was higher than in less effective teams. This study also aimed to provide a greater understanding of virtual leadership.

Implicit Leadership Theories

The essence of the implicit leadership theories is that leadership is a cognitive phenomenon that resides in the minds of both leaders and their subordinates (Eden and Leviatan 1975; Schilling 2001). According to this view, both leaders and followers have preconceived implicit leadership theories, which are essentially cognitive schemas (i.e., mental models) comprised of the individual's expectations, preconceptions, and beliefs about leadership. Bass further describes ILTs as "cognitive frameworks" that are used by leaders and subordinates "during information processing to encode, process and recall specific events and behaviors" (1990, 376). Thus, by determining how leaders and subordinates process information, ILTs influence how leaders and subordinates interpret and make sense of events and behaviors.

Since the ILT approach focuses specifically on the cognitive side of leadership, it provided an ideal fit for our first research question, so this literature was explored for how managers "see" and "think" about virtual leadership. For the sake of simplicity, this paper refers to the managers' perceptions of virtual leadership as their implicit theories of virtual leadership (ITVL). Table 8.1 provides a list of all the ITVLs induced from the managers in this research study. A detailed explanation of the induction method is provided in the methods section.

Behavioral Theories of Leadership

Unlike the ILT approach with its emphasis on cognition, behavioral theories of leadership focus on leaders' behaviors (i.e., what leaders actually do in order to lead). The focus of many of these behavioral leadership theories (e.g., Bass 1985; Blake and Mouton 1964; Burns 1978; Mintzberg 1973; Tichy and Devanna 1986; Yukl 1989) is to identify and to categorize leaders' behaviors into a series of taxonomies that researchers use in order to investigate whether particular combinations of leaders' behaviors differentiate effective from ineffective leadership.

Among the numerous taxonomies of leadership behaviors that have been developed in the last three decades, one of the most highly regarded is Yukl's (1989) taxonomy of managerial practices that categorizes leadership behaviors into fifteen different categories. Developed on the basis of rigorous empirical research (Yukl 1987), Yukl's taxonomy (1989) has been shown to be highly reliable and accurate, and therefore it was selected in order to explore the behaviors used by the virtual team managers in this study, as we describe in detail in the research methods section (cf. Table 8.2).

While enjoying widespread acceptance, the behavioral approach to leadership has been criticized because it fails to take into account the interaction between leaders' behaviors and contextual variables, such as the nature of the task at hand or the teams' characteristics. Aiming to address this shortcoming, the contingency approach to leadership (e.g., Fiedler's theory [1964, 1967], least preferred coworker [LPC] Evans's path-goal theory [1970]; House and Mitchell 1974) and expectancy theory (Vroom 1964) assume that effective leadership is determined not only by a leader's behaviors but also by the fit between the leader and the situation.

In spite of the high face validity of contingency theories, they have been criticized in the past for the tendency to be far too simplistic, particularly because they do not consider that numerous leadership styles may be effective across a wide variety of situations. For instance, because the focus of most contingency theories is on leader-subordinate relations, they fail to take into account that a leader's behavior that is ineffective with subordinates may very well be effective with other stakeholders, such as peers, superiors, or clients.

Reacting to the shortcomings of contingency approaches to leadership, the more recent BCLT (Hooijberg 1996) argues that in order to be effective, leaders in the complex, modern workplace must possess a broad portfolio of leadership behaviors (a behavioral repertoire) and be able to identify when to enact a given behavior (behavioral differentiation). According to this theory of leadership, effective leaders are those who possess broad portfolios of leadership behaviors and who can juggle these behaviors across a complex variety of situations and relations with multiple stakeholders.

Several empirical studies have found support for behavioral complexity theory (Hooijberg 1996; Dennison et al. 1995; Hart and Quinn 1993, 1996). The main thrust of behavioral complexity theory is moreover supported by some empirical work on virtual teams. In a study of global virtual teams of students, Kayworth and Leidner (2002) found that effective team leaders are capable of dealing with paradox and contradiction by performing multiple leadership roles simultaneously.

Virtual Communication

The extensive literature on technologically mediated technology contains a wide range of theories examining various dimensions of technology-mediated communication, ranging from the ability of different technologies to transmit rich information (e.g., Daft and Lengel 1986) to the behavioral impacts of different communication technologies (e.g., Sproull and Kiesler 1986) and individuals' abilities to adapt to virtual communication (e.g., Carlson and Zmud 1999; Walther 2002).

Given the aims of our study, we found media richness theory (Daft and Lengel 1986) especially useful. Media richness theory proposes that communication technologies vary in their ability to transmit rich information and that, therefore, the suitability of communication media varies depending on the situation and the purpose for which they are used. According to the media richness literature (Daft et al. 1987), rich information, which includes nonverbal, social, and feedback cues, is far better than nonrich information at reducing ambiguity and uncertainty and at communicating shared meanings. For this reason, communication media that have the capability to transmit rich information (e.g., face-to-face meetings or videoconferencing) are considered to be more suitable for uncertain situations or ambiguous tasks than nonrich communication media.

Based on this literature, there could be a relationship between the managers' ITVLs and the media richness of the different types of communication channels they choose in order to communicate with their subordinates since their ITVLs could be related to their preferred communication technologies or channels.

This paper considered all means of communication that have the ability to transmit nonverbal, social, and feedback cues as high in media richness. According to this definition, face-to-face communication is high in media richness because it allows for a maximum of nonverbal information and social cues to be transmitted. Although not as highly media rich as face-to-face communication, teleconferencing and videoconferencing also have a relatively high degree of media richness since they also allow for the transmission of nonverbal information and social cues. Relative to face-to-face communication, teleconferencing, or videoconferencing, technologies that allow for a limited transmission of nonverbal and social cues (e.g., voice mail or e-mail) were considered to be low in media richness.

The introduction of the World Wide Web and of internal computer networks linking workers together within organizations has revolutionized methods of communicating and working. This study also distinguished between Web-based means of communication (i.e., communication means that are based on computer networks often linked to the World Wide Web and that did not exist before the concept of linking computers together into networks was introduced) and those that are not. Specifically, e-mail, intranet, and groupware were defined as Web-based media, while letters, telephone, voice mail, and fax were non-Web-based.

METHOD

Background

The research study described in this chapter was part of a broad, two-year-long, inductive study of communication and leadership in virtual teams in the Swiss IT industry. A detailed overview of the study appears in the unpublished final, internal report (in German) that was compiled at the end of the study (Manchen-Spörri et al. 2002). For an overview (in German) of selected key findings, please refer to Grote et al. (2004). This overview does not include the analyses linking managers' ITVLs with their choice of virtual communication, team attributes, and team performance but does include the findings of the bulk of the team data that are beyond the scope and aims of this chapter.

Design and Research Sample

In total, twenty-nine managers and the thirty-five virtual teams they led agreed to participate in the project. One manager led two teams and a second manager led five teams. These teams belonged to a total of fifteen organizations in the Swiss IT industry. Of these virtual teams, 51.6 percent developed software, 32.3 percent handled networking projects, and 16.1 percent provided computer consulting services. The teams varied in their degree of virtuality—that is, the extent to which they were distributed and the extent to which they relied on communication technologies in order to complete tasks. Forty percent of the teams were comprised of team members who were completely distributed across different countries, cities, or various work sites. Sixty percent of the teams were not completely distributed since some members within the teams worked at the same location. All the teams in the study, however, had to work virtually, using various combinations of communication technologies in order to communicate and to complete their work tasks.

Those teams whose members were completely distributed were categorized as high-virtuality teams, and teams whose members were not completely distributed were categorized as low-virtuality teams. In the case of the two managers who led multiple teams, it turned out that all those teams had the same level of virtuality; neither manager led both a high-virtuality and a low-virtuality team. For instance, the manager who led two teams had two high-virtuality teams.

Two out of the twenty-nine managers in the study were women. The ages were grouped as follows: 38 percent of the managers were between thirty and forty years old, 38 percent were between forty and fifty years old, and 20 percent were fifty or older. Half of the managers had completed a university-level degree and the other half had completed a technical degree. Two-thirds of the managers had a technical background (e.g., computer science, electronics, or physics) and the rest had a background in business or social science.

Considering the teams themselves, the average size of the teams (not including the managers) was 8.5 members. Ten percent of the team members were women. Thirty-six percent of the team members worked in teams with more than three technical specializations, 16 percent in teams with three, and 26 percent in teams with two specializations. At the time of data collection, the teams had been in existence between 2 and 240 months. On average, the teams had been in existence for 28.6 months.

Data

The data used to answer the core research questions of this paper consisted of semistructured interviews conducted with the twenty-nine managers and responses to a questionnaire administered to the team members. The semistructured interviews with the managers included general questions about the organization (e.g., questions about the organizational structure), the team, the managers' perceptions of virtual and nonvirtual teams, the leadership instruments and practices they used to solve problems, the problems they encountered, and their beliefs about leading virtual and nonvirtual teams, as well as any other ideas expressed by the managers that appeared to be relevant at the time of the interview. On average, the interviews lasted ninety minutes.

The team questionnaire included items on leadership, communication, team climate, and team members' perceptions of performance. The response rate within teams was 71.7 percent. In total, 134 team members completed the questionnaire. In alignment with the third research question, only the measure of the teams' perceptions of performance is included in this paper. For further analyses of the questionnaire data that are not included in this paper, please refer to Manchen-Spörri et al. (2002). Since several teams either dropped out of the study or failed to fill out the questionnaire, only twenty-four of the twenty-nine interviews carried out with the managers had enough matching data from the team questionnaire to be analyzable. The team data used in this chapter are drawn from this smaller subset of twenty-four teams.

Measures

The measure of the teams' perceptions of performance used to address the third research question of this study consisted of a one-item question ("in your opinion, what is your team's current level of performance compared with its maximum possible performance?") that asked the team members to assess their perceptions of team performance on a scale from 0 to 100 percent, where 100 percent corresponded to the team's best possible performance. Although at the onset of the project the intention was to collect actual team performance data, it proved impossible to collect these data since some managers refused to disclose the data while others did not collect systematic team performance data.

The degree of interrater agreement within the teams was checked using James,' Demaree, and Wolf's (1993) interrater reliability statistics (rwg) index. The rwg for these data was 0.3. Additionally, the level of within-team versus between-team agreement was compared by carrying out a standard analysis of variance (ANOVA) test where the dependent variable was our measure of performance and the independent variable the team ID. The ANOVA was significant ($F = 1.937$, $p < 0.01$). Additionally, the ICC computed as 0.1 for the data. Although the rwg for these data is quite low, the results of the ANOVA test in combination with the positive ICC led to the conclusion that there was at least more variance between teams than within teams to make aggregation at the team level defensible.

Data Analysis

As we explained in the introduction, given the exploratory nature of the study and the lack of empirical research on virtual leadership, an inductive approach was selected as the most appropriate method for the data analysis.

Coding of the Interview Data

The managers' statements about their beliefs about virtual leadership and the managerial practices they use were coded using an inductive and theoretical approach. Since in the interviews the managers described their beliefs and philosophies of virtual leadership as well as the actual, concrete, managerial practices they use to lead a virtual team, these two different dimensions of virtual leadership were categorized with the labels "implicit theories of virtual leadership" and "managerial practices," respectively.

In order to code the interviews, two of the researchers read the interviews and free-coded the statements that referred to the ITVLs. A list of six mutually exclusive ITVL codes (cf. Table 8.1) was developed and the interviews were coded once more. In order to code the managers' statements about managerial practices, Yukl's (1989) list of managerial practices was utilized. Three additional managerial practices (norm and value setting, sensing, and vision setting) that were detected in the interviews are not part of Yukl's original list. Those practices were added to the list of managerial practices (cf. Table 8.2).

In order to analyze the coded ITVL data, only the existence or nonexistence of a code was considered in each interview. In this way, a measure was obtained of whether each manager in the study had adopted each of the managerial practices and ITVL or not. This binary coding scheme was chosen because ITVLs are highly abstract constructs that are not easy to quantify, and it would have been easy to introduce biases using frequency counts (e.g., erroneously inferring that a given manager exhibits a stronger leadership style than another because he or she mentions their beliefs more often).

In order to code the managers' statements about the types of communication channels and technologies they use to lead their teams, a list was compiled of all the different types of channels and technologies they claimed to use in the interviews. This list included face-to-face communication in a group, one-on-one face-to-face communication, e-mail, telephone, fax, letter, groupware, videoconferencing, teleconferencing, and voice mail. The interviews were then coded by counting the number of times that each manager described the use of a given communication technology for a given purpose. If during the course of the interview a manager repeated using a given communication medium for a purpose or situation that had already been mentioned, this statement was not included in the frequency count. In this way, double-counting was avoided. In contrast to the binary coding scheme, used for the managers' statements about leadership, frequency counts were used for the statements about media types because, unlike the more abstract managerial practices and the highly abstract ITVLs, communication technology use is comparatively easier to understand and quantify. In this case, the biases introduced by frequency counts were assumed to be relatively small and to convey meaningful information. In order to assess the reliability of the coding scheme, a research assistant recoded four randomly selected interviews. Average reliability for the four recoded interviews was 80 percent.

Table 8.1

Descriptions of Implicit Theories of Virtual Leadership and Degree of Adoption by Managers

Leadership styles	Degree of adoption by manager (percent)	Description of leadership style	Examples from the interviews
Directive leader	48	Directive leaders are managers with a top-down philosophy of leadership who believe in commanding subordinates rather than engaging in participative leadership.	"At some point you have to say, 'Sorry, this is the direction we're going' . . . So at some point you have to be a pretty strong leader." S.P., CEO, STM
Empowerer	79	Empowerers emphasize giving a great deal of autonomy and responsibility to subordinates. They expect subordinates to play a proactive role, participating actively in decision making, and are interested in furthering their subordinates' development.	"Put the right people according to their strength into an environment where they can really work and develop and do something on their own." H.A., CEO, NewNet
Team player	28	Team players think of themselves as being "one of the team" and tailor their leadership strategies to that conceptualization. They possess an extremely egalitarian philosophy of leadership and tend to shun the directive approach.	"Even if there is a hierarchy I don't quite see it like that. Either we work as a team or we all go under." S.R., manager, RCN
Parent	17	Parents see themselves as the team's symbolic father or mother. While they believe that they know best, rather than employing a completely directive style they also emphasize nurturing their subordinates, protecting them, and bonding with them.	"A manager's job includes at least half, how shall I say it, fatherly skills." W.W., manager, Technology Inc.
Intuitor	14	Intuitors are managers with a philosophy of leadership that emphasizes relying on instinct and intuition. In relating to subordinates or others, they emphasize doing what feels right rather than relying on intellectual rationalizations.	"[About leadership] It's intuitive." Z.P., manager, ISI
Role model	21	Role models are managers whose conceptualization of leadership centers on self-presentation and being a figurehead for the team.	"I am perhaps a role model in many ways . . . I find leading by example good." T.V., manager, Software Systems

Table 8.2

Descriptions of Managerial Practices and Degree of Adoption by Managers

Managerial practices[a]	Definition	Degree of adoption by managers (percent)
Planning and organizing	Determining long-term objectives and strategies, allocating resources according to priorities, determining how to use personnel and resources efficiently to accomplish a task or project, and determining how to improve coordination, productivity, and effectiveness	82.76
Problem solving	Identifying work-related problems, analyzing problems in a systematic but timely manner to determine causes and find solutions, and acting decisively to implement solutions and resolve crises	51.72
Clarifying	Assigning work, providing direction in how to do the work, and communicating a clear understanding of job responsibilities, task objectives, priorities, deadlines, and performance expectations	75.86
Informing	Disseminating relevant information about decisions, plans, and activities to people who need the information to do their work	65.51
Monitoring	Gathering information about work activities and external conditions affecting the work, checking on the progress and quality of the work, and evaluating the performance of individuals and the effectiveness of the organizational unit	79.31
Motivating	Using influence techniques that appeal to logic or emotion to generate enthusiasm for work, commitment to task objectives, and compliance with requests for cooperation, resources, or assistance; also setting an example of proper behavior	72.41
Consulting	Checking with people before making changes that affect them, encouraging participation in decision making, and allowing others to influence decisions	34.48
Recognizing	Providing praise and recognition for effective performance, significant achievements, and special contributions	6.89
Supporting	Acting friendly and considerate, being patient and helpful, and showing sympathy and support when someone is upset or anxious	65.51
Managing conflict and team-building	Facilitating the constructive resolution of conflict and encouraging cooperation, teamwork, and identification with the organizational unit	89.66
Networking	Socializing informally, developing contacts with people outside the immediate work unit who are a source of information and support, and maintaining contacts through periodic visits, telephone calls, correspondence, and attendance at meeting and social events	13.79
Delegating	Allowing subordinates to have substantial responsibility and discretion in carrying out tasks and other work activities and giving them the authority to make important decisions	51.72
Developing and mentoring	Providing coaching and career counseling and facilitating a subordinate's skill acquisition and career advancement	55.1
Rewarding	Providing tangible rewards such as a pay increase or promotion for effective performance and demonstrated competence by a subordinate	31.03
Sensing*	Using intuition or nonrational gut feelings to obtain information about a given situation	65.51
Vision setting*	Developing and disseminating a bigger picture to subordinates	41.38
Norm and value setting*	Developing and establishing norms and values	27.58

[a]Adapted from Yukl (1989).
*Additional managerial practices added to Yukl's (1989) original list are marked with an asterisk.

Table 8.3

Induction Table Relating Managers' Managerial Practices, Implicit Theories of Virtual Leadership (ITVLs), and Virtual Leadership Portfolios (VLPs)

Sum of managerial practices	Parent	Empowerer	Directive leader	Team player	Role model	Intuitor	Sum of ITVLs	VLP
9							0	Practitioner
10							0	Practitioner
5		X					1	Specialist
13		X					1	Specialist
9		X					1	Specialist
7		X					1	Specialist
12		X					1	Specialist
8		X					1	Specialist
8						X	1	Specialist
17		X	X				2	Dualist
12		X	X				2	Dualist
10		X	X				2	Dualist
10		X	X				2	Dualist
13		X		X			2	Dualist
11		X		X			2	Dualist
10		X			X		2	Dualist
9		X			X		2	Dualist
7		X				X	2	Dualist
5			X	X			2	Dualist
12			X	X			2	Dualist
7			X		X		2	Dualist
6		X	X			X	3	Diversifier
12	X	X	X		X		3	Diversifier
5	X	X	X				3	Diversifier
13	X	X	X	X			3	Diversifier
12	X	X	X	X			4	Diversifier
10	X	X		X	X		3	Diversifier
11	X	X	X			X	4	Diversifier
13	X	X	X	X	X		4	Diversifier

Data Analysis

In keeping with the inductive, exploratory approach and the small number of cases in the sample, patterns and relationships in the coded data were explored using standard qualitative techniques used in inductive data analysis (e.g., Creswell 1998; Miles and Huberman 1994). These analyses involved creating induction tables relating variables of interest from the manager interview data and the team data in order to identify meaningful patterns in the data (e.g., Table 8.3). Additionally, a series of supporting exploratory statistical analyses (chi-square tests and one-way ANOVAs) was executed, investigating the relationships between the managers' ITVLs, their managerial practices, use of communication technology, team performance, and various team attributes that could influence how managers led their teams (i.e., degree of team virtuality, the age of the team, the diversity of the team, and the size of the team).

In order to carry out chi-square tests, the continuous team attribute data was dichoto-

Table 8.4

Descriptive Statistics of Team Attributes and Performance Data ($N = 24$)

Team attributes	Mean	SD	1	2	3	4	5
Size (number of members) (1)	5.80	5.60		0.18	−0.01	−0.12	0.23
Average number of technical specializations per team member (2)	3.06	0.48			0.42*	−0.04	0.03
Team age (in months) (3)	29.50	22.64				−0.27	0.23
Percent of women (4)	16.29	27.06					0.11
Perceived team performance (5)	77.77	8.37					

*$p < 0.05$.

Table 8.5

Descriptive Statistics of Communication Technology Use

Communication media type	Descriptions of communication media	Minimum	Maximum	Mean	SD
Web-based medium media richness	Groupware	0	1.00	0.14	0.35
Web-based low media richness	Intranet, e-mail	1.00	7.00	3.55	1.92
Non-Web-based high media richness	Face-to-face one-on-one, face-to-face group, teleconferencing, videoconferencing	0	13.00	5.03	3.63
Non-Web-based medium media richness	Telephone, cell phone, voicemail	0	5.00	2.1	1.63
Non-Web-based low media richness	Letter, fax	0	2.00	0.17	0.47

Note: We found no communication media used that could be categorized in the Web-based, high media richness category.

mized by computing the mean for each team attribute (team diversity was operationalized using two variables: the percentage of women on the team and the average number of technical specializations in each team) and using the mean of each team attribute as a cutoff to dichotomize each variable into high and low. Table 8.4 provides descriptive statistics of the teams' attributes.

In order to explore a possible relationship between managers' ITVLs and their use of communication technology, the different types of communication technologies used by the managers were divided into six categories depending on the media richness levels of the technology (low, medium, high) and whether the technology was Web-based or not (Table 8.5). We did not identify any communication technologies that fitted into the Web-based, high media richness category.

RESULTS

Virtual Team Managers' ITVLs and Managerial Practices

Addressing the first two core research questions, as Tables 8.1 and 8.2 show, on average, all of the managers in the study appear to exhibit a wide variety of ITVLs and managerial practices. For instance, while 79 percent of the managers seem to have developed an empowering ITVL, at the same time almost half of the managers also seem to have developed a directive ITVL (cf. Table 8.1). This result means that a significant proportion of managers are simultaneously espousing both empowering and directive approaches to leadership. Although at first blush this contradiction may appear somewhat counterintuitive, a possible explanation for this finding is that although many managers leading virtual teams embrace empowerment to a certain extent, a large number of them may either simultaneously conceptualize leadership as a directive, top-down influence process or may feel the need to revert to a directive style in certain situations.

In relation to the managerial practices that the virtual team managers use, some managers appear to use more managerial practices than others, and, on average, some managerial practices appear far more popular than others. For instance, as Table 8.2 shows, in order of importance, the top five managerial practices used by over 70 percent of the managers are team building, planning and organizing, monitoring, clarifying, and motivating. In contrast, the least popular practices (used by less than 35 percent of the managers) are consulting, rewarding, norm setting, networking, and recognizing.

This finding suggests that virtual managers' choice of managerial practices may be somewhat inconsistent. For instance, in contradiction to the widely held, popular perception that virtual teams are highly empowered, autonomous teams, most of the managers in our study emphasized monitoring their subordinates. Furthermore, consulting with subordinates does not appear to be a widely used practice, and, somewhat surprisingly, only about half of the managers appear to delegate tasks to their subordinates.

The chi-square tests carried out to explore whether there were significant differences between the ITVLs of managers leading high-virtuality teams and those leading low-virtuality teams were all nonsignificant. Similarly, the analyses exploring whether there were significant differences between the managerial practices used by managers leading high-virtuality teams and those leading low-virtuality teams were also nonsignificant. None of the other team attributes were significantly related to the managers' ITVL or their managerial practices, and no meaningful patterns were detected qualitatively.

Virtual Leadership Portfolios

When the managers in the sample were further grouped on the basis of their ITVLs and managerial practices, qualitatively a clear pattern was detected showing that the managers could be categorized into one of four different virtual leadership portfolios (VLPs) based on the number of ITVLs they had developed (cf. Table 8.3). No clear patterns emerged with respect to the managerial practices used with the exception that managers

Table 8.6

Descriptive Statistics of the Amount of Managers' Communication by Virtual Leadership Portfolios ($N = 29$)

Virtual leadership portfolio	N	Mean	SD
Practitioner	2	7.50	3.54
Specialist	7	10.43	6.45
Dualist	12	11.58	5.37
Diversifier	8	13.38	5.29

who had developed a greater number of ITVLs also appear to use a few more managerial practices (this difference was not statistically significant, however). The labels given to these virtual leadership portfolios are as follows:

- *Practitioners:* Managers who tend to focus exclusively on managerial practices and who have not developed any ITVLs whatsoever.
- *Specialists:* Managers who employ a wide range of managerial practices and who develop only one ITVL.
- *Dualists:* Managers who employ a wide range of managerial practices and who have developed two ITVLs.
- *Diversifiers:* Managers who adopt a wide range of managerial practices and who have developed three or more ITVLs.

Virtual Leadership Portfolios and Communication Technologies

As Table 8.6 and Figure 8.1 show, when relating the communication technology data to the managers' VLPs, a pattern emerged suggesting that managers' VLPs may be related to their communication technology use. Specifically, it appears that managers with broader portfolios tend to communicate more and tend to use a somewhat greater number of communication technologies of different types than managers with narrow portfolios.

In contrast, managers with narrow VLPs (practitioners) use fewer communication technologies of different types. A possible explanation for this pattern is that managers with broad leadership portfolios may be better communicators and more adept at skill-fully handling a wide variety of different communication technologies than managers with narrower portfolios. Although the pattern in the data was fairly clear, it was not statistically significant. Therefore, it would be necessary to test it empirically using a larger research sample in order to establish its validity and generalizability. Nevertheless, given the clarity of the pattern observed, proposition 1 is formulated as follows:

Proposition 1: The breadth of managers' virtual leadership portfolios will be correlated with the degree to which they communicate with their subordinates and with the number of communication technologies of different types that they employ to manage the team.

Figure 8.1   **Managers' Virtual Leadership Styles and Communication Media Use by Type**

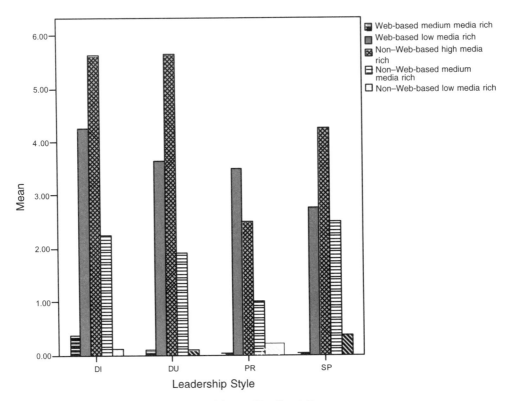

DI = Diversifier, DU = Dualist, PR = Practitioner, SP = Specialist.

Virtual Leadership Portfolios and Team Attributes

In exploring the relationship between managers' virtual leadership portfolios and the characteristics of their teams (i.e., team diversity, age, size, degree of virtuality) qualitatively, no patterns were observed. The chi-square tests computed were also not statistically significant. Further relating the managers' VLPs to the teams' attributes and the teams' perceptions of performance, all the statistical tests were nonsignificant with the exception of an ANOVA test relating degree of virtuality to perceived team performance using the nondichotomized perceived team performance variable as the dependent variable. This analysis showed that high-virtuality teams' perceptions of team performance are significantly higher than those of low-virtuality teams (cf. Table 8.7).

Further exploring the relationship between degree of team virtuality, managers' VLPs, and perceived performance qualitatively, a pattern in the data was detected although this pattern was not statistically significant. Although the pattern is somewhat weak, the patterns in the data suggest that high-virtuality teams perceived as high-performing are more likely to be led by managers with broad VLPs (i.e., dualists or diversifiers). Spe-

Table 8.7

Results of One-Way Analysis of Variance for Teams' Perceptions of Performance by Degree of Virtuality

df	F	p
23	4.816	.039*

$p * > 0.05.$

Contrast coefficients

	Degree of virtuality	
Contrast	Low	High
1	1	−1

Contrast tests

		t	df	p
Perceived team performance	Assuming equal variances	−2.195	22	.039*
	Not assuming equal variances	−2.314	21.971	.030*

$p * > 0.05.$

cifically, in the high-virtuality condition, out of eight managers with broad leadership portfolios (four dualists and four diversifiers), six led teams perceived as high performers (all four of the diversifiers led teams perceived as high performers) and only two dualists led teams perceived to be low performers. It is therefore proposed that:

Proposition 2: Managers with broad virtual leadership portfolios are more likely to lead high-virtuality, high-performing virtual teams than managers with narrow virtual leadership portfolios.

DISCUSSION AND CONCLUSIONS

The research described in this chapter sought to (1) explore how managers who are actually leading virtual teams conceptualize virtual leadership (i.e., their ITVLs), (2) pinpoint the managerial practices that managers are currently using to lead virtual teams, (3) explore the relationship between managers' ITVLs and the communication technologies they use, and (4) explore the relationship between leadership and virtual team performance. In this section, we briefly discuss the findings of the study and provide some conclusions.

Informing the first two core research questions, this study supports the view held by some researchers that in practice virtual leadership in the workplace may be very similar to nonvirtual leadership in purpose and content. This conclusion is lent support by the findings that: (1) a large proportion of the managers in this study simultaneously embrace the empowerer and the directive leader ITVLs, (2) very few managers have adopted the team player ITVL, and (3) relatively few managers appear to delegate or to consult with their subordinates. Hence, these findings lead us to conclude that, like traditional managers, virtual managers still believe that a key dimension of their job is to control and to direct subordinates.

In relation to the third core research question, the patterns in the data suggest that the breadth of managers' virtual leadership portfolios may be related to the extent to which they communicate with their subordinates and to the number of communication technologies they use. This finding further implies that in order to be successful, virtual leaders must manage numerous communication technologies in synergy with different ITVLs and managerial practices in a way that does not lead to confusion, ambiguity, role conflict, or miscommunication.

Addressing the relationship between degree of team virtuality and performance, from a theoretical standpoint this study lends some support to Kayworth and Leidner's (2002) findings and to BCLT (Hooijberg 1996). Specifically, our findings suggest that managers with broader (i.e., more complex) VLPs tend to lead teams with higher perceptions of performance than those led by managers with narrow portfolios (at least in the high-virtuality condition). Nevertheless, in contrast to Kayworth and Leidner's findings and to BCLT, this study additionally suggests that virtual team managers' performance may be influenced by contextual variables (e.g., the degree of team virtuality).

REFERENCES

Avolio, B.J., and Kahai, S.S. 2002. Adding the "e" to e-leadership: How it may impact your leadership. *Organizational Dynamics* 31, 4, 325–338.

Axtell, C.M., Fleck, S.J., and Turner, N. 2004. Virtual teams: Collaborating at a distance. In I.T. Robertson and C.L. Cooper (eds.), *International Review of Industrial and Organizational Psychology*. San Francisco: Jossey Bass, 205–248.

Bass, B.M. 1985. Good, better, best. *Organizational Dynamics,* 13, 3, 26–40.

———. 1990. *Bass and Stogdill's Handbook of Leadership.* New York: Free Press.

Bell, B.S., and Kozlowski, S.W.J. 2002. A typology of virtual teams: Implications for effective leadership. *Group and Organization Management* 27, 1, 14–49.

Blake, R.R., Mouton, J.S. 1964. *The Managerial Grid.* Houston: Gulf Publishing.

Burns, J.M. 1978. *Leadership.* New York: Harper & Row.

Carlson, J.R., and Zmud, R.W. 1999. Channel explosion theory and the experiential nature of media richness perceptions. *Academy of Management Journal* 42, 2, 153–170.

Cascio, W.F. Managing a virtual workplace. *Academy of Management Executive,* 14, 3 (2002), 81–90.

Cascio, W.F., and Shurygailo, S. 2002. E-leadership and virtual teams. *Organizational Dynamics* 31, 4, 362–376.

Creswell, J.W. *Qualitative Inquiry and Research Design.* Thousand Oaks, CA: Sage, 1998.

Daft, R.L., and Lengel, R.H. 1986. Organizational information requirements, media richness and structural design. *Management Science* 32, 5, 554–571.

Daft, R.L., Lengel, R.H., and Trevino, L.K. 1987. Message equivocality, media selection, and manager performance: Implications for information systems. *MIS Quarterly* 11, 3, 355–366.

Dennison, D.R., Hooijberg, R., and Quinn, R.E. 1995. Paradox and performance: A theory of behavioral complexity in managerial leadership. *Organization Science* 6, 5, 524–540.

Duarte, D.L., and Snyder, N.T. 1999. *Mastering Virtual Teams.* San Francisco: Jossey-Bass.

Eden, D., and Leviatan, U. 1975. Implicit leadership theory as a determinant of the factor structure underlying supervisory behavior scales. *Journal of Applied Psychology* 60, 736–741.

Evans, M.G. 1970. The effect of supervisory behavior on the path-goal relationship. *Organizational Behavior and Human Performance* 5, 277–298.

Fiedler, F.E. 1964. A contingency model of leadership effectiveness. In L. Berkowitz (ed.), *Advances in Experimental Social Psychology,* vol. 1. Orlando, FL: Academic Press.

———. 1967. *A Theory of Leadership Effectiveness.* New York: McGraw-Hill.

Grote, G., Manchen-Spörri, S., and Springall, L. 2004. Telemanagement: Notwendigkeit für ein komplexes Verhaltensrepertoire. *Arbeit* 1, 48–60.

Hart, S.L., and Quinn, R.E. 1993. Roles executives play: CEOs, behavioral complexity, and firm performance. *Human Relations* 46, 5, 543–574.

Hertel, G., Konradt, U., and Orlikowski, B. 2004. Managing distance by interdependence: Goal setting, task interdependence and team-based rewards in virtual teams. *European Journal of Work and Organizational Psychology* 13, 1, 1–28.

Hooijberg, R. 1996. A multidimensional approach toward leadership: An extension of the concept of behavioral complexity. *Human Relations* 49, 7, 917–946.

Hooijberg, R., Hunt, J.G, and Dodge, G.E. 1997. Leadership complexity and development of the leaderplex model. *Journal of Management* 23, 3, 375–408.

House, R.J., and Mitchell, T.R. 1974. Path-goal theory of leadership. *Journal of Contemporary Business* 3, 81–97.

House, R.J., Hanges, P.J., Ruiz-Quintanilla, S.A., Dorfman, P.W., Javidan, J., Dickson, M.W., Gupta, et al. 1999. Cultural influences on leadership and organizations: Project GLOBE. In W.H. Mobley, M.J. Gessner, and V. Arnold (eds.), *Advances in Global Leadership.* Greenwich, CT: JAI Press, 171–233.

James, L.R., Demaree, R.G., and Wolf, G. 1993. r-sub(wg): An assessment of within-group interrater agreement. *Journal of Applied Psychology* 78, 306–309.

Jarvenpaa, S.L., and Tanriverdi, H. 2002. Leading virtual knowledge networks. *Organizational Dynamics* 31, 4, 403–412.

Kayworth, T.R., and Leidner, D.E. 2002. Leadership effectiveness in global virtual teams. *Journal of Management Information Systems* 18, 3, 7–40.

Lipnack, J., and Stamps, J. 1997. *Virtual Teams: Reaching Across Space, Time, and Organizations with Technology.* New York: Wiley.

Manchen-Spörri, S., Springall, L., and Grote, G. 2002. Führung und Kommunikation in virtuellen Teams der IT-branche. Abschlussbericht-Projekt Telemanagement. Institut für Arbeitspsychologie, Eidgenössische Technische Hochschule Zürich.

Miles, M.B., and Huberman, A.M. 1994. *Qualitative Data Analysis.* Thousand Oaks, CA: Sage.

Mintzberg, H. 1973. *The Nature of Managerial Work.* New York: Harper.

Schilling, J. 2001. *Wovon sprechen Führungskräfte, wenn sie über Führung sprechen? Eine Analyse subjektiver Führungstheorien.* Hamburg: Kovac.

Sproull, L., and Kiesler, S. 1986. Reducing social-context cues: Electronic mail in organizational communication. *Management Science* 32, 11, 1492–1512.

Staples, S.D., Hulland, J.S., and Higgins, C.A. 1998. A self-efficacy theory explanation for the management of remote workers in virtual organizations. *Journal of Computer Mediated Communication* 3, 4, 1–22.

Tichy, N., and Devanna, M. 1986. *Transformational Leadership.* New York: Wiley.

Vroom, V.H. 1964. *Work and Motivation.* New York: McGraw-Hill.

Walther, J.B. 2002. Time effects in computer-mediated groups: Past, present, and future. In S. Kiesler (ed.), *Distributed Work.* Cambridge, MA: MIT Press, 235–259.

Yukl, G. 1987. Development of a new measure of managerial behavior: Preliminary report on validation of the MPS. Paper presented at Eastern Academy of Management, Boston.

———. 1989. *Leadership in organizations.* Englewood Cliffs, NJ: Prentice-Hall.

———. 1999. An evaluative essay on current conceptions of effective leadership. *European Journal of Work and Organizational Psychology* 8, 33–48.

Zaccaro, S.J., and Bader, P. 2002. E-leadership and the challenges of leading E-teams. *Organizational Dynamics* 31, 4, 377–387.

Zaleznik, A. 1977. Managers and leaders: Are they different? *Harvard Business Review* 55, 5, 67–80.

Zigurs, I. 2002. Leadership in virtual teams: Oxymoron or opportunity? *Organizational Dynamics* 31, 4, 339–351.

CHAPTER 9

CONVERGENCE IN VIRTUAL TEAMS

CHRISTEL G. RUTTE

Abstract: Virtual teams are groups of geographically and/or organizationally dispersed coworkers who collaborate primarily through some combination of communication and information technologies. The extant literature shows that virtual teams are more effective on divergent tasks than face-to-face teams but less effective on convergent tasks. The aim of this chapter is to generate a series of theoretical propositions that explain why virtual teams are less effective at convergent tasks than face-to-face ones and to suggest interventions to support virtual teams.

Keywords: Virtual Teams, Communication, Trust, Status

INTRODUCTION

Teamwork is a widespread and popular phenomenon in organizations worldwide. Examples of organizational teams are management teams, production teams, sales teams, research and development teams, self-managing teams, and project teams. The general definition of an organizational team is "a group of individuals who see themselves and are seen by others as a social entity, who are interdependent because of tasks they perform as members of a group, who are embedded in one or more larger social systems, and who perform tasks that affect others" (Guzzo and Dickson 1996, 308–309). Teams can be set up as temporary or permanent structures.

Virtual teams are groups of geographically and/or organizationally dispersed coworkers who collaborate using telecommunications and information technologies to accomplish an organizational task. Virtual teams rarely, if ever, meet in a face-to-face setting (Townsend et al. 1998; Beyerlein et al. 2001). Forecasts are that virtual teams will become the dominant organizational form of the twenty-first century (Windsor 2001).

Although few pure virtual team forms exist today, aspects of virtuality occur in many teams and organizations. According to DeSanctis and Monge (1999), three dimensions of virtuality can be distinguished: (1) the proportion of time that team members work virtually compared to face to face, (2) the proportion of team members at each location, and (3) the proportion of time that team members spend working on their virtual team task compared to other duties. The more time that team members work together virtually as compared to face to face, the more virtual team members are spread over different locations, and the more time that team members work on virtual tasks, the more virtual the nature of work is.

The increase in virtual work forms is facilitated by the information revolution. Internet and intranet, desktop videoconferencing systems, and collaborative software systems allow team members to collaborate without meeting face to face. However, such technological advances are not the only reason that organizations move from traditional teams to virtual teams. Townsend et al. (1998) mention five trends that push organizations from face-to-face teams to virtual teams.

The first trend is the increasing prevalence of flattened organization structures. Teams are made responsible for their own way of working and performance and no longer operate under close supervision. If teams are largely self-managing, it is increasingly possible for organizations to operate in a structurally and geographically distributed way. The second trend is the increase in interorganizational cooperation. Information and communication technologies help strategic partners in such collaboration to work effectively and efficiently together as if they were one organization, without having to move the partners to one location. As a result of this trend, groups of firms cooperate in a structurally and geographically distributed way. A third trend is changes in workers' expectations about teleworking. The levels of education and technological sophistication of employees have increased in past decades and nowadays much of the work is office work. Work can also be done at home or at an office location closer to home. Increasing numbers of employees expect their organizations to allow them to telework. A fourth trend is the shift from production to service and knowledge work. Service processes are often less permanent in structure than production processes and do not require a fixed location. Service firms can be more flexible in the composition of the service teams and business units. Knowledge activities like research and development are also more dynamic in nature because they are often organized as temporary projects with teams differing in composition depending on the content of the project. Flexibility in team composition is a great advantage of virtual teams. Experts can be part of the team no matter where they are physically located. A final relevant trend is business globalization. Due to fierce competition, many organizations have relocated parts of their business processes to countries where salaries are lower or new consumer markets are opened. The result is that geographically distributed subunits within one organization have to collaborate.

As a result of these five trends and enabled by information and communication technologies, organizations thus move from traditional face-to-face teams to virtual teams. For organizations, working virtually has several advantages: flexibility in team composition, access to global markets, increased productivity and profit, improved service, and cost reductions (Cascio 1999). All these advantages, however, presuppose that virtual teams perform at least as well in their tasks as face-to-face teams.

PERFORMANCE OF VIRTUAL TEAMS

Whether virtual teams perform as well as face-to-face teams is dependent on the type of task. A distinction can be made between divergent and convergent tasks (McGrath 1984).

Figure 9.1   **Proposed Determinants of Virtual Team Performance**

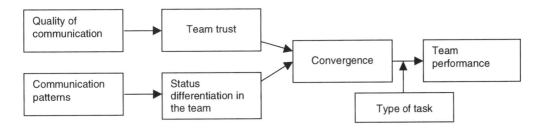

On divergent tasks, teams perform well if the team members come up with many different contributions. Examples of divergent tasks are brainstorming tasks, where the goal is to generate as many ideas or plans as possible. The more ideas or plans the team members generate, the better the performance. On convergent tasks, team members perform well if they are able to reach closure. Team members have to come to an agreement on which of all the different ideas or plans is the best and what it will take to make that idea or plan work. Solving problems, deciding issues, or resolving conflicts are examples of convergent tasks.

A consistent finding in the empirical literature is that groups are more effective in divergent tasks when communicating electronically rather than face to face. Convergent tasks are better done face to face than electronically (Barefoot and Strickland 1982; Gallupe et al. 1992; Gallupe et al. 1988; Hiltz et al. 1986; Valacich and Schwenk 1995). Many tasks of virtual teams have both divergent and convergent elements. Based on the empirical literature, it may thus be expected that virtual teams will be more effective on the divergent elements of their tasks than face-to-face teams but less effective on the convergent elements.

The remainder of this chapter proposes a series of theoretical propositions that explain why virtual teams are less effective at convergent tasks than face-to-face ones and suggest interventions to support virtual teams on convergent tasks. Two main reasons are proposed as to why virtual teams are less effective at convergent tasks. The first reason lies in the quality of the communication between virtual team members. The second reason lies in the patterns of communication between team members. The proposed theoretical model is schematically represented in Figure 9.1.

The figure shows that quality of communication is expected to be related to the emergence of trust in the team, and trust, in turn, to convergence. Here, convergence is used in the sense of "coming to closure as a team." The figure also shows that patterns of communication are expected to be related to the emergence of status differentiation in the team, and status differentiation, in turn, to convergence. Finally, the figure shows that convergence is expected to be related to team performance, depending on the type of task.

Quality of Communication and Trust

Trust is believed to be based on shared norms, repeated interactions, shared experiences, and shared anticipation of future interactions (Mayer et al. 1995). Face-to-face meetings are believed to be indispensable to build trust (Handy 1995). In virtual teams there is typically limited, if any, face-to-face interaction. Therefore, according to classical trust theory, it will be very difficult, if not impossible, to build trust in virtual teams. Jarvenpaa et al. (1998) and Jarvenpaa and Leidner (1999) conducted exploratory studies about trust in global virtual teams. These researchers analyzed and described the communication processes of several global virtual teams in detail. Their analyses suggest that building trust is not impossible in virtual teams (see also Walther 1996). In particular, Jarvenpaa and her associates suggest that in order to build up and maintain trust, teams should begin with an extensive social dialogue, teams should show great enthusiasm through the entire project, and team members should react to each other's contributions predictably and on time. All in all, trust appears to be related to the quality of communication between virtual team members. In this view, quality of communication depends on the content (social), tone (enthusiastic), and timeliness of the information exchanged between team members.

According to social presence theory (Chidambaram 1996; Short et al. 1976), members of virtual teams tend to have a reduced feeling that others are truly present in the interaction. This impression will generally lead to a lesser quality of communication in virtual teams than in face-to-face teams. Virtual team members are, therefore, less likely to engage in social dialogues, to show enthusiasm, and to react to each other's contributions on time and predictably; therefore, chances increase that there will be little trust among team members.

> **Proposition 1:** The more virtual team members engage in social dialogue, the more enthusiasm team members will show, and the timelier and more predictable communication is, the higher the level of trust will be among team members.

Note that this proposition does not state that communication should be limited to a social focus. A task focus in the communication is also important for the development and functioning of virtual teams (Hart and McLeod 2003).

Trust and Convergence

When there is lack of trust, team members will not believe that others will stick to agreements and act beneficially for the team (Cummings and Bromiley 1996; Deutsch 1958; Mayer et al. 1995). Lack of trust is therefore likely to make convergence in virtual teams more difficult (Potter and Balthazard 2002). If team members who have to solve problems, decide on issues, or resolve conflicts do not trust each other, they will doubt each other's efforts and intentions to reach a good decision or arrive at a good solution for the problem or conflict. They may also doubt each other's honesty in conflict negotiations and may believe that other team members will take advantage, given the opportunity (Cummings and Bromiley 1996). If, on the other hand, trust is present, convergence may be facilitated considerably.

Proposition 2: Trust has a positive effect on convergence in virtual teams.

Patterns of Communication and Status Differentiation

The second reason for less effective convergence in virtual teams is proposed to lie in the patterns of communication between team members. The primary interaction of virtual teams is through some combination of electronic communication systems (Cascio 2000), which influences the patterns of communication in virtual teams. Team members can send messages to each other undisturbed by others. Moreover, they can communicate all at the same time using these systems, or they can communicate at different times and fellow team members can read the messages at their convenience. As a result, electronic media may overload team members with messages and information, and individuals are less likely to attend fully to all communications (Miranda and Saunders 2004).

Electronic communication differs considerably from face-to-face communication. When communicating face to face, team members cannot send messages to each other undisturbed. In face-to-face teams, members have to wait their turn, giving some group members the chance to dominate over others. According to Weisband et al. (1995), the fact that every member in a virtual team can send messages undisturbed by others in electronic communication gives more equal influence opportunities to all team members (see also France et al. 2001). As a result, a status or influence structure is less likely to evolve in virtual teams. This effect is likely to be reinforced by the fact that electronic communication technologies attenuate the status cues that are available in face-to-face conversation (Kiesler et al. 1984; Short et al. 1976). A typical electronic message, for example, identifies senders and receivers by surname and address but not by job titles, social importance, organizational hierarchy, departmental affiliation, race, age, appearance, first name, or gender. In addition, it lacks a situational definition and reminders of the social setting. Several empirical studies indeed demonstrated that participation and influence are more equally distributed in virtual than in face-to-face teams (Dubrovsky et al. 1991; McGuire et al. 1987; Siegel et al. 1986). This phenomenon is also known as the "status equalization effect" (Dubrovsky et al. 1991). All in all, status or influence structure appears to originate in the communication patterns among team members.

Proposition 3: The less differentiated the patterns of communication between the virtual team members are, the less differentiated the status or influence structure of the team will be.

Status Differentiation and Convergence

A status or influence structure is an important regulating force in convergent tasks. Teams can be more effective when they accurately identify their more expert members, give them an appropriate status position, and allow them to influence the team process (Bunderson 2003). According to expectation states theory (Berger et al. 1972; Berger et al. 1977; Ridgeway 1984), once group members perceive status differences, they adjust their targets, the tone and content of their communications, and their social behavior to fit the situation. Members with high status in face-to-face teams talk more, have more control over the agenda, and have more influence than low-status members have. Team members with low status talk less and have less influence. This status structure reduces overload of communications in the team and makes it easier to weigh the relative importance of contributions. These behaviors lead to team efficiency and satisfaction (Berger et al. 1977).

In divergent tasks, lack of status differences may be helpful for team effectiveness because it increases the number of contributions (Silver et al. 1994). Since in virtual teams, team members will be less aware of social differences in the team, it is easier for low-status members to contribute because they will feel less psychologically inhibited by high-status members. Thus, low- and high-status members will contribute more equally, and this influx will increase the total number of contributions (Kiesler et al. 1984; Short et al. 1976). In convergent tasks, lack of status differences may be detrimental for effectiveness because of the increased number of contributions and the difficulties of weighing their relative importance. If all members contribute about equally and there is no status structure to facilitate determining which contributions are more worthwhile, converging might prove very difficult in a team (Montoya-Weiss et al. 2001; Poole et al. 1991).

> **Proposition 4:** Lack of status differentiation makes convergence in virtual teams more difficult.

Note that this proposition does not imply that status differentiation necessarily makes team members converge on high-quality decisions or solutions. This convergence will be the case only if higher status or influence is given to the more expert members in the team (Bunderson 2003).

Convergence and Team Performance

The issue of convergence in virtual teams is important because a relationship can be expected with team performance. The relationship between convergence and team performance will be moderated by type of task. If the task is of a convergent type (like solving problems, deciding issues, or resolving conflicts), not being able to converge within given time limits can be expected to be negatively related to team performance. Teams perform well on convergent tasks if they come to a high-quality decision or solution for the problem or conflict at hand within given time limits. If teams are unable to converge on time, a high-quality decision or solution is less likely. However, if the task is of a divergent type (like generating ideas or plans), not being able to converge within given time limits will not be detrimental for team performance. Teams perform well on divergent tasks to the extent that they are able to generate a high quantity of ideas or plans. Converging is not necessary to be effective on those tasks.

> **Proposition 5:** The relationship between convergence and team effectiveness is moderated by type of task.

SUGGESTIONS FOR INTERVENTIONS TO SUPPORT
VIRTUAL TEAMS

According to the extant literature, virtual teams are less effective on convergent tasks than face-to-face teams. Note that in this chapter it is assumed only that in virtual teams converging is more difficult than in face-to-face teams, not that it is impossible. It is important to understand why converging is more difficult because many tasks of virtual teams have convergent aspects, and it will often not be feasible to colocate team members every time they have to work on a convergent task, as media richness theory suggests. Media richness theory (Daft and Lengel 1986; Dennis and Kinney 1998; Hollingshead and McGrath 1995; Hollingshead et al. 1993) deals with the type of communication medium appropriate for different types of tasks. According to the theory, convergent-type tasks need rich communication media (e.g., face-to-face communication) and divergent-type tasks need less rich communication media (e.g., electronic communication). If groups want to be effective, media richness theory suggests that they fit the communication medium to the type of task at hand. Often, however, virtual teams will not have the choice to do divergent tasks electronically and convergent tasks face to face because team members may be dispersed geographically (DeSanctis and Poole 1994). Under those circumstances, it may be too costly and/or too time-consuming to meet face to face. It is, therefore, important to support virtual teams to be effective on convergent tasks without having to meet face to face.

By better understanding why converging is more difficult for virtual teams, interventions may be designed to support them and make them more effective.

If quality of communication is related to trust, and trust, in turn, to convergence, then it is worthwhile to try to improve the quality of communication between team members. According to social presence theory (Chidambaram 1996; Short et al. 1976), communication behaviors in virtual teams that are less positive than in face-to-face teams are caused by the circumstance that members of virtual teams tend to have a reduced feeling that others are truly present in the interaction. Increasing the social presence of team members may therefore increase the quality of the communication. Social presence could be increased, for example, by adding features to the information technology that personalize other team members. One example would be to add pictures, names, nicknames, or avatars to messages. Another example would be that information technology could inform team members, each time they log in, which team member worked at what time on which subtask and who is waiting for a reaction from the team member who has logged in. This communication would make the other group members and their actions more present.

If the patterns of communication are related to status differences, and status differences, in turn, to convergence, then it is also worthwhile to try to influence the patterns of communication between team members. According to expectation states theory (Berger et al. 1972; Berger et al. 1977; Ridgeway 1984), once group members perceive status differences, they adjust their communication behavior to fit the situation. Patterns of communication may, therefore, be influenced by bringing diffuse or specific status characteristics more to the fore, such that status differences are more readily perceived. Messages, for example, could automatically identify senders and receivers not only by name and address but also by status characteristics like job titles, seniority, or expertise. Messages could also include reminders of the social setting, for example, by adding special features to messages from group members with higher status to make these messages more readily identifiable as originating from a higher-status group member. Increasing the visibility of diffuse or specific status characteristics may influence communication patterns in virtual teams.

One could also try to influence patterns of communication more directly, by manipulating which communication channels are available for team members. According to Weisband et al. (1995), the fact that every member in a virtual team can send electronic messages undisturbed by others gives more equal influence opportunities to all team members. One way to influence the status structure would be to manipulate the information technology by restricting the available communication channels so messages cannot be sent to all team members undisturbed by others. One could, for example, force virtual teams—at certain points in time—to work synchronously and take turns while communicating. This synchronization would make communication more similar to face-to-face communication. One could also restrict the communication channels such that team members, for example, can send messages only to one central team member who summarizes them all, decides on their importance or has a team vote on that, and does everything necessary to help the team converge. Thus, a status or influence structure would be imposed on the team.

Designing technological interventions is a promising avenue along which one can try to support virtual teams. It is by no means the only avenue; another one is selecting, training, appraising, and rewarding team members for displaying attitudes and behaviors required for effective virtual teams. Virtual teams could be composed of team members who are able to express themselves and understand others in an environment with less social presence. Cascio (2000) argues that virtual team members should have excellent social skills (e.g., be able to communicate easily, show appreciation to others, apologize if they have not delivered what was promised, ask for feedback), communication skills (e.g., be able to exchange ideas without criticism, paraphrase unclear sentences, use emoticons, acknowledge receipt of messages, react on time), and collaboration skills (e.g., agree on activities, set interim deadlines, meet deadlines). Team members could be selected who already have these skills, or otherwise they could be trained. In addition, managers could appraise and reward these behaviors and skills. Thus, next to technological interventions, human resource management instruments like selection, training, appraising, and rewarding could be brought into action to support virtual teams.

CONCLUSION

Organizations are moving increasingly from traditional face-to-face teams to virtual teams. As a result of several trends (like flattened organizational structures, an increase in interorganizational cooperation, a shift from production to service and knowledge work, increased globalization of corporate activity, and changes in workers' expectation about teleworking), virtual teams are forecasted to become the dominant organizational form of the twenty-first century. Many economic advantages are attributed to virtual teams. However, these advantages can be attained only if virtual teams are at least as effective as traditional face-to-face teams. The extant literature suggests that virtual teams are more effective on divergent tasks than face-to-face teams but less effective on convergent tasks. Many organizations, however, have no choice. They introduce virtual teams because they are forced to carry out tasks in a distributed fashion. This necessity makes the question of whether virtual teams are better or worse than face-to-face teams less relevant than the question of how to increase the effectiveness of virtual teams. In the present chapter, a theoretical model has been proposed on which suggestions are based for interventions to increase the effectiveness of virtual teams on convergent tasks. By improving the quality of the communication (i.e., social content, enthusiastic tone, and predictability), the development of team trust, and thereby convergence, would be facilitated. By influencing the communication patterns, status differentiation can be emphasized in order to facilitate convergence. Finally, quality of communication and patterns of communication can be influenced not only by technological interventions but also by human resource management instruments.

REFERENCES

Barefoot, J., and Strickland, L.H. 1982. Conflict and dominance in television mediated interactions. *Human Relations* 35, 559–566.

Berger, J.M., Cohen, B.P., Zelditch, M.J. 1972. Status conceptions and social interaction. *American Sociological Review* 37, 241–255.

Berger, J.M., Fisek, M.H., Norman, R.Z., and Zelditch, M. 1977. *Status Characteristics and Social Interaction: An Expectation-States Approach,* New York: Elsevier.

Beyerlein, M.M., Johnson, D.A., and Beyerlein, S.T. (eds.). 2001. *Virtual Teams. Advances In Interdisciplinary Studies of Work Teams,* vol. 8. London: Elsevier Science/JAI Press.

Bunderson, J.S. 2003. Recognizing and utilizing expertise in work groups: A status characteristics perspective. *Administrative Science Quarterly* 48, 557–591.

Cascio, W.F. 1999. Virtual workplaces: Implications for organizational behavior. In C.L. Cooper, and D.M. Rousseau (eds.). *The Virtual Organization.* Trends in Organizational Behavior, vol. 6. New York: John Wiley, 1–14.

———. 2000. Managing a virtual workplace. *Academy of Management Executive* 14, 81–90.

Chidambaram, L. 1996. Relational development in computer-supported groups. *MIS Quarterly* 20, 143–165.

Cummings, L.L., and Bromiley, P. 1996. The organizational trust inventory (OTI): Development and validation. In R.M. Kramer, and T.R. Tyler (eds.), *Trust in Organizations: Frontiers of Theory and Research.* Thousand Oaks, CA: Sage, 302–330.

Daft, R., and Lengel, R. 1986. Organizational information requirements, media richness, and structural design. *Management Science* 32, 135–138.

Dennis, A.R., and Kinney, S.T. 1998. Testing media richness theory in the new media: The effects of cues, feedback, and task equivocality. *Information Systems Research* 9, 256–274.

DeSanctis, G.J., and Monge, P. 1999. Introduction to the special issue: Communication processes for virtual organizations. *Organization Science* 10, 693–703.

DeSanctis, G.J., and Poole, M.S. 1994. Capturing the complexity in advanced technology use: Adaptive stucturation theory. *Organization Science* 5, 121–147.

Deutsch, M. 1958. Trust and suspicion. *Journal of Conflict Resolution* 2, 265–279.

Dubrovsky, V.J., Kiesler, S., and Sethna, B.N. 1991. The equalization phenomenon: Status effects in computer-mediated and face-to-face decision-making groups. *Human-Computer Interaction* 6, 119–146.

France, E.F., Anderson, A., and Gardner, M. 2001. The impact of status and audio conferencing technology on business meetings. *International Journal of Human-Computer Studies* 54, 857–876.

Gallupe, R.B., Dennis, A.R., Cooper, W.H., Valacich, J.S., Bastianutti, L.M., Nunamaker, J.F. 1992. Electronic brainstorming and group size. *Academy of Management Journal* 35, 350–369.

Gallupe, R.B., DeSanctis, G., and Dickson, G.W. 1988. Computer-based support for group problem finding: An experimental investigation. *MIS Quarterly* 12, 277–298.

Guzzo, R.A., and Dickson, M.W. 1996. Teams in organizations: Recent research on performance and effectiveness. *Annual Review of Psychology* 47, 307–338.

Handy, C. 1995. Trust and the virtual organization. *Harvard Business Review* 73, 40–50.

Hart, R.K., and McLeod, P.L. 2003. Rethinking team building in geographically dispersed teams: One message at a time. *Organizational Dynamics* 31, 352–361.

Hiltz, S.R., Johnson, K., and Turoff, M. 1986. Experiments in group decision-making: Communication process and outcome in face-to-face versus computerized conferences. *Human Communication Research* 13, 225–252.

Hollingshead, A.B., and McGrath, J.E. 1995. Computer-assisted groups: A critical review of the empirical research. In R.A. Guzzo, et al. (eds.). *Team Effectiveness and Decision Making in Organizations.* San Francisco: Jossey-Bass, 46–78.

Hollingshead, A.B., McGrath, J.E., and O.Connor, K.M. 1993. Group task performance and communication technology. *Small Group Research* 24, 307–333.

Jarvenpaa, S.L., Knoll, K., and Leidner, D.E. 1998. Is anybody out there?: The antecedents of trust in global virtual teams. *Journal of Management Information Systems* 14, 4, 29–65.

Jarvenpaa, S.L., and Leidner, D.E. 1999. Communication and trust in global virtual teams. *Organization Science* 10, 791–815.

Kiesler, S., Siegel, J., and McGuire, T.W. 1984. Social psychological aspects of computer-mediated communication. *American Psychologist* 39, 1123–1134.

Mayer, R.C., Davis, J.H., and Schoorman, F.D. 1995. An integrative model of organization trust. *Academy of Management Review* 20 (3), 709–734.

McGrath, J.E. 1984. *Groups: Interaction and Performance.* Englewood Cliffs, NJ: Prentice Hall.

McGuire, T.W., Kiesler, S., and Siegel, J. 1987. Group and computer-mediated discussion effects in risk decision making. *Journal of Personality and Social Psychology* 52, 917–930.

Miranda, S.M., and Saunders, C.S. 2004. The social construction of meaning: An alternative perspective on information sharing. *Information Systems Research* 14, 1, 87–106.

Montoya-Weiss, M.M., Massey, A.P., and Song, M. 2001. Getting it together: Temporal coordination and conflict management in global virtual teams. *Academy of Management Journal* 44, 1251–1262.

Poole, M.S., Holmes, G., and DeSanctis, G. 1991. Conflict management in a computer-supported meeting environment. *Management Science* 37, 926–953.

Potter, R.E., and Balthazard, P.A. 2002. Virtual team interaction styles: Assessments and effects. *International Journal of Human Computer Studies* 56, 423–443.

Ridgeway, C.L. 1984. Dominance, performance, and status in groups: A theoretical analysis. *Advances in Group Processes* 1, 59–93.

Short, J.E., Williams, B., and Christie, B. 1976. *The Social Psychology of Telecommunications.* London: John Wiley.

Siegel, J., Dubrovsky, V., Kiesler, S., McGuire, T.W. 1986. Group processes in computer-mediated communication. *Organizational Behavior and Human Decision Processes* 37, 157–187.

Silver, S.D., Cohen, B.P., and Crutchfield, J.H. 1994. Status differentiation and information exchange in face-to-face and computer-mediated idea generation. *Social Psychology Quarterly* 57, 108–123.

Townsend, A.M., DeMarie, S.M., and Hendrickson, A.R. 1998. Virtual teams: Technology and the workplace of the future. *The Academy of Management Executive* 12, 17–29.

Valacich, J.S., and Schwenk, C. 1995. Devil's advocacy and dialectical inquiry effects on face-to-face and computer-mediated group decision-making. *Organizational Behavior and Human Decision Processes* 63, 158–173.

Walther, J.B. 1996. Computer-mediated communication: Impersonal, interpersonal, and hyperpersonal interaction. *Communication Research* 23, 3–43.

Weisband, S.P., Schneider, S.K., and Conolly, T. 1995. Computer-mediated communication and social information: Status salience and status differences. *Academy of Management Journal* 38, 1124–1151.

Windsor, D. 2001. International virtual teams: Opportunities and issues. In M.M. Beyerlein, D.A. Johnson, and S.T. Beyerlein (eds.), *Virtual Teams. Advances in Interdisciplinary Studies of Work Teams*, vol. 8. London: Elsevier Science/JAI Press, 1–39.

CHAPTER 10

USAGE OF INTERNET-BASED CAREER SUPPORT

Svetlana N. Khapova, Jörgen S. Svensson,
Celeste P.M. Wilderom, and Michael B. Arthur

Abstract: *The contemporary era of shifting employment arrangements invites more career self-management and greater individualized career support over the Internet. This study examines the usage of one such Web-based career support (WBCS) system, within an almost ideal setting for the usage of such technology: the information technology (IT) sector. The WBCS system was designed to support aspiring European IT professionals to make a career change toward or within the IT sector. A careful monitoring of the actual usage of the system showed, however, that full usage of the system was not reached. Although a large number of people signed up for the free-of-charge system, the actual usage of the system's career functionalities was quite limited. In the discussion section, this discrepancy between assumed career support needs and actual use is explored.*

Keywords: *Web-based Career Support, IT Professionals, Career Support System, Integrated Career Support*

INTRODUCTION

The dynamics of the postindustrial information age challenge workers with employment uncertainty. Fluctuations in the economy cause periods of labor shortages to be followed by periods of oversupply and vice versa. At the same time, the industrial model of long-term employer-employee relationships is fading (Cappelli 1999), while rapid changes in technology render existing skills obsolete (Agarwal and Ferratt 2002). As a result, we witness the emergence of the so-called do-it-yourself career (Trommel 1997, 1999). Individuals no longer opt for a lifelong commitment or loyalty to a single employer but take a more independent approach to their own careers (Arthur et al. 1999).

Despite the numerous literatures that point out the emergence of these "new careers," not every aspiring professional is born with the necessary prerequisites for career self-management. Especially, people who are seeking to enter or reenter a certain professional field may lack the insight, experience, and knowledge to make appropriate career decisions. In such circumstances, external career support may be required. Traditional forms of career support and career counseling are expensive and often unavailable to the average worker; therefore, alternative forms of support are desired. As various career scholars and practitioners suggest, the Internet can offer such alternatives (Kleiman and Gati 2004).

On the Internet there is an explosion of so-called e-recruiting (Kumar 2003), and also the Internet's training and career counseling potential has been recognized (Boer 2001; Clark et al. 2000; Harris-Bowlsbey et al. 1998). Therefore, predictable attempts have been made to develop Web-based career support (WBCS). WBCS is provided via the Internet or an intranet. WBCS systems offer, electronically, a combination of key career counseling and support functions:

- appraisal support through personality assessment and skills assessment, including some degree of personalized feedback (Oliver and Zack 1999; Reile and Harris-Bowlsbey 2000);
- informational support through advising users on available career paths (Gati and Asher 2001; Gati et al. 2003);
- instrumental support through Web-based recruiting (Kumar 2003) and e- or Web-based learning opportunities (Reile and Harris-Bowlsbey 2000);
- social and emotional support, in online forums and self-moderating discussion groups (Gati et al. 2003).

While integrated career-support systems continue to emerge, this chapter will address the actual use of this type of system. The following research question is pursued:

> To what extent do individuals make use of integrated Web-based career support when it is offered?

Why is this question important to address? Widespread literatures exist on the new demands of postindustrial labor markets (e.g., Trommel 1997, 1999; Soidre 2004). A key question in those discussions is to what extent these new demands are recognized by the relevant individual labor market participant. The academic observation that employees need to take responsibility for their careers by no means implies that everyone already recognizes this circumstance. Given the strength of industrial institutions, many professionals and companies continue to rely on in-company training and traditional, company-oriented career management. Moreover, a deep gap exists between people's recognition of a potential career problem and their own concrete action (Amundson 2002). Individuals may recognize a change in labor market functioning but will not show any great change in their career-orienting behaviors.

The actual use of the newly emerging WBCS systems might be further complicated by the complex nature of the career-counseling task. Moreover, the cognitive and emotional intricacies of electronic support in career self-management have not yet been fully explored. Today, many if not most computer-aided guidance systems are designed to be used on a stand-alone basis, often at a distance, without the support of a human counselor (Watts 2002, 144–145). This mode of application, however, will fit the cognitive capabilities and personal preferences of only certain types of individuals. Other individuals may experience technical, affective, or cognitive constraints that hinder such usage (Savard et al. 2002). They may require additional assistance operating these complex systems, selecting the appropriate information, or initiating interaction with others, such as career counselors. In this respect, most experts advocate the integration of computer-aided guidance into more broadly based guidance services that provide additional interaction with a human counselor (Barak 2003). However, the empirical questions of whether and how people use either integrated or stand-alone WBCS remain unanswered.

CHANGE2IT: A WBCS SYSTEM FOR IT PROFESSIONALS

This research consists of case study of the actual use of a WBCS system within the information technology (IT) sector. This case study was conducted in the specially selected field of aspiring IT professionals and was focused on a specific WBCS system: Change2IT.

In this section, the specifics of the case selection are discussed, after which the methodology of examining the usage of this specific case of WBCS is presented.

The Field of Aspiring IT Professionals

The field of aspiring IT professionals was selected for this case study. This field was chosen above others because of the likelihood that WBCS ought to succeed. There are several reasons for expecting success of a WBCS system within the IT field:

1. Within this relatively new labor market, and especially for those employed by small and medium enterprises, structures for delivering traditional types of career support are weak.
2. People aspiring to a career change into a new sector lack knowledge about that sector because of limited access to existing professional networks.
3. Aspiring IT professionals are expected to be more open to the idea of using Web-based technology for acquiring personal services than workers in other sectors.

Various scholars and practitioners suggest that the IT sector differs greatly from other business sectors of the present economy (e.g., Saxenian 1996). Due to rapid economic changes and continuous emergence of new technologies, the IT sector performs under especially dynamic conditions. New companies and competencies are constantly being formed, while outdated or nonviable ones are closing down. For most of its employees— IT professionals—working for the IT sector offers numerous advantages, such as creative work environments with flexible working hours. It also offers numerous challenges, for instance, frequent interfirm mobility and career instability (Saxenian 1996).

Given the small size of most IT companies, there are relatively few organizational structures that provide individuals with opportunities for growth. Most of the learning is offered as part of the job. Professionals are expected to learn as they participate in projects. Moreover, projects are the only formal structures through which the performance of employees can be quantified or assessed. In these "weak situations" (ambiguous situations with few salient guidelines for action), IT professionals are challenged to take on responsibility not only for their careers but also for the design of structures and process of the employing organization (Weick 1996, 43).

The circumstances in which IT professionals perform invite them to seek career support outside their employing organizations. Established professionals may seek support within their informal networks, often comprised of former project coworkers, team leaders or bosses, and their peer professionals. However, the characteristics of the IT sector suggest a high possibility that people aspiring to make a career change to the IT sector will experience serious challenges in making career decisions. These challenges are due to limited knowledge about the sector and limited access to existing professional networks. In this respect, career support provided through the Internet may assist in entering the industry. Moreover, given that aspiring IT professionals are generally experienced IT users, they are likely to seek career assistance through the Internet. Finally, they are likely to be able to understand systems such as newly developed WBCS systems.

So, all in all, the field of aspiring IT professionals can be regarded as a field with a relatively strong likelihood to adapt to the usage of a WBCS system.

The WBCS System: Change2IT

Within the selected field, our case study focuses on a newly developed WBCS system, named Change2IT. This system was developed with support from the European Commission and introduced throughout Europe in 2004. The goal is to provide integrated career support to individuals who are seeking a suitable job in the IT sector. Not only are current IT professionals invited to use this system, but also people with any other background who intend to start working within the IT sector.

This particular WBCS system combines several approaches to make career support viable. Requirements for users include the following:

1. posting a curriculum vitae (CV posting) to provide employers with details about the user's employment preferences and relevant work and educational experiences;
2. undergoing three role diagrammic approach (RDA) tests to measure the values, behavioral tendencies, and personal skills of the users. These tests are expected to provide the users (and, if given permission, also potential employers) with information about a user's suitability for a desired job;
3. taking IT skill tests, aimed at determining the user's level of IT knowledge and skills;
4. participating in online community activities to provide a meeting point for individuals interested in pursuing a career in IT.

In addition, Change2IT provides information about and links to e-learning courses and information about IT labor market trends. It also matches CV profiles against labor market demand for any of the IT profiles. Finally, a sophisticated job-matching function of Change2IT continuously and automatically matches CV profiles of its users with new IT vacancies. All services are publicly accessible and free of charge. The system is fully digitalized and aims to provide career support services any time and any place. Furthermore, a core assumption behind Change2IT is that it can be used independently of any other support by human experts or career counselors. In other words, it is considered an example of "pure," integrated WBCS.

Research Design and Measurements

The specific objectives of the research were (1) to monitor the behavior of users with respect to the whole Change2IT system and its separate functions; and (2) to evaluate users' acceptance of the system. The research was carried out during a period of six months after the system was launched in 2003, in four European countries: Austria, Greece, Italy, and the Netherlands. The users of the system were the participants in the evaluation. They were recruited through similar, national marketing efforts within each of the participating countries. All individuals interested in finding a suitable job in IT were invited to become users of Change2IT. The recruiting was carried out through national and local media outlets, official networks of IT professionals, conferences, and other events through which Change2IT was promoted.

The actual usage of Change2IT and its functions were monitored electronically. After a six-month period, all users were contacted with an e-questionnaire. The questionnaire aimed to collect data about users' views on Change2IT. It included questions about users' sense of the system's usefulness, its ease of use, and whether it was worth their time. Users were also queried on their perceived frequency of Change2IT usage, motivation to use the system, and self-reported usage of the various Change2IT functions.

Three criteria—"useful," "easy to use," and "worth the time"—were used to measure users' perceived acceptance of Change2IT. According to various researchers on technology acceptance, the criteria "useful" and "easy to use" provide a reasonable view of users' satisfaction with IT applications (e.g., Davis 1989; Davis et al. 1989; Taylor and Todd 1995). Perceived usefulness is the degree to which a person believes that using a particular system may enhance his or her career. This reference follows from the definition of the word *useful:* "capable of being used advantageously." Thus, a system high in perceived usefulness is one for which a user believes in the existence of a positive use-performance relationship. In contrast, perceived ease of use refers to the degree to which a person believes that using a particular system would be free of effort. This reference follows from the definition of *ease:* "freedom from difficulty or great effort." All else being equal, an application perceived to be easier to use than another is more likely to be accepted and used. We chose to add a third criterion, regarding whether each separate Change2IT treatment was worth the user's time. With this additional criterion, we wanted to examine whether users perceived value in what was being offered in various system functions, in contrast to the effort of coproduction (e.g., filling in their CVs and taking personality tests).

Thus, users' perceived acceptance of the system was measured on a five-point scale (1, not at all, to 5, to the maximum extent) with three single-item questions that measured "usefulness," "ease of use," and "worth the time" of each of the system's functions. A typical question is: "To what extent do you perceive the following functions as *useful?*" The possible answers regarded the various functions within Change2IT (e.g., CV posting).

The perceived frequency of the Change2IT usage was measured through one question: "How regularly have you used Change2IT?" The multiple-choice answers included "only once," "sporadically (a few times in total)," "regularly (at least once a week)," "often," and "daily."

The motivation to use Change2IT was measured on a five-point scale (1, disagree completely, to 5, agree completely) with the question: "Please indicate what motivated you to use Change2IT." Eight possible answers were provided. An example is "I was interested to find a new job." All items are included in Table 10.4.

Self-reported usage of the different functions of Change2IT was measured on a five-point scale (1, not at all, to 5, to the maximum extent) through the question: "To what extent have you used the following functions of Change2IT?" The five core functions of Change2IT were then listed (i.e., CV posting, RDA personality tests, IT skills test, e-learning, and online community).

EMPIRICAL RESULTS

The following analyses were carried out in relation to the evaluation of Change2IT:

1. actual usage of the Change2IT functions;[1]
2. user satisfaction with Change2IT; and
3. the relation between user satisfaction and actual usage of Change2IT.

In the following subsection, the results of the analyses are reported.

Actual Usage of Change2IT

The actual usage of Change2IT was assessed for the 2,089 users registered in the Change2IT system. (See Table 10.1.) System usage data yielded the following:

1. Among the 2,089 registered users, only 855 users (or 41 percent) posted their CVs on the system.
2. About 4 percent of all users took one or more of the RDA personality tests.
3. About 13 percent (or 276) of all users entered the online community.

Furthermore, the monitoring of the actual usage revealed information on *patterns* of usage. A usage pattern is defined as the combination of Change2IT functions selected

Table 10.1

Actual Usage of the Change2IT Functions (*N* = 2,089)

Usage (in percent)	CV posting	RDA values test	RDA behavior test	RDA skill test	Online community
Used	41	4	3	1	13
Not used	59	96	97	99	87
Total	100	100	100	100	100

Table 10.2

Patterns of Actual Usage of Change2IT Functions (*N* = 2,089)

Number of persons	Percent	Change2IT functions				
		CV posting	RDA values test	RDA behavior test	RDA skills test	Online community
1,196	57	—	—	—	—	—
33	2	—	—	—	—	X
1	0	—	—	—	X	—
2	0	—	—	X	—	—
1	0	—	—	X	—	X
1	0	—	X	—	—	—
529	25	X	—	—	—	—
175	8	X	—	—	—	X
2	0	X	—	—	X	—
3	0	X	—	—	X	X
43	2	X	—	X	—	—
27	1	X	—	X	—	X
39	2	X	X	—	—	—
37	2	X	X	—	—	X
2,089	100	855	77	73	6	276

and used by a single subject. Table 10.2 presents the results of the patterns of usage for Change2IT. By viewing the data in terms of patterns of usage, additional insights emerge. Table 10.2 shows that no single user of Change2IT made use of all the system's career support functions. Hence the key logic of the system's developers—that this career support system integrates five interdependent career support functions—has not been fully exploited or accepted by its users.

The information about system logins in Table 10.3 provides additional insights. The login data indicate that users varied in terms of intensity of system usage. There were 602 users (or 29 percent) who registered but never came back. There were 805 persons (or 39 percent) who logged in once after registration, most probably to post their CV. There were 422 persons who logged in to Change2IT two or three times. Assuming that logins above four are frequent usage, 260 persons (or 13 percent) logged in between four and thirty-three times during our six-month observation period. This frequency shows some fledgling interest in more than mere CV posting. Thus, despite the lack of familiarity with career services beyond e-recruiting, these users had taken the time to try to get familiar with the relatively unknown other functions that Change2IT was offering.

Table 10.3

Login Frequencies of Change2IT Users (*N* = 2,089)

Login frequencies	Users (in percent)
0	29
1	38
2	14
3	6
4–8	10
9–16	2
17–33	1
Total	100

Table 10.4

Motivations to Join Change2IT

	Mean	Standard deviation
I was interested to find a new job.	4.4	1.1
I was interested to post my CV in Change2IT.	4.3	1.0
I was interested to get personalized career advice.	3.8	1.2
I was interested to join the online community.	3.5	1.3
I was interested to test my IT skills.	3.3	1.4
I was interested to get information about e-learning.	2.8	1.5
I was just curious.	2.5	1.5
I was urged to become a user of Change2IT.	2.3	1.5

Note: All items were measured on a five-point scale: 1 = disagree completely; 5 = agree completely.

In sum, our analysis of the usage patterns of Change2IT led to the following results:

- More than half of the registered persons have not used any of the functionalities (these are called registered nonusers).
- About one quarter of the persons who did register used the CV posting function only.
- About 12 percent of the users have used a combination of two or three functions.
- None of the registered users have used all functions in combination.
- A rather limited number of users (13 percent) visited the site frequently.

User Satisfaction

User evaluation of Change2IT was carried out with the e-questionnaire sent to all users. The legible response consisted of ninety-three users, which is about 11 percent of the total number of persons who really used the system, that is, at least posted their CVs (*N* = 855).

The respondents indicated various reasons for joining Change2IT (Table 10.4). Most users were attracted to Change2IT as a way to find a new job (*N* = 60 out of *N* = 93).

Table 10.5

Users' Evaluations of Change2IT

	Useful		Easy to use		Worth the time	
	Mean	SD	Mean	SD	Mean	SD
CV posting	4.5	0.8	4.0	1.1	4.4	0.9
RDA (overall)	3.4	1.2	3.5	1.3	3.4	1.3
IT skills test	3.6	1.2	3.4	1.3	3.5	1.3
E-learning	3.3	1.2	3.3	1.3	3.3	1.2
Online community	3.1	1.2	3.3	1.3	3.3	1.2
Change2IT (as a whole)	3.6	0.8	3.5	1.0	3.6	0.9

Note: All items were measured on a five-point scale: 1 = not at all; 5 = to the maximum extent.

Among the ninety-three users who responded to the posttest questionnaire, thirty-four were interested in receiving personalized career advice, and twenty-three users were interested in testing their IT skills. Twenty-four users were interested in joining the online community, and fourteen users were somewhat interested in getting information about e-learning. Eleven users indicated that curiosity was the main reason for them to join Change2IT. The majority of Change2IT users (65 percent) intended to get a new job.

To find out the degree of users' acceptance of Change2IT, the users were asked to evaluate the Change2IT offerings in terms of "usefulness," "ease of use," and "worth the time" (Table 10.5). In general, users are most positive about the CV posting function (with mean scores: 4.5 for "useful," 4.0 for "easy to use," and 4.4 for "worth the time"). The other functions are evaluated more neutrally.

In sum, the results of the user satisfaction analysis are similar to the results from the actual usage of Change2IT functions: the users of Change2IT were mainly interested in the system as a sole recruiting facility. Most users indicated that they came to use Change2IT with the idea of finding a new job. Also, of all Change2IT functions, they graded CV posting as most useful, easy to use, and worth their time.

Relation Between Satisfaction and Usage

A final analysis focuses on the relationship between usage of the individual functions and the perception of these functions as presented above: to what extent is usage related to the perception of usefulness, ease of use, and worth the respondent's time? Table 10.6 offers an interesting result: although the total use of the system is not significantly related to these perceptions, the usage of different functions often is. Especially for the CV posting function, there is a clear indication that people use it more when they judge it as useful and worth their time ($R = .36^{**}$; .27; and $.31^{**}$ for "useful," "easy to use," and "worth the time," respectively).

In sum, the analysis of the relationship between the usage of the individual functions and the perception of these functions suggests that users made more intensive usage of those functions that they perceive as "useful," "easy to use," and "worth the time."

Table 10.6

Self-Reported Usage of the WBCS and Its Evaluation

| Function | Self-reported usage | | Correlations between self-reported usage and its evaluation as | | |
	Mean	SD	Useful (R)	Easy to use (R)	Worth the time (R)
CV posting	4.3	1.0	.36**	.27	.31**
RDA tests	2.7	1.6	.20	.18	.18
IT skill tests	1.9	1.4	.06	.19	.17
E-learning	1.6	1.0	.25*	.26*	.31**
Online community	1.7	1.2	.28*	.28*	.32**
Change2IT (as a whole)	2.5	0.8	.08	.18	.18

* Sign level = < 0.05; ** sign level = < 0.01.

DISCUSSION

During the first six months, Change2IT attracted a substantial number of registered participants. Nearly 2,100 people registered as users of the system, so in this sense, the system may be called a success. More careful observation, however, shows that of the 2,089 registered people, only some 43 percent actually used any of the system's functionalities. Moreover, most of these 43 percent were in effect superficial or one-dimensional users who used only some of the functionality, especially CV posting.

When this last observation is compared with the intentions of the designers of the system, there is reason to be dissatisfied. As far as the objective of Change2IT was to provide *integrated* career support, it has not succeeded so far. Why? This question may be answered, in part, by interpreting the results of the evaluative survey. Although the survey concerns a relatively small proportion of the total user population of Change2IT, it revealed two things:

- Limited usage does not seem to be the simple result of lack of interest since a substantial number of users in the survey indicated that they were motivated to improve their careers.
- Limited usage does not mean necessarily a general dissatisfaction with the system since the average evaluation of the system is mildly positive and many users seem to enjoy it.

What then may cause the reported limited usage? As the results of the analysis of the relationships between usage and user evaluations suggest, one answer might be that the system allowed its users the opportunity for selective usage.[2] The users of Change2IT used those functions within Change2IT that they considered useful, easy to use, and worth their time. Other functions, evaluated to be of lesser importance, have generally been skipped. From the perspective of the individual, this choice is a rational and justifiable behavior. People used the system for their personal purposes and invested their own time and effort to do so. Why invest in a function they do not feel they need?

Figure 10.1 **Simplified Process of Traditional Career Counseling**

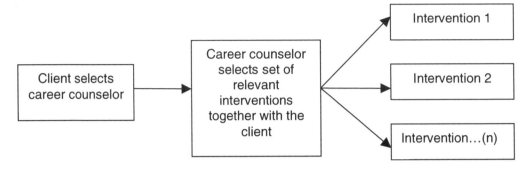

This practice of selective usage is interesting to compare to practices of personal career support by human career counselors. Could the same explanation be applied in such an interpersonal context? Would a human career counselor accept the idea of this type of selective usage by clients?

The literature on traditional (or nonvirtual) career counseling (e.g., Amundson 2002; Gati and Asher 2001; Flores 2003) suggests that interaction between a career counselor and a client is usually led by the former. The interaction includes several career counseling stages during which the problem of the client is explored with a rational decision-making process and actual action planning. The change may even be supported through "verbal persuasion" (Amundson 2002, 138). The input of career counselors is complex. First, career counselors are expected to distinguish a client's career problems from personal problems (Herr 1997). Often problems related to depression or selection of an occupation within the social circle of family and friends may influence career indecisiveness (or difficult career decision making). Second, career counselors are expected to create for their client an environment in which the client will feel welcome and important (Schlossberg et al. 1989). The goal is to create an inviting, warm climate, prompting clients to fully tell or express their story. Third, counselors are expected, using their own creativity and imagination, to help clients to imagine new career possibilities (Amundson 2002).

Of course, a human career counselor does not forcibly engage clients in counseling interventions. However, counselors lead the clients—through the process of counseling, explaining, and persuading—to use assessment tests, card sorts, and other counseling techniques.

While we do not expect selective usage in interpersonal career counseling, the context of career counseling through Web-based systems seems quite different. Here the freedom to choose is—thus far—much larger. In order to serve latent career support needs of working individuals, a WBCS system may need a better introduction, stronger marketing, or an established reputation before its use will become commonplace.

Figures 10.1 and 10.2 summarize the processes applicable to receiving career support from a traditional or nonvirtual career counselor and from a WBCS system. In both cases the processes are presented in a simplified version.

Figure 10.2 **Simplified Process of Web-Based Career Support**

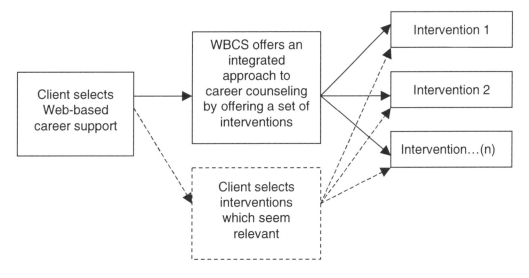

Within nonvirtual career counseling, a client is responsible only for initiating the interaction with a career counselor. After that initiation, the responsibility of the career counselor is to steer the discussion in order to reveal insights important for the client's future. In this discussion with the client, the career counselor selects the most relevant counseling interventions that will assist in further career decision making.

In the context of career support provided through the Web, the client is responsible for finding a career support system that he or she is willing to use. A WBCS system, designed to offer a generalized, integrated career support approach such as Change2IT, offers a set of what its designers see as effective interventions. However, given that electronic or Web-based systems are not capable (or have not yet been designed to be capable) of communicating interactively with their clients and persuading them about which interventions would be most appropriate for their career decision making, the clients independently select interventions that they perceive as relevant. This independence usually limits the client's choice to a minimal or narrow selection of interventions, if any at all. As stated earlier, the selective usage of WBCS functions or interventions raises questions about the effectiveness of the career support provided through the Web.

Further complications stem from the plethora of Web-based choices that face prospective WBCS clients, the lack of commitment they need to show to any system that they choose, and the lack of personal guidance about which Web-based system to pick and why. These complications add to the fundamental problem reported here, that WBCS systems as presently developed are at risk of losing touch with established career counseling practice.

In this respect, three basic recommendations may help to increase usage and acceptance of Change2IT and other WBCS systems currently under development: (1) strengthening the system's design, (2) better consideration of users' needs and characteristics, and (3) availability of human support.

1. *Strengthening the design.* Although Change2IT seems to have a solid design, the question is whether its design is sufficiently understood by its users. Hardly anyone is used to working with an integrated career support site. Perhaps, to some extent, this design logic could be better clarified by the system itself. The designers could, for instance, introduce mechanisms that more or less force the users into the intended optimal pattern of use (it should be stressed that this control would invite other unintended consequences.) In this respect, the system may also require a higher degree of system intelligence. If a system (like Change2IT) aims to provide career support as is normally provided by career counselors and human resources experts, it needs to be an adequate substitute for the traditional human approach. This goal is, at present, unrealistic.

2. *Considering users' needs and characteristics.* It may well be that aspiring IT professionals will differ from other target groups in their career ambitions and the preparedness to reflect on and invest in them. However, this specific target group was actually selected because of the assumption that they were excellently suited for this type of innovative career support. A system like Change2IT may be even less likely to succeed with other, less computer-literate clients. This system may also be ahead of its time; awareness among the working population about the possibilities of WBCS is only beginning to grow. The idea of employing a structured method in order to better think about one's own career is new. So too, for many, is the thought that they need to become "agents of their own development" (Weick 1996, 45).

3. *Accompanying e-services with human support.* At the moment, purely Web-based or virtual career support may be a bridge too far. However, based on the fledgling and serious interest among members of the target group, the question may be raised whether now and in the foreseeable future people with a need for career counseling are willing to rely fully on electronic systems. Although the use of electronic support in nonvirtual career counseling has become indisputable, the availability of non virtual, human expertise may also be essential for most users. A pressing question in this respect is whether purely virtual forms of career counseling will be able to handle the various motivational and attitudinal aspects of clients' job searches. A point of reference might be the experience of ten years of research and evaluation work conducted on e-learning. E-learning seems to be most effective if supported by good rapport with the teachers, as the experts who deliver customized feedback, support, coaching, and referrals (Frank et al. 2003).

CONCLUSION

Web-based career support systems are being developed to assist individuals in their task of career self-management. The study reported in this chapter examined one such system: Change2IT. The system's goal was to support aspiring IT professionals in career change toward or within the IT sector. Change2IT offers an integrated career support service and has attracted a number of users in first few months of existence. The evaluation of Change2IT's actual usage and perceived acceptance by users showed that, although the users themselves appeared to be pleased with the system, they in fact used little of what the designers of the system offered. Instead of using Change2IT as a career development tool, most users merely used it as just another online recruiting service.

The results of this study propose that current Web-based career support systems allow for selective usage of the system's functions, or "cherry-picking." WBCS provides the freedom to use only the functions that people find relevant to their career development and career decision making. This freedom of choice is the user's right; but if users of WBCS do not adopt the design logic of the system developers, the system's benefits may disappoint. WBCS systems do not yet appear to be adequately designed either for stand-alone use or use with a career counselor. More research is needed to increase the effectiveness of the next generation of WBCS systems.

NOTES

1. Please note that IT skill tests became available on Change2IT only during the second half of the evaluation; thus data about actual usage are missing in Tables 10.1 and 10.2.

2. An interesting aspect of the results reported in this chapter is that they do not stand by themselves. In an earlier pilot evaluation of a similar WBCS system, roughly the same results were found. This system, called iCIS Community (i.e., "Integrated e-training and recruiting community for IT professionals and IT SMEs [subject matter experts]") was designed to assist European IT professionals in their career development, providing them with a similar set of integrated career support functions: CV posting, RDA personality tests (values, behavior, and skills), IT skill tests, and free e-learning courses. The pilot ran for about two months in the Netherlands, Portugal, and Italy. The evaluation was set up in a similar manner. Although in the iCIS Community only a total of forty-five persons became registered users (and their motivations were slightly different), the results, in terms of usage, were almost identical. With the exception of one person, the complete, integrated iCIS Community career support was not used either, although other functions than mere CV posting were used more than in Change2IT.

REFERENCES

Agarwal, R., and Ferratt, T. 2002. Enduring practices for managing IT professionals. *Communications of the ACM* 45, 9, 73–79.

Amundson, N.E. 2002. Coloring outside the lines: Boundary issues for counselors. *Journal of Employment Counseling* 39, 138–144.

Arthur, M.B., Inkson, K., and Pringle, J.K. 1999. *The New Careers: Individual Action and Economic Change.* London: Sage.

Arthur, M.B., and Rousseau, D.M. 1996. *The Boundaryless Career.* New York: Oxford University Press.

Barak, A. 2003. Ethical and professional issues in career assessment on the Internet. *Journal of Career Assessment* 11, 3–21.

Boer, P.M. 2001. *Career Counseling over the Internet.* Mahwah, NJ: Erlbaum.

Cappelli, P. 1999. *The New Deal at Work: Managing the Market-Driven Workforce.* Boston: Harvard Business School Press.

Clark, G., Horan, J.J., Tompkins-Bjorkman, A., Kovalski, T., and Hackett, G. 2000. Interactive career counseling on the Internet. *Journal of Career Assessment* 8, 85–93.

Davis, F.D. 1989. Perceived ease of use, and user acceptance of information technology, *MIS Quarterly* 13, 319–339.

Davis, F.D., Bagozzi, R.P., and Warshaw, P.R. 1989. User acceptance of computer technology: A comparison of two theoretical models. *Management Science* 35, 8, 982–1002.

Flores. L.Y. 2003. Practice and research in career counseling and development. *Career Development Quarterly* 52, 2, 98–131.

Frank, M., Reich, N., and Humphreys, K. 2003. Respecting the human needs of students in the development of e-learning. *Computers and Education* 40, 1, 57–70.

Gati, I., and Asher, I. 2001. Prescreening, in-depth exploration, and choice: From decision theory to career counseling practice-effective techniques. *Career Development Quarterly* 50, 2, 140–157.

Gati, I., Kleiman, T., Saka, N., and Zakai, A. 2003. Perceived benefits of using an Internet-based interactive career planning system. *Journal of Vocational Behavior* 62, 272–286.

Harris-Bowlsbey, J., Riley, D.M., and Sampson, J.P. 1998. *The Internet: A Tool for Career Planning.* Columbus, OH: National Career Development Association.

Herr, E.L. 1997. Perspectives on career guidance and counseling in the 21st century. *Educational and Vocational Guidance Bulletin* 60, 1–15.

Kleiman, T., and Gati, I. 2004. Challenges of Internet-based assessment: Measuring career decision-making difficulties. *Measurement and Evaluation in Counseling and Development* 37, 1, 41–55.

Kumar, S. 2003. Managing human capital supply chain in the Internet era. *Industrial Management and Data Systems* 103, 4, 227–237.

Oliver, L.W., and Zack, J.S. 1999. Career assessment on the Internet: An exploratory study. *Journal of Career Assessment* 7, 323–356.

Reile, D.M., and Harris-Bowlsbey, J. 2000. Using the Internet in career planning and assessment. *Journal of Career Assessment* 8, 1, 69–84.

Savard, R., Gingras, M., and Turcotte, M. 2002. Delivery of career development information in the context of information computer technology. *International Journal for Educational and Vocational Guidance* 2, 173–191.

Saxenian, A. 1996. Beyond boundaries: Open labor markets and learning in Silicon Valley. In M.B. Arthur and D.M. Rousseau (eds.), *The Boundaryless Career.* New York: Oxford University Press, 40–57.

Schlossberg, N.K., Lynch, A.Q., and Chickering, A.W. 1989. *Improving Higher Education Environments for Adults.* San Francisco: Jossey-Bass.

Soidre, T. 2004. Unemployment risks and demands on labour-market flexibility: An analysis of attitudinal patterns in Sweden. *International Journal of Social Welfare* 13, 2, 124–133.

Taylor, S., and Todd, P.A. 1995. Understanding information technology usage: A test of competing models. *Information Systems Research* 6, 2, 144–176.

Trommel, W.A. 1997. *De Doe-Het-Zelf-Loopbaan: Arbeid, Zekerheid en Solidariteit in de Risicosamenleving.* Amsterdam: Welboom.

———. 1999. *ICT en Nieuwe Arbeidspatronen: Een Literatuurstudie.* Den Haag: Rathenau Instituut.

Watts, A.G. 2002. The role of information and communication technologies in integrated career information and guidance systems: A policy perspective. *International Journal for Educational and Vocational Guidance* 2, 139–155.

Weick, K.E. 1996. Enactment and the boundaryless career: Organizing as we work. In M.B. Arthur and D.M. Rousseau (eds.), *The Boundaryless Career.* New York: Oxford University Press, 40–57.

CHAPTER 11

MENTORING TRANSFORMED VIA THE INTERNET

Effects on Career Management

VERONICA M. GODSHALK

Abstract: *Web-based mentoring, online mentoring, telementoring, or e-mentoring: call it what you will, the Web is transforming mentor-protégé relationships. Since the time of Odysseus, the mentor-protégé relationship has been described as a close association between individuals that allows them to learn from each other. Mentoring involves an experienced individual (mentor) who promotes the career development and professional advancement of a junior colleague (protégé) by providing psychosocial, role modeling, and vocational support functions. The setting and pursuit of goals for personal and professional development is an important element in the transfer of learning in mentor-protégé relationships, and mentors often offer feedback and information to help the protégés attain their goals. The purpose of this chapter is to describe what e-mentoring is, create an e-mentoring typology based on the computer-mediated communication (CMC) literature, describe the levels of developmental support offered within the CMC environment, and discuss the benefits and potential challenges associated with e-mentoring. Anecdotal evidence gathered from many e-mentoring sites will be used to illustrate e-mentoring relationships. Since e-mentoring is a new avenue by which individuals are transforming their careers via the Internet, an investigation of this phenomenon is warranted.*

Keywords: Online Mentoring, e-Mentoring, Career Management

WHAT IS MENTORING?

Mentors provide protégés with three broad functions: career development (i.e., exposure and visibility, coaching, protection, sponsorship, challenging assignments), psychosocial support (i.e., acceptance and confirmation, counseling, friendship), and role modeling (demonstrating, articulating, and counseling regarding appropriate behaviors implicitly or explicitly) (Kram 1985; Scandura 1992). The career development functions provide vocational support and are associated with protégé outcomes including enhanced knowledge, skills, and abilities, opportunities for promotion, and increased compensation. Vocational support is also provided through role modeling, which allows protégés to understand appropriate interpersonal behavior and culture within the organizational context and aids protégés in performing tasks and communicating well with superiors, peers, and subordinates. The psychosocial functions provide socioemotional (social) support and are associated with protégé outcomes such as job and career satisfaction, career balance, and increased expectations of career success.

Much is known about the protégé's learning opportunities within mentoring relationships. For example, individuals who are mentored report higher levels of overall compensation, promotions, and career advancement, enhanced career mobility, and career satisfaction (Dreher and Cox 1996; Fagenson 1989; Ragins 2002; Scandura 1992; Turban and Dougherty 1994; Wanberg et al. 2003; Wilson and Elman 1990). Mentors' career development support has been shown to be a predictor of managerial promotions and career aspirations (Tharenou 2001). Protégés' satisfaction with their mentoring relationship was positively related to their career and organizational commitment, job satisfaction, perceived opportunities for promotion (Ragins et al. 2000), and increased socialization and organizational citizenship behavior (Chao 1997; Donaldson et al. 2000). Godshalk and Sosik (2003) found that protégés with high levels of learning goal orientation similar to their mentors' reported high levels of psychosocial support.

Mentors, too, benefit from relationships with their protégés. Allen et al. (1997) found that mentors reported development of a support network, new knowledge, and job-related assistance. Mentoring may reduce career plateauing (Chao 1990). Ragins and Scandura (1999) identified a range of potential outcomes, including a rewarding psychological experience, an opportunity to develop a loyal base of trusting followers, an opportunity for generativity, improved job performance, and increased recognition by others. In sum, mentor-protégé relationships provide many career-enhancing learning opportunities for both mentors and protégés.

While mentoring has been considered primarily a dyadic relationship, Higgins and Kram (2001) noted that this conceptualization is short-sighted because (1) it limits the protégé's relationship to a single mentor, (2) the relationship's context is organizationally based, and (3) it does not consider today's available technology. Higgins and Kram, therefore, call mentoring researchers to investigate the individual's developmental network, or "the set of people a protégé names as taking an active interest in and action to advance the protégé's career by providing" vocational and psychosocial support functions (2001, 268). Ensher et al. (2003) posit e-mentoring as one way to overcome the obstacles associated with traditional mentoring. E-mentoring may be the avenue by which individuals transform their careers through the use of developmental relationship networks or "constellations" that can be created, maintained, and expanded over time using computer-mediated communication (CMC) technology.

WHAT IS E-MENTORING?

E-mentoring is a new outgrowth of the traditional mentoring relationship that utilizes the Internet, e-mail, and instant messaging for interfacing mentor and protégé. In practice, e-mentoring appears to be flourishing and a common alternative to traditional dyadic mentoring relationships. A recent survey of the Internet (specifically searches in Google and MSN) produced Web links to approximately 2.4 million sites. While many of these sites may be the same, clearly e-mentoring has proliferated in many industries and organizations throughout the world. E-mentoring appears to provide valuable assistance to a variety of individuals. For example, e-mentoring joins women with similar professional interests (e.g., MentorNet and Women of NASA) and children who aspire to specific professions (e.g., Cyber-sisters.org and TeachingKidsBusiness.com). E-mentoring provides networks of peer vocational assistance (e.g., Electronic Emissary and Mighty Mentors) and adult vocational assistance for youth (e.g., Mentorplace and icouldbe.org). Also, underserved youth and those with disabilities are finding support through e-mentoring relationships (e.g., iMentor and Connecting to Success). A summary of these Web sites is located in Table 11.1.

However, e-mentoring has yet to have an agreed-upon definition. Clearly, e-mentoring conceptually follows the above-noted functions that traditional mentors provide for protégés: vocational support through career development, and role modeling, and psychosocial support. Ensher et al. (2003) have begun to define the e-mentoring context by using the CMC literature to categorize the types of e-mentoring relationships that exist. Ensher et al. have differentiated e-mentoring from other online relationships, including online business coaching, friendships, counseling, and learning. These relationships strive to provide a particular service to the recipient that may be entirely different from the range of vocational and psychosocial support offerings that protégés receive.

A CMC-only e-mentoring relationship occurs when the mentor and protégé exclusively use e-mail for correspondence. CMC-only relationships often occur because of large geographic or spatial (different organizations, industries) distance between partners. A CMC-primary e-mentoring relationship arises, when geographically feasible, if the dyad augments e-mail with telephone or face-to-face interactions. In CMC-primary relationships, some geographic or spatial distance is present but not to the degree of CMC-only relationships. Finally, a CMC-supplemental e-mentoring relationship happens when the majority of dyad interactions are done in person, and e-mail and instant messaging are additional modes of communication.

Contextual variations exist in the formality and frequency of mentor-protégé interactions. A review of the literature suggests that informal, frequent contacts in traditional mentoring relationships provide protégés with greater mentoring functions than those relationships that are more formal or have fewer interactions (Allen et al. 1997; Ensher and Murphy 1997). E-mentoring relationships should follow similar contextual guidelines. Therefore, the more frequent and informal the interaction between e-mentor and e-protégé, the greater the likelihood of vocational and psychosocial support received by the e-protégé.

Because of the simplicity and ease of use associated with CMC technology, this environment allows e-mentoring relationships to flourish (Walther 1996). The online environment allows dyad members to be honest and objective in a neutral emotional environment (Harrington 1998). Ensher et al. (2003) suggest that an e-mentoring relationship can be built on trust, identified goals, and outcome achievement. It allows for

Table 11.1

E-Mentoring Web Sites

E-Mentor organization	URL	Mission
Peer-to-peer e-mentoring		
Electronic Emissary	http://emissary.wm.edu/	Teachers provide peers with creative and new ways to engage their students in authentic learning experiences.
Mighty Mentors	http://mightymentors.com/	Teachers help other teachers improve their teaching techniques and troubleshoot classroom problems.
Women in Coaching (Coaching Association of Canada)	www.coach.ca/women/e/mentor/index.htm	Women coaches at all levels receive feedback from and exchange ideas with an experienced coach.
Gender-specific e-mentoring		
MentorNet	www.mentornet.net/	College women studying science and engineering are paired with industry or academic e-mentors to help them navigate career options.
Women of NASA	www.quest.arc.nasa.gov/women/won-chat.html	Women of NASA mentors and project participants discuss issues related to gender equity and/or specific topics relating to particular fields of study in which the Women of NASA engage.
Adult-youth e-mentoring		
IBM's Mentorplace	www.mentorplace.org/	A partnership between IBM Corporation and EdReach, Inc.; IBM employee-volunteers provide public school students with academic assistance and technical career counseling.
TeachingKids Business.com	www.teachingkids business.com/ementoringprogram.htm	Kids between nine and fourteen explore a variety of careers and begin their career preparation process with an e-mentor. Site helps make the transition to business careers easier by arming kids with advice, knowledge, and confidence.
Underserved youth e-mentoring		
icouldbe.org	http://www.icouldbe.org/	icouldbe.org has steered 2,500 underserved teens toward careers they never imagined.
Cargill Cares	www.cargill.com/news/news_releases/2002/020307_cnfoundation.htm	Cargill Cares program has matched more than 330 employees and students from an inner-city Minneapolis middle school to encourage successful work and study habits and friendship.
Special needs e-mentoring		
DO-IT	www.washington.edu/doit/	Serves to increase the success of people with disabilities in college and careers by partnering with e-mentors.
Connecting to Success	http://ici.umn.edu/ementoring/	Connecting to Success is designed to promote successful transition of youth with disabilities to adult life.

Figure 11.1   **E-Mentoring Development Network Definition and Computer-Mediated Communication Typology**

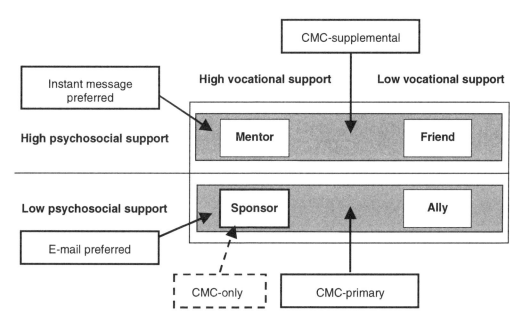

improved performance, better goal setting, and enhanced ability to adapt to one's environment. E-protégés' ability to set and achieve business goals and balance work and family has also been suggested as a benefit (Harrington 1998).

E-mentoring appears to be a necessary form of relationship given the technology-dependent environment of today's workers. Relying solely on face-to-face mentors may become impossible given the globalized workforce and geographically dispersed subject matter experts. As noted above, many researchers have suggested that savvy professionals would be well advised to develop a network of developmental relationships (Baugh and Scandura 1999; Higgins and Kram 2001). This network can include individuals within and outside a person's organization or industry. The network allows the individual to consult experienced professionals who might aid in navigating complex organizational and career path issues. E-mentoring increases the network's structural diversity, that is, the range and density of a professional's network (Higgins 2004).

Figure 11.1 offers a refined e-mentoring definition based on Higgins and Kram's (2001) and Higgins's (2004) work. First, e-mentoring needs to adopt the broader Higgins and Kram definition of developmental network or constellation of individuals actively offering vocational and psychosocial support to e-protégés. Second, Higgins provides a framework that articulates the context of vocational and psychosocial support offered. These contexts vary in levels of support presented and thereby differentiate mentors from sponsors, friends, and allies. According to Higgins, a *mentor* is a "special case of a developmental relationship that provides high amounts of both" vocational and psychosocial support (2004, 13). A *sponsor* offers mainly vocational assistance, while a *friend* offers primarily psychosocial assistance. Although an *ally* offers low levels of both vocational and psychosocial support, that may be "due to a low level of emotional closeness or low frequency of communication" (13).

Finally, the e-mentoring definition, including the developmental network perspective and context support framework, can then be overlaid by the CMC typology.

Each e-mentor relationship can be characterized as CMC-only, CMC-primary, or CMC-supplemental in nature. It is expected that true *mentor* and *friend* relationships will use CMC in a supplemental way. For the closeness, friendship, and high levels of psychosocial support that develop in these relationships, CMC must be supplemented with face-to-face or phone interactions. It is also expected in these e-relationships that instant messaging will become a preferred mode of CMC due to the speed, convenience, and intimacy of that vehicle.

In *sponsor* and *ally* e-relationships, CMC-primary is expected to be a sufficient mode of interaction because of the low levels of psychosocial support that may be readily offered via e-mail. *Sponsors* may have already developed a personal relationship with the e-protégé, may now offer vocational support exclusively, and may maintain that relationship via CMC. CMC-only relationships may exist in *sponsor* e-relationships for similar reasons. CMC-only relationships may not flourish in *mentor* and *friend* e-relationships, due to the high levels of psychosocial support these relationships offer. In *ally* e-relationships, CMC-primary is sufficient due to the laissez-faire attitudes and levels of support offered in these dyads.

In all, CMC offers a mechanism whereby e-mentors and e-protégés may correspond with each other. The depth and breadth of the e-mentoring relationship will vary as levels of vocational and psychosocial support vary. E-mentoring partners may prefer certain CMC modes (e-mail or instant messaging) above others, based on what their relationship needs. Finally, while the types of CMC interactions may dictate the e-mentoring relationships individuals partake in, there is still too little research to attempt to understand these influences.

E-Mentoring Benefits

E-mentoring may enable protégés who were previously facing barriers in developing mentoring relationships. These barriers include a lack of available mentors in a given organization, location, or profession; professional and personal time demands placed on mentors; lack of perceived similarity in attitude, demography, and/or communication style; and misplaced expectations on part of either dyad member (Allen et al. 1997; Ensher et al. 2003; Ragins 2002). E-mentoring opens up a world of professionals who may share common interests and vocational desires. E-mentoring may lower or eliminate the above noted barriers, particularly for minorities and women.

Initial evidence from e-mentoring program evaluations and scholarly work (Emery 1999; Lewis 2002) suggests that e-mentoring is beneficial to mentors and protégés. In an online environment, mentors reported experiencing new learning, increased commitment to their profession, and a sense of renewal. Mentors can learn some heartfelt lessons from their protégés too. One said, "I learned a lot about myself. I found that the MentorNet experience really made me reflect on my career and honestly evaluate how I dealt with various situations in the workplace" (www.mentornet.net). Dwayne Dreakford, IBM Software Group and IBM Mentorplace coordinator, agreed: "I learned that it really doesn't take much to make a difference in another person's life. I also learned that the learning process itself is a two-way street. Communicating with my student taught me as much about myself as I learned about him" (www.mentorplace.org).

African American and Latina protégés report the highest degree of satisfaction with their mentoring experience when compared to their white counterparts; for these women of color, their mentor was a top motivator for staying in school and continuing studies in their chosen field (www.mentornet.net). An illustrative example is Marilyn, a Hispanic high school student, who used the icouldbe.org site:

> "I am the first person from my family to be born in the United States. Now, I will also be the first to attend college. I have had a narrow field of exposure to careers in my life because the women in my family have all been certified home attendants. I saw myself following along in those footsteps. Logging onto icouldbe.org changed the direction of my future! . . . I immediately e-mailed [my e-mentor] more questions like, "How does your personality fit into your work?," "What does a work week look like?," "Is it an exciting or stressful job?," "Do you love your work?" The dialogue just went on and on. I began to daydream about the world of a stockbroker. . . . Without [my e-mentor's] advice, I would not have the focus I have in school now. I know now that in order to entertain the idea of becoming a stockbroker I must do well in high school to attend a university to study finance. The encouragement I receive from the mentor helps me to stay motivated and to keep working towards my goal, which is the focus of our conversations. (www.icouldbe.org/newsletter/testimonials/index.html)

IBM's Mentorplace is another example of a Web site where minority children are learning from their minority e-mentors: "It was a good opportunity to work with Hispanic children and learn from them about what they need in school and [their] community," said Manuel Monserrate, IBM Retail Store Solutions. "The program was a good way to strengthen [children]'s self-esteem, to motivate them to look ahead and see the importance of education and embracing technology." Luis Freeman, IBM Personal Computer Division, agrees. "IBM Mentorplace was a chance to make a difference. I decided to participate because, as a Hispanic, I feel the need to influence other Hispanics to keep studying. Most of the Hispanic population, unfortunately, doesn't even finish high school" (www.mentorplace.org/Feature.htm).

A study of teacher survey data suggests that e-mentoring is making a measurable difference for secondary students. A high percentage of teachers witnessed significant improvement in writing skills (95 percent), self-directed learning (88 percent), critical thinking skills (75 percent), career and workplace knowledge (57 percent), desire to go to college (46 percent), increase in subject grades (45 percent), and science comprehension and ability (44 percent) (www.telementor.org). Preliminary findings also suggest that CMC

can be used to initiate and sustain both peer and mentor-protégé relationships and alleviate barriers to traditional communications due to time and schedule limitations, physical
distances, and disabilities of participants (Burgstahler and Cronheim 2001). One e-mentor explains, "I try to tell the DO-IT [physically or mentally challenged] kids to listen to
their hearts and think about what they really want to do. Don't listen to people who say no,
you can't do this or that, or you should be thinking only about this kind of work; just think
about what you really want to do, what turns you on, and go for it" (www.washington.edu/
doit/Brochures/Technology/doors.html).

Learning and role modeling appear to be key positive characteristics of the outcomes
e-protégés experience in their relationships with e-mentors. These vocational support
functions aid in the protégés' career development. The following examples from female
e-mentoring relationships demonstrate women helping women with issues as broad as
office politics, diversity, and work-family balance.

"Rachel [the e-mentor] kept up a steady stream of talk about how work was going,
and how she was solving different relationship problems with coworkers. It was good to
hear how she was dealing with her project work, of course, but the office politics piece
was really interesting to me, because that's the part of work life that I find difficult,"
Patricia says. "In a field [engineering] where women are so outnumbered, it's hard to
know whether someone is treating you the way they're treating you because you're a
woman or because they're that way with everyone. Sharing stories and examples is a
valuable way of learning about that."

"Mary looks at things from a long-term perspective, and she is a great role model for
me," Christina says. "Our e-mail exchanges have empowered and motivated me to succeed and live a balanced life."

"I feel I can really trust Elaine when I talk about things, because I know that she keeps
our exchanges confidential," Kiri says. "She's always made me feel comfortable coming
to her with anything." While they are very different people, a married, midlife Jewish
woman from New York City raising a teenage daughter and a young woman from rural
Utah who loves astronomy and photography, Elaine and Kiri both come from worlds
where going to college was not the norm. "That has made Elaine's support particularly
important," Kiri says. "Elaine has been a real role model for me."

"As a woman scientist, I sometimes feel very alone," Karri says. "I had support from
a professor in the biology department at KSU, and if I hadn't had her to talk to over the
last few years, I'd be so dejected right now. It was important to have her as a role model
and to hear her say about some insensitive professors, 'They're just not used to having
women in the program. Hang in there'" (www.mentornet.net/documents/about/experi-
ences/Insights).

The CMC environment allows intimate relationships to develop, albeit they may take
some time (Chidambaram 1997). When online dyad members highly identify with their
partners, due to a shared interest or profession, they may perceive their e-mentoring
relationship a more favorable one than their face-to-face relationship (Walther 1996).

Afroz describes her approach to e-mentoring as more like friendship, less like business.
"In e-mentoring, you occasionally share very deep and intimate details and emotions,"

she says. "There's definitely the service level of mentoring, where an e-mentor writes, 'This is what I do. How are your classes going?' But I thought we could have more, and I didn't hold back in describing my experiences. I would think back to my freshman year and write, 'This is what such and such was like for me. How is it for you?' Faith and I came to have an easy back-and-forth interaction, with no lapses between emails, and very free-flowing" (www.mentornet.net/documents/about/experiences/Insights).

E-mentoring allows for the discussion of goals and directions the protégé wants. Several examples confirm these e-mentoring benefits: "I was working with someone I wasn't really enjoying, and I asked Eden if she'd worked in less-than-optimal conditions like that before," Lisa says. "She validated that I was doing the right thing by making the best of a bad situation, and we talked about focusing on common goals with co-workers rather than, in this case, on what I found objectionable about this person. She also suggested that when I'm working with people I enjoy, to recognize that and try to get on more projects with them. In short, focus on the positive" (www.mentornet.net/documents/about/experiences/Insights).

Dorcas describes how her e-mentor was instrumental in supporting her and finding a challenging internship assignment.

> When I started logging onto icouldbe.org, I looked under all types of law related fields: police officer, legal secretary, etc. Eventually, I saw a couple of [e-mentor] profiles that seemed interesting to me. They were both lawyers. I e-mailed them, introducing myself, and started asking them if they like their careers as lawyers. I received real positive responses within days. I started e-mailing two of them on a regular basis and I was always receiving good replies. We had conversations about their work environments, salary, how they got into the field, what do they like most about being a lawyer and more.
>
> I enjoy talking with two different lawyers because I feel that it gives me a better representation of what is out there. My mentors even helped me get an internship position. It's at a firm that is involved with marriage and immigration law. Before the interview I wrote my mentors and asked them about the interview process. I got the pointers I needed in order to get the job. They shared with me their opinions from "what I should wear" to "how to answer certain questions." (www.icouldbe.org /newsletter/testimonials/index.html).

Finally, e-mentoring surveys suggest that one of the most valuable benefits of having a mentor is obtaining information about industry (www.mentornet.net).

It is apparent from these examples that e-mentoring provides for a focus on goal achievement through communication between e-mentor and e-protégé. Both psychosocial and vocational support functions seem to be present in these CMC contexts. Learning is provided for through discussions on topics that are immediate issues for the e-protégé. It may be that given the immediate responses that the CMC context allows, e-protégés and mentors are tackling tough issues when they present themselves, instead of having to wait to discuss them at a face-to-face meeting (when the issues might be forgotten).

Discussions with Carol Muller, PhD, CEO of MentorNet, revealed that e-mentors and protégés were challenged to discover goals and long-term desired outcomes of the relationship as soon as a rapport was built between e-mentoring partners (Muller 2004). While vocational support and role modeling were considered key outcomes of the relationship, goal commitment, achievement, and psychosocial support were equally important outcome opportunities. "Coaching messages are offered for e-mentors on a weekly basis, helping them to develop objectives for the relationship," Muller said. "This focus on objectives, expectations, and goal development allows for success via the [e-mentoring] conversation."

This discussion begins to uncover the benefits of e-mentoring relationships within a CMC environment. Many of these reports have not empirically examined the significant antecedent and outcome variables affecting the e-mentoring relationships. Also, the contextual influences of the CMC environment need to be addressed. Some areas for future e-mentoring research include its effect on learning and role modeling, lowering barriers for minorities, increased commitment to profession or organization, increased time flexibility, increased opportunities for the disabled, the level of intimacy that develops, and increased goal attainment. Should future research examine these factors, a greater understanding of the benefits of e-mentoring will accrue.

E-Mentoring Problem Areas

Developing relationships is similar in both CMC and face-to-face, in that individuals go through the same process of gathering information and forming impressions about each other. However, this process may be slowed in the CMC environment by the way information is exchanged and the lack of visual cues (Walther 1996). Often, online partners overinterpret the few cues they receive, further complicating the communication process. This complication may affect the e-mentor relationship in the long term since enthusiasm for development of the e-relationship may wane. Researchers have found that individuals who have experienced communication via the Internet, such as those in newsgroups or listservs, are more likely to develop future online relationships (Carlson and Zmud 1999) because of their assurance with the medium. However, those who do not communicate well online, who lack computer proficiency, or who often experience computer malfunctions may not serve as effective e-mentors or protégés (Esher et al. 2003).

Other issues that may cause problems for the e-mentoring relationship include privacy, confidentiality, and ethical dissemination of the information provided online. In formal e-mentoring programs, dyad partners are often asked to sign a confidentiality agreement (Emery 1999; MentorNet 2004). Given this litigious society and the fact that the e-mentoring relationship occurs in a written mode, both e-mentors and protégés have cause to be anxious.

It may be that to circumvent these problem areas, protégés would be wise to create a developmental network of mentors. An e-mentoring network could pick up the slack in areas where one mentor might fall down or where another mentor is more trusted, providing the e-protégé with alternatives. Another option would be for the protégé to build a face-to-face network, augmenting e-mentoring relationships with traditional face-to-face mentor relationships. This interaction will ease the physical separation between the e-mentor and protégé and would allow for visual cues as well. For example, one e-protégé, Lisa, created an online network of mentors to fulfill her many needs. Lisa's e-mentor said, "MentorNet suggests establishing expectations with your protégé, and Lisa, who had had a MentorNet mentor previously, knew what she was looking for and helped shape our relationship. That gave me confidence. Also, I believe that it's good to have multiple mentors, and I was happy to be one of Lisa's." Lisa explained, "Since my first mentor had only been out of graduate school for about a year, it was very easy for us to identify with each other. For my second year participating the program, I wanted to have contact with a woman who was further along in her career—someone to help me imagine where I'll be not only a few years down the road, but also 20 years down the road," (MentorNet 2004). Developing a network of e-mentors gave Lisa multiple points of view.

There are several problem areas associated with e-mentoring relationships within a CMC environment. While some of these reports have empirically examined the variables, many significant relationships affecting e-mentoring outcomes still need to be addressed. Future research opportunities to understand problems associated with mentoring include studying how e-relationships develop over time, how trust is established, how communication in CMC-only or CMC-primary e-relationships can be enhanced, how e-relationships can be maintained and professionally concluded, and how confidentiality can be preserved. Future research on these issues will further our understanding of e-mentoring.

Implications

While many of the anecdotal examples offered herein are from organizations, like MentorNet, which exclusively focus on creating e-mentoring networks, it should be noted that e-mentoring is transforming the workplace as well. According to Grace Suh, the global program manager of IBM's Mentorplace, IBM has created a worldwide online community of over 36,000 internal volunteers who offer themselves as mentors to local schools and communities (Suh 2004). During any year, 5,000 e-mentors are matched with e-protégés. The program, started in 1999, now has participants in over twenty-five countries across the world. E-mentoring allows volunteers to give back to their communities in a preferred way, since less time and effort are taken away from normal business activities. Often the IBM e-mentoring relationships involve a minimal face-to-face component so that e-mentors and e-protégés are able to establish relationships with each other. In all, IBM feels strongly about being a partner in locales where it has offices, so Mentorplace is a conduit for making the connection between the company, its employees, and the community.

Organizations may want to develop in-house programs. Human resource managers are advised to consider the degree of comfort both the e-mentor and protégé have with an online environment. Appropriate matching may forestall problems (www.mentornet.net). Training and guidance may be necessary to allow both e-mentor and e-protégé to establish goals that each member in the relationship wishes to achieve.

Organizations may not have the resources IBM has to establish e-mentoring relationships for employees. It would behoove human resource professionals to offer e-mentoring networks, like Electronic Emissary and Mighty Mentors, to their employees so they may receive vocational assistance with little company interaction.

An implication for employees is that there are more resources available to them than they probably realize. E-mentoring networks cover many industries and professions. E-mentoring is transforming the careers of countless individuals, and through some investigation and soul-searching, anyone can become either an e-mentor or an e-protégé.

CONCLUSION

This chapter has examined how the traditional mentoring functions of psychosocial and vocational support are provided for in an e-mentoring environment. The chapter described what e-mentoring is, created an e-mentoring typology based on the computer-mediated communication literature, described the levels of developmental support offered within the CMC environment, and discussed the benefits and potential challenges associated with e-mentoring. Future research opportunities associated with e-mentoring were offered. Anecdotal evidence was used to illustrate many of the positive outcomes associated with e-mentoring. As Carol Muller said, "It is possible to see e-mentoring throughout the education pipeline in the future" (2004). E-mentoring is destined to become an opportunity for all individuals, whether they are children or adults, to transform their careers via the Internet.

REFERENCES

Allen, T.D., Poteet, M.L., and Burroughs, S.M. 1997. The mentor's perspective: A qualitative inquiry and future research agenda. *Journal of Vocational Behavior* 51, 70–89.

Baugh, S.G., and Scandura, T.A. 1999. The effects of multiple mentors on protégé attitudes toward the work setting. *Journal of Social Behavior and Personality* 14, 4, 503–521.

Burgstahler, S., and Cronheim, D. 2001. Supporting peer-peer and mentor-protégé relationships on the Internet. *Journal of Research on Technology in Education 34*, 1, 59–74.

Carlson, U.R., and Zmud, R.W. 1999. Channel expansion theory and the experiential nature of media richness perceptions. *Academy of Management Journal* 42, 13–170.

Chao, G.T. 1997. Mentoring phases and outcomes. *Journal of Vocational Behavior* 51, 15–28.

———. 1990. Exploration of the conceptualization and measurement of career plateau: A comparative analysis. *Journal of Management* 16, 1, 181–193.

Chidambaram, L. 1997. Relational developments in computer-supported groups. *MIS Quarterly* 20, 143–160.

Donaldson, S.I., Ensher, E.A., and Grant-Vallone, E. 2000. Longitudinal examination of mentoring relationships and organizational commitment and citizenship behavior. *Journal of Career Development* 26, 4, 233–248.

Dreher, G.F., and Cox, T.H. 1996. Race, gender, and opportunity: A study of compensation attainment and the establishment of mentoring relationships. *Journal of Applied Psychology* 81, 297–308.

Emery, K.A. 1999. Online mentoring: A review of literature and programs. www.homestead.com/prosites-ffy/files/onlinementoring.htm.

Ensher, E.A., Heun, C., and Blanchard, A. 2003. Online mentoring and computer-mediated communication: New directions in research. *Journal of Vocational Behavior* 63, 264–288.

Ensher, E.A., and Murphy, S.E. 1997. Effects of race, gender, perceived similarity, and contact on mentor relationships. *Journal of Vocational Behavior* 50, 460–481.

Fagenson, E.A. 1989. The mentor advantage: Perceived career/job experiences of protégés versus nonprotégés. *Journal of Organizational Behavior* 10, 309–320.

Godshalk, V.M., and Sosik, J.J. 2003. Aiming for career success: The role of learning goal orientation in mentoring relationships. *Journal of Vocational Behavior* 63, 417–437.

Harrington, A. 1998. A sounding board in cyberspace. *Fortune* 138, 6, 301–302.

Higgins, M.C. 2004. *Developmental Network Questionnaire* (9–404–105). Boston: Harvard Business School Publishing.

Higgins, M.C., and Kram, K.E. 2001. Reconceptualizing mentoring at work: A developmental network perspective. *Academy of Management Review* 26, 264–288.

Kram, K.E. 1985. *Mentoring at Work.* Glenview, IL: Scott, Foresman.

Lewis, C.W. 2002. *International Telementoring Report.* www.telementor.org.

MentorNet. 2004. 2002–2003 Program Evaluation Highlights. www.mentornet.net/documents/files/Eval.0203.Report.pdf.

Muller, C. 2004. Personal communication.

Ragins, B.R. 2002. Understanding diversified mentoring relationships: Definitions, challenges and strategies. In D. Clutterbuck and B. Ragins (eds.) *Mentoring and Diversity: An International Perspective.* Oxford, UK: Butterworth-Heinemann, 23–53.

Ragins, B.R., Cotton, J.L., and Miller, J.S. 2000. Marginal mentoring: The effects of type of mentor, quality of relationship, and program design on work and career attitudes. *Academy of Management Journal* 43, 1177–1194.

Ragins, B.R., and Scandura, T.A. 1999. Burden or blessing? Expected costs and benefits of being a mentor. *Journal of Organizational Behavior* 20, 493–509.

Scandura, T. 1992. Mentorship and career mobility: An empirical investigation. *Journal of Organizational Behavior* 13, 169–174.

Suh, G. 2004. Personal communication.

Tharenou, P. 2001. Going up? Do traits and informal social processes predict advancing in management? *Academy of Management Journal* 44, 1005–1017.

Turban, D.B., and Dougherty, T.W. 1994. Role of protégé personality in receipt of mentoring and career success. *Academy of Management Journal* 37, 688–702.

Walther, J.B. 1996. Computer mediated communication: Impersonal, interpersonal, and hyperpersonal interaction. *Communication Research* 23, 3–43.

Wanberg, C.R., Welsh, E.T., and Hezlett, S.A. 2003. Mentoring research: A review and dynamic process model. *Research in Personnel and Human Resources Management* 22, 39–124.

Wilson, J.A., and Elman, N.S. 1990. Organizational benefits of mentoring. *Academy of Management Executive* 4, 4, 88–94.

PART III

CHANGING TROUBLING
TRANSFORMATIONS INTO
PROMISING ONES

CHAPTER 12

CONTROLLING INTERNET ABUSE
IN THE WORKPLACE

A Framework for Risk Management

KIMBERLY S. YOUNG

Abstract: *As more businesses rely upon information systems to run almost every facet of their business, the potential costs of employee Internet abuse is rising. Last year alone, industry analysts estimated that billions of dollars in lost revenue were attributed to employee Internet abuse, and new trends suggest that lost productivity and corporate liability have emerged as new workplace concerns due to such cyberslacking. This chapter reviews the corporate costs associated with employee Internet abuse and presents a comprehensive framework for risk management. Specifically, the chapter outlines current business practices that employ both information technology and human resources departments in controlling Internet abuse and corporate online management strategies from policy development to software monitoring and management training.*

Keywords: *Employee Internet Abuse, Internet Addiction, Risk Management, Internet Use Policies, Employee Monitoring*

INTRODUCTION

The benefits of the Internet in the workplace as an information and communication tool certainly outweigh the negatives for any company, yet there is a definite concern that it is a growing distraction among employees. Any misuse of time in the workplace creates a problem for managers, especially as corporations are providing employees with a tool that can easily be abused. As corporations rely upon management information systems to run almost every facet of their business, employee Internet abuse has become a potential business epidemic and corporations have become increasingly concerned about its potential costs. A survey of human resources directors showed that approximately 70 percent of companies provide Internet access to more than half of their employees and that such widespread corporate reliance on the Internet has spurred increasing concern about the prevalence of employee abuse (Net Monitoring Survey 2000).

In a survey of 1,439 workers by Vault.com, an online analyst firm, 37 percent admitted to surfing constantly at work, 32 percent surfed a few times a day, and 21 percent surfed a few times a week (Adschiew 2000). In a survey of 224 corporations by Websense Inc., an electronic monitoring firm, 64 percent of the companies have disciplined and more than 30 percent have terminated employees for inappropriate use of the Internet (Websense 2000). Specifically, accessing pornography (42 percent), online chatting (13 percent), gaming (12 percent), sports (8 percent), investing (7 percent), and shopping (7 percent) at work were the leading causes for disciplinary action or termination. In an online usage report conducted in 2000 by eMarketer.com, 73 percent of U.S. active adult users accessed the Web at least once from work, 41 percent access the Web a majority of the time at work, and 15 percent go online exclusively at work (McLaughlin 2000). New studies show that employees who abuse the Internet during work hours cost corporations billions in lost revenue, lost productivity, drains on network resources, job turnover, negative publicity, and possible legal liability.

COSTS OF INTERNET ABUSE

Lost Productivity

Employee Internet abuse translates into billions of dollars in lost revenue for employers (Stewart 2000). Vault.com estimated that employee Internet abuse cost $54 billion annually in lost productivity (Adschiew 2000). Computer Economics notes that online shopping, stock trading, car buying, looking for a new house, and even visiting pornographic sites have become daily practices for about 25 percent of workers, costing companies $5.3 billion in lost productivity due to recreational Internet surfing in 1999. For example, after the peak of the Clinton-Lewinsky scandal, ZDNet reported that industry experts estimated that American companies lost $470 million in productivity to employees reading the Starr report online (Swanson 2001). Similarly, in 2001, lingerie company Victoria's Secret posted a forty-four-minute, mid-workday Webcast with an estimated 2 million viewers, costing an estimated $120 million in lost productivity (Nielsen Net Ratings 2000).

Network Slowdowns

Employees who abuse the Internet during work hours not only underperform, but cause a drain on network resources. In one study, a large technology firm conducted an internal network audit to review online transmissions for one week: only 23 percent was work-related (Machlis 1997). The remainder was for personal use: viewing sports sites, news sites, gaming sites, and pornography sites. Employees who use the Internet for other than job tasks place a significant drain on network energy, decreasing the responsiveness of the system for job-related functions. Access to the Internet costs money, either in fees to support servers, Internet service providers, or in hardware costs necessary to accommodate increased network traffic and data storage. An employee's inappropriate use may negatively affect other employees' speed of access or storage space for work product. Or worse, system slowdowns can delay data retrieval and result in network malfunction or failure due to overload (Ching 2003).

Job Turnover

In some high-profile cases, employee Internet abuse has led to job termination. Broker-age firm Edward Jones fired nineteen employees and gave warnings to forty-one more for sending jokes and non-business-related messages by electronic mail (Newsbytes 1999). Xerox terminated forty workers for spending work time surfing pornographic and shop-ping sites on the Web (Associated Press 2000). Dow Chemical fired fifty employees and suspended another 200 without pay after an e-mail investigation uncovered hard-core pornography and violent subject matter (Collins 2000) and Merck, a prominent pharma-ceutical firm, dismissed multiple contractors for inappropriate Internet use (DiSabatino 2000). When confronted with cases of overt Internet abuse, many managers quickly react with job suspensions or dismissals. While these actions put an end to an employee's abuse of the Internet, they generate hidden costs for the employer such as increased turnover rates and recruitment and retraining expenses. These actions can also create a climate of fear, distrust, and resentment in the workplace that will undermine productiv-ity and cooperation among those workers who are using their Internet accounts properly, and this type of negative publicity can cause customers to become less trustful of the integrity of the company.

Negative Publicity

Telemate.Net Software Inc., a provider of Internet usage management and e-business intelligence solutions, surveyed more than 700 companies from a diverse cross-section of industries (Business Wire 2000). Survey respondents included executives, senior in-formation technology (IT) professionals, and human resources managers. Findings indi-cated that 83 percent of companies were concerned about inappropriate employee usage of the Internet and the resulting negative publicity. The fear of Internet abuse in the workplace and its associated public costs was consistent across industries, company size, and job titles of respondents.

Such negative publicity can hurt a firm's reputation as a strong and reliable company and its reputation for quality and customer service. When wired workers surf during work hours, they are slower to respond to customer needs, are unable to meet deadlines, and fail to complete tasks (Griffiths 2003). These deficiencies translate into poor quality and customer service, which eventually hurt corporate credibility. Organizational effi-ciency is compromised because the firm is unable to meet consumer needs and/or de-liver quality products. Over time, these problems will create a negative brand image as the reputation of the company becomes tarnished and the firm is labeled unreliable and unresponsive (McClausland 2004).

Legal Liabilities

Jokes e-mailed to coworkers may seem an innocent way to brighten up another person's day. However, these jokes can lead to costly harassment suits if the e-mail is perceived to be sexually or racially discriminatory, and the company may be liable if the e-mail was sent over a firm's intranet or network mailing system. In one notable case, Chevron was liable for $2 million in damages in a class action suit when a former manager sent a discriminatory e-mail over the corporate e-mail system (Overly 1999).

A recent study commissioned by Elron Software found that one out of every five employees was sent offensive e-mail (Marson 2000), and beyond e-mail, other types of discrimination and harassment issues can also emerge. For instance, sexually explicit material in the form of pictures, video, sound, and text abounds in cyberspace. If such material is brought into the workplace, it carries the potential to create a hostile work environment, thereby presenting a potential risk of exposure to the employer under federal or state prohibitions against sex discrimination. Increased corporate liability means that firms must be extra vigilant about the type of information distributed online. Recent legislation amending harassment and stalking laws to include e-mail has been passed in Washington, Arizona, California, Indiana, Michigan, New Hampshire, and Wyoming, placing companies at further risk. California also legislated against spoofing with fines of $1,000 and jail terms of up to six months (Overly 1999).

Most alarming for corporations is the growing legitimacy of Internet addiction as a disorder, placing corporations who use the Internet under significant liability under the Americans with Disabilities Act (ADA) (Young and Case 2004). Under the ADA, former workers have sued an employer for wrongful termination, claiming that they suffer from a mental disorder and holding the company responsible for providing access to the "digital drug." While such a claim seems frivolous and even ludicrous to employers, more cases are being seen in court each year.

A FRAMEWORK FOR RISK MANAGEMENT

Managers question the best way to respond effectively to incidents of abuse. Should they simply suspend the employee's Internet privileges or set an example by taking the more drastic measure of firing the employee? If they fire the employee, what will be the impact on employee morale? How much will customer and investor goodwill be affected if the media report on the firings? Managers today must carefully shape and structure decisions related to effective employee Internet management in order to cultivate a positive corporate culture that will maximize productivity and reduce liability. Using a model first conceptualized by Case and Young (2001), this chapter outlines a comprehensive theoretical framework of employee Internet management explained as a range or continuum of approaches (Figure 12.1).

Based upon this model, employee Internet management can be approached from the extremes of a proactive perspective to a reactive perspective. Four management behaviors include practices relating to hiring, prevention, enforcement, and termination or rehabilitation.

Proactively, hiring practices that incorporate screening prospective employees for Internet misuse tendencies in the form of a survey instrument or interview can be used to assess the potential for online abuse among new hires. Prevention examines policy de-

Figure 12.1 **Framework for Internet Management from Proactive to Reactive Approaches**

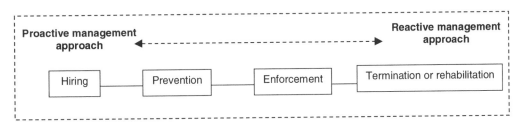

velopment, communication, and reinforcement. Prevention efforts include developing policies that outline acceptable practices of Internet use in the workplace, education initiatives to increase employee compliance, and management training in early detection of employee Internet abuse. Moving along the continuum, enforcement examines the technological infrastructure within the firm, including electronic monitoring of networks, filtering that blocks inappropriate Web sites, and layered computer security to track employee Internet use. Finally, termination or rehabilitation examines the effects of firing or rehabilitation. Of interest are the legal implications of termination and the potential loss of an otherwise productive employee. The research framework is important from both the academic and practitioner perspectives. From an academic standpoint, the framework is useful in providing research direction in a presently fragmented area. From a practitioner orientation, results may be used to improve employee Internet management to maximize productivity, limit risk, and minimize negative behavior.

Hiring Practices

Corporations have begun to incorporate hiring practices that screen for potential online abuse among new hires. Recruiters incorporate questions that evaluate a candidate's prior Internet behavior or attitudes toward stealing company bandwidth and other electronic material as a means to identify potential employees who might be at risk to abuse the Internet. Upon interview, candidates who demonstrate negative attitudes toward technology-related integrity or negligence about online security may be turned down for key positions or, if hired, monitored carefully regarding their online usage.

One government agency screened all applicants using a structured interview that evaluated Internet citizenship behavior, including questions about antisocial versus prosocial behavior, patterns of online use (volume of e-mail, types of Web sites browsed, overall online habits), vigilance about security and viruses, and attitudes toward information security. The agency found that preemployment screening enabled it to detect applicants at risk for online abuse and reduced the risk of information security breaches and compromised access to protected databases. Screening to identify at-risk hires serves as a proactive response to managing worker online abuse; over time, such innovative hiring practices can reduce potential incidents of abuse, decrease future job turnover, and improve overall organizational efficiency.

Until recently, standardized assessment instruments to measure or predict the potential of employee online abuse were not available. However, Davis et al. (2002) introduced the first theory-driven, multidimensional scale to measure problem Internet use. The online cognition scale (OSC) was validated using college students, and a confirmatory factor analysis indicated that problematic Internet use consisted of four dimensions: diminished impulse control, loneliness or depression, social comfort, and distraction. Early studies showed that the OCS predicted all the study variables in the expected directions and focused on procrastination, poor impulse control, and social rejection as key elements of problematic Internet use. Use of the scale in a work sample detected aspects of these risk factors, and a history of being reprimanded for inappropriate Internet usage was predicted by scores on the scale. With further study, the utility of the OCS can be used by organizations as a standardized preemployment screening measure to identify potential employees who are likely to abuse the Internet in the workplace.

PREVENTION

Policy Development

Business use of the Internet has experienced extraordinary growth in this decade. It is now commonplace for employees to have access to the Internet, and as the United States moves ever closer to an information and service economy, even more workers will need access to the Internet to do their job effectively. Given the rise of employee Internet abuse, many employers have recognized that unrestricted use of the Internet by employees has the potential to drain rather than enhance productivity. The solution may be to implement a policy outlining the permissible parameters of employee Internet use.

According to the Society for Human Resource Managers, attorneys advise companies to write policies on e-mail, Internet use, and electronic monitoring procedures (SHRM 2002). A formal Internet use policy serves as a written agreement that establishes the permissible workplace uses of the Internet. In addition to describing permissible uses, an effective Internet use policy should specify prohibited uses, rules of online behavior, and access privileges. Penalties for violations of the policy, including security violations and vandalism of the system, should also be covered. Anyone using a company's Internet connection should be required to sign the policy and know that it will be kept on file as a legally binding document. SHRM also advises employers to alert employees regularly that their online activities may be monitored and that inappropriate use may result in disciplinary action. A growing trend suggests that corporations rely upon Internet use policies to cut recreational use of the Internet during work hours and mitigate legal liability regarding such misuse. The American Management Association (AMA) found that 83 percent of companies have some form of an Internet use policy (AMA 2001). Such policies combat abuse, shield the employer from possible harassment suits, prevent drains on network resources for frivolous use, and reduce corporate liability in the event of legal action taken by an employee terminated for abuse.

Education Initiatives

In the past, companies relied upon written communication alone to convey the importance of appropriate Internet use in the workplace. However, as statistics reveal, employee Internet abuse is on the rise despite the implementation of an acceptable Internet use policy. Another difficulty that companies face is the need to communicate policy updates that stay current with new technologies in the workplace. For instance, if a firm moves from intranet-based e-mail access to a wireless system, supplying employees with Blackberry Palm devices to access Web accounts, the corporation must then modify its Internet acceptable use policies to incorporate these new applications. However, corporations often upgrade workplace technologies without updating policies, leaving themselves at great corporate risk if an employee abuses the new technology and no policy specifically prohibits its abuse (Flynn 2000).

How do corporations effectively communicate and update policies to employees? New trends emerging in the field find that corporate training regarding employee Internet use and its potential for abuse is effective to communicate policies and aid in the prevention of Internet abuse (Case and Young 2002a). Akin to sensitivity training for sexual harassment or diversity training, corporate training programs are designed to increase employee awareness of the issues, reduce occurrence of future incidents, and decrease corporate liability.

Ultimately, corporate seminars are a proactive means of educating employees about how to use technology responsibly. Firms that employ educational initiatives cover such topics as defining what is acceptable and unacceptable Internet use, identifying the warning signs of abuse in the workplace, and identifying risk factors in an employee's life that may contribute to Internet abuse (Young 1999). In one instance, a mid-level technology firm found that educating employees on the dynamics of online abuse complemented written policies with didactic instruction that reinforced the message, and providing training to long-time employees as well as new hires increased employee compliance with acceptable Internet use policies. With continued use, education and training can increase employee accountability and ethical integrity when online, enhance employee interdependency with workplace technologies, and reduce corporate risk and liability when violations occur.

Management Training in Early Detection

Early detection of problems reduces a firm's risk that employee Internet abuse will occur. As more companies in industries from engineering to journalism are venturing online every day, it is important for effective managers to learn the early warning signs that differentiate healthy from abusive patterns of Internet use among employees. Based upon a study of 600 workers who abused the Internet during work, Young (1999) described five changes in behavior related to an employee's Internet use that can serve as warning signs of online abuse during work hours.

Decrease in productivity: While many factors can contribute to a worker's diminished capacity to get the job done, companies that recently adopted the Internet should be especially sensitive to the possibility that output may be sagging because workers are getting hooked by the Internet's interactive applications. Workers likewise should know that if they are not producing as much, those fun new games and chat rooms may be getting in the way.

Increase in mistakes: Most workers getting hooked on the Internet tend to shift back and forth rapidly between legitimate work and interactive Net play. This switching makes it more difficult to concentrate on work details, especially when employees are spending a lot of time playing interactive games or talking in chat rooms, where little care is given to correct grammar, spelling, punctuation, or even logical thought patterns. Anything goes on the Internet but not so with work details. An unaware manager may assume wrongly that a sudden rise in employee error is being caused by stress at home, when it is really triggered by bad habits cultivated on the Internet.

Less interaction with coworkers: Employees spending a great deal of time online may ignore all other social activity because of a growing obsession with the Internet. Once sociable employees suddenly shun all coffee break chatter or friendly morning greetings or turn down invitations for shared lunches or after-hours socializing in favor of spending more time on the Internet.

Startled looks when approached at their stations: If employees enjoy relative privacy during their computer usage, the manager should notice how they respond when approached unaware. Many workers hop in their chairs, shift their bodies, or quickly type a command to change what is on their computer screens. If a manager notices employees who suddenly become secretive about their online activities, it may indicate that they are using the computer for recreation rather than business.

Excessive fatigue: Employees who work extra hours to compensate for their Internet activities often get exhausted by the effort. Employees may be tired all the time at work, not because their employer gave them more work to do, but rather because they have given themselves more activities to keep up with in the form of personal Internet usage at work and late night logins at home.

Enforcement

Once a policy is appropriately communicated, employers must develop a system to monitor employee Internet accounts in order to enforce Internet use policies. After all, what is the effectiveness of a policy that a firm is unable to enforce? Many corporations rely upon filtering software and firewalls for blocking access to inappropriate areas of the Internet and employ monitoring software to detect employee Internet abuse. Filters are an effective deterrent as they disable an employee from accessing sites that the corporation finds unproductive or objectionable. In the past, the main target has been online pornography sites; however, any problematic Web site or area of the Internet can be filtered. While filters are effective, however, they are not invincible, as computer-savvy employees can disable the filter or pass through the firewall with ease.

In 2002, the AMA noted that 74 percent of corporations used monitoring software

(Seltzer 2000). Moreover, the AMA estimated that 45 percent of companies with a thousand or more employees monitored electronic communications from workers (SR *PC Magazine* 2000). Employers can also monitor employee Internet accounts with software that generates Internet usage reports that track an employee's online activities such as Web sites visited and duration of use. Time spent at entertainment sites, sports sites, gaming sites, or adult entertainment sites can be tracked. Here again, however, computer-savvy employees may be able to apply software to erase their Internet tracks, cleaning away traces of inappropriate or objectionable online use.

Given the complexity of the issue, management should consider several factors in order to implement an optimal technological infrastructure that will effectively minimize employee Internet misuse and abuse. According to the AMA, companies must carefully consider what type of filtering and/or monitoring software is right for their firm. Given the size and scope of the firm, management must consider what type of network solutions to employ. Does the firm need to install special application-oriented terminals or can a general-purpose terminal be used for computer security and employee monitoring? What types of operators will use the terminals? Will additional training be necessary? Are proposed terminals compatible with existing equipment? Are Web hosting modifications necessary?

Management must then evaluate how best to maintain records and manage databases collected from employee monitoring. Managers must also consider how monitoring will increase overall organizational efficiency and what projected impact this monitoring will have on production, sales, and revenue for the business. Ultimately, management must consider its funding limitations in order to select a monitoring software package that will provide maximum utility for the least long-term cost. The additional funds in hardware, software, and labor to install and maintain these monitoring systems are considerable; therefore, a thorough cost analysis must be conducted. Many companies try to cut corners, especially in a down market, only to install a system that does not provide adequate employee monitoring or blocking capability. While this penury saves on initial costs, corporations may end up spending more in the long run on network upgrades because the current firewall and monitoring systems are ineffective.

Managers must consider a range of factors in order to evaluate the data produced by the employee monitoring efforts before taking any disciplinary action. How long has the abuse been occurring? Is the abuse just a one-time event or is it chronic? How long has the employee been employed with the firm? Has the employee's Internet misuse significantly reduced job performance? What is this employee's work history? If the employee's work history has always been below average, then most likely the employee has always been a slacker and abusing the Internet is just another way to waste time. But if the employee has shown exemplary performance in the past, then he or she may be dealing with a new problem—for example, a recent divorce, the death of a loved one, or problems at home—and turning to the Internet as way to escape (Young 1998, 21). Certainly, it is important to place the violation in some sort of context so that management can make the best and most informed disciplinary decisions.

As Flynn (2000) notes, management must also decide who should be monitored. Should all employees be monitored or should job status influence that decision? If everyone is to be monitored, how will senior management and the policy makers themselves feel about being monitored? To deal with this issue, many corporations monitor only middle to lower management, skilled labor, clerical staff, and the like, offering unrestricted Internet access as a perk to senior management. The belief is that senior managers will not abuse the Internet because of their job responsibilities within the firm. However, senior executives are equally likely, if not more vulnerable, to develop an unhealthy or addictive habit toward the Internet (Young 2001, 21). Often, senior executives are placed in situations that lend themselves easily to the development of abusive use of the Internet. They have unlimited and unsupervised access, often in a private office. Having such job independence most likely means that this person is free from supervision by a corporate "big brother," making it that much easier for problems to develop since counterproductive and maladaptive online behavior can be easily concealed. It may not be until job productivity is significantly compromised before colleagues and coworkers detect that there is a problem.

Rehabilitation Versus Termination

Similar to the manner in which alcoholism or drug dependence is handled in the workplace, employers may chose to rehabilitate rather than terminate employees who abuse the Internet. Before taking any direct action, employers should consider a referral to the firm's employee assistance program (EAP) to assess the employee for the presence of an underlying addiction to the Internet. Employers must consider the costs involved in such rehabilitation efforts and the costs of possible litigation.

Studies estimate that nearly 6 percent of online users suffer from Internet addiction (Greenfield 1999), which can lead to significant occupational, social, familial, and psychological problems (e.g., O'Reilly 1996; Scherer 1997). Internet addiction may seem a little far-fetched to those who use the Internet for work purposes only and even to those who sometimes use the Internet to unwind. However, for those who have lost jobs, ruined marriages, or alienated themselves from their friends in order to spend "just five more minutes" on the Internet, Internet addiction is a very real and frightening condition (Young 1998, 49).

An employer may be willing to acknowledge the legitimacy of Internet addiction and may even be prepared to implement fair and appropriate strategies to offset productivity losses caused by inappropriate use of the Internet, rather than impose zero tolerance policies that alienate employees and leave the employer susceptible to litigation. The problem then becomes a lack of information about how to create and implement an Internet use policy that incorporates rehabilitation. Managers must therefore develop a concrete strategy to handle critical incidences of abuse to ensure fair, appropriate treatment of the situation.

In one instance, a Fortune 500 company employed detailed record forms and reporting methods to monitor critical incidences of worker online abuse. Factors such as an employee's work history, length of employment, and job status were used to evaluate the action taken against an employee for a violation. Employees who had greater longevity with the firm and positive performance appraisals in the past were offered job redesign options and clinical rehabilitation through the corporate EAP. Job redesign took the form of new duties that did not entail use of the Internet, and selective monitoring of online use was initiated after the employee received treatment through the EAP. Over time, by offering rehabilitation as an alternative to termination, the firm was able to reduce potential job turnover, reduce recruitment costs, and better protect itself from possible legal risk.

CONCLUSION

Employee Internet abuse costs billions of dollars in lost productivity, lost goodwill, and lost potential sales. Therefore, corporations must employ effective Internet use management strategies ranging from policy development to employee monitoring and training seminars. Collectively, these efforts will enhance employees' interdependency with workplace technologies and enable firms to integrate the Internet within the organization successfully.

The rapid reliance upon the Internet has future implications on employee Internet management, especially with the proliferation of mobile computing and wireless Internet appliances. Cahners In-Stat Group reports that the Internet access devices market (which includes personal computers, mobile telephones, and smart Internet devices) is expected to grow at an annual rate of 41.6 percent between 2001 and 2005 (Abdur-Razzaq 2002). Mobile and wireless computing will make detecting incidents of misuse even more difficult for corporations, emphasizing the need to utilize an array of risk management strategies to prevent abuse.

REFERENCES

Abdur-Razzaq, B.M. 2002. Boom times. *PC Magazine* 1, 5, 30.

Adschiew, B. 2000. A Web of workers. *NBC Nightly News.* June.

American Management Association. 2001. AMA Study: Workplace monitoring and surveillance. www.amanet.org/research/pdfs/ems_short2001.pdf.

Associated Press. 2000. Dow chemical fires 50 over offensive e-mail. *CNET News.* July 27.**<<ok?>>** http://news.cnet.com/news/01007-200-2372621.html.

Business Wire. 2000. A landmark survey by Telemate.Net Software shows that 83 percent of companies are concerned with the problem of Internet abuse. Business Wire, July, 12–13.

Case, C.J., and Young, K.S. 2001. Employee Internet misuse: An epidemic in need of a research framework. *Journal of Business and Information Technology* 1, 1, 30–36.

———. 2002a. Employee Internet use policy: An examination of perceived effectiveness. *Issues in Information Systems* 3, 82–88.

———. 2002b. Employee Internet management: Current business practices and outcomes. *CyberPsychology and Behavior* 5, 4, 355–361.

Ching, K.M. 2003. Should you be concerned with employee Internet abuse? jobstreet.com. http://ph.jobstreet.com/career/issues/work20.htm.

Collins, L.A. 2000. Dow Chemical fires 50 over e-mail. Associated Press, July 27. news.excite.com/news/ap/000727/18/dow-chemical-e-mail.

Davis, R.A., Flett, G.L., and Besser, A. 2002. Validation of a new scale for measuring problematic Internet use: Implications for pre-employment screening. *CyberPsychology and Behavior* 5, 4, 331–345.

DiSabatino, J.A. 2000. E-mail probe triggers firings. *Computerworld,* July 27, 1–2.

Flynn, N.L. 2000. *The E-Policy Handbook: Designing and Implementing Effective E-Mail, Internet, and Software Policies.* New York: American Management Association.

Greenfield, D. 1999. Psychological characteristics of Internet addiction: A preliminary analysis. *CyberPsychology and Behavior* 2, 5, 403–412.

Griffiths, M.D. 2003. Internet abuse in the workplace: Issues and concerns for employers and employment counselors. *Journal of Employment Counseling* 40, 87–96.

Machlis, S. 1997. Gotcha! Monitoring tools track Web surfing at work. *Computerworld,* April 7, 2–3.

Marson, C.D. 2000. Employee study cites rampant Internet abuse. *Network World,* 9–13.

McClausland, V. 2004. Employee Internet use and abuse: How it's affecting organizations. *Supplier Spotlight* (February), 9–10.

McLaughlin, L. 2000. Bosses disapprove, but employees still surf. October 31. www.business2.com/articles/web/0,1653,15120,FF.html.

Net Monitoring Survey. 2000. *InformationWeek.com* 805, September 25, 211, 56–57.

Newsbytes. 1999. Edward Jones fires 19 workers for e-mail abuse. May 7. www.exn.ca/Stories/1999/05/07/04.asp.

Nielsen Net Ratings. 2000. Secret lingerie broadcast grabs 1.1 million Internet viewers. http://banners.noticiasdot.com/termometro/boletines/docs/audiencias/niel>sen-netratings/2000/0200/netratings_pr_000211.htm.

O'Reilly, M. 1996. Internet addiction: A new disorder enters the medical lexicon. *Canadian Medical Association Journal* 154, 1882–1883.

Overly, M.R. 1999. *E-Policy: How to Develop Computer, E-Policy, and Internet Guidelines to Protect Your Company and Its Assets.* New York: American Management Association.

Scherer, K. 1997. College life online: Healthy and unhealthy Internet use. *Journal of College Development* 38, 655–665.

Seltzer L. 2000. Monitoring software. *PC Magazine* 20, 5, 26–28.

Society of Human Resource Managers. 2003. Technology and privacy use. www.shrm.org/trends/visions/0300c.asp=0300c.asp.

SR. 2000. Snoop at your peril. *PC Magazine* 9, 17, 86. www.pcmag.com/article2/0,4149,481811,00.asp.

Stewart, F. 2000. Internet acceptable use policies: Navigating the management, legal, and technical issues. *Information Systems Security* 9, 3, 46–53.

Swanson S. 2001. Beware: Employee monitoring is on the rise. *InformationWeek,* August 20, 57–58.

Websense Inc. 2000. Survey on Internet misuse in the workplace. March, 1–6.

Young, K.S. 1998. *Caught in the Net: How to Recognize Internet Addiction and a Winning Strategy for Recovery.* New York: Wiley.

———. 1999. Internet misuse in the workplace. *Credit Union Management,* 42–43.

———. 2001. *Tangled in the Web: Understanding Cybersex from Fantasy to Addiction.* Bloomington, IN: 1st Books Library, Fall 1999, quarterly.

Young, K.S., and Case, C.J. 2004. Internet abuse in the workplace: New trends in risk management. *CyberPsychology and Behavior* 7, 1, 105–111.

CHAPTER 13

WORK COMMITMENT AND EMPLOYEES' MISUSE OF THE INTERNET IN THE WORKPLACE

ABRAHAM CARMELI

Abstract: In a knowledge-based society, the Internet becomes a necessity for any organization. Despite its importance in advancing organizational efficiency and effectiveness, organizations encounter the phenomenon of individuals who use organizational facilities, in general, and the Internet at work, in particular, to generate personal benefits. Misuse of the Internet at work is defined as behavior that falls outside both the reference group and the hypernorms' sets of norms. Such misbehavior not only causes serious economic damages but also socially undermines the work environment and the core values and practices on which the organization itself has been built. Organizational responses aimed at coping with such misbehavior have concentrated on disciplinary actions and technical solutions to block employees' access to the Internet and e-mail programs but have enjoyed only limited success. To better cope with such misconduct, an organization must look beyond the current conventional responses to the roots of individual behavior in the workplace. In this chapter, the theory of work commitment is used to explore how distinct forms of work commitment may promote or diminish the likelihood of inappropriate individual use of the Internet in the workplace.

Keywords: Work Commitment, Deviance, Workplace Misbehavior, Misuse of the Internet

INTRODUCTION

In a knowledge-based society, the Internet becomes an important tool used by organizations daily to enhance efficiency and effectiveness. However, organizations encounter the phenomenon of individuals who use organizational facilities, in general, and the Internet, in particular, for their own benefit.

Recent reports indicate that this is a large-scale phenomenon. The French research agency Benchmark Group surveyed 600 experienced French Internet users during June 2002 and found that about 23 percent of the employees who had Internet access in the workplace spent more than one hour each day surfing the Web for personal use, and 72 percent of those who admitted surfing the Web at work reported that it was done on the firm's time. The UCLA Internet Report (2001) on Internet and e-mail use reveals an increase of 5.7 percent (from 52.4 percent to 58.1 percent) in the number of employees who use organizational facilities for personal e-mail at work and an increase of 10 percent (from 50.7 percent to 60.7 percent) in the number of employees who visit Web sites or surf the Web for personal use.

Employees acknowledge that the Internet at work makes them less productive or unproductive mainly because of the time spent surfing sites that are unrelated to work. However, many employees believe it is appropriate to use the Internet at work for personal needs. The story of Adam Dreyfus demonstrates this belief well. Dreyfus, booking manager at Tech TV in San Francisco, was desperately behind on his shopping one morning when he set out to test his "near-total belief that the Internet can solve all my problems." Using the Internet for his personal needs at work posed no problem for Dreyfus, who argued that it was appropriate given the long hours he spends at work (Richtel 2002).

Evidence shows that many organizations have not yet established a comprehensive written policy by which this phenomenon may be addressed effectively (Mills et al. 2001; Stewart 2000). Clearly, organizational policies may play a role in diminishing the scope of this phenomenon. However, attempts to cope with Internet misuse by employees at work have thus far gained only very limited, if any, success.

In general, these attempts have taken the form of deterrence, prevention, detection, and remedies (Mirchandani and Motwani 2003; Sipior and Ward 2003). In particular, organizations tend to adopt rigid policies and disciplinary actions, to install software to detect improper use of the Internet, and to block access to specific domain sites (e.g., pornography). These methods may be useful to a certain extent; however, they deal only with the symptoms.

The story told by Jeff Middleton, the president of Computer Focus, a one-man consulting firm in New Orleans (Cohen 2000b) demonstrates the ineffectiveness of such actions. Middleton was asked by his clients to detect the improper behavior of employees who surf the Web when they should be working. Responding to his client, an architectural design group, required a look at its server logs (server logs provide a record of all the Internet activity on a network, indicating what users visited what Web site, how long they stayed, what they looked at, what they searched for, and where they went next). By viewing the server logs, Middleton found that half the staff viewed porn sites from their desktops. One employee even came in on weekends to surf sex sites. The architectural design group had already taken some steps (establishing a clear policy that Web access was to be used for business purposes only and that violators would be subject to disciplinary action) to prevent such misuse. The top management team called a meeting in which Middleton's findings were presented and organizational members were asked to sign new written policies. Not surprisingly, within weeks some were back to their improper behavior.

This story and many more, along with the simple fact that this issue is a growing worldwide phenomenon, demonstrate the need to explore new avenues by which organizations can better understand reasons for misuse and discover ways of coping with the root causes. One such avenue, presented by Anandarajan (2002), argued that a social contract balanced between organizational and employee needs and expectations may lead to the desired end—productive Internet usage. Alternatively, excessive freedom or excessive control would yield productive Internet misuse (e.g., misuse that results in or prevents creative solutions, exposure to new information, and obtaining important knowledge). Hence, Anandarajan's suggestion of balanced social contracts may explain how social contracts among organizational members may satisfy both the organization's and its members' needs. This congruence has implications for employee commitment toward the work and the organization.

This chapter presents the theory of work commitment in order to explore how distinct forms of work commitment may promote or diminish the likelihood of improper individual use of the Web in the workplace. Augmenting work commitment is suggested as a key process by which improper Internet use at work would be diminished. The chapter attempts to advance recent efforts to build a theory around the management of Internet usage, in general, and Internet misuse, in particular (Anandarajan and Simmers 2002).

WHAT IS EMPLOYEE MISUSE OF THE INTERNET?

When is a specific behavior considered to be appropriate or inappropriate? Work behavior is any action taken by an individual in the workplace. The appropriateness of work behavior is often determined by the degree to which it deviates from the formal and informal rules, values, and norms of the organization. Deviance often entails negative or destructive consequences. It is defined as "voluntary behavior that violates significant organizational norms and in so doing threatens the well-being of an organization, its members, or both" (Robinson and Bennett 1995, 557). However, Warren (2003) argues against the shortcomings of this definition, indicating that deviance may be constructive as much as compliance may be destructive. As Warren (2003) shows, there is a wide variety of negative (e.g., lying, sabotage) and positive (e.g., organizational citizenship behavior, creative disobedience) characterizations of deviance in organizational science. Considering whether a specific behavior is appropriate or inappropriate depends on the reference points by which it is being evaluated. In other words, what is considered as inappropriate in a particular social context may be well accepted in another setting. To overcome this inherent difficulty in the evaluation of deviance, Warren suggests using Donaldson and Dunfee's (1999) concept of hypernorms. Hypernorms go beyond the universal dimension to capture social values and norms globally. This global system of values and norms is shaped by global institutions, such as the United Nations (Donaldson and Dunfee 1999). Drawing on the reference group and hypernorms perspectives, Warren (2003) suggests the following: "behavior that falls outside both sets of norms (reference group and hypernorms) is *destructive deviance*" (131).

Drawing on Vardi and Wiener's (1996) definition of organizational misbehavior[1] and Warren's conceptualization of deviance, misuse of the Internet at work is defined as behavior that falls outside both the reference group and the hypernorms' sets of norms and, thus, may be considered destructive deviance. This definition of Internet misuse is similar to the definition of *cyberslacking,* used by Mills et al. to denote "recreational web surfing on the job or using the Internet at work for one's own purposes" (2001, 34).

In general, an employee who surfs the Internet while at work to fulfill personal needs, such as shopping and gambling, exhibits a form of destructive deviance because this behavior falls outside both sets of norms (reference group and hypernorms). This type of behavior contrasts with the norm of devoting one's time at work to the completion of organizational tasks, which is embraced by both sets of norms.

THE THEORY OF WORK COMMITMENT: IMPLICATIONS FOR INTERNET MISUSE

The theory of work commitment (Becker 1992; Meyer and Allen 1997; Morrow 1983, 1993) has been central in the field of organizational behavior for its significance in explaining both individual and group behaviors and outcomes in the workplace, presuming that highly committed employees would advance organizational performance. Whereas much research has been dedicated to the effect of employee commitment to the organization and work behaviors (e.g., organizational citizenship behavior) and outcomes (e.g., turnover, job performance) (e.g., Carmeli and Gefen 2005; Cohen 2000a), little effort has been directed toward the impact of work commitment on misbehavior in the workplace. Particularly, researchers have not explored how work commitment may augment or diminish employees' misuse of the Internet at work. This chapter suggests that work commitment may have an important role in diminishing a costly and growing phenomenon —misuse of the Internet on the job—with which organizations have been trying to cope without significant success thus far.

The rationale for concentrating on a limited number of forms of work commitment is as follows. Growing interest in work commitment has yielded the construction of about twenty-five commitment-related definitions and scales (Morrow 1983). This development may be attributed to the recognition that (1) employees exhibit different forms of work commitment (Becker 1960), (2) employees experience each form of work commitment with respect to particular work behavior and outcomes (Wiener and Vardi 1980), and (3) the experience of certain forms of work commitment by employees is usually in accordance with their own benefit (Ritzer and Trice 1969). Though the construction of these twenty-five definitions and scales is an impressive outcome, it has, unfortunately, not been accompanied by a careful reliance on existing scales and definitions (Morrow 1983). This digression is problematic because it makes it difficult to establish a coherent theory for work commitment.

To overcome this difficulty, Morrow (1983, 1993) has suggested directing research efforts at establishing the empirical validity of work commitment constructs. Accordingly, Morrow (1993) has argued that a better validated and generalized work commitment definition could be accomplished by concentrating on four fundamental constructs termed universal forms of work commitment. The term *universal* is meant to "identify forms of work commitment relevant to as many employees as possible" (Morrow 1993, 160). The four universal constructs of work commitment are work ethic endorsement (also referred to as Protestant work ethic), job involvement, career commitment, and organizational commitment. Following well-established agreement among researchers

Figure 13.1   **Direct Effect of Work Commitment Forms on Employees' Misuse of the Internet at Work**

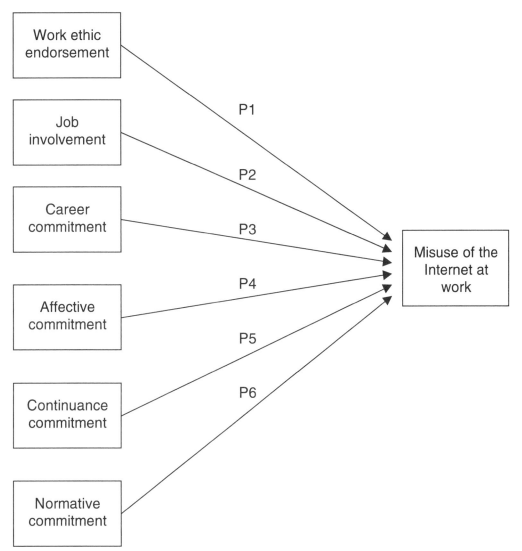

(Allen and Meyer 1996; Becker 1992; Mathieu and Zajac 1990; Meyer and Allen 1984), organizational commitment is considered as a multidimensional construct that consists of three distinguishable forms—affective commitment, continuance commitment, and normative commitment. Hence, this chapter defines and examines six forms of work commitment—work ethic endorsement, career commitment, three dimensions of organizational commitment (affective commitment, continuance commitment, and normative commitment) job involvement—and explores their effect on employees' misuse of the Internet at work. Figure 13.1 presents the direct effect of each form of work commitment on employees' misuse of the Internet at work.

Work Ethic Endorsement

Work ethic endorsement is the extent to which one believes that hard work is important and that leisure and excess money are detrimental (Blood 1969; Mirels and Garrett 1971; Morrow 1993). Work ethic endorsement is considered a "relatively fixed attribute over the life course" (Morrow 1983, 495). Employees with a high level of work ethic conceive their work as being central to their life; work shapes their identity and they value it as being a worthy end in itself (Weber 1958).

Employees who believe in the virtue of hard work think that it makes them better people. As such, they would strongly reject the use of organizational facilities for personal benefit. Furthermore, surfing porn or game sites at work goes against the very essence of the work ethic because individuals with a strong work ethic believe that leisure time diminishes the meaningfulness of life and is not good for people. In other words, individuals who have a high level of work ethic would reject misconduct in the workplace because it undermines the virtue of work, the very essence of their self-conception. Using the Internet at work to gain individual benefit at the expense of one's employers means a corruption of valued working time and conflicts with the personal values of the employee. On the basis of this logic, the following is proposed:

Proposition 1: Work ethic endorsement would be negatively related to employees' misuse of the Internet at work.

Job Involvement

Job involvement is "a belief descriptive of the present job and tends to be a function of how much the job can satisfy one's present needs" (Kanungo 1982, 342). It appears to demonstrate a moderate level of stability (Morrow 1983, 495). Job-involved workers may be described as those for whom work is a very important part of life and those who are very much personally affected by their whole job situation (i.e., the work itself, their coworkers, the organization for which they work) (Rabinowitz and Hall 1977, 266). As such, job involvement as a function of the situation and of personality should be discussed with regard to employees' misuse of the Internet at work.

To be highly involved in the job, employees need to adapt themselves to job conditions to the extent that the conditions do not contradict the workers' self-conception. For example, job-involved individuals need to have a feeling of personal success, in general, and organizational success, in particular (Rabinowitz and Hall 1977). It is therefore unlikely that job-involved employees will exhibit misbehavior that has the potential to undermine their feeling of pride in job achievement and to damage the organization's performance. Thus, using the Internet at work for personal use rather than for organizational purposes would be strongly rejected from a moral perspective. On the basis of this logic, the following proposition is suggested:

Proposition 2: Job-involvement would be negatively related to employees' misuse of the Internet at work.

Career Commitment

Career commitment is defined as "one's attitude toward one's profession or vocation" (Blau 1985, 20). It denotes the magnitude of an employee's motivation to work in a particular occupation (Hall 1971). Career-committed employees devote much effort to advance their professional status. As such, they would devote themselves to enhance their professional skills through professional activities as part of their self-definition.

Clearly, career-committed employees are not likely to engage in misuse behavior that is perceived as intrusive by the organization as a whole and that therefore would jeopardize their career advancement. Surfing the Web at work for non-career-related benefits would not fit in with their professional activities aimed at advancing their career and, by implication, their self-concept. On the basis of this logic, the following proposition is suggested:

Proposition 3: Career commitment would be negatively related to employees' misuse of the Internet at work.

Affective Organizational Commitment

Affective commitment is defined as "positive feelings of identification with, attachment to, and involvement in the work organization" (Meyer and Allen 1984, 375). Employees with strong affective commitment remain on the job because they *want* to, not because they need or must remain. These workers are emotionally attached to the organization and identify with what the organization represents.

Affective committed employees are likely to exhibit organizational citizenship behaviors such as altruism and compliance. Employees with a high compliance behavior are not likely to misuse the Internet at work for their own benefit because such misbehavior might produce negative effects—both tangible (e.g., on productivity) and intangible (e.g., on image)—on the organization and their coworkers. Being part of and closely attached to a group is too important to employees with strong affective organizational commitment for them to risk their job by any sort of misbehavior. Although there is a lack of studies examining the relationship between affective commitment and misuse of the Internet at work, researchers have linked affective commitment with citizenship behaviors. O'Reilly and Chatman (1986) provided initial support that employees who are psychologically attached to, identified with, and involved in their organization are likely to be "good" citizens. This argument has received wide support in the literature (Bergami and Bagozzi 2000). On the basis of this logic, the following proposition is suggested:

Proposition 4: Affective commitment would be negatively related to employees' misuse of the Internet at work.

Continuance Organizational Commitment

Continuance commitment is defined as "the extent to which employees feel committed to their organizations by virtue of the costs that they feel are associated with leaving" (Meyer and Allen 1984, 375). Scholars have indicated that continuance commitment should be studied as a two-dimensional construct. The first dimension is continuance commitment due to employees' belief that they have has few alternatives (hereafter, low-alternative), while the second dimension is continuance commitment due to employees' recognition that leaving the organization will be a big sacrifice (hereafter, high-sacrifice), given their investment during the years of work within the organization (for a review, see Allen and Meyer 1996).

Because employees who are high in continuance commitment remain in their organization because they need to (having few alternatives and not willing to make a high sacrifice), they are likely to exhibit instrumental (cost) behavior. As such, they would engage in misbehavior only to the extent that would not require a high sacrifice and would recognize the few alternatives they have. Their behavior is very much contextual-based because they are constantly occupied with observing changes regarding their alternatives and the sacrifices they are willing to make. On the basis of this logic, we suggest the following proposition:

Proposition 5: Continuance commitment would be moderately positively related to employees' misuse of the Internet at work.

Proposition 5a: Low-alternative-based continuance commitment would be moderately positively related to employees' misuse of the Internet at work.

Proposition 5b: High-sacrifice-based continuance commitment would be moderately positively related to employees' misuse of the Internet at work.

Normative Organizational Commitment

Normative commitment refers to commitment based on one's sense of obligation to the organization. Employees with strong normative commitment remain because they feel they *ought* to (Allen and Meyer 1996, 253). Employees who are high in normative commitment would not use the Internet at work for private purposes rather than for organizational purposes because of this feeling of obligation toward the organization and the feeling of organizational belongingness. Normative committed employees are not likely to engage in misbehavior due to the burden of guilt they may not be able to bear. The sense of guilt would occur as a result of breaching the obligation they feel for their organization. On the basis of this logic, the following proposition is suggested:

Proposition 6: Normative commitment would be negatively related to employees' misuse of the Internet at work.

EXISTING MODELS OF WORK COMMITMENT

Though understanding how distinct forms of work commitment directly affect work behaviors and outcomes is important, it limits knowledge regarding the interrelationships among work commitment constructs. As noted by Randall and Cote, "by failing to consider the larger web of relationships encompassing the various work commitment constructs, researchers may incorrectly identify the strength and direction of the relationship between these constructs" (1991, 194). This subject has only recently attracted scholars (Cohen 2000a; Hackett et al. 2001; Morrow 1993) who direct their research agendas toward establishing theoretical and empirical relationships among work commitment constructs.

Theoretically, the most established commitment models are those of Morrow (1993) and Randall and Cote (1991). Morrow's model considers the relationships among the following forms of work commitment: work ethic endorsement, career commitment, job involvement, affective commitment, and continuance commitment. Randall and Cote's model examines the following forms of work commitment: work ethic endorsement, work group attachment, organizational commitment, career commitment, and job involvement. Except for work group attachment, the other forms correspond to the forms of work commitment employed by Morrow (1993). Additionally, Randall and Cote (1991) employ one dimension of organizational commitment—affective commitment. These models are presented and discussed in the next sections.[2]

Morrow's Model

In Morrow's model, work ethic endorsement influences both career commitment and continuance commitment. Career commitment affects both continuance commitment and affective commitment. Continuance commitment augments affective commitment. Finally, both affective and continuance commitment affect job involvement and mediate the relationship between work ethic endorsement and job involvement and the relationship between career commitment and job involvement.

Randall and Cote's Model

Randall and Cote's model is presented in Figure 13.2. These researchers were the first to explicitly advocate the adoption of "a multivariate approach to work commitment research [that] will advance the understanding of how various pieces of the commitment puzzle fit together and how constellations of work commitment constructs influence outcome variables" (1991, 209).

As indicated above, Randall and Cote's model evaluates a slightly different web of work commitment. Following previous studies (Cohen 1999; Hackett et al. 2001), the focus should be given to the four commitment forms that are universal: work ethic endorsement, job involvement, career commitment, and organizational commitment.

Figure 13.2 **Randall and Cote's Commitment Model**

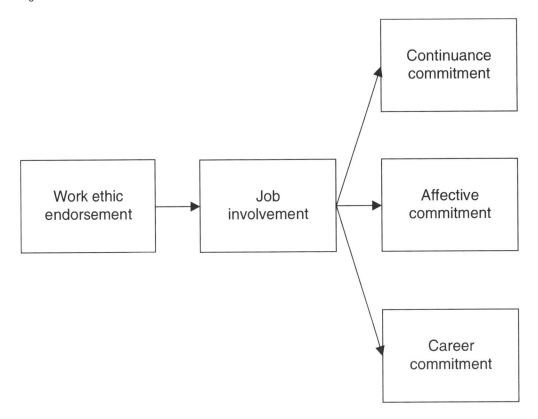

The main difference in Randall and Cote's model is the role of job involvement. Randall and Cote attribute a "pivotal" role to job involvement as a mediator in the work ethic endorsement/career commitment relationship and the work ethic endorsement/ organizational commitment relationship.

Rationale of Morrow and Randall and Cote's Models

As mentioned, the major difference between these models is the role of job involvement. This is a reflection of different perspectives regarding the essence of job involvement. Morrow holds that job involvement is mainly a function of situational conditions whereas Randall and Cote hold that job involvement is mainly a product of individual character- istics. Neither of these perspectives is incorrect. In their profound review, Rabinowitz and Hall (1977) clearly indicate that there are three theoretical perspectives on job in- volvement: (1) job involvement as a personal characteristic (fits with Randall and Cote's approach), (2) job involvement as a function of the situation (fits with Morrow's ap- proach), and (3) job involvement as an individual-situation interaction.

Morrow suggests that work ethic endorsement influences career commitment and continuance commitment. Employees who possess a strong work ethic are likely to pursue a career as part of their belief in hard work (Greenhaus 1971; Morrow 1983). Such employees are likely to pursue careers that fulfill their personality (Hogg and Terry 2000; Tsui et al. 1992), especially regarding professions that demand work values (Furnham 1990). Employees who possess a strong work ethic are likely to develop continuance commitment because they would not want to lose their work setting, an act that contradicts their substance and their personality.

According to Morrow's (1993) model, career commitment influences organizational commitment. Career committed employees would develop commitment to their organization for the potential that their employment in a particular organization may have in the advancement of their career (McGee and Ford 1987; Meyer et al. 1990). Though sociologists saw an inherent conflict between career commitment and organizational commitment, meta-analyses have indicated quite a strong positive relationship between these variables (Mathieu and Zajac 1990; Wallace 1993). More recently, a meta-analysis conducted by Lee et al. (2000) has shown similar results regarding the relationship between career commitment and affective commitment (corrected $r = .449$). However, Lee et al. found a weak inverse relationship between career commitment and continuance commitment (corrected $r = -.092$). This result, however, is based on a very limited number of samples ($k = 5$) and therefore requires caution when interpreting this finding.

Job involvement is in the outermost circle of Morrow's model. According to Morrow, job involvement is affected by both affective and continuance commitments. Morrow assumes that the involvement of an employee in a job is affected mainly by situational conditions. According to Rabinowitz and Hall (1977), this approach is rooted in the human relations movement as well as in motivation theories that regard organizational policies (e.g., rewards) as the main antecedents of employee behavior (Argyris 1964; McGregor 1960; Vroom 1964). Employees who develop affective commitment are attached to their organization as they identify with its values, goals, and practices. A high degree of identification is created through a linkage between employees and their work settings (for an in-depth discussion, see Rabinowitz and Hall 1977) and is likely to generate a higher degree of job involvement (Reichers 1986). As explained earlier, continuance-based commitment means that employees are attached to their organization because they feel they *need* to be attached. Therefore, employees who are committed to their career are likely to develop continuance commitment to the organization as a means of maintaining their career and their job involvement. This commitment would happen either because the employees do not have attractive alternatives and/or because they are not willing to make the sacrifice needed based on a cost-benefit assessment. The meta-analysis conducted by Brown (1996) provides some support for this relationship. It has found a strong positive relationship between job involvement and organizational (affective) commitment (corrected $r = .511$) and a medium positive relationship between job involvement and organizational (continuance) commitment (corrected $r = .287$).[3]

Randall and Cote's (1991) model postulates that work ethic endorsement directly affects job involvement. This approach conceives job involvement as an individual characteristic that is not influenced by situational factors. An employee with a strong work ethic is thus likely to be involved in the job regardless of the situational context (Rabinowitz and Hall 1977). Randall and Cote (1991) have taken a situational approach to assume the direct effect of job involvement on organizational commitment and career commitment. Situational advocaters argue that motivation is primarily a consequence rather than an antecedent of job involvement (Brown 1996, 238). The positive events that an employee experiences at work augment identification with the organization. Positive experiences at work also foster calculative attachment to the organization as well as normative commitment, which has been developed and strengthened throughout the period an employee spends in a particular work setting.[4]

Randall and Cote (1991) attribute a mediator role to job involvement for the relationships between work ethic endorsement and organizational commitment and career commitment. Mowday et al. (1982) provide some rationale for this argument. They argue that employees first become familiar with and involved in a particular job and only later, once their needs are fulfilled, develop commitment to the organization. It is also true for commitment to a career. Employees who are highly involved in the job accumulate experiences that lead them to conceive their career as being more salient in their life and to develop higher commitment to it.

A PROPOSED MODEL OF WORK COMMITMENT AND EMPLOYEE'S MISUSE OF THE INTERNET

Drawing on the models proposed by Morrow (1993) and Randall and Cote (1991), an extended and reconciled work commitment model of employee's misuse of the Internet at work is presented. The proposed model extends Morrow's and Randall and Cote's models by including the three dimensions of organizational commitment (affective, continuance, and normative). Furthermore, it attempts to reconcile the differences in their models. This reconciliation, however, is done with respect to employees' misuse of the Internet at work and thus implies that any proposed commitment model is contextual. The proposed model of work commitment is presented in Figure 13.3. In the next paragraphs, the rationale of the model is discussed.

The model postulates a direct effect of work ethic endorsement on both job involvement and career commitment. Employees with strong work ethics consider the work as an end in itself, a significant part of their identity and personality. Such employees will be highly involved in the job and engaged in career building because it fits their fundamental belief in the virtue of work.

The model also postulates that rather than conceptualizing job involvement, career commitment, and affective commitment as causes and effects of one another, it is theoretically more accurate and better conceptualized to view them as reciprocals. That is, they augment one another rather than being a cause and effect of each other. Job involvement enhances career commitment due to the positive experience an employee accumulates in a particular job setting. Employees are not always fortunate enough to choose the particular job setting that fully fits their career aspirations. However, once they are in a particular job setting, they come to know the particular career their job reflects, and even

Figure 13.3 **Work Commitment Model of Employee's Misuse of the Internet at Work**

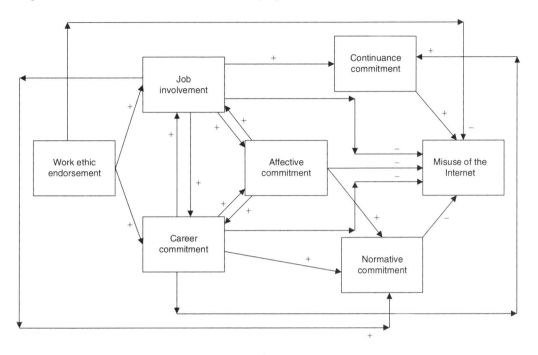

if they had no previous intentions to pursue this career, they now become aware of its values and drawbacks. The same holds true for the possibility that career commitment enhances job involvement. Employees who are highly committed to a particular career find themselves involved in a particular job that fits well with their career expectations.

As suggested by Randall and Cote (1991), job involvement may enhance affective commitment due to the positive events that employees experience in a particular job setting, leading them to develop an affect toward the organization. Over time, a cognitive attachment may lead to an affective attachment. The opposite, of course, is plausible as well. Employees may feel emotionally attached to an organization because of social relationships. Organizational members usually interact within groups and subgroups; they feel a higher level of commitment to their group than to the whole (see Lawler 1992), and their involvement in the job is created after they develop a sense of commitment to their group or subgroup. Finally, people may become attached to an organization before their entry. It is only after their entrance that they would be highly involved in the job.

The model in Figure 13.3 also postulates a reciprocal connection between career commitment and affective commitment. Career committed employees seek organizations in which their career will be advanced and fulfilled (Lee et al. 2000). Hence, career commitment may enhance affective commitment. Affective commitment may also enhance career commitment. Young people do not always have a clear career orientation, or they may believe they know what kind of career they wish to pursue but after a while find themselves facing serious doubts. In any of these cases, these employees may find themselves affectively attached to work settings that open up new career orientations and opportunities. In pursuing these opportunities, they may find themselves both affectively attached to the organization and highly committed to their career.

The model also suggests that continuance commitment is influenced by both job involvement and career commitment. Employees who are highly committed to their career, especially in a specialized profession that requires unique skills, may feel that they have low alternatives or that the sacrifice is too high, and therefore they tend to develop high continuance commitment. Highly job-involved individuals value their job to the point that they would not risk it, recognizing that other alternatives that would enable such a degree of involvement are few.

Normative commitment is influenced by job involvement, career commitment, and affective commitment. Employees who are highly involved in the job and feel affective commitment to the organization are likely to feel an obligation to the organization. Regardless of whether they are cognitively or psychologically attached to the organization, trying to leave their organization would present a moral conflict for them. However, a stronger positive relationship is expected between affective commitment and normative commitment than between job involvement and normative commitment. Career committed employees who think that the organization they work for has been advancing their career will feel morally attached and obligated to it. Career development does not depend only on the individual; rather, it is the interaction between the individual's aspirations and efforts and organizational needs and efforts. Normative commitment is not expected to be affected by continuance commitment. Employees who are high on continuance commitment choose to stay because they have low alternatives or are not willing to make significant sacrifices associated with quitting. These two aspects are not likely to augment moral obligation to an organization.

The model postulates a mediation relationship between work ethic endorsement and the three dimensions of organizational commitment (affective, continuance, and normative). The main reason for this mediation is the stability or instability of the constructs. Work ethic endorsement is a relatively fixed attribute, career commitment and job involvement demonstrate moderate levels of stability, and organizational commitment is highly unstable and context-based. It is difficult to assume a positive or negative connection between work ethic endorsement and organizational commitment, whereas, as explained above, a positive connection between work ethic endorsement and career commitment and job involvement is likely.

Finally, the model suggests complex relationships—direct and indirect—between work commitment and employees' misuse of the Internet at work. Though the direct effects of work commitment on Internet misuse, as explained above, are important, the complex interrelationships among major forms of work commitment can better explain how joint forms of work commitment are associated with employees' misuse of the Internet at work. For example, the model assumes a positive relationship between work ethic endorsement and employees' misuse of the Internet at work. However, organizations seeking to diminish such misbehavior must recognize that recruiting work ethic–oriented individuals would only be an initial phase. Understanding the process by which affective commitment, job involvement, career commitment, and normative commitment are developed and associated with one another to diminish misbehavior is critical for any organizational policy.

The model implicitly suggests that work ethic, job involvement, and career commitment have an influence on employees' misuse of the Internet at work, but this impact is rather moderate. The other forms in Figure 13.3 are expected to have a higher impact on employees' misuse of the Internet at work. As can be seen, the model postulates a positive relationship between continuance commitment and employees' misuse of the Internet at work. Individuals who have low alternatives and are not willing to leave because of the high sacrifice involved are likely to be constantly engaged in behavior that explores new alternatives and reduces the level of sacrifice. On the other hand, employees who develop high affective commitment and normative commitment are not likely to engage in such misbehavior because it conflicts with their moral obligation and their emotional attitude toward the organization.

AVENUES FOR FUTURE RESEARCH

This chapter should be considered as an initial effort to provide explanations rooted in the area of organizational behavior for the growing phenomenon in which employees misuse the Internet and e-mail at work. It suggests that traditional responses (e.g., technical and disciplinary) have had only limited success because of their failure to explore the reasons for the misbehavior itself. Drawn from the theory of work commitment, this chapter attempts to provide a basic understanding as to how forms of work commitment facilitate employees' behavior in organizations. Yet this chapter is limited in scope. Future research may explore the effect of types of work environment on employees' misuse of the Internet. Organizations may benefit from a coherent human resources policy aimed at reducing the motivation of employees to engage in improper behavior.

This chapter emphasizes the negative effect of employees' misbehavior at work. However, it has not addressed a fundamental issue—how much misuse of the Internet is acceptable? Surfing the Web at work does not necessarily mean that the employee is concentrating only on porn or game sites; it may expose employees to useful sites as well. This is a critical question for organizational policy in general and for the formation of strategic human resources policies in particular. It involves issues of empowerment, autonomy, and rigidity, among others. This chapter suggests that employees' misuse of the Internet is not a simple phenomenon to address as it incorporates individual, organizational, and national characteristics. For example, does culture at the national level play a role? It seems that this topic provides an intriguing area of research to explore. Finally, this model needs empirical examination.

ACKNOWLEDGMENTS

I wish to thank the editors, Murugan Anandarajan, Claire Simmers, and Thompson Teo. I also thank three anonymous reviewers for their helpful comments and suggestions.

NOTES

1. Organizational misbehavior is any intentional action by members of organizations that defies and violates (1) shared organizational norms and expectations and/or (2) core societal values, mores, and standards of proper conduct (Vardi and Wiener 1996, 153).

2. Randall and Cote's (1991) model was adapted to the universal forms of work commitment (omitting work group attachment). Unlike both of the original models, organizational commitment is considered a three-dimensional construct (i.e., affective commitment, continuance commitment, and normative commitment).

3. It should be noted that Brown (1996) does not consider organizational commitment as a predictor of job involvement; rather, he conceives organizational commitment as being influenced by job involvement. This concept is in line with Randall and Cote's (1991) approach.

4. Randall and Cote's (1991) model refers only to organizational commitment that reflects the affective dimension of this construct and thus does not provide any rationale as to how job involvement affects continuance commitment and normative commitment.

REFERENCES

Allen, N.J., and Meyer, J.P. 1996. Affective, continuance, and normative commitment to the organization: An examination of construct validity. *Journal of Vocational Behavior* 49, 3, 252–276.

Anandarajan, M. 2002. Internet abuse in the workplace. *Communications of the Association of Computing Machinery (ACM)* 45, 1, 53–54.

Anandarajan, M., and Simmers, C. (eds.). 2002. *Managing Web Usage in the Workplace: A Social, Ethical and Legal Perspective.* Hershey, PA: Idea Group Publishing.

Argyris, C. 1964. *Integrating the Individual and the Organization,* New York: Wiley.

Becker, H.S. 1960. Notes on the concept of commitment. *American Journal of Sociology* 66, 1, 33–42.

Becker, T.E. 1992. Foci and bases of commitment: Are they distinctions worth making? *Academy of Management Journal* 35, 232–244.

Bergami, M., and Bagozzi, R.P. 2000. Self-categorization, affective commitment and group self-esteem as distinct aspects of social identity in the organization. *British Journal of Social Psychology* 39, 555–577.

Blau, G.J. 1985. The measurement and prediction of career commitment. *Journal of Occupational Psychology* 58, 277–288.

Blood, M.R. 1969. Work values and job satisfaction. *Journal of Applied Psychology* 53, 456–459.

Brown, S.P. 1996. A meta-analysis and review of organizational research on job involvement. *Psychological Bulletin* 120, 2 235–255.

Carmeli, A., and Gefen, D. 2005. The relationship between work commitment models and employee withdrawal intentions. *Journal of Managerial Psychology* 20, 2, 63–86.

Cohen, A. 1999. Relationships among five forms of commitment: An empirical assessment. *Journal of Organizational Behavior* 20, 285–308.

———. 2000a. The relationship between commitment forms and work outcomes: A comparison of three models. *Human Relations* 53, 3, 387–417.

———. 2000b. No Web for you! *Fortune,* October 30, 10.

Donaldson, T., and Dunfee, T. 1999. *The Ties That Bind.* Boston: Harvard University Press.

Furnham, A. 1990. *The Protestant Work Ethic.* New York: Routledge.

Greenhaus, J.H. 1971. An investigation of the role of career salience in vocational behavior. *Journal of Vocational Behavior* 1, 209–216.

Greenspan, R. December 3, 2002. Internet abuse drains time and money. *Internetnews.com.* www.internetnews.com/stats/article.php/1551411.

Hackett, R.D., Lapierre, L.M., and Hausdorf, P.A. 2001. Understanding the links between work commitment constructs. *Journal of Vocational Behavior* 58, 392–413.

Hall, D. 1971. A theoretical model of career subidentity development in organizational settings. *Organizational Behavior and Human Performance* 6, 50–76.

Hogg, M.A., and Terry, D.J. 2000. Social identity and self-categorization in organizational contexts. *Academy of Management Review* 25, 1, 121–140.

Kanungo, R.N. 1982. Measurement of job and work involvement. *Journal of Applied Psychology* 67, 3, 341–349.

Lawler, E.J. 1992. Affective attachment to nested groups: A choice process theory. *American Sociological Review* 57, 327–339.

Lee, K., Carswell, J.J., and Allen. N.J. 2000. A meta-analytic review of occupational commitment: Relations with person- and work-related variables. *Journal of Applied Psychology* 85, 5, 799–811.

Mathieu, J.E., and Zajac, D.M. 1990. A review and meta-analysis of the antecedents, correlates, and consequences of organizational commitment. *Psychological Bulletin* 108, 171–194.

McGee, G.W., and Ford, R.C. 1987. Two (or more) dimensions of organizational commitment: Reexamination of the affective and continuance commitment scales. *Journal of Applied Psychology* 72, 638–642.

McGregor, D. 1960. *The Human Side of Enterprise.* New York: McGraw-Hill.

Meyer, J.P., and Allen, N.J. 1984. Testing the 'side-bet theory' of organizational commitment: Some methodological considerations. *Organizational Behavior and Human Performance* 69, 3, 372–378.

Meyer, J.P., and Allen, N.J. 1997. *Commitment in the Workplace: Theory, Research, and Application.* Thousand Oaks, CA: Sage, 1997.

Meyer, J.P., Allen, N.J., and Gellaty, I.R. 1990. Affective and continuance commitment to the organization: Evaluation of measures and analysis of concurrent and time-lagged relations. *Journal of Applied Psychology* 75, 710–720.

Mills, J.E, Hu, B., Beldona, S., and Clay, J.M. 2001. Cyber slacking: A wired workplace liability issue. *The Cornell Hotel and Restaurant Management Quarterly* 42, 5, 34–47.

Mirchandani, D., and Motwani, J. 2003. Reducing Internet abuse in the workplace. *SAM Advanced Management Journal* 55 (Winter), 22–26.

Mirels, H.L., and Garrett, J.B. 1971. The protestant ethic as a personality variable. *Journal of Consulting and Clinical Psychology* 36, 1, 40–44.

Morrow, P.C. 1983. Concept redundancy in organizational research: The case of work commitment. *Academy of Management Review* 8, 486–500.

———. 1993. *The Theory and Measurement of Work Commitment.* Greenwich, CT: JAI Press.

Mowday, R.T., Porter, L.M., and Steers, R.M. 1982. *Employee-Organizational Linkage: The Psychology of Commitment, Absenteeism, and Turnover.* New York: Academic Press.

O'Reilly, C.A., III, and Chatman, J. 1986. Organizational commitment and psychological attachment: The effects of compliance, identification, and internalization on pro-social behavior. *Journal of Applied Psychology* 71, 492–499.

Rabinowitz, S., and Hall, D.T. 1977. Organizational research on job involvement. *Psychological Bulletin* 84, 2, 265–288.

Randall, D.M., and Cote, J.A. 1991. Interrelationships of work commitment constructs. *Work and Occupations* 18, 194–211.

Reichers, A.E. 1986. Conflict and organizational commitment. *Journal of Applied Psychology* 71, 508–514.

Richtel, M. 2002. Net shoppers log on from work: Some risk violating company policy on use of computers. *New York Times,* December 24.

Ritzer, G., and Trice, H.M. 1969. An empirical study of Howard Becker's side-bet theory. *Social Forces* 47, 4, 475–478.

Robinson, S., and Bennett, R. 1995. A typology of deviant workplace behaviors: A multidimensional study. *Academy of Management Journal* 38, 555–572.

Sipior, J.C., and Ward, B.T. 2003. A strategic response to the broad spectrum of Internet abuse. *Information Systems Management* 19, 4, 71–79.

Stewart, F. 2000. Internet acceptable use policies: Navigating the management, legal, and technical issues. *Information System Security* 9, 3, 46–52.

Tsui, A.S., Egan, T.D., and O'Reilly, C.A. III. 1992. Being different: Relational demography and organizational attachment. *Administrative Science Quarterly* 37, 549–579.

UCLA Internet Report. 2001. *Surveying the Digital Future: Year 2.* Los Angeles: UCLA Center for Communication Policy.

Vardi, Y., and Wiener, Y. 1996. Misbehavior in organizations: A motivational framework. *Organization Science* 7, 151–165.

Vroom, V. 1964. *Work and Motivation.* New York: Wiley.

Wallace, J.E. 1993. Professional and organizational commitment: Compatible or incompatible? *Journal of Vocational Behavior* 42, 333–349.

Warren, D.E. 2003. Constructive and destructive deviance in organizations. *Academy of Management Review* 28, 4, 622–632.

Weber, M. 1958. *The Protestant Ethic and the Spirit of Capitalism.* New York: Scribner.

Wiener, Y., and Vardi, Y. 1980. Relationships between job, organization and work outcomes: An integrative approach. *Organizational Behavior and Human Performance* 26, 81–96.

CHAPTER 14

UNDERSTANDING DYSFUNCTIONAL CYBERBEHAVIOR

The Role of Organizational Justice

CONSTANT D. BEUGRÉ

Abstract: This chapter develops a model of dysfunctional cyberbehavior, which contends that information technology can be used as a medium for dysfunctional behaviors in organizations. The model considers dysfunctional cyberbehavior as a multifaceted construct, including cyberdestruction, cyberincivility, cyberloafing, and cybertheft. The model also analyzes dysfunctional cyberbehavior through the lens of organizational justice. Specifically, it suggests that perceptions of distributive, procedural, and interactional justice would reduce the likelihood of dysfunctional cyberbehavior, whereas perceptions of distributive, procedural, and interactional injustice would increase the likelihood of dysfunctional cyberbehavior. However, the potential negative effect of perceptions of unfairness would be mitigated by control mechanisms, such as organizational policies related to computer and Internet usage and computer monitoring. The model's implications for practice and research are discussed.

Keywords: Dysfunctional Cyberbehavior, Cyberdestruction, Cyberincivility, Cyberloafing, Cybertheft, Organizational Justice

INTRODUCTION

In 1998, "Lockheed Martin's e-mail system crashed for six hours after an employee sent 60,000 co-workers an e-mail (with e-receipt requested) about a national prayer day" (Naughton et al. 1999, 52). "The New York Times Company in 1999 discharged 23 employees in its Norfolk, Virginia, processing center for disseminating sexually explicit pictures through its e-mail system. The Xerox Corporation in 2000 discharged 40 employees for spending excessive time visiting non-work-related or sexually oriented sites" (Gomez-Mejia et al. 2004, 465). "In 2003, Bank One Corporation filed a lawsuit alleging that five former employees took confidential information on wealthy clients when they left for new jobs with Smith Barney. Before they quit, according to the lawsuit, the five defendants used their e-mail to transfer confidential customer information from their Bank One computers to outside personal e-mail addresses" (*Wall Street Journal* 2003).

As these examples illustrate, information technology is a double-edged sword (e.g., Anandarajan 2002; Beugré 2003; Simmers 2002). For instance, employees can use the Internet to improve their job performance, but those same employees can easily become distracted by the many available interesting and tempting Web pages (Mills et al. 2001). Employee recreational Web surfing costs employers $5.3 billion annually (Bronikowski 2002). Using information technology for non-work-related activities represents a particular form of dysfunctional behavior (Beugré 2003). "Dysfunctional behavior in organizations refers to motivated behavior by an employee or group of employees that has negative consequences for an individual within the organization, a group of individuals within the organization, and/or the organization itself" (Griffin et al. 1998, 67). Although this new paradigm—information technology as a source of dysfunctional behavior—may seem provocative, it describes a new organizational reality. Employees may use company computer systems to line their own pockets, to seek revenge because they did not get a promotion, or to avenge perceived slights (Carley 1992). Although information technologies per se do not lead to dysfunctional behaviors, they can be used as weapons to perpetrate behaviors that are detrimental to other employees and the organization itself.

This chapter focuses on information technology because information and communication technologies are dominant technologies in today's economy. In this information age, most companies use some form of information technology in their operations (Gunasekaran et al. 2001). However, if mismanaged, information technology can become a liability rather than an asset. Although information technology includes a vast array of technologies, such as phone, fax, voice mail, and video conferencing, the present chapter focuses only on computer-based information technologies. As Oates puts it, "the growth of the information age and the globalization of Internet communication and commerce have significantly affected the manner in which economic crimes are committed, the frequency with which these crimes are committed, and the difficulty of apprehending the perpetrators" (2001, 93). The construct of dysfunctional cyberbehavior is used to account for dysfunctional behavior displayed through the use of computer devices. The focus is only on dysfunctional cyberbehaviors perpetrated by organizational members since insiders commit most dysfunctional cyberbehaviors. Hackers are a threat but insiders are a more pressing threat (Hoffer and Straub 1989). Indeed, 85 percent of computer fraud and theft can be traced to employees or contractors of the organization (Wooley 1998). In addition, organizations can design mechanisms that monitor and may prevent dysfunctional cyberbehaviors perpetrated by organizational insiders.

Understanding dysfunctional cyberbehavior has both theoretical and practical implications. The U.S. economy, including the rapidly expanding area of e-commerce, is increasingly threatened by computer economic crimes (Oates 2001). Information technology researchers (Anandarajan et al. 2000; Boone and Ganeshan 2001; Brynjolfsson 1993; Dewett and Jones 2001; Dos Santos and Sussman 2000; Folster and Flynn 1984; Hitt and Brynjolfsson 1996) have focused on the effects of technology on organizational efficiency and effectiveness. Technological advancements have also multiplied the opportunities that employees have to be unproductive at work. Yet the research into computer misuse lags far behind its prevalence in today's workplace (Bennet and Robinson 2003). The present chapter is an attempt to build a bridge between the literatures in organizational behavior and information technology. From the practical standpoint, a model of dysfunctional cyberbehavior may provide a guideline for managers, specifically in helping them to design electronic and managerial mechanisms to prevent such dysfunctional behaviors.

This chapter is divided into four sections. The first section analyzes the nature and forms of dysfunctional cyberbehavior. The second section reviews the extant literature on organizational justice. Although this review is far from comprehensive, it helps lay the groundwork for the development of a model of dysfunctional cyberbehavior. The third section describes the model of *dysfunctional cyberbehavior*. The main thrust of the model is that information technology can become a medium for dysfunctional behaviors in organizations. The fourth section discusses the model's implications for management practice and research.

NATURE AND FORMS OF DYSFUNCTIONAL CYBERBEHAVIOR

Definition

Dysfunctional cyberbehavior is any intentional behavior perpetrated by means of computer devices that harms organizational members and/or the organization itself. Dysfunctional cyberbehavior does not necessarily occur when a person is connected to a computer network. For instance, playing computer games using a desktop or a laptop is an example of dysfunctional cyberbehavior. Dysfunctional cyberbehavior is behavior that (1) is perpetrated using information technology; (2) has the potential to cause harm to members of the organization or the organization itself; and (3) has the intention to cause harm.

This definition presents two advantages. First, it puts all the terms used to describe the misuse of the computer and the Internet at work under the unique umbrella of dysfunctional cyberbehavior. "Cyberslacking, cyberloafing, and cyberludging are terms used to describe the activities involved in wasting time on the Internet while people are supposedly at work" (Mills et al. 2001, 34). The construct of dysfunctional cyberbehavior captures all these counterproductive behaviors. Second, the definition is broader and more inclusive than that of cyberloafing since it includes behaviors such as sabotaging computer equipment or programs, deleting files, and stealing software that may not necessarily require the use of the Internet.

The conceptualization of dysfunctional cyberbehavior is similar to Griffin et al.'s (1998) definition of dysfunctional work behaviors. Indeed, the authors note that dysfunctional work behaviors result in negative consequences and that to be considered dysfunctional the behavior must be motivated in some way. Intentionality is key to distinguishing dysfunctional behavior from accidents, errors, or mistakes (Griffin et al. 1998). Thus, dysfunctional cyberbehavior is a subset of dysfunctional work behaviors. The difference, however, lies in the medium used. Dysfunctional cyberbehavior is a behavior displayed through computer devices, whereas dysfunctional behavior in general refers to any behavior that is detrimental to an organization or its members regardless of the medium through which it is committed.

Dysfunctional work behaviors include a vast array of behaviors, such as theft (Greenberg 1990, 1993; Greenberg and Alge 1998), sabotage (Ambrose et al. 2002), incivility (Andersson and Pearson 1999), deviance (Robinson and Bennett 1995), workplace aggression (Baron and Neuman 1996), and spreading rumors (Baron and Neuman 1999). Some of these behaviors may be perpetrated using computer-based information technologies. For instance, an employee may sabotage the work of a company by deleting computer files or spreading viruses in computer programs. Likewise, an employee may spread rumors about a colleague or boss through e-mail messages or by posting damaging information on the company Web site. Thus, dysfunctional cyberbehavior may be considered an extension of known forms of dysfunctional behavior albeit with a computer and/or Internet twist. As dysfunctional behaviors are multifaceted, so are dysfunctional cyberbehaviors. To facilitate the discussion, dysfunctional cyberbehaviors are classified into four categories, including cyberincivility, cyberloafing, cyberdestruction, and cybertheft. In the following sections each of these categories of dysfunctional cyberbehavior is defined and explained. Although this classification may seem subjective, it draws in part from the previous discussion on dysfunctional behavior and aims to capture the essence of dysfunctional cyberbehaviors that are prevalent in today's workplace.

Cyberincivility

Cyberincivility refers to dysfunctional cyberbehaviors that show a lack of respect for others within the company and violate accepted rules of common decency. These behaviors include sending threatening and derogatory electronic messages to others, harassing others electronically, and illegally accessing others' computer files. The definition of cyberincivility is similar to the definition of incivility as an organizational concept. As an example of dysfunctional behavior, workplace incivility is mistreatment that may breach relationships and erode empathy (Pearson et al. 2000). It involves interacting with disregard for others in the workplace, in violation of workplace norms for respect (Andersson and Pearson 1999).

Although electronic communication represents a gateway to disseminate company information, it is also a vehicle for various forms of harassment and threats. E-mail is now the most common method of workplace bullying and harassment (Shabi 2000). Sexual harassment and disclosure of confidential information account for 75 percent of the problems with the Internet and e-mail abuse (Verespej 2000). For instance, Microsoft Corporation settled for $2.2 million a sexual harassment suit involving pornographic messages sent within the company via e-mail (Verespej 2000). *Business Week* (2001) reported the case of a pink-slipped worker who sent bawdy e-mails, complete with pornographic pictures attached, to everyone at the high-tech company where he had worked. Such actions are considered dysfunctional since they clearly demonstrate a lack of civility and may be detrimental to interpersonal relations at work.

Cyberloafing

Cyberloafing refers to any voluntary act of employees using their companies' Internet access during office hours to surf non-work-related Web sites for nonwork purposes and to access (including receiving and sending) non-work-related e-mail (Lim et al. 2002, 67). Examples of such activities include sending and reading personal e-mail messages, online shopping, online trading, and reading newspapers. In a study conducted in Singapore, Lim et al. (2002) found that employees involved in cyberloafing typically used the Internet to send and receive personal e-mails, visit general news Web sites, and download non-work-related information. Cyberloafing is dysfunctional when its purpose is to intentionally shirk and reduce personal work input. Cyberloafing is the information technology way of idling on the job (Lim 2002).

Cyberdestruction

Cyberdestruction consists of actions in which the perpetrator physically or electronically destroys computer documents. Such behaviors include deleting computer files, sabotaging computer equipment, and spreading a computer virus. Computer viruses are malicious software written to produce undesirable effects on the system, user, or organization (Loch et al. 1992). Disgruntled employees may retaliate against unfair work practices by deleting critical information that the company needs. Employees may also destroy files that contain information that is detrimental to them. At an import-export outfit, the CEO cannot access any of his old e-mails because a former employee wiped them all out (*Business Week* 2001). Cyberdestruction may have more damaging effects on organizations than other forms of dysfunctional cyberbehavior. Spreading destructive viruses has a stronger negative impact on computer uses than software copying (Harrington 1989).

Cybertheft

Cybertheft refers to stealing from the company by means of computer devices. Such activities include electronically embezzling funds, deleting information, stealing trade secrets, stealing software, copying software, and computer fraud. Computer fraud methods include establishing fictitious vendors, establishing fictitious jobs, and unilaterally raising the perpetrator's salary (Wilson 1984). Cybertheft also includes stealing computer hardware and modifying data.

The four components described here make dysfunctional cyberbehavior a multifaceted phenomenon. Studying dysfunctional cyberbehavior requires answering the following question: Why do employees engage in dysfunctional cyberbehavior? In other words, why do employees use information technology to engage in activities that are detrimental to their organization and colleagues? The literature on dysfunctional behavior offers some clues in attempting to answer this question. Previous research (Greenberg 1990, 1993) considered perceived injustices as an important determinant of counterproductive work behaviors. Organizational justice is a promising perspective for understanding counterproductive workplace behaviors (Greenberg and Alge 1998). Recent research on cyberloafing (Lim 2002; Lim et al. 2001; Lim et al. 2002) found that perceived injustices played an important role in the occurrence of cyberloafing. Not only do employees cyberloaf when they feel overworked and underpaid (Lim et al. 2002), but this sense of injustice gives them a moral justification for their counterproductive activities (Lim et al. 2001; Lim 2002). Thus, the study of dysfunctional cyberbehavior is inextricably linked to an understanding of employee perceptions of justice in the workplace.

ORGANIZATIONAL JUSTICE

Organizational justice refers to perceptions of fairness in organizations (Greenberg 1990, 1993) and encompasses three dimensions: distributive justice, procedural justice, and interactional justice. Discussion of each of these three dimensions follows. Although this literature review on the three dimensions of justice is not intended to be exhaustive, it aims to explain the link between employee perceptions of justice and the occurrence of dysfunctional cyberbehavior.

Distributive Justice

Distributive justice refers to perceptions of outcome fairness (Adams 1965). This component of organizational justice is similar to equity theory (Adams 1965) since both theories deal with outcome distribution. Equity theory postulates that in an exchange relationship, a person compares their input/output ratios to those of another person. A balance between yours and the other person's ratios leads to a feeling of equity. However, perceived inequity creates tension within individuals, who are then motivated to restore equity by engaging in a variety of behaviors including reducing effort, quitting the exchange relationship, or changing the comparison person (Adams 1965).

Distributive injustice occurs when a person does not get the amount of reward expected in comparison to the reward some other person receives (Deutsch 1985). Greenberg (1990, 1993) found a significant correlation between distributive injustice and employee theft. Employees who felt unfairly rewarded tended to steal as compared to those who felt fairly rewarded. Feelings of distributive injustice would be further exacerbated by the existence of unfair procedures and an insensitive manner in which outcomes are announced (Brockner and Wiesenfeld 1996; Folger and Skarlicki 1998; Greenberg and Alge 1998). According to Folger (1993), two factors predict when people will respond most negatively to unfair outcomes: the severity of the loss and the inappropriateness of the conduct by a supervisor or an agent of authority. Thus, judgments about outcome fairness also entail judgments about the fairness of procedures.

Procedural Justice

Procedural justice refers to the fairness of decisions underlying the outcome distribution (Leventhal 1976; Thibaut and Walker 1975). Leventhal (1976) and Leventhal et al. (1980)

identified six procedural justice rules: consistency (procedures must be consistent to ensure fairness), bias suppression (procedures must be developed and implemented without considering the self-interests of those who elaborated them), accuracy (procedures must be based on accurate information), correctability (procedures must allow room for correction), representativeness (procedures must integrate the interests of all parties), and ethicality (procedures must follow moral and ethical standards). According to the authors, a procedurally fair decision should include all these characteristics. In addition to Leventhal's procedural justice framework, the process control model or instrumental model (Thibaut and Walker 1975) and the group-value model or relational model (Lind and Tyler 1988; Tyler and Lind 1992) help explain procedural justice.

Process control refers to control over the development and selection of information that will constitute the basis for resolving the dispute (Thibaut and Walker 1975). Individuals value justice when they have control over the decision process and, subsequently, the outcome. Procedures are perceived to be most fair when disputants have outcome control and the opportunity to participate in developing the options that will be considered for the dispute's outcome. The group-value model contends that people expect the group and its authorities to treat them in ways that affirm their self-esteem by indicating that they are valued members of the group who deserve treatment with respect, dignity, and politeness (Lind and Tyler 1988; Tyler and Lind 1992).

Procedural justice has especially strong effects on attitudes about institutions or authorities as opposed to attitudes about the specific outcome in question (Lind and Tyler, 1988; Folger and Konovsky 1989). Folger and Konovsky (1989) found that perceptions of the procedures used to determine pay raises uniquely contributed to such factors as organizational commitment and trust in supervision, whereas perceptions of distributive justice were uniquely associated with one's own pay satisfaction. "The perception that unfair treatment is embedded in the policy of the organization may lead to feelings of hopelessness, anger at supervisors, and protests against the system, and/or it may negatively affect employees' self-worth" (DeBoer et al. 2002, 192). Anger and resentment associated with perceptions of unfair procedures may energize individuals to engage in retaliation (Skarlicki and Folger 1997).

Interactional Justice

Interactional justice refers to the quality of interpersonal treatment people receive during the implementation of a procedure (Bies and Moag 1986). Interactional justice includes such aspects as treating employees with respect and dignity (Cropanzano and Greenberg 1997) and providing explanations for a decision (Bies 1987). Bies and Moag (1986) found that job candidates believed that corporate recruiters treated them fairly to the extent that the recruiters presented honest and candid information and reasonable justifications for the decisions they made. Fair treatment by the other party symbolizes to people that they are being dealt with in a dignified and respectful way, thereby bolstering their sense of self-identity and self-worth (Brockner et al. 1992).

Perceptions of interactional injustice tend to lead to retaliation directed toward the tar-

Figure 14.1   **A Model of Dysfunctional Cyberbehavior**

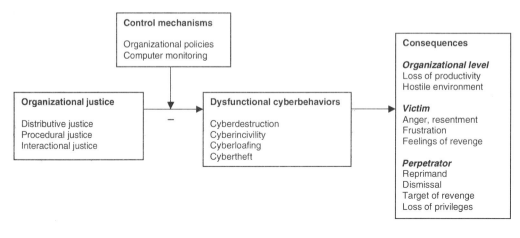

get (Skarlicki and Folger 1997). However, when the perpetrator of an injustice provides causal explanation of an unfair decision, this justification may mitigate the negative intentions the victim might attribute to the perpetrator (Bies 1987). In an experimental study designed to analyze the effects of mitigating circumstances on anger and aggression, Johnson and Rule (1986) found that participants who learned of mitigating circumstances before being provoked exhibited smaller increases in physiological arousal and reported less annoyance than did those who learned of mitigating circumstances after insult. Johnson and Rule also found that participants evaluated their provoker more favorably and retaliated less when they learned of mitigating circumstance information beforehand.

Although distinct, these three justice dimensions interact to influence employee behavior in the workplace. Employees do care about the fairness of the outcomes they receive, the formal procedures underlying the distribution of these outcomes, and the fairness of interpersonal treatment from managers. Failure to meet these expectations of justice may lead to dysfunctional behaviors, such as retaliation (Skarlicki and Folger 1997), theft (Greenberg 1990, 1993), sabotage (Ambrose et al. 2002) and workplace aggression (Baron et al. 1999). As a subset of dysfunctional behavior, dysfunctional cyberbehavior may be explained by perceptions of organizational justice. Thus, the following model links dysfunctional cyberbehavior and organizational justice.

A MODEL OF DYSFUNCTIONAL CYBERBEHAVIOR

The negative sign in Figure 14.1 indicates that the model anticipates a negative relationship between organizational justice and dysfunctional cyberbehavior. High levels of distributive, procedural, and interactional justice would reduce the likelihood of dysfunctional cyberbehavior, whereas low levels of distributive, procedural, and interactional justice would increase the likelihood of dysfunctional cyberbehavior. When employees feel unfairly treated, they may use computers as a medium to retaliate against the harm-doer or the organization itself. Lim et al. (2001), Lim et al. (2002), and Lim (2002) found that employees engaged in cyberloafing as a result of perceptions of unfair treatment. Employees are willing to cyberloaf when they perceive that they are overworked and underpaid. For example, one research participant stated: "It is all right for me to use the Internet for non-work reasons at work. After all, I work overtime without receiving extra pay from my employer" (Lim et al. 2002, 69).

Perceptions of distributive injustice, procedural injustice, and interactional injustice may have different effects on different dimensions of dysfunctional cyberbehavior. Greenberg (1993) found that employees use theft to retaliate against situations of inequitable payment. Thus, perceptions of distributive injustice may lead to cybertheft. In this case, cybertheft may represent an attempt to even the score when the employee is a victim of perceived distributive injustice. Such dysfunctional cyberbehavior would be oriented toward the organization or its representative responsible for the outcomes distribution. People are more likely to blame individuals rather than systems when making attributions for unfair outcomes (Aquino et al. 1999).

Procedural injustice, however, may lead to cyberloafing or cyberdestruction. The enactment of formal procedures is often attributed to the organization and its managers. Since the perpetrator of injustices is the organization or someone identified with it, the victim may retaliate by using a form of dysfunctional cyberbehavior that targets the organization or its representative. *Business Week* (2001) reports retaliatory actions committed by disgruntled former employees. In one case, an axed systems administrator hacked back into his former company's computers, then published user IDs, passwords, and secret company information in public chat rooms. Interactional injustice, however, may be likely to lead to cyberincivility if the perpetrator is directly identified. Thus, the following proposition is formulated:

Proposition 1: Employees who report high levels of distributive, procedural, and interactional justice would be less likely to engage in dysfunctional cyberbehaviors than employees who report low levels of distributive, procedural, and interactional justice.

Moderators

The model considers control mechanisms as potential moderators of the relationship between organizational justice and dysfunctional cyberbehavior. Control mechanisms include organizational policies and computer monitoring.

Organizations may prevent dysfunctional cyberbehavior by developing and implementing clear policies related to computer use and Internet and intranet access during work time. Organizations should explain behaviors that are considered dysfunctional and thus detrimental to the organization. Wen and Lin (1998) suggest that employers should determine what are acceptable amounts of time to spend online, what material should and should not be accessed, and what materials can be downloaded. Developing such policies would allow organizations to successfully control Internet access. Enacting policies governing computer use is important because when people do not have rules governing their behavior, they tend to make up their own rules. The existence of policies may serve as both guidelines and deterrents. As guidelines, organizational policies may discipline computer use and Internet access, helping employees understand what behaviors are acceptable or not. As deterrents, organizational policies may prevent employees from displaying behaviors that management considers unacceptable.

The likelihood of being punished when caught may prevent employees from abusing the computer system. As Straub and Welke put it, "Active and visible policing is thought to lower computer abuse by convincing potential abusers that there is too high a certainty of getting caught and punished severely" (1998, 441). Even if employees perceive that they have been unfairly treated and are willing to contemplate revenge by engaging in dysfunctional cyberbehavior, they may refrain from doing so if organizational policies related to such behaviors exist and are effectively enforced. For instance, Weisband and Reinig (1995) note that organizations that explicitly stipulate e-mail practices reduce the frequency of inappropriate messages, especially when the policies are routinely enforced. Thus, the following proposition is formulated.

> **Proposition 2:** The existence and enforcement of policies regulating the use of computers and the Internet at work may mitigate the negative impact of perceived injustices on dysfunctional cyberbehavior.

A second moderating variable included in the model is computer monitoring. Computer monitoring refers to the use of computer software to track employee computer usage and Internet activities. Computer monitoring may occur in two ways: building control devices within the system and monitoring employee computer behavior. The former is less invading than the latter. Building control devices into the system limits employee access to certain sites and the likelihood of cyberloafing. The second process involves a concurrent control, which occurs while the employee is working on the computer. Such control helps to monitor employee behavior. A third type of control mechanism occurs when the employee finishes working on the computer. It includes reading an employee's e-mail messages or tracking the Web activities to collect information about the sites visited.

Hoffer and Straub (1989) found that the use of operating system controls, such as passwords, security locks, integrity rules, and extra security software, cuts down on computer abuse. According to some employees, the lack of security in computer systems can be used as rationalization for computer abuse: "If you can't secure it, accept the consequences" (Harrington 1995). This assumption may be extended here: "If you can't monitor it, accept the consequences." Internet monitoring provides the employer with the ability to track an employee's Internet movements and report on them (Wen and Lin 1998). Although such methods may not eliminate dysfunctional cyberbehavior in organizations, they may reduce its frequency and consequently improve the efficiency and effectiveness of information technology. Thus, computer monitoring may act as a deterrent and therefore mitigate the negative impact of perceptions of unfairness.

> **Proposition 3:** Computer monitoring would mitigate the negative impact of perceived injustices on dysfunctional cyberbehavior.

Consequences of Dysfunctional Cyberbehavior

Dysfunctional cyberbehavior may have negative consequences for the victim, the organization, and the perpetrator.

Dysfunctional cyberbehavior may lead to frustration, resentment, and a desire for retaliation in the victim. These feelings may have a negative impact on the victim's work performance and affect relations with the perpetrator. As a way of protesting against an unfair treatment, the victim of a dysfunctional cyberbehavior may reduce inputs, report the aggressive acts, and/or seek revenge. Research on retaliation in organizations (Skarlicki and Folger 1997) suggests that when people feel offended, they tend to retaliate against the perpetrator of the perceived injustice.

Organizational outcomes affected by dysfunctional cyberbehavior include productivity and work climate. Although the consequences of obvious forms of dysfunctional cyberbehavior, such as destruction of computer files, may be tangible and measurable for the organization, the consequences of subtle forms of dysfunctional cyberbehavior, such as cyberincivility, may be difficult to quantify. Dysfunctional cyberbehavior may reduce organizational performance in the sense that time spent surfing the Web for non-work-related activities is time wasted.

Dysfunctional cyberbehavior may also create a hostile work environment characterized by suspicion and lack of interpersonal trust. Such a hostile atmosphere reduces the likelihood of cooperation between employees. To the extent that employees depend on each other for work-related information, a lack of cooperation and knowledge sharing may negatively impact their performance.

The negative consequences of dysfunctional cyberbehavior are not limited to the victim or the organization. The perpetrator may suffer its negative consequences as well, in the form of reprimand, dismissal, loss of privileges and future opportunities, or retaliatory actions. A perpetrator of dysfunctional cyberbehavior may face verbal reprimands from management for minor violations and possibly dismissal for more severe forms of dysfunctional cyberbehavior. The perpetrator may also face retaliation from the victim, hence escalating the conflict, or suffer from a tarnished reputation. The victim may retaliate by using similar computer devices or other more traditional means, such as verbal attacks or physical assaults, or may report the incident to a higher-status third party. Thus, dysfunctional cyberbehavior may backfire since the perpetrator may become a victim in turn. For instance, sending an offensive e-mail to a boss can threaten a career, torch morale, and reveal a woeful lack of professionalism (Sandberg 2003).

IMPLICATIONS FOR PRACTICE AND RESEARCH

Implications for Management Practice

The model described in this chapter contends that dysfunctional cyberbehavior is an organizational reality that is heavily influenced by perceptions of justice. In addition, the model considers that organizational policies and computer monitoring may mitigate the negative impact of perceptions of injustice on dysfunctional cyberbehavior. This model presents several lessons for managers, including creating fair working environments, developing and enforcing computer usage policies, and computer monitoring.

Managers may reduce dysfunctional cyberbehaviors by enhancing perceptions of distributive, procedural, and interactional justice. For instance, if employees use cyberloafing because they feel underpaid, then managers may reduce cyberloafing by administering equitable payment. Likewise, managers may also reduce dysfunctional cyberbehavior by treating employees with respect and dignity and by providing explanations underlying their decisions. Managers may also increase perceptions of fairness when designing and implementing organizational policies related to Internet usage and computer monitoring. They may improve the fairness of such policies by explaining to employees the goals of the policies and the types of computer activities to be monitored and by seeking their input.

Managers may also reduce dysfunctional cyberbehavior by developing and enforcing computer usage policies. A strategy for thwarting dysfunctional cyberbehavior is the development of a cyber code of conduct. A cyber code of conduct is a company booklet spelling out acceptable rules for computer use and Internet access. This code may be part of a company handbook or a separate document. Such a code serves two purposes. First, it guides employees concerning acceptable ways of using computers and the Internet. Second, it serves as a standard against which to evaluate employee behavior. Although organizations provide advice concerning the use, dissemination, and classification of sensitive information, rarely do they provide employees with detailed information about computer use and Internet access. Codes are believed to deter computer abuse because they keep employees abreast of laws and regulations and clearly define unacceptable or illegal conduct. Without them, it may be easier for employees to rationalize irresponsible action (Harrington 1996).

Based on the model of dysfunctional cyberbehavior, a prevention program containing five steps is suggested (see Figure 14.2). These steps include (1) recognition of the probability of dysfunctional cyberbehavior, (2) risk analysis, (3) development of alternative measures, (4) selection and implementation of the best alternative, and (5) enforcement of policies. First, managers should recognize the possibility that employees may misuse computer equipment and Internet access. Recognition of such problems would lead to the development of measures of prevention. Second, managers should analyze the possible risks involved in misusing computer equipment. This analysis may concern both technology and people. Third, once managers have identified deficiencies in the system, they should develop a list of possible solutions to prevent the occurrence of dysfunctional cyberbehavior. Fourth, managers should implement the best alternative. Finally, for the implementation to be successful in the long run, appropriate measures should be taken. One such measure is the enforcement of policies related to computer use and Internet access. Managers should play a key role in successfully deterring, preventing, and detecting computer abuse as well as pursuing remedies and/or punishing offenders for abuse (Straub and Welke 1998).

Finally, managers may reduce dysfunctional cyberbehavior by relying on computer

Figure 14.2 **Stages in the Development of a Dysfunctional Cyberbehavior Prevention Program**

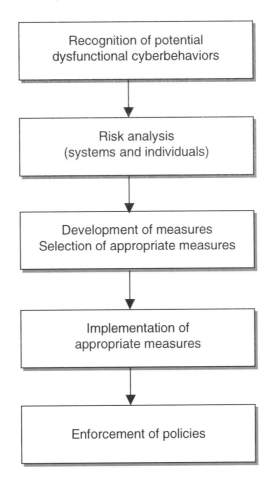

monitoring. In a survey administered to 103 companies, Hoffman et al. (2003) found that 92 percent of these companies had a monitoring system in place. These companies also notified their employees in advance. Indeed, employee notification is important because it enhances the fairness of the monitoring system. The monitoring system should also be consistent and applicable to all employees. However, to ensure fairness, any electronic monitoring of potential dysfunctional behaviors should specify work standards and unacceptable work behaviors, involve employees in the design of the process, and determine the measurement process of dysfunctional behaviors.

Computer monitoring may incur tangible as well as intangible costs for the company. Tangible costs include the software used, personnel employed, and time spent monitoring employees. Intangible costs may include employee distrust and ethical issues. Computer monitoring may also increase the degree of mistrust between management and employees and raise ethical issues (Hartman 2001; Introna 2002). Such mistrust may be overcome by providing clear explanations related to the goals and procedures of computer monitoring. Computer monitoring may pose problems for employees, who may consider it an invasion of privacy. However, if the management of a company is respectful of the employees, manages their expectations realistically, and is frank about the company's objectives, it can cultivate an atmosphere of trust and transparency in which employees may be more likely to view the monitoring process as serving a business need than as a sinister intrusion (Hoffman et al. 2003).

Implications for Research

Three lines of research can be gleaned from the dysfunctional cyberbehavior model based on the propositions formulated earlier. A first line of research concerns the effects of fairness perceptions on dysfunctional cyberbehavior. To what extent do perceptions of distributive, procedural, and interactional unfairness lead to dysfunctional cyberbehavior? Lim (2002) and Lim et al. (2001) note that employees who are disgruntled because they perceive that their employers have treated them unfairly would be inclined to get even with their employers through cyberloafing. Researchers could also study the extent to which each justice dimension is related to a particular form of dysfunctional cyberbehavior. Such studies may prove fruitful in explaining how organizational justice influences dysfunctional cyberbehavior.

A second line of research concerns the role of the potential moderators discussed in the model, organizational policies and computer monitoring. Researchers could analyze the extent to which the existence of organizational policies and computer monitoring mitigates the negative impact of perceived injustices. A third line of research focuses on the multidimensional nature of dysfunctional cyberbehavior. Although the present model has identified four types of dysfunctional cyberbehavior—cyberdestruction, cyberincivility, cyberloafing, and cybertheft—future research may identify other forms of dysfunctional cyberbehaviors. Most important, this classification needs empirical validation. Such validation requires the development of an instrument measuring these four components. A factor analysis could then determine whether these four categories overlap or represent separate forms of dysfunctional cyberbehavior.

Several methodologies may be used to analyze the relationship between organizational justice and dysfunctional cyberbehavior. Previous studies on cyberloafing (Lim 2002; Lim et al. 2001, 2002) used a survey methodology. Although this methodology garners useful information, it may prevent participants from fully disclosing their counterproductive activities even if anonymity is guaranteed. One way of overcoming this drawback is to ask respondents to report the extent to which such events have occurred in their workplace. In studying the frequency of aggressive behaviors in the workplace, Baron and Neuman (1999) asked respondents to report the extent to which they had observed such behaviors in the workplace in addition to asking them if they had engaged in such behaviors themselves. One possible advantage of this methodology is that employees would be likely to disclose information concerning actions committed by others rather than themselves, particularly if these actions are perceived as negative. Other methodologies include scenario analysis or critical incidents. Whatever the methodology used, it should be guided by a clear operationalization of the construct of dysfunctional cyberbehavior and the formulation of specific research hypotheses.

CONCLUSION

This chapter has introduced a new construct, dysfunctional cyberbehavior, in the organizational science literature and developed propositions that may lead to empirical inquiry. In an era in which computer usage is ubiquitous in organizations, it is important for organizational scholars to assess the extent to which information technology can be a double-edged sword. Although information technology can facilitate communication, improve efficiency, and foster productivity, it can also be misused. It is hoped that the present discussion will spark future theoretical and empirical studies on the phenomenon of dysfunctional cyberbehavior.

REFERENCES

Adams, S.J. 1965. Inequity in social exchange. In L. Berkowitz (ed.), *Advances in Social Experimental Psychology,* vol. 2. New York: Academic Press, 267–299.

Ambrose, M.L., Seabright, M.A., and Schminke, M. 2002. Sabotage in the workplace: The role of organizational injustice. *Organizational Behavior and Human Decision Processes* 89, 947–965.

Anandarajan, M. 2002. Internet abuse in the workplace. *Communications of the ACM* 45, 1, 53–54.

Anandarajan, M., Simmers, C., and Igbaria, M. 2000. An exploratory investigation of the antecedents and impact of Internet usage: An individual perspective. *Behavior and Information Technology* 19, 69–85.

Andersson, L.M., and Pearson, C.M. 1999. Tit-for-tat: The spiraling effect of incivility in the workplace. *Academy of Management Review* 24, 452–471.

Aquino, K., Lewis, M., and Bradfield, M. 1999. Justice constructs, negative affectivity, and employee deviance: A proposed model and empirical test. *Journal of Organizational Behavior* 20, 1073–1091.

Baron, R.A., and Neuman, J.H. 1999. Workplace violence and workplace aggression: Evidence on their relative frequency and causes. *Aggressive Behavior* 22, 161–173.

Baron, R.A., Neuman, J.H., and Geddes, D. 1999. Social and personal determinants of workplace aggression: Evidence for the impact of perceived injustice and the Type A behavior pattern. *Aggressive Behavior* 25, 281–296.

Bennet, R.J., and Robinson, S.L. 2003. The past, present, and future of workplace deviance research. In J. Greenberg (ed.), *Organizational Behavior: The State of the Science.* 2nd ed. Mahwah, NJ: Lawrence Erlbaum Associates, 247–281.

Beugré, C.D. 2003. Information technology as a double-edged sword: A model of cyber dysfunctional behavior. Published paper presented at Proceedings of the Eastern Academy of Management Meeting, April 30–May 3, Baltimore, Maryland, 1–28.

Bies, R.J. 1987. The predicament of injustice: The management of moral outrage. In L.L. Cummings and B.M. Staw (eds.), *Research in Organizational Behavior.* Greenwich, CT: JAI Press, 289–319.

Bies, R.J., and Moag, J.S. 1986. Interactional justice: Communication criteria of fairness. In R.J. Lewicki, B.H. Sheppard, and M.H. Bazerman (eds.), *Research on Negotiation in Organizations,* vol. 1. Greenwich, CT: JAI Press, 43–55.

Boone, T., and Ganeshan, R. 2001. The effect of information technology on learning in professional service organizations. *Journal of Operations Management* 19, 485–495.

Brockner, J., Tyler, R.T., and Cooper-Schneider, R. 1992. The influence of prior commitment to an institution on reactions to perceived unfairness: The higher they are, the harder they fall. *Administrative Science Quarterly* 37, 241–261.

Brockner, J., and Wiesenfeld, B.M. 1996. An integrated framework for explaining reactions to decisions: Interactive effects of outcomes and procedures. *Psychological Bulletin* 120, 189–208.

Bronikowski, L. 2002. Esniff.com sniffs out cyberslacking. *ColoradoBiz* 27, 11, 46.

Brynjolfsson, E. 1993. The productivity paradox of information technology. *Communications of the ACM* 36, 12, 67–77.

Business Week. 2001. Revenge of the downsized nerds. July 30, 40.

Carley, W. 1992. Rigging computers for fraud or malice is often an inside job. *Wall Street Journal,* August 27.

Cropanzano, R., and Greenberg, J. 1997. Progress in organizational justice: Tunneling through the maze. In C.L. Cooper and I.T. Robertson (eds.), *International Review of Industrial and Organizational Psychology.* New York: John Wiley, 317–372.

DeBoer, E.M., Bakker, A.B., Syroit, J.E., and Schaufeli, W.B. 2002. Unfairness at work as a predictor of absenteeism. *Journal of Organizational Behavior* 23, 181–197.

Deutsch, M. 1985. *Distributive Justice: A Social-Psychological Perspective.* New Haven: Yale University Press.

Dewett, T., and Jones, G.R. 2001. The role of information technology in the organizations: Review, model, and assessment. *Journal of Management* 27, 313–346.

Donaldson, T. 2001. Ethics in cyberspace: Have we seen this movie before? *Business and Society Review* 106, 4, 273–291.

Dos Santos, B., and Sussman, L. 2000. Improving the return on IT investment: The productivity paradox. *Internal Journal of Information Management* 20, 429–440.

Folger, R. 1993. Reactions to mistreatment at work. In K. Murnighan (ed.), *Social Psychology in Organizations: Advances in Theory and Research.* Englewood Cliffs, NJ: Prentice Hall, 161–183.

Folger, R., and Baron R.A. 1996. Violence and hostility at work: A model of reactions to perceived injustice. In G.R. VandenBos and E.Q. Bulato (eds.), *Workplace Violence.* Washington, DC: American Psychological Association, 51–85.

Folger, R., and Konovsky, M.A. 1989. Effects of procedural and distributive justice on reactions to pay raise decisions. *Academy of Management Journal* 32, 115–130.

Folger, R., and Skarlicki, D.P. 1998. A popcorn metaphor for employee aggression. In R.W. Griffin, A. O'Leary-Kelly, and J. Collins (eds.), *Dysfunctional Behavior in Organizations,* vol. 1: *Violent Behaviors in Organizations.* Stamford, CT: JAI Press, 43–81.

Folster, L.W., and Flynn, D.M. 1984. Management information technology: Its effects on organizational form and function. *MIS Quarterly* 8, 229–236.

Gomez-Mejia, L.R., Balkin, D.B., and Cardy, R.L. 2004. *Managing Human Resources,* 4th ed. Upper Saddle River, NJ: Prentice Hall, 2004.

Greenberg, J. 1990. Employee theft as a reaction to underpayment inequity: The hidden costs of pay cuts. *Journal of Applied Psychology* 75, 561–568.

Greenberg, J. 1993. Stealing in the name of justice: Informational and interpersonal moderators of employee reactions to underpayment inequity. *Organizational Behavior and Human Decision Processes* 54, 81–103.

Greenberg, J., and Alge, B.J. 1998. Aggressive reactions to workplace injustice. In R.W. Griffin, A. O'Leary-Kelly, and J. Collins (eds.), *Dysfunctional Behavior in Organizations,* vol. 1: *Violent Behaviors in Organizations.* Greenwich, CT: JAI Press, 119–145.

Griffin, R.W., O'Leary-Kelly, A., and Collins, J.M. 1998. Dysfunctional work behaviors in organizations. In D.M. Rousseau and C. Cooper (eds.), *Trends in Organizational Behavior,* vol. 5. London: John Wiley, 65–82.

Gunasekaran, A., Love, P.E.D., Rahimi, F., and Miele, R. 2001. A model for investment justification in information technology projects. *International Journal of Information Management* 21, 349–364.

Hartman, L. 2001. Technology and ethics: Privacy in the workplace, *Business and Society Review* 106, 1, 1–27.

Harrington, S.J. 1989. Why people copy software and create computer viruses: Individual characteristics or situational factors? *Information Resources Management Journal* 2, 3, 28–37.

———. 1995. Computer crime and abuse by IS employees. *Journal of Systems Management* 46, 2, 6–11.

———. 1996. The effects of codes of ethics and personal denial of responsibility on computer abuse judgments and intentions. *MIS Quarterly* 20, 257–278.

Hellriegel, D., Slocum, J.W., Jr., and Woodman, R.W. 2001. *Organizational Behavior,* 9th ed. Cincinnati: South-Western College Publishing.

Hitt, L., and Brynjolfsson, E. 1996. Productivity, business profitability, and consumer surplus: Three different measures of information technology value. *MIS Quarterly* 20, 121–142.

Hoffer, J.A., and Straub, D.W., Jr., 1989. The 9 to 5 underground: Are you policing computer crimes? *Sloan Management Review* 30, 4, 35–44.

Hoffman, W.M., Hartman, L.P., and Rowe, M. 2003. You've got mail . . . and the boss knows: A survey by the Center for Business Ethics of Companies' e-mail and Internet monitoring. *Business and Society Review* 108, 3, 285–307.

Introna, L.D. 2002. The (im)possibility of ethics in the information age. *Information and Organization* 12, 71–84.

Johnson, T.E., and Rule, B.G. 1986. Mitigating circumstance information, censure, and aggression. *Journal of Personality and Social Psychology* 50, 537–542.

Jung, B., Han, I., and Lee, S. 2001. Security threats to Internet: A Korean multi-industry investigation. *Information and Management* 38, 487–498.

Leventhal, G.S. 1976. The distinction of rewards and resources in groups and organizations. In L. Berkowitz and E. Walster (eds.), *Advances in Experimental Social Psychology,* vol. 9. New York: Academic Press, 91–131.

Leventhal, G.S., Karuza, J., and Fry, W.R. 1980. Beyond fairness: A theory of allocation preferences. In G. Mikula (ed.), *Justice and Social Interaction.* New York: Springer-Verlag, 167–218.

Lim, V.K.G. 2002. The IT way of loafing on the job: Cyberloafing, neutralizing, and organizational justice. *Journal of Organizational Behavior* 23, 675–694.

Lim, V.K.G., Loo, G.L., and Teo, T.S.H. 2001. Perceived injustice, neutralization and cyberloafing at the workplace. Paper presented at the Academy of Management, Washington, DC, August 5–8.

Lim, V.K.G., Teo, T.S.H., and Loo, G.L. 2002. How do I loaf here? Let me count the ways. *Communications of the ACM* 45, 1, 66–70.

Lind, E.A., and Tyler, T.R. 1988. *The Social Psychology of Procedural Justice.* New York: Plenum Press.

Loch, K.D., Carr, H.H., and Warkentin, M.E. 1992. Threats to information systems: Today's reality, yesterday's understanding. *MIS Quarterly* 17, 173–186.

Mills, J.E., Hu, B., Beldona, S., and Clay, J. 2001. Cyberslacking: A liability issue for wired workplaces. *Cornell Hotel and Restaurant Administration Quarterly* 42, 34–47.

Naughton, K., Raymond, J., Shulman, K., and Struzzi, D. 1999. Cyberslacking: The Internet has brought distractions into cubicles, and now corporate America is fighting back. *Newsweek,* November 29, 62–65.

Oates, B. 2001. Cyber crime: How technology makes it easy and what to do about it. *Information Systems Management* 18, 3, 92–96.

Pearson, C.M., Andersson, L.M., and Porath, C.L. 2000. Assessing and attacking workplace incivility. *Organizational Dynamics* 29, 123–137.

Robinson, S.L., and Bennett, R.J. 1995. A typology of deviant workplace behaviors: A multidimensional scaling study. *Academy of Management Review* 38, 555–572.

Sandberg, J. 2003. Workplace e-mail can turn radioactive in clumsy hands. *Wall Street Journal,* February 12.

Shabi, R. 2000. The spying game. *Financial Management,* September, 32–33.

Simmers, C.A. 2002. Aligning Internet usage with business priorities. *Communications of the ACM* 45, 1, 71–74.

Skarlicki, D.P., and Folger, R. 1997. Retaliation in the workplace: The role of distributive, procedural, and interactional justice. *Journal of Applied Psychology* 82, 434–443.

Straub, D.W., and Welke, R.J. 1998. Coping with systems risk: Security planning models for management decision making. *MIS Quarterly* 22, 441–469.

Thibaut, J.W., and Walker, L. 1975. *Procedural Justice: A Psychological Analysis.* Hillsdale, NJ: Lawrence Erlbaum Associates.

Tyler, T.R., and Lind, E.A. 1992. A relational model of authority in groups. In M.P. Zanna (ed.), *Advances in Experimental Social Psychology,* vol. 25. San Diego, CA: Academic Press, 115–191.

Verespej, M.A. 2000. Inappropriate Internet surfing. *Industry Week,* February 7, 59–64.

Wall Street Journal Online. 2003. Bank One says ex-employees stole confidential client data. www.wsj.com.

Weisband, S.P., and Reinig, B.A. 1995. Managing user perceptions of e-mail privacy. *Communications of the ACM* 38, 12, 40–47.

Wen, H.J., and Lin, B.S. 1998. Internet and employee productivity. *Management Decision* 36, 395–398.

Wilson, G.T. 1984. Computer systems and fraud prevention. *Journal of Systems Management* 35, 9, 36–39.

Wooley, D. 1998. Electronic robbery: How to prevent huge losses in nanoseconds. *Journal of Retail Banking Services* 20, 2, 49–53.

CHAPTER 15

CYBERLOAFING AND ORGANIZATIONAL JUSTICE

The Moderating Role of Neutralization Technique

VIVIEN K.G. LIM AND THOMPSON S.H. TEO

Abstract: *This study focuses on cyberloafing—the act of employees using their companies' Internet access for personal purposes during work hours. Using the theoretical framework offered by research on neutralization techniques, we develop a model that suggests that when individuals perceive their organizations to be distributively, procedurally, and interactionally unjust, they are likely to invoke a specific neutralization technique, i.e., the metaphor of the ledger, to legitimize their subsequent engagement in the act of cyberloafing. Data were collected with the use of an electronic questionnaire and focus group interviews from 188 working adults with access to the Internet at the workplace. Results of moderated regression analyses provide empirical support for the moderating role of neutralization technique on the relationship between cyberloafing and the three types of organizational justice (distributive, procedural, and interactional). This indicates that employees tend to neutralize their cyberloafing behavior. The results have important implications for organizational Internet policies on cyberloafing.*

Keywords: *Cyberloafing, Organizational Justice, Internet Use, Internet Misuse*

INTRODUCTION

The Internet has played an important role in helping businesses reduce costs, shorten product cycle times, and market products and services effectively (Anandarajan et al. 2000). Recent evidence suggests that the Internet is a double-edged sword that companies should deploy freely to employees with caution. For example, an online survey reported that about 84 percent of employees sent non-job-related e-mail, while another 90 percent surfed the Internet for recreational Web sites using time when they should have been working (Sharma and Gupta 2004). Additionally, a survey of 1,000 workers in the United States revealed that 64 percent of those surveyed surf the Internet for personal interest during working hours (*Straits Times* 2000).

Reports in the mass media lend further support to this worrying and costly trend of employees misusing the Internet while on the job. For example, a study by research firm

Computer Economics found that when employees accessed the Internet on company time with company computers for personal reasons, as much as US$5.3 billion in costs may be incurred (Young and Case 2004).

Besides these direct costs, intangible costs in the form of productivity losses can result from employees' misuse of the Internet. For example, a majority of the 250 executives polled in a study reported that their employees' productivity levels are being impaired because these employees use the Internet for non-job-related purposes (Lichtash 2004). Further, another study reported that Internet misuse at work is costing American corporations more than $85 billion annually in lost productivity (Websense 2003). Thus, taken together, these figures provide evidence regarding the prevalence or, at the very least, the potential of employees misusing the Internet access provided at the workplace.

Extant studies examining employees' misuse of the Internet, to date, remain largely atheoretical and provide little insight as to why this phenomenon occurs. To the extent that employees' misuse of the Internet entails considerable costs to organizations and affects employees' productivity, it is important to understand what motivates individuals to engage in this behavior so that effective organizational intervention programs and policies may be developed and implemented to deter or limit its occurrence. The present study represents an initial attempt to examine employees' misuse of the Internet.

We used the theoretical frameworks offered by organizational justice and neutralization studies to explain why employees may be motivated to misuse their companies' Internet access, specifically in the form of cyberloafing, and the mechanisms through which this behavior is facilitated. The contributions of our study are twofold. First, extant studies in the emerging literature related to the Internet have largely examined the possible benefits that this global communications tool offers (e.g., Anandarajan et al. 2000). Work on the darker side of the Internet, excluding studies of Internet addition (e.g., Armstrong et al. 2000), tend to be anecdotal and descriptive in nature. Thus, our study attempts to fill this void in the literature by proposing a model based on the organizational justice framework to extend our understanding of cyberloafing in the work setting.

Second, by approaching the issue from not only the theoretical perspectives offered by organizational justice, but also in particular, neutralization techniques—defined as rationalizations that individuals invoke in order to convince themselves and others that their deviant behaviors are justifiable and/or excusable—this study aims to further our understanding as to why misbehavior among employees continues to prevail in organizations, despite the presence of extensive organizational rules and procedures designed and implemented precisely to keep such misbehavior to a minimum. As noted by Robinson and Kraatz (1998), there is the possibility that employees are using underlying mechanisms (i.e., neutralization) to facilitate their engagement in questionable behaviors. However, to date, the concept of neutralization has largely been applied to understanding misbehavior among delinquents. To this end, therefore, the present study seeks to extend the existing workplace deviance literature by examining a new form of employee misbehavior, i.e., cyberloafing within the framework offered by neutralization. Specifically, we examined the role of the metaphor of the ledger, a specific form of neutralization technique in moderating the relationship between (1) distributive justice, (2) procedural

Figure 15.1   **Research Model**

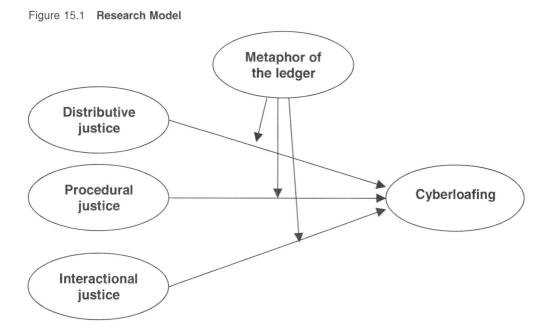

justice, and (3) interactional justice and cyberloafing. Figure 15.1 depicts the relation-ships among variables in our study.

DEFINITION OF CONSTRUCTS

Cyberloafing Defined

Consistent with previous research, (e.g., Lim 2002; Lim et al. 2002), we conceptualized and operationalized cyberloafing to include any voluntary act of employees' using their companies' Internet access during office hours to surf non-job-related Web sites for per-sonal purposes and to check (including receiving and sending) personal e-mail. Both of these activities constitute an unproductive use of time in that they detract employees from carrying out and completing their main job duties (Lim et al. 2002).

According to this definition, therefore, cyberloafing can and will be considered a deviant workplace behavior in our study. Workplace deviance refers to voluntary acts undertaken by organizational members that violate significant organizational norms, such that the well-being of organizations and/or their members are usually adversely affected (Robinson and Bennett 1995). While cyberloafing has not been empirically examined in the area of workplace deviance, our definition of cyberloafing categorizes it under the rubric of production deviance, which includes organizational misbehaviors that are counterproductive in nature.

Production deviance in the form of loafing is a perennial and costly phenomenon that has existed in organizations since time immemorial, as is evident from Snyder et al.'s study (1990), where employees admitted to various forms of malingering on the job. In fact, as early as two decades ago, the *ABA Banking Journal* (1983) proposed a comprehensive list to describe the various types of people who loaf at work: these include the telephone chatters, the restroom-minded, and the long lunchers, among others.

With the availability of the Internet, however, production deviance has evolved to take on a new form. Employees can now engage in loafing on the job by maintaining the guise of being hard at work in the real world while, in effect, traveling through cyberspace by surfing Web sites for personal interests and purposes. Cyberloafers need not be absent from the office for inexplicably long periods of time, as long lunchers do. Cyberloafers also need not worry as much about the visibility of their loafing compared to the restroom-minded or those who hang out by the watercooler to chat. Indeed, Bennett and Robinson (2003) noted that with the advent of technology, the opportunities for employees to be unproductive at work have been multiplied and that cyberloafing is a production deviance that employers should be increasingly concerned with.

Cyberloafers can inadvertently end up spending a lot of time surfing the Internet, moving from one Web site to another simply with a click of the mouse. Also, cyberloafers in their virtual travels may—unwittingly or otherwise—visit sites that expose the organization to legal liabilities and to the dangers posed by computer viruses. These factors taken together suggest that cyberloafers may pose a greater "threat" to organizations in terms of productivity losses and costs incurred, relative to other types of loafers.

The advent of technology has thus revolutionized loafing. Specifically, cyberloafing is the information technology (IT) way of idling on the job. Therefore, while access to the Internet may not result in an increase in production deviance with more people engaging in loafing per se, the temptation to do so is certainly higher since the Internet makes it so easy and convenient to loaf in this manner.

Metaphor of the Ledger as a Neutralization Technique

Scholars explain that people generally possess an innate desire to present themselves favorably both to themselves and to others (Greenberg 1998; Copes 2003). Neutralization techniques are a priori rationalizations that individuals invoke in order to convince themselves and others that their deviant acts are excusable and/or justifiable (Sykes and Matza 1957). Individuals undertake these strategies in order to reconcile the discrepancies between their deviant behavior and the positive self-image they wish to project, as well as to protect themselves from self-blame and guilt (Robinson and Kraatz 1998). In this way, neutralization makes it easier for people to engage in deviant acts.

While various neutralization techniques have been put forth and conceptualized by researchers, in this study we focused on the technique known as the metaphor of the ledger. When individuals engage in neutralization through the metaphor of the ledger, they rationalize that they are entitled to indulge in deviant behaviors because of past good behaviors, which have led to accrual of credits that they can "cash in" (Klockars 1974). Premised upon this idea, therefore, employees who have expended resources in the form of time and effort in fulfilling or even going beyond their job duties would expect their employers to respond in kind by allocating outcomes to them in a favorable manner or ensuring that the procedures in the outcome allocations are just by treating them in a just and fair manner. Employees would view services provided as accumulated credits to be cashed in in exchange for organizational rewards—both tangible and intangible—that have been implicitly and explicitly promised. According to organizational justice theory, therefore, it makes sense that individuals who feel that they have been shortchanged in some way in the employment relationship would invoke this neutralization technique when they want to exercise the penalty of taking back something in an effort to restore some semblance of justice in the relationship. The role of justice violations in invoking the metaphor of the ledger as a neutralization technique will be discussed in greater detail in the next section.

THEORETICAL BACKGROUND

The relationship between the justice variables and cyberloafing can be understood from theoretical perspectives provided by the literature on organizational justice. Organizational justice refers to how fair an organization is in its conduct toward its employees. Existing research largely suggests that organizational justice takes three different forms, which govern both the outcomes as well as the processes leading to these outcomes.

The first type of organizational justice is distributive justice, which refers to the perception of fairness relating to allocation of outcomes or resources. The second is procedural justice, which refers to the perceived fairness of the processes used to determine outcome allocation. Interactional justice, the third type of organizational justice, refers to the quality of interpersonal treatment (i.e., interpersonal sensitivity and explanations or social accounts) received by employees.

Extant research in the area of organizational behavior has established theoretical arguments as well as empirical evidence that violations of any type of organizational justice often lead to the occurrence of workplace deviance (e.g., Fox et al. 2001; Greenberg and Barling 1998; Masterson et al. 2000). In general, results of such studies suggest that the perceived lack of organizational justice consistently predicts employees' propensity to redress their felt grievances through either property or production deviance, or both. For example, Colquitt et al. (2001) found that all three justice constructs were significant predictors of deviant behaviors directed against both the organization and other organizational members.

Organizational injustice has also been found to have significant effects on employee theft. Greenberg and Scott (1996) established a framework whereby employee theft was conceptualized as a response to distributive injustice. More specifically, Greenberg and Scott proposed that in social exchange relationships, such as employment relationships, individuals are motivated to maintain equilibrium between the outcomes they receive and the inputs they provide. For example, individuals who were made to work late and were not reimbursed for their transportation costs were found to take money from their employers' cash register because they viewed it as an entitlement (Analoui and Kakabadse 1991).

It can thus be seen that a considerable amount of evidence has been found in support of the relationship between perceived organizational injustice and employee misconduct. Indeed, the main effects of the different types of organizational justice on workplace deviance have been frequently examined and consistently demonstrated; hence, we do not make any formal hypotheses along this line (for a detailed discussion of the relationship between organizational justice and cyberloafing, see Lim [2002]). Rather, in this study, we are more interested in examining if the metaphor of the ledger, a specific neutralization technique, would moderate the relationship between the different types of organizational justice and cyberloafing.

As discussed earlier, inherent in the metaphor of the ledger as a neutralization technique is the idea that individuals are entitled to indulge in deviant behavior insofar as they have accrued good credits in the past that can be cashed in later to excuse the misbehavior. The individuals' guilt would thus be assuaged since good credits are cashed in for bad ones, leading to equilibrium between good and evil acts (Hollinger 1991).

Extending this line of reasoning, we argue that while the justice theory suggests that perceptions of unfairness at the workplace predispose individuals toward the possibility of retaliation through misbehaving in the form of cyberloafing, neutralization theory goes one step further and suggests that insofar as employees feel that the time and effort they put in for their organizations (i.e., accumulated good credits) have not been fairly evaluated, rewarded, and appreciated, individuals will invoke the metaphor of the ledger as a neutralization technique to mitigate any guilt they may experience. While these employees may be aware that what they plan to do is not right, they neutralize their actions such that these actions become acceptable; that is, to themselves as well as to others, when they misbehave at the workplace, they are merely cashing in their accrued credits. Thus, we argue that the metaphor of the ledger moderates the relationships between perceived injustice and cyberloafing.

Hypothesis 1a: In the context of Internet usage at work, the metaphor of the ledger moderates the relationship between distributive justice and cyberloafing; the relationship becomes stronger when neutralization is high and weaker when neutralization is low.

Hypothesis 1b: In the context of Internet usage at work, the metaphor of the ledger moderates the relationship between procedural justice and cyberloafing; the relationship becomes stronger when neutralization is high and weaker when neutralization is low.

Hypothesis 1c: In the context of Internet usage at work, the metaphor of the ledger moderates the relationship between interactional justice and cyberloafing; the relationship becomes stronger when neutralization is high and weaker when neutralization is low.

METHOD

Procedures and Respondent Characteristics

Data were obtained through the use of an online survey that was posted on the Internet. This method of data collection was deemed appropriate for our study for three reasons.

First, it provided us with access to an enormous pool of employed adults who were Internet-savvy—that is, individuals who were able to cyberloaf if they are inclined to do so.

Second, previous research has shown that people exhibit lower social desirability when they respond to an online rather than a paper-based questionnaire (e.g., Lee 1993). Therefore, given that we were trying to elicit responses to behaviors (i.e., cyberloafing) that may reflect negatively on respondents, we decided to use an electronic questionnaire in order to ensure that social desirability was kept to a minimum and anonymity maintained.

A third consideration that guided us in the selection of our sample and data collection procedure was the generalizability of our findings. By targeting employed individuals who had Internet access at the workplace and were Internet savvy, we would be able to generalize our findings to this population of Internet users.

Prior to the design of the questionnaire, interviews were held with several working adults to ensure that the cyberloafing items were easily understood by them. Issues, concerns, and suggestions raised by the interviewees were noted. The revised instrument was then pretested with two undergraduate Internet users. While no major problem was detected, several minor modifications were made based on their feedback regarding the clarity of some items as well as the overall presentation of the survey.

The second round of pretest was conducted using three working adults. No major adverse comments were raised by these workers. Thus, the survey instrument was deemed ready for actual respondents.

The survey site was publicized in various newsgroups. To encourage participation in the survey, a token phone card was offered as an incentive to the first hundred participants. A total of 188 surveys were received. Since these received surveys were fully completed by respondents, all 188 surveys were used in our data analyses.

Of these 188 respondents, about 47 percent were men. The average age of respondents was 30 years (SD = 7). About 85 percent of respondents had at least a high school diploma or a bachelor's degree. Respondents reported that, on average, they use the Internet while at work for about 2.4 hours each day (SD = 2) and have been using the Internet for about 2.6 years (SD = 2).

We compared our sample characteristics with those studies conducted on Internet users both in Singapore (e.g., Teo et al. 1997) and in the United States (e.g., Graphics, Visualization, and Usability [GVU] Center 1998). Respondents in all these studies were predominantly male (89 percent for Teo et al.'s study and 66 per cent for GVU). However, GVU's study reported an increasing trend in the number of women users, particularly in Europe. Thus, it is possible that the almost even distribution of men and women in our study was due to the local government adopting a proactive stance toward IT adoption here.

Our sample was also comparable to those in previous research in terms of age and educational level. For example, most of the respondents in Teo et al.'s (1997) study were between sixteen and thirty years old, while the respondents in GVU's (1998) study averaged about thirty-eight years old. Additionally, both studies also found that the general Internet user was college (or its equivalent) educated.

Measures

Organizational Justice

The three justice variables were measured using scales developed by Moorman (1991). Distributive justice was measured with five items ($\alpha = 0.95$) pertaining to individuals' perceptions of the extent to which they were fairly rewarded by their organizations based on items such as "the responsibilities you have," "the stresses and strains of your job," and "the work that you have done well."

Procedural justice was assessed with seven items ($\alpha = 0.95$) pertaining to respondents' perceptions regarding the fairness of organizational procedures. One item, for example, was this: "How fairly are the organizational procedures designed to (a) Provide opportunities to appeal against or challenge a company's decision; (b) Hear the concerns of everyone affected by a company's decision; and (c) Generate standards so that decisions can be made with consistency." Items for both distributive and procedural justice were scored on a five-point scale ranging from (1) very unfair to (5) very fair.

The scale for interactional justice included six items pertaining to whether organizational procedures were enacted properly and fairly by supervisors. Items, which were scored on a five-point scale ranging from (1) strongly disagree to (5) strongly agree, included the following: "My supervisor (a) Provides me with timely feedback about decisions and their implications; (b) Is able to suppress personal bias; and (c) Treats me with kindness and consideration." The Cronbach's alpha for this scale was 0.93.

The Metaphor of the Ledger

We assessed this variable using the scale developed by Hollinger (1991). This scale consisted of seven items ($\alpha = 0.88$) pertaining to respondents' perception that good credits may be accumulated and cashed in subsequently to neutralize the employees' deviant behaviors. Respondents were asked to indicate, on a five-point scale ranging from (1) strongly disagree to (5) strongly agree, the extent to which they agreed or disagreed with statements such as "I should not feel guilty about using the Internet for non-job-related reasons if I: (a) Have to put in extra work because I do not receive enough help and equipment; (b) Were asked to do excessive amounts of work; and (c) Have to put in extra effort to find enough information to get the job done."

Cyberloafing

This variable was assessed with eleven items developed by Lim et al. (2002) and Teo et al. (1997). Respondents were asked to indicate how often they engaged in activities such as using the Internet to surf non-job-related Web sites and sending personal e-mails (1 = never to 5 = constantly) during working hours.

We conducted factor analyses to ascertain the underlying factor structure for the eleven cyberloafing items. Two factors accounting for about 59 percent of the variance were

Table 15.1

Results of Factor Analyses for Cyberloafing

Items	Loadings
Browsing activities Eigenvalue = 5.08, variance explained = 46.2 percent, α = 0.85	
1. Sports-related Web sites	0.87
2. Investment-related Web sites	0.82
3. Entertainment-related Web sites	0.80
4. General news sites	0.75
5. Non-job-related Web sites	0.73
6. Download non-work-related information	0.68
7. Shop online for personal goods	0.60
8. Adult-oriented (sexually explicit) Web sites	0.55
E-mailing activities Eigenvalue = 1.46, variance explained = 13.3 percent, α = 0.90	
1. Check non-work-related e-mail	0.90
2. Send non-work-related e-mail	0.87
3. Receive non-work-related e-mail	0.85

Table 15.2

Means, Standard Deviations, Correlations, and Reliabilities

Variables	Mean	SD	1	2	3	4	5
Distributive justice	3.15	1.13	(.95)				
Procedural justice	3.01	1.02	0.75***	(.95)			
Interactional justice	3.60	0.95	0.62***	0.61***	(.93)		
Metaphor of the ledger	3.26	0.95	−0.43***	−0.41***	−0.37***	(.88)	
Cyberloafing	3.02	0.96	−0.38***	−0.38***	−0.29***	0.39***	(.88)

N = 188. The numbers in parentheses on the diagonal are coefficient alphas.
***$p < .001$.

retained. The first factor, browsing activities, consisted of eight items ($\alpha = 0.85$) pertaining to how often individuals used the Internet during working hours to surf various non-job-related Web sites, such as those which were investment-, sports-, or entertainment-related. The second, e-mailing activities, included three items ($\alpha = 0.90$) assessing how often respondents sent and checked personal e-mail during working hours. The results of factor analyses are shown in Table 15.1.

ANALYSIS AND RESULTS

The means, standard deviations, correlations, and reliabilities of the variables in this study are presented in Table 15.2. The results of correlational analyses suggest that in general, the variables in our study were significantly correlated in the expected directions.

Table 15.3

Results of Moderated Regression Analyses

Outcomes	R^2	ΔR^2	ΔF
Cyberloafing			
Distributive justice + Neutralization using metaphor of the ledger	0.35		
Distributive justice + Neutralization using metaphor of the ledger + Distributive justice × Neutralization using metaphor of the ledger	0.36	0.01	2.98*
Procedural justice + Neutralization using metaphor of the ledger	0.35		
Procedural justice + Neutralization using metaphor of the ledger + Procedural justice × Neutralization using metaphor of the ledger	0.37	0.02	3.99*
Interactional justice + Neutralization using metaphor of the ledger	0.34		
Interactional justice + Neutralization using metaphor of the ledger + Interactional justice × Neutralization using metaphor of the ledger	0.36	0.02	4.19*

$N = 188; {}^*p < 0.05.$

Moderating Role of Metaphor of the Ledger as a Neutralization Technique

Moderated regression analyses were used to examine the moderating effect of the metaphor of the ledger as a neutralization technique on the relationship between the three justice variables and cyberloafing. A summary of the results, as shown in Table 15.3, suggests that the neutralization technique significantly moderated the relationships between cyberloafing and distributive justice, procedural justice, and interactional justice. The gains in the amount of variance explained were 0.01, 0.02 , and 0.02, respectively.

To determine whether the patterns characterizing the interactions conform to the directions as proposed in the research hypotheses, separate regressions of cyberloafing were performed on the three justice predictors for respondents who engaged in low levels of techniques of neutralization and for those who engaged in high levels of techniques of neutralization. The low and high distinction was defined as scores on neutralization technique that fell one standard deviation above and below the mean of the scores on neutralization technique. This procedure was recommended by Cohen and Cohen (1983) for all interaction cases.

Figure 15.2 depicts graphically the interaction effect of neutralization technique on the relationship between distributive justice and cyberloafing. The interaction is ordinal in nature. As shown in the figure, the directions of the relationship are in line with those proposed in hypothesis 1a in that the slope of the regression line of distributive justice and cyberloafing for high neutralization technique is steeper than the slope of the regression line for low neutralization technique. Figure 15.3 reveals that, consistent with hypothesis 1b, the relationship between procedural justice and cyberloafing becomes stronger when neutralization technique is high and weaker when neutralization technique is low. The graph in Figure 15.3 depicts an ordinal interaction.

Figure 15.4 shows the interaction effect for hypothesis 1c. The graph suggests an ordinal interaction, supporting our hypothesis that the relationship between interactional

Figure 15.2   **Relationship Between Distributive Justice and Cyberloafing for High Neutralization and Low Neutralization**

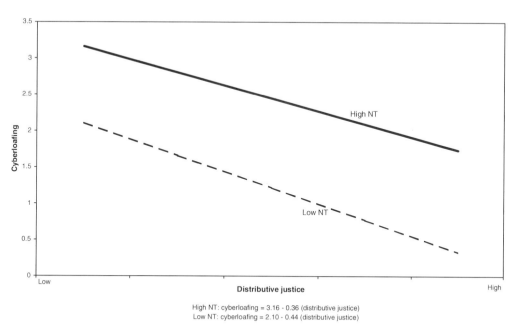

High NT: cyberloafing = 3.16 - 0.36 (distributive justice)
Low NT: cyberloafing = 2.10 - 0.44 (distributive justice)

justice and cyberloafing becomes stronger when neutralization technique is high and weaker when neutralization technique is low.

While all hypotheses were supported, it is worthwhile to note that the interactions accounted for a small percentage of the variance in the outcome variables and were statistically significant due to the large sample size in the present study. Such small increments in R square as a result of the interactions are not unusual in moderated regression analyses. Several researchers have noted that the test of the interaction term is essentially a very conservative one as it accounts for the variance left over "after the stronger main effects have been partialled out" (Pierce et al. 1993, 283). Nevertheless, Chaplin (1991) noted that even very small interaction effect sizes might be important in the context of a well-articulated theory. Hence, although small, the interaction effects in the present study are theoretically interesting in that they shed light on the potential moderating role of neutralization technique in the relationship between perceived injustice and cyberloafing—i.e., while perceived injustice may motivate individuals to retaliate by engaging in cyberloafing, individuals do make use of the metaphor of the ledger as a neutralization technique to assuage their experienced guilt and to legitimate otherwise unacceptable behavior.

DISCUSSION

Our study examined the misuse of the Internet at the workplace by employees (i.e., cyberloafing) from the combined perspectives offered by organizational justice and neu-

Figure 15.3   **Relationship Between Procedural Justice and Cyberloafing for High Neutralization and Low Neutralization**

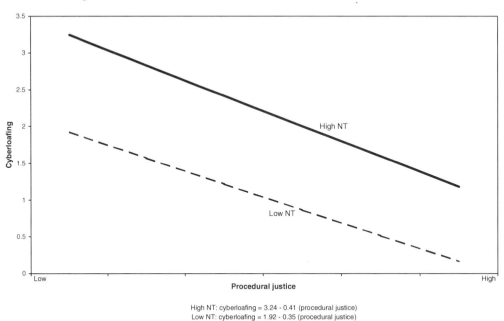

High NT: cyberloafing = 3.24 - 0.41 (procedural justice)
Low NT: cyberloafing = 1.92 - 0.35 (procedural justice)

tralization. Specifically, our findings suggest that when organizations are distributively, procedurally, and interactionally unjust in their treatment of their employees (i.e., organizations have not given expected rewards or fair treatment in exchange for fair work), these employees are more likely to invoke the neutralization technique—the metaphor of the ledger—to legitimate their subsequent engagement in the act of cyberloafing. Since neutralization enables them to justify their otherwise deviant actions, employees thus exhibit a greater propensity to engage in cyberloafing.

Our results are noteworthy in that they suggest that exchange principles governing relationships are applicable to the understanding of new problems posed by new technology. That is, employees who are disgruntled because they perceive an imbalance in the employment relationship as a result of unjust treatment would be inclined to reinstate an equitable relationship through cyberloafing. Our findings further highlight the interesting possibility that before employees do so, they would actually neutralize their questionable actions via the metaphor of the ledger in an attempt to ameliorate any feelings of guilt that they may experience.

Individuals may make an effort to neutralize their guilt prior to cyberloafing for several reasons. One plausible explanation is that while employees may be unhappy with their employers as a consequence of perceived injustice, they may still retain some form of commitment to the norm of generally avoiding any wrongdoing. Thus, by rationalizing that what they are contemplating (e.g., cyberloafing) is not unacceptable and, in fact, perfectly justifiable since they have already put in time and effort to perform their job duties (i.e., neutralization through the metaphor of the ledger), employees are able to

Figure 15.4   **Relationship Between Interactional Justice and Cyberloafing for High Neutralization and Low Neutralization**

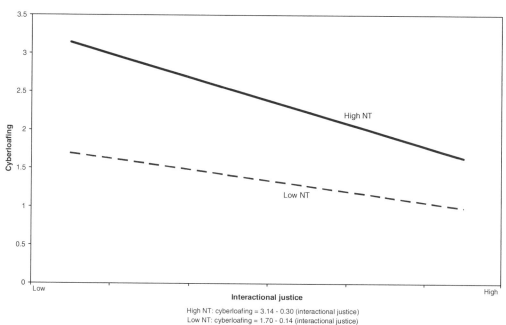

High NT: cyberloafing = 3.14 - 0.30 (interactional justice)
Low NT: cyberloafing = 1.70 - 0.14 (interactional justice)

cyberloaf without feeling guilty and to convince others that they are merely taking what they deserve. That is, they perceive themselves to be fully entitled to use the time that should be spent working to surf the Internet, since they had already put in time to do work that has not been fully appreciated and/or rewarded by their employers. Indeed, comments from respondents who were interviewed provided support to this line of reasoning: for example, "Personally, I think that although using the Internet at work for personal purpose is wrong in principle, I would still do it because it is actually a type of payment in kind from the company for the work I do."

In addition, we acknowledge that it is possible that employees may choose to retaliate against their employers for perceived injustice through other means. However, given the convenience of using the Internet and the difficulty of detecting cyberloafing, it seems highly plausible that employees would take advantage of this evolved form of production deviance as a way of discreetly imposing some form of penalty on their employers for not having reciprocated the employees' input(s) into the employment relationship. Comments from our respondents who were interviewed further highlighted the apparent ease with which cyberloafing in particular may be neutralized through the metaphor of the ledger and thus easily engaged in. One respondent said, "It is all right for me to use the Internet for personal reasons at work. After all, I do work overtime without receiving extra pay from my employer." Another commented, "I don't see anything wrong with using the company's Internet access for nonwork purposes as long as I do not do it too often and complete my work as required by my boss." Thus, the results of our study provide preliminary evidence suggesting that employees do cyberloaf when they feel that they have not been justly treated and after legitimating the act of cyberloafing by invoking the metaphor of the ledger.

THEORETICAL IMPLICATIONS

Our results provide encouraging evidence that suggests that neutralization theory may be useful in shedding light on why workplace deviance continues to be a pervasive problem in organizations. To date, however, only a few studies have attempted to use neutralization theory as a framework for understanding employees' misbehavior at the workplace (e.g., Hollinger 1991). Previous studies have established that employees are motivated to redress perceived inequilibrium in the employment relationship through various forms of misbehavior when they perceive themselves to have been unfairly treated. Drawing in part from neutralization theory, our study examined the possibility that a plausible explanation of why employee cyberloafing is commonplace is that employees may invoke the metaphor of the ledger to justify their actions to themselves as well as to other organizational members.

Results suggest that this is indeed the case. That is, employees can easily convince themselves that by cyberloafing, their misbehavior is acceptable since they have accrued sufficient credits previously through the time and effort that they put into completing their work. Cyberloafing is simply a means of cashing in these accumulated credits and is viewed as a fair entitlement. In this manner, employees will find it all too easy to cyberloaf while at work.

MANAGERIAL IMPLICATIONS

The findings of our study are instructive because they not only highlight that cyberloafing does indeed occur at the workplace, but also that neutralization is at work in the organizational setting. The latter is especially noteworthy as employees may be neutralizing not only cyberloafing but also other more potentially detrimental deviant acts at the workplace. Managers need to be aware of this possibility and take the necessary steps to forestall these neutralization techniques in their attempts to keep cyberloafing and other deviant behaviors to a minimum level within their own organizations.

The results of our study suggest that to the extent that employees put in time and effort to fulfill their job duties, they expect to be fairly treated by their employers. When employers fail to reciprocate by treating these employees in a just manner, it becomes all too easy for employees to invoke the metaphor of the ledger and neutralize their subsequent attempt to take time back from their employing organizations through such acts as cyberloafing. Thus, managers need to realize that despite the tremendous changes that have been wrought upon the workplace by technology, the quaint and simple norm of reciprocity is still very much in operation.

To make it more difficult for employees to justify the illegitimate and costly act of cyberloafing, employers need to ensure that employees are not tempted to utilize the metaphor of the ledger to justify cyberloafing. This can be done by treating employees fairly and ensuring that the work environment is adequately conducive for productive work to take place in order to reciprocate employees' investment of time and effort in their work.

According to Robinson and Kraatz (1998), neutralization techniques are more easily invoked in organizational cultures in which there are few or weak norms governing what constitutes acceptable behaviors. Thus, another way in which organizations can eliminate the possibility of employees indulging in the use of neutralization techniques would be to establish clear, explicit guidelines with regard to behaviors that the organizations deem tolerable or otherwise. In this case, to curb employees from invoking the metaphor of the ledger to rationalize cyberloafing, organizations should develop and implement a workplace policy governing the acceptable use of the Internet while at work. Some of the issues that need to be addressed include the Web sites that can be accessed in the work premises using Internet access provided by the company regardless of whether the sites are visited during work or nonwork hours. For example, organizations may choose to block access to adult-oriented Web sites altogether. Organizations also need to decide whether it is appropriate for employees to use the Internet for personal purposes during lunch hours and after office hours.

Another issue that the organizational policy on Internet regulation will need to address is monitoring. If organizations decide to track their employees' movements in cyberspace and monitor the e-mails that are being sent and received via the company server, this must be explicitly stated in the policy. This frankness will prevent disgruntled employees from thinking that their privacy has been secretly invaded by monitoring or that monitoring reflects a lack of trust in them. As Taillon (2004) notes, while various forms of monitoring would enable organizations to determine if employees were actually working, monitoring may in fact be counterproductive as it can cause resentment in employees. Comments elicited from respondents who were interviewed lend support to this concern. One respondent commented, "If there is a need to regulate, the company is better off not providing Internet access to its employees." Another worker noted, "I guess the company could track the sites visited by the employees . . . but I think it [tracking] shows that the company doesn't respect their employees' privacy!"

Furthermore, organizational Internet policies need to outline clearly the disciplinary consequences that employees will face if they flout the guidelines stated explicitly in the policy. As with all other types of organizational policies, disciplinary actions must be meted out accordingly; otherwise, the purpose of creating the policy in the first place would be defeated. Finally, for such a policy to be effective, it must be communicated to all employees as soon as they join the company and also every time the policy is updated. Only then will employees find it difficult to bend the rules through such neutralization techniques as the metaphor of the ledger.

LIMITATIONS AND DIRECTIONS FOR FUTURE RESEARCH

Our research, while providing insightful results, is not without its limitations that should be taken into consideration in its interpretation. First, our study relies exclusively on cross-sectional, self-reported data. The use of cross-sectional data precludes the possibility of making causal inferences about the relationships among the variables examined. Thus, a longitudinal design in future research would provide further confidence in our ability to make causal inferences. While the nature of the variables under study renders the use of self-reports appropriate, relying entirely on self-reports raises the issue of whether results may have been inflated due to common method bias. Thus, we acknowledge that future studies should further reduce the potential of common method bias by supplementing the self-reports with reports from other sources. For example, a clearer picture of the justice climate that prevails in the organizations might be captured by obtaining managers' responses with regard to this issue.

In addition, although examining the metaphor of the ledger in relation with the other variables included in our study was viewed as particularly suitable, there may be concerns regarding the focus on only one technique of neutralization in our study. Therefore, future work that integrates the neutralization and workplace deviance research would further enhance our understanding of both topics by incorporating and operationalizing other relevant neutralization techniques, such as those originally proposed by Sykes and Matza (1957) (e.g., denial of victim, condemnation of condemners, and appeal to higher loyalties) or those proposed by Greenberg (1998), and Robinson and Kraatz (1998).

Third, it is also possible that there exist predictors of cyberloafing other than organizational justice. For example, some individuals may be inherently more inclined to cyberloaf thus, individual traits such as Machiavellianism, should be examined in conjunction with cyberloafing. In addition, situational variables such as frustration arising from work may also influence individuals' tendency to cyberloaf. Hence, future research may also want to take into account the effects of situational variables.

In line with Robinson and Bennett's (1995) typology of workplace deviance, which suggests that deviant behaviors vary along two dimensions, namely (1) minor versus serious and (2) interpersonal versus organizational, future research may want to extend this study by investigating cyberloafing activities that are specifically targeted at harming the organization and those that are intended to harm its members (e.g., sending inflammatory personal e-mails to coworkers). It is plausible that individuals invoke different neutralization techniques to exonerate themselves from engaging in the different types of cyberloafing acts.

CONCLUSION

Workplace Internet usage is increasing dramatically around the world. While this rapid growth has focused much attention on the impact of Internet usage on productivity, much of the work in this area has thus far largely examined the positive productivity influences brought about by the Internet. Our research is thus noteworthy in that it represents one of the few empirical endeavors to study how the Internet has not only revolutionized the ways in which work can be done, but also transformed the ways in which loafing can be done.

Despite the limitations inherent in our study, its findings are instructive in that they focus attention on one of the possible unforeseen negative consequences of the technology-enabled workplace (i.e., cyberloafing). Additionally, our results highlight the intricacies surrounding employees' actual engagement in deviant behaviors at the workplace. Specifically, while some employers may view cyberloafing as a trivial activity that can be overlooked, our study shows that employees very easily neutralize (i.e., rationalize) cyberloafing as an activity in which they may freely indulge with few or no qualms. Furthermore, employees' propensity to cyberloafing, while motivated by perceived imbalances in the social exchanges that characterize the employment relationship, may in fact be further facilitated by the invocation of neutralization techniques. Thus, while existing research suggests that employers need to be fair in order to minimize the occurrence of workplace deviance, the results of our study highlight how neutralization techniques, like the metaphor of the ledger, make it all too easy for employees to misbehave in the organizational context.

From a researcher's perspective, while neutralization theory may be into its fifth decade of existence since being first proposed by Sykes and Matza (1957), the results of our study indicate that the theory may be applied to further our understanding of workplace deviance in future organizational behavior research. From a practitioner's perspective, our findings suggest that managers need to understand and fully appreciate the cumulative effects of the occurrence of cyberloafing in their organizations. With the introduction of the Internet at the workplace, a very easy way of loafing under the guise of being hard at work is now placed in the hands of employees. Although it is important to trust employees to use this productivity tool properly, managers must also understand the cognitive processes underlying employees' deviant behaviors such as cyberloafing in order to fully deal with these recalcitrant behaviors and ensure that the Internet works for and not against the company.

REFERENCES

ABA Banking Journal. 1983. Getting the goods on time thieves. March 22.

Analoui, F., and Kakabadse, A. 1991. *Sabotage.* London: Mercury.

Anandarajan, M., Simmers, C., and Igbaria, M. 2000. An exploratory investigation of the antecedents and impact of Internet usage: An individual perspective. *Behavior and Information Technology* 19, 69–85.

Armstrong, L., Phillips, J.G., and Saling, L.L. 2000. Potential determinants of higher Internet usage. *International Journal of Human Computer Studies* 53, 537–550.

Bennett, R.J., and Robinson, S.L. 2003. The past, present and future of workplace deviance research. In J. Greenberg (ed.), *Organizational Behavior: The State of the Science.* 2nd ed. Mahwah, NJ: Lawrence Erlbaum Associates. 247–281.

Chaplin, W.F. 1991. The next generation of moderator research in personality psychology. *Journal of Personality* 52, 143–178.

Cohen, J., and Cohen, P. 1983. *Applied Multiple Regression for the Behavioral Sciences.* Hillsdale, NJ: Lawrence Erlbaum Associates.

Colquitt, J.A., Conlon, D.E., Wesson, M.J., Porter, C.O.L.H., and Ng, K.Y. 2001. Justice at the millennium: A meta-analytic review of 25 years of organizational justice research. *Journal of Applied Psychology* 86, 425–445.

Copes, H. 2003. Societal attachments, offending frequency and techniques of neutralization. *Deviant Behavior* 24, 101–127.

Fox, S., Spector, P.E., and Miles, D. 2001. Counterproductive work behavior in response to job stressors and organizational justice: Some mediator and moderator tests for autonomy and emotions. *Journal of Vocational Behavior* 59, 291–309.

Graphics, Visualization and Usability (GVU) Center. 1998. www.static.cc.gatech.edu/user_surveys.

Greenberg, J. 1998. The cognitive geometry of employee theft: Negotiating "the line" between taking and stealing. In R. Griffin, A. O'Leary-Kelly, J. Collins J (eds.), *Dysfunctional Behavior in Organizations:* vol. 2. *Nonviolent Behaviors in Organizations.* Stamford, CT: JAI Press, 147–193.

Greenberg, J., and Scott, S.K. 1996. Why do employees bite the hand that feed them? Employee theft as a social exchange process. In L.L. Cummings and B.M. Staw (eds.), *Research in Organizational Behavior,* vol. 18. Greenwich, CT: JAI Press, 111–156.

Greenberg, L., and Barling, J. 1998. Predicting employee aggression against co-workers, subordinates and supervisors: vol. 2. The role of person behaviors and perceived workplace factors. *Journal of Organizational Behavior* 20, 897–913.

Hollinger, R.C. 1991. Neutralizing in the workplace: An empirical analysis of property theft and production deviance. *Deviant Behavior* 12, 169–202.

Klockars C.B. 1974. *The Professional Fence.* New York: Macmillan.

Lee, R. 1993. *Doing Research on Sensitive Topics.* London: Sage.

Lichtash, A. 2004. Inappropriate use of e-mail and the Internet in the workplace: The arbitration picture. *Dispute Resolution Journal* 59, 26–36.

Lim, V.K.G. 2002. The IT way of loafing on the job: Cyberloafing, neutralizing and organizational justice. *Journal of Organizational Behavior* 23, 675–694.

Lim, V.K.G., Teo, T.S.H., and Loo, G.L. 2002. How do I loaf here? Let me count the ways: Cyberloafing in an Asian context. *Communications of the Association for Computing Machinery* 45, 66–70.

Masterson, S.S., Lewis, K., Goldman, B.M., and Taylor, M.S. 2000. Integrating justice and social exchange: The differing effects of fair procedures and treatment on work relationships. *Academy of Management Journal* 43, 738–748.

Moorman, R.H. 1991. Relationship between organizational justice and organizational citizenship behaviors: Do fairness perceptions influence employee citizenship? *Journal of Applied Psychology* 76, 845–855.

Pierce, J.L., Gardner, D.G., Dunham, R.B., and Cummings, L.L. 1993. Moderation by organization-based self-esteem of role condition-employee response relationships. *Academy of Management Journal* 36, 271–288.

Robinson, S.L., and Bennett, R.J. 1995. A typology of deviant workplace behaviors: A multidimensional scaling. *Academy of Management Journal* 38, 555–572.

Robinson, S.L., and Kraatz, M.S. 1998. Constructing the reality of normative behavior: The use of neutralization strategies by organizational deviants. In R. Griffin, A. O'Leary-Kelly, J. Collins (eds.), *Dysfunctional Behavior in Organizations:* part I. *Violent and Deviant Behavior.* Stamford, CT: JAI Press, 203–220.

Sharma, S.K., and Gupta, J.N.D. 2004. Improving workers' productivity and reducing Internet abuse. *Journal of Computer and Information Systems* 44, 74–78.

Snyder, N.H., Blair, K.E., and Arndt, T. 1990. Breaking the bad habits behind time theft. *Business* 40, 31–33.

Straits Times. 2000. Cyberslackers at work. April 28.

Sykes, G.M., and Matza, D. 1957. Techniques of neutralization: A theory of delinquency. *American Sociological Review* 22, 664–670.

Taillon, G. 2004. Controlling Internet use in the workplace. *CPA Journal* 74, 16–17.

Teo, T.S.H, Lim, V.K.G., and Lai, R.Y.C. 1997. Users and uses of the Internet: The case of Singapore. *International Journal of Information Management* 17, 325–336.

Websense. 2003. Key Internet usage statistics.

Young, K.S., and Case, C. J. 2004. Internet abuse in the workplace: New trends in risk management. *Cyber Psychology and Behavior* 7, 105–112.

CHAPTER 16

HOFSTEDE'S CULTURAL DIMENSIONS OF PERSONAL WEB USAGE ACTIVITIES IN THAILAND AND THE UNITED STATES

PRUTHIKRAI MAHATANANKOON, H. JOSEPH WEN,
AND MURUGAN ANANDARAJAN

Abstract: *This study compares Hofstede's four dimensions of culture (collectivism/ individualism, power distance, masculinity/femininity, and uncertainty avoidance) and their impact on personal Web usage behaviors between two samples of natives of Thailand and natives of the United States. An initial sample of 79 Thai top-level managers and 100 Thai employees was compared to a similar sample of 94 U.S. top-level managers and 116 U.S. employees. The results support the existence of cultural differences between the two samples in terms of three of Hofstede's cross-cultural dimensions, with the masculinity/femininity dimension as the exception. Evidence suggests that personal Web usage activities could be influenced by cultural factors and that management must take those cultural factors into consideration when developing an interorganizational Internet usage policy.*

Keywords: *Cross-cultural Dimensions, Personal Web Usage, Internet, Hofstede's Dimensions*

INTRODUCTION

Recent cases of nonproductive Internet usage in the workplace have led many organizations to adopt various Internet usage policies to reduce the effects of slacking employees. As a deterrent strategy, organizations publicize their Internet usage policy with the objective of increasing the productivity of their employees. Various strategies have been implemented, ranging from allocation of personal Web time, filtering of offensive Web sites, examining server logs, and monitoring corporate e-mails. Although effective against Internet abuses (pornography, offensive, and illegal Web sites), these strategies are inadequate to inhibit casual non-work-related Internet surfing, such as reading online newspapers, visiting travel Web sites and searching for travel information, or performing online banking. The vagueness of what can be categorized as non-work-related Internet usage raises new issues regarding individual factors that contribute to such behaviors.

Non-work-related Internet usage in the workplace, depending on the severity of the deviant behavior, is broadly defined as Internet abuse in the workplace (Anandarajan 2002), cyberloafing (Lim 2002), problematic Internet usage (Davis 2001; Davis et al. 2002), or even Internet addiction (Case and Young 2002; Greenfield 1999). Considering many publicized cases of employees abusing their Internet access, organizations have applied several tactics to cultivate productive Internet usage. Although excessive Internet usage is not entirely a positive behavior at work, some researchers consider moderate non-work-related Internet usage as a motivational factor enhancing workplace satisfaction and performance (Belanger and Van Slyke 2002; Oravec 2002). This chapter will refer to non-work-related Internet usage behaviors as personal Web usage in the workplace (PWU): voluntary online Web behaviors during working time using any of the organization's resources for activities outside current customary job or work requirements (Anandarajan and Simmers 2002).

DIVERGENCE VERSUS CONVERGENCE

We suggest that apart from organizational policies and individual factors that affect personal Web usage in the workplace, cultural factors could also influence an individual's Internet activities. More important, what employees consider as personal usage "norms" could be based on both organizational and cultural settings. Evidence shows support for divergence theory, suggesting there are differences of personal Web usage activities across nations (Simmers and Anandarajan 2004). Edberg et al. (2001) identify five key issues for global information systems management: language, culture and geography, systems development and support, legal regulations and enforcement, and level of technology. In contrast, there are comparable differences between Western and Eastern countries in terms of information technology (IT) usage (Martinsons and Westwood 1997).

Various studies related to culture and IT usage support either the divergence theory or the convergence theory. Hill et al. (1998) conclude from structured interviews with members of the Arab-American business community and people in five Arab nations that sociocultural factors are powerful. The researchers observe that the highly Americanized Arab businessmen evidence strong identification with their Arab culture. Kandelin et al. (1998) administered a survey to Indonesian managers and discovered strong similarities among their attitudes toward computer systems, implying that culture, education, and familiarity with technology contribute to the acceptance of information systems. Straub et al. (2001) studied the influence of cultural beliefs and values on the transference of IT in the Arab world. The authors developed a cultural influence model of IT transfer (ITT) that presupposes the effect of culture, price attractiveness, top management support, and required staff time on ITT. This study suggests that differences in cultural background could also influence the nature of personal Web usage behaviors.

While divergence theorists argue that there are differences across nations regarding IT usage, the opposite is true for convergence theorists. Other findings suggest that the effects of culture on IT have not been consistent with the divergence theory (McLeod et al. 1997). Dirksen (2001), constructing a meta-analysis of previous research, notes that the universal applicability of IT is a "myth." Couger (1986) reports, based upon a survey of computer analysts in Singapore and the United States, that there are more cultural similarities than differences and that these similarities are very surprising given the demographic differences involved.

Since the impact of personal Web usage activities in the workplace has led to the implementation of many deterrent strategies in many nations, practitioners and researchers must understand how cross-cultural norms may influence personal Web usage behaviors so that better strategies can be adapted to different cultural settings. By examining personal Web usage behaviors of people in Thailand and in the United States, this chapter relates Hofstede's four dimensions of culture to such behaviors. The objectives of this chapter are to explain how the following concepts are influenced by Hofstede's cultural dimensions: (1) work-related Web usage and personal Web usage; (2) organizational Internet usage policies and Internet monitoring; and (3) the differences between top manager and employee personal Web usage behaviors.

CULTURE AND PERSONAL WEB USAGE

Culture gives people a sense of who they are, of where they belong, of how they should behave, and of what they should be doing. It provides a learned, shared, and interrelated set of symbols, codes, and values that direct and justify human behavior. It encompasses a set of fundamental values that distinguishes one group from another (Hofstede and Bond 1988) and these values can act as a strong determinant of managerial ideology that consequently affects organizational performance (Luna et al. 2002). Values are enduring beliefs about important goals in life, which serve as guiding principles in people's lives (Rokeach 1973; Schwartz 1994). They serve as criteria for determining what is good and bad, for choosing among available alternatives. Though values may alter in response to major changes in technology, economy, and politics, they are fairly stable (Schwartz 1992). People from different cultures may hold different values with varying degrees of intensity and direction (Hofstede 1980).

The creation and sharing of cultural beliefs and values is an integral part of being human, and this notion is also true for the World Wide Web. Internet usage management is receiving increasing attention by organizations. The reason for this interest is productivity of employees. Many employees are spending more and more time on the Internet during work hours for reasons that are not job-related. However, most employees consider personal Web usage as "normal" in the workplace because they reason that these behaviors have few consequences on productivity. Such a rationale may also be influenced by different cultural usage norms, especially when the Internet is used in businesses around the world. The issue of which behavior is acceptable and which is not becomes unclear. More important, in some cultures, the mere adoption of information technology does not invariably lead to effective usage (Gannon 1994).

To solve this problem, organizations have tried implementing Internet usage policies (IUPs), installing Internet monitoring software, or restricting Web site access. Although these strategies may reduce Internet abuse and improve employees' productivity, the impact on cross-cultural issues is still unclear. Should organizations consider cross-cultural issues when they try to establish an IUP or Internet monitoring software?

To examine this issue, Internet usage management must fall under the same multicultural scrutiny and research as previous information systems and IT. The following literature on personal computer usage provides support and rationale for the divergence theory. Harris and Davison (1999) find considerable differences in personal computer (PC) involvement surveys across users in China, Hong Kong, Malaysia, New Zealand, Tanzania, and Thailand; the researchers attribute some of those differences to culture. Rose and Straub (1998), using the technology acceptance model (TAM) to compare perceived usefulness and actual use of computers across national borders, conclude that cultural biases play a role in TAM when applied to PC use. Prior findings conclude that people with different cultural backgrounds, personality types, and developmental experiences vary in their propensity to trust. Research in the area of PC skills and acceptability may play a major role in understanding personal Web usage.

HOFSTEDE'S DIMENSIONS AND PERSONAL WEB USAGE

This study adopts Hofstede's dimensions. In his landmark research of work-related values in fifty countries, Hofstede (1980) identifies four dimensions against which the nationally held values of his sample could be classified. These dimensions include power distance, collectivism/individualism, uncertainty avoidance, and masculinity/femininity. According to our study, Thailand is a high-power-distance, collectivist, feminine, and strong-uncertainty-avoidance society, while the United States is a low-power-distance, individualistic, masculine, and weak-uncertainty-avoidance society (Hofstede 1997). The following pages summarize and compare each of the cultural dimensions between the two countries.

Power Distance Index

Power distance index (PDI) is the "extent to which the less powerful members of institutions and organizations within a country expect and accept that power is distributed unequally" (Hofstede 1997, 28). It is a culture's willingness to accept a difference in power over various members of the culture. Thus, high-power-distance cultures tend to be willing to accept differences in the distribution of power across cultural members. However, low-power-distance cultures will strive for an equal distribution of power. While inequality may exist within any culture, the degree to which it is accepted varies considerably across cultures. Thus, individuals who come from cultures exhibiting high power distances, such as Malaysia, Guatemala, Panama, the Philippines, Thailand, and Mexico, might consider themselves unequal and expect to be directed. On the other hand, those who come from cultures with low power distances, such as the Scandinavian nations, New Zealand, Israel, Austria, and the United States (Hofstede 1991), may feel less dependent upon their superiors. According to Hofstede, the United States ranks thirtieth of fifty, while Thailand ranks twenty-first. Thus, in Hofstede's typology, Thailand is identified as a relatively high-power-distance culture, whereas the United States is a comparatively low-power-distance culture.

In high PDI countries, organizations centralize power within the top management, and employees are expected to follow rules. Privileges and status symbols for managers are both expected and popular. Personal Web usage is often perceived as a privilege of management. However, in low-power-distance countries, these luxuries meet with disapproval, and everyone is assumed to have equal rights. Therefore, managers in low PDI countries have less freedom and are more restricted in their personal Web usage. In other words, managers in high PDI countries spend more time on personal Web usage activities than their employees do, while managers and employees in low PDI countries spend equal amounts of time on personal Web activities.

Hypothesis 1a: Thai managers spend more time on PWU activities than their employees do.

Hypothesis 1b: U.S. managers spend more time on PWU activities than their employees do.

Individualism/Collectivism

Individualism (IDV) describes the degree to which the connections between individuals are loose; people are expected to look after themselves and their immediate family (Hofstede 1997). Individualists can be expected to experience relatively little pressure from others tending to be universalistic and apply the same standards to all. "Collectivism . . . pertains to societies in which people from birth onwards are integrated into strong, cohesive groups, which throughout people's lifetime continue to protect them in exchange for unquestioning loyalty" (Hofstede 1997, 51). Individuals in a collective culture are presumed to look after the interest of their group before themselves. Thus, collectivists display great loyalty to their group and are biased toward protecting the interests of its members. As a result, individuals prefer cohesive and tightly knit social frameworks, group harmony, and reduced levels of intragroup confrontation.

In high IDV cultures, speaking one's mind is a virtue. In collectivist or low IDV cultures, harmony is more important. High IDV nations include the United States, Australia, Great Britain, Canada, and the Netherlands. The United States ranks first in the IDV index. The lowest IDV nations are nations of the Pacific Rim and several Central American countries. Thailand ranks thirty-ninth of fifty. According to Hofstede, high IDV employees are expected to act according to their own interest before that of their employer. Therefore, in an individualist collectivist society, the personal Web usage activities should prevail over the task. However, in a collectivist society, PWU behaviors depend on how employees' peers and organizations view such behaviors.

Hypothesis 2a: Thai employees adhere to peers' PWU norms more than U.S. employees do.

Hypothesis 2b: Thai employees adhere to organizational controls of PWU more than U.S. employees do.

Uncertainty Avoidance

Uncertainty avoidance index (UAI) measures the "extent to which the members of a culture feel threatened by uncertain or unknown situations" (Hofstede 1997, 113). It refers to a society's lack of tolerance for uncertainty and ambiguity, which expresses itself in high levels of anxiety and energy release, strong needs for formal roles and absolute truth, and lack of tolerance for people or groups with deviant ideas or behaviors. In countries with a high UAI, people feel emotional resistance to change. Employees and managers in such cultures feel comfortable in structured environments that attempt to prevent uncertainty and ambiguity in people's behavior. People in high UAI cultures could be presumed to provide socially acceptable responses that are condoned by a large percentage of the population and thus serve to reduce personal risk while being more likely to resist innovative ideas. These individuals seek to avoid ambiguity and therefore develop rituals and rules for virtually every possible situation.

On the other hand, countries that are characterized by low uncertainty avoidance are less conservative and rule-bound, more willing to take risks and accept conflict and dissent. Organizations in low-uncertainty-avoidance cultures have less structuring of activities, fewer rules, and managers who are more interpersonally oriented and flexible in their style (Hofstede 1980). Persons from a low-uncertainty-avoidance culture might be more reflective and relatively broad-minded, resulting in less need for social approval and increased openness in intercultural communication, leading to additional risk taking, tolerance toward deviant behavior, and acceptance of innovative ideas.

A need for predictability and a predisposition for written and unwritten rules express this dimension. Uncertainty avoidance leads to a reduction of ambiguity. According to Hofstede, the emotional need for rules in strong UAI nations can result in an affinity for precision and punctuality, especially where the power distance is relatively small. Strategic planning demands a greater tolerance for ambiguity. Low UAI cultures are more likely to stimulate innovation and tolerate unorthodox ideas. Greece, Portugal, Guatemala, Uruguay, and Belgium are the highest in UAI, while Hong Kong, Sweden, Denmark, Jamaica, and Singapore score the lowest. The United States ranks forty-third of fifty nations, while Thailand ranks thirtieth. Straub (1994) studied the effect of culture on e-mail and fax technologies in Japan and the United States. He used Hofstede to hypothesize that high UAI and the structural features of the Japanese written language could explain the differences.

Hypothesis 3a: Companies operating in Thailand have more written rules regarding Internet usage policies (IUP) than those operating in the United States.

Hypothesis 3b: Companies operating in Thailand have more Internet monitoring and filtering software installed than those operating in the United States.

Masculinity/Femininity

Masculinity (MAS) is defined as an index pertaining to societies in which "social gender roles are clearly distinct (i.e., men are supposed to be assertive, tough and focused on material success . . .)" (Hofstede 1997, 82). Hofstede (1997) positions nations along a continuum from masculine to feminine. Nations that are high in the masculinity index attach the most importance to earnings, recognition for doing a job well, the opportunity for advancement, and challenging work. A low MAS index reflects the importance of a "good working relationship with the direct supervisor, cooperation with fellow employees, an acceptable family space, and employment security" (Hofstede 1997, 81–82). Masculine traits are attributes such as strength, assertiveness, competitiveness, task achievement, and the acquisition of things. Feminine traits are attributes such as affection, compassion, nurturance, and emotionality (Hofstede 1984). More specifically, this index measures the degree to which respondents of both sexes within a country tend to endorse goals usually more popular among men (high masculinity) or among women (high femininity). Masculinity is expected to be associated with traditionalism (Tian and Emery 2002), and countries that have a high masculinity index have fewer women in high-paying jobs requiring high qualifications. There are greater value differences between men and women in the same jobs than in countries with a low masculinity index. These social differences are caused by cultural sanctions, educational barriers, legal restrictions, corporate obstacles, and women's disinterest in pursuing a traditional masculine career (Adler and Bartholomew 1992). Moreover, generally there is more sex-role differentiation and inequality in masculine cultures compared with feminine cultures (Hofstede 1991).

High MAS countries include Japan, Austria, Venezuela, and Italy. The ranking of the United States, Greece, and England are very close in Hofstede's MAS index. The United States ranks fifteenth of fifty nations. Low MAS nations are Denmark, the Netherlands, Norway, and Sweden. Thailand ranks forty-fourth. Feminine societies stress quality of work life and interpersonal relationships while masculine societies stress competition and job performance. Therefore, it is likely that employees at feminine workplaces will spend more time on personal Web usage activities than at masculine workplaces.

Hypothesis 4a: Thai employees spend more time on personal Web activities than U.S. employees.

Hypothesis 4b: Thai managers spend more time on personal Web activities than U.S. managers.

METHODS

Data Collection and Sample Profile

A Web-based survey was conducted to allow access to potential respondents who were savvy Internet users. To collect the data, e-mails with a URL link to the questionnaire

Table 16.1

Sample Characteristics

Percentages	Thai		United States	
	Managers (N = 79)	Employees (N = 100)	Managers (N = 94)	Employees (N = 116)
Age				
20–29	11.4	63.0	26.6	53.4
30–39	36.7	29.0	31.9	22.4
40–49	39.2	4.0	16.0	13.8
> 50	12.7	4.0	25.6	10.4
Education				
Some college	11.4	18.0	6.4	11.2
Bachelor's degree	46.8	59.0	20.2	27.6
Some graduate study	11.4	3.0	24.5	35.3
Graduate or professional degree	30.4	20.0	48.9	25.9
Gender				
Male	74.7	48.0	69.1	61.2
Female	25.3	52.0	30.9	38.8
Working hours per day	9.57 SD = 1.402	9.20 SD = 1.563	9.34 SD = 1.448	8.20 SD = 1.627

and a request for participation in the Internet usage study were sent directly to forty companies in Thailand and the United States. The respondents were guaranteed anonymity and confidentiality of their responses. There were 389 respondents, yielding an approximate response rate of 17 percent. Table 16.1 divides the sample characteristics into four demographic categories. The chi-square test of independence showed nonsignificant results of gender differences between Thai managers and U.S. managers ($\chi^2 = .648$, $p = .420$), and Thai employees and U.S. employees ($\chi^2 = 3.786$, $p = .052$). There were, however, significant results showing differences in age and educational level.

Operationalization

Table 16.2 shows how Hofstede's cultural dimensions influence the nature of PWU behaviors and characteristics. Since culture is the most difficult factor to isolate, define, and measure (Hasan and Ditsa 1999), the study uses demographics variables and modifies existing measures from Anandarajan and Simmers (2000) and Taylor and Todd (1995).

To test hypotheses 1a and 1b and 4a and 4b, respondents (managers and employees) were asked to what extent they visited work-related and non-work-related Web sites while at work (Anandarajan et al. 2000). Work-related Web sites include competitors, suppliers, and customers' Web sites. Non-work-related Web sites include arts and entertainment, travel and leisure, living and consumer, and sports and news Web sites. Hypotheses 2a and 2b were tested using the constructs modified from Taylor and Todd

Table 16.2

Hofstede's Cultural Dimensions and Personal Web Usage Characteristics

United States	Thailand
Small power distance • Equalities among personal Web usage activities are expected among managers and employees • Internet usage privileges are frowned upon	**Large power distance** • Inequalities of personal Web usage activities are expected between managers and employees • Internet usage privileges are expected
Individualist • PWU behaviors are based on individual interests • Work-related Web usage and personal Web usage are not based on organizational norms • Psychological contract between employer and employee is based on mutual advantage	**Collectivist** • Social norms determine PWU behaviors • Personal Web usage activities prevail over work-related Web usages if part of norms • Psychological contract between employer and employee is based on perceived moral terms
Weak uncertainty avoidance • Internet usage policy and Internet monitoring tools are not prevalent • Fewer rules governing deviant behaviors	**Strong uncertainty avoidance** • Internet usage policy and Internet monitoring tools are prevalent • Strict rules governing deviant behaviors
Masculine • Work-related Web usage is related to increasing competition among colleagues and performance • "Live in order to work"	**Feminine** • Personal Web usage activities are related to improving the quality of work life • "Work in order to live"

(1995) to reflect peer norms and organizational behavioral control. For hypothesis 3a and 3b, comparisons were made with how many U.S. and Thai companies are currently implementing Internet and e-mail usage policy and Internet and e-mail monitoring software. (See Appendix.) Table 16.2 shows how each of Hofstede's cultural dimensions are related to the nature of PWU activities.

Data Analysis

Questionnaire responses were analyzed using of the SPSS V11.0 statistical package. The analysis focused upon the calculation of descriptive statistics, chi-square, and independent-samples t-test statistics to determine the differences on the basis of country with regard to each cultural dimension. The independent-samples' t-test identifies differences between the means of independent categories using group variables (U.S. managers, U.S. employees, Thai managers, Thai employees) and test variables (work-related and non-work-related Web sites). Each hypothesis is evaluated to what extent the mean value of the test variable for one group differs significantly from the mean value of the test variable for the second group. To test hypothesis 3a and 3b, chi-square statistic is used to determine the differences among U.S. and Thai companies' Internet usage and monitoring policy.

Table 16.3

Descriptive Statistics Based on Activities and Types of Roles

Countries	Roles	Work-related Web sites		Personal-related Web sites		t-test
		Mean	SD	Mean	SD	
United States	Managers	2.067	.9257	2.795	1.096	−5.803*
	Employees	2.621	1.247	2.575	.999	.337
Thailand	Managers	2.283	.920	2.718	.939	−3.419*
	Employees	2.507	1.070	2.310	.873	1.743

*$p < 0.001$.

RESULTS

Table 16.3 characterizes the descriptive results based on countries and types of employees. The table shows that, on average, employees from both countries spent more of their time on work-related Web sites than on personal-related Web sites. This difference, however, was not statistically significant. The study found that managers from both countries were spending more time on personal-related Web sites than on work-related Web sites ($t = -5.803$, $p < .001$; $t = -3.419$, $p < .001$, respectively). An independent-sample t-test was conducted to evaluate hypotheses 1a and 1b for any differences between how managers and employees spend time on PWU activities. The test was significant ($t = 2.98$, $p < 0.01$) for the Thai sample, but the U.S. sample did not show any statistical significance. The strong significant result ($t = 3.338$, $p = 0.001$) from hypothesis 2a also showed that the PWU behaviors of the Thai sample are consistent with Hofstede's individualistic and collectivist dimension. The support for hypothesis 3b ($\chi^2 = 4.124$, $p = .042$) indicated that the companies operating in Thailand had more Internet monitoring and filtering software installed than those operating in the United States, suggesting the impact of Hofstede's uncertainty avoidance dimension on organizational policies. The last hypothesis testing detected that Thai employees were spending more time on PWU activities than U.S. employees were. The test was significant ($t = -2.05$, $p < 0.05$) for the employees' groups but not for the managerial groups. The results of statistical tests are presented in Table 16.4.

DISCUSSION AND IMPLICATIONS

The results of this study indicated that Hofstede's cross-cultural dimensions affect the way that employees perform PWU behaviors. In Table 16.4a, the nonsignificant result from the U.S. respondents suggests no differences in the overall personal Web usage of managers and employees; this result is not surprising in low PDI societies. However, there is a significant difference between U.S. managers and employees in work-related Web access ($t = 3.687$, $p < .001$), with employees reporting more of this type of usage

Table 16.4a–d

Results from Hypothesis Testing

Table 16.4a

Thai managers	Hypothesis 1a	Thai employees		
Mean SD	Thai managers spend more time on PWU	Mean	SD	t-test
2.718 .9392	activities than their employees do.	2.310	.8727	2.980**

U.S. managers	Hypothesis 1b	U.S. employees		
Mean SD	U.S. managers spend more time on PWU	Mean	SD	t-test
2.795 1.0962	activities than their employees do.	2.575	.9996	1.503

Table 16.4b

Thai employees	Hypothesis 2a	U.S. employees		
Mean SD		Mean	SD	t-test
3.170 .9593	Thai employees adhere to peers' PWU norms more than U.S. employees do.	2.746	.8859	3.358***

Thai employees	Hypothesis 2b	U.S. employees		
Mean SD		Mean	SD	t-test
3.410 .8084	Thai employees adhere to organizational controls of PWU more than U.S. employees do.	3.388	.8775	.192

Table 16.4c

	Hypothesis 3a		
Internet usage policy	Companies operating in Thailand have more written rules regarding Internet usage policies than those operating in the United States.	Chi-square =	0.074; p = .785

	Hypothesis 3b		
Internet monitoring software	Companies operating in Thailand have more Internet monitoring and filtering software installed than those operating in the United States.	Chi-square =	4.124; p = .042

Table 16.4d

Thai employees	Hypothesis 4a	U.S. employees		
Mean SD		Mean	SD	t-test
2.310 .8727	Thai employees spend more time on personal Web activities than U.S. employees do.	2.575	.9996	−2.084*

Thai managers	Hypothesis 4b	U.S. managers		
Mean SD		Mean	SD	t-test
2.718 .9391	Thai managers spend more time on personal Web activities than U.S. managers do.	2.795	1.0962	−0.497

$*p < 0.05$; $**p < 0.01$; $***p < 0.001$.

than managers. We speculate that the increased usage of the group of employees is related to job demands and task assignments. It is likely that employees, by nature of their job requirements, spend more time than managers on work-related Web sites.

However, this result was not the case for Thailand, where there were significant supports for the inequalities of personal Web usage activities between Thai managers and Thai employees. Although managers from both countries were spending more time on personal-related Web sites than on work-related Web sites, only the Thai respondents showed a significant difference between managers and employees in terms of personal-related Web site access ($t = 2.98$, $p < 0.01$). Privileges and status symbols for managers are expected in large-power-distance countries (Hofstede 1997). In modern offices, these privileges may include computer terminals with Internet and e-mail access, which are a status symbol in large-power-distance countries.

The verb *to abuse* sometimes means, among other interpretations, "to put [a privilege] to a wrong or improper use." In such cases, Internet abuse in large-power-distance countries is more frequent than in small-power-distance countries; however, these "abuses" are tolerated because of societal values. The degree of personal Web usage inequality in the workplace raises the possibility that different attitudes exist toward personal Web usage activities among managers and subordinates; these differences in attitude increase as the power distance index increases.

While Thai employees adhered to organizational controls more than U.S. employees did, the result was not significant (Table 16.4b). Nevertheless, there was a strong support for peers' norms on personal Web usage among Thai employees ($t = 3.358$, $p < .001$), which is evidence of a collectivist society. Thai managers were tested for adherence to their peers' norms more than U.S. managers. The result showed adequate support for this hypothesis, however, with a lower level of significance ($t = 2.101$, $p < 0.05$). Based on these results, organizations may now have better deterrent strategies for excessive personal Web usage. Organizations could utilize the effects of peer influence to discourage unacceptable behaviors. Prior research suggests that informal social controls through peer influence are more effective in controlling employees' behaviors than managerial controls (Hollinger and Clark 1982). This control is more apparent in collectivist societies where the psychological contract between employers and employees is based on perceived moral terms. Limiting non-work-related Internet usage in a collectivist society should focus on psychological bonds reinforced by peer influence, such as loyalty and respect for the general welfare, while in an individualist society, organizations should advocate a fair Internet usage policy. In any case, the balance between work-related and non-work-related Internet access is essential for maintaining employee satisfaction.

Companies operating in Thailand had more Internet monitoring and filtering software installed than those operating in the United States ($\chi^2 = 4.124$, $p = .042$). The result suggested that Hofstede's uncertainty avoidance dimension might have an impact on how organizations monitors employees' Internet usage behaviors; workplace monitoring tools should be widespread in strong-uncertainty-avoidance societies but not in weak-uncertainty-avoidance societies. According to Hofstede (1997), the rules and regulations in strong-uncertainty-avoidance countries serve as a "psycho-logic" as employees have been "programmed" to feel comfortable in structured workplace settings. However, in weak-uncertainty societies, rules and regulations are based on absolute need; they are enforced only when there is a need to ensure that employees are behaving properly. Therefore, organizations should be careful when it comes to workplace Internet monitoring. Internet monitoring and filtering software are useful tools to keep employees consistent with organizational norms, but organizations should also be concerned with establishing a sound, balanced rationale for employees' productivity and employees' privacy rights, especially in weak-uncertainty-avoidance societies. The freedom to explore and to build a successful career is one of the most important factors in Internet workplace management.

Workplaces in feminine societies emphasize equality, solidarity, and quality of work life while those in masculine societies put stress on equity, competition, and performance. We find that U.S. employees spent more time on personal-related Web sites than the Thai did ($t = -2.084$, $p < 0.05$), which was contradictory to our prediction. Thai managers spent more time on personal Web activities than the U.S. managers did; however, this difference was not statistically significant. Based on the masculine/feminine cultural dimension, masculine societies would be expected to spend less time on personal Web activities and more time on work-related Web sites, based on Table 16.3. Another t-test statistic was executed to compare the means of work-related Web site access between employees from both countries, and no support was discerned; they spent a similar amount of time on their work-related Web sites. One explanation for these contradictory findings could be that the U.S. employees rationalize that because of the time they have spent on work-related Web sites, they deserve some relaxation and personal Web surfing. This explanation is highly consistent with individualist societies in which the psychological contract between the employer and employee is based on mutual advantage.

The results of this study indicate that the propensity to access non-work-related Web sites could be caused by the differences among workplace cultures. In other words, Hofstede's cross-cultural dimensions could explain the differences in the results of our statistical findings. It is recommended that Internet management practices should be modified to fit different cultural and organizational contexts.

LIMITATIONS AND FUTURE RESEARCH

There are several limitations to this study. First of all, the results are based on a convenience sampling method. Both of the samples differed in terms of age and educational level. However, these differences are inherent in the nature of the disparities between developed and developing countries. Generally, employees in developed countries have higher educational levels than employees in developing countries with ranks being equal. Also, age is not really a determining factor for managerial positions in the United States; however, seniority is an important factor for such positions in Thailand. Second, since the questionnaire was based on self-reported items, there was a possibility that the results were somewhat biased toward positive behaviors, even though the questionnaire specified clearly that it maintained anonymity and confidentiality. Finally, PWU had been indirectly operationalized in terms of Holstede's cultural dimensions. These findings could yield better results if the questions were asked based on these dimensions.

While cross-cultural studies such as the present one are useful in identifying the patterns of relationships among the relevant variables, a longitudinal research design is essential to confirm the causal linkages among the study variables. The strengths of the findings would be enhanced by the use of objective measures of Internet usage, such as collecting Web information from an existing server log. It is also plausible that other environmental factors, such as economics and telecommunication infrastructure, have direct effects on non-work-related or personal Web usage behaviors. Internet connections in the workplace are generally faster than dial-up connections in homes, especially in third-world countries. This factor could motivate employees to use "free" workplace Internet connections for personal reasons, such as downloading software or personal digital contents. Future research could focus on these issues, as well as on how organizational norms, job characteristics, motivation, and cross-cultural work ethics influence the nature of unproductive Internet usage. Another issue that needs more attention is antecedent motivational factors. Researchers could investigate employees' motivation by examining the intrinsic rewards that come from engaging in leisure Internet activities. New cross-cultural research will help researchers predict the Internet usage patterns of employees and advise better filtering and monitoring strategies to fit their jobs and organizational needs.

CONCLUSION

The purpose of this research was to investigate the cultural issues related to employees' behaviors toward accessing work-related and personal-related Internet activities based on Hofstede's four dimensions of culture: collectivism/individualism, power distance, masculinity/femininity, and uncertainty avoidance. It compares personal Web usage behaviors between Thailand and the United States. Thailand is a high-power-distance, collectivist, feminine, and strong-uncertainty-avoidance society, while the United States is a low-power-distance, individualistic, masculine, and weak-uncertainty-avoidance society. Personal Web usage behaviors are assumed to be influenced by peers and organizational expectations in Thailand, expectations that may not always coincide with employees' interests. However, in the United States, employees are expected to act according to their own interest, and personal Web usage is conducted in a way that involves a balance between the interests of the employees and those of the organization. In Thailand, the attitude toward personal-related Web site access differs greatly between managers and subordinates compared to those in the low-power-distance spectrum. There is also a need for workplace Internet monitoring in Thailand as the culture feels more comfortable with rules governing Internet usage behaviors. The study shows little support for the masculine/feminine dimension. Understanding different cultural backgrounds could lead to new and effective organizational strategies to cope with these emerging workplace behaviors.

APPENDIX: QUESTIONNAIRE

1. Age

2. Gender [male, female]

3. Which of the following categories best describes your current position?
   [Top/middle manager, administrative support/technical position]

4. Where are you presently working? [United States, Thailand]

5. On average, how many hours do you spend on your organization's work per day?

6. Does your organization have an Internet and/or e-mail usage policy? [yes, no]

7. Does your organization implement Internet and/or e-mail monitoring software?
   [yes, no]

8. Please indicate how likely you would be to access the following types of Web pages for work-related versus non-work-related activities while at work.

Work-related Web sites:

	Very unlikely	Some-what unlikely	Neither likely nor unlikely	Some-what likely	Very likely
• Competitor's Web site for work activities	—	—	—	—	—
• Supplier's Web site for work activities	—	—	—	—	—
• Customer's Web site for work activities	—	—	—	—	—

Non-work-related Web sites:

	Very unlikely	Some-what unlikely	Neither likely nor unlikely	Some-what likely	Very likely
• Arts and entertainment Web sites for nonwork activities	—	—	—	—	—
• Travel and leisure Web sites for nonwork activities	—	—	—	—	—
• Living and consumer Web sites for nonwork activities	—	—	—	—	—
• Sports and news Web sites for nonwork activities	—	—	—	—	—

9. Please indicate your opinion about using the Internet and e-mail at work.

	Strongly disagree	Disagree	Neutral	Agree	Strongly agree
• My coworkers or colleagues who influence my behavior would think that I should use the Internet and/or e-mail for work-related tasks only.	—	—	—	—	—
• People who are important to me would think that I should use the Internet and/or e-mail for work-related tasks only.	—	—	—	—	—
• Using the Internet and/or e-mail is entirely within my control.	—	—	—	—	—
• The Internet usage policy or Internet monitoring and filtering software does not restrict my usage of the Internet and/or e-mail.	—	—	—	—	—

REFERENCES

Adler, N.J., and Bartholomew, S. 1992. Managing globally competent people. *Academy of Management Executive* 6, 3, 52–65.

Anandarajan, J. 2002. Internet abuse in the workplace. *Communications of the ACM* 45, 1, 53–54.

Anandarajan, J., and Simmers, C. 2002. Factors influencing Web access behavior in the workplace. In M. Anandarajan and C. Simmers (ed.), *Managing Web Usage in the Workplace: A Social, Ethical and Legal Perspective.* Hershey, PA: Ideal Group Publishing, 44–66.

Anandarajan, M., Simmers, C., and Igbaria, M. 2000. An exploratory investigation of the antecedents and impact of Internet usage: An individual perspective. *Behavior and Information Technology* 19, 1, 69–85.

Belanger, F., and Slyke, C.V. 2002. Abuse or learning? *Association for Computing Machinery: Communications of the ACM* 45, 1, 64.

Case, C.J., and Young, K.S. 2002. Employee Internet management: Current business practices and outcomes. *CyberPsychology and Behavior* 5, 4, 355–361.

Couger, J. 1986. Effect of cultural differences on motivation of analysts and programmers: Singapore vs. the United States. *MIS Quarterly* 10, 2, 189–196.

Davis, R.A. 2001. A cognitive-behavioral model of pathological Internet use. *Computers in Human Behavior* 17, 2, 187–195.

Davis, R.A., Flett, G.L., and Besser, A. 2002. Validation of a new scale for measuring problematic Internet use: Implications for pre-employment screening. *CyberPsychology and Behavior* 5, 4, 331–345.

Dirksen, V. 2001. The cultural construction of information technology. *Journal of Global Information Management* 9, 1, 5–10.

Edberg, D., Grupe, F., and Kuechler, W. 2001. Practical issues in global IT management: Many problems, a few solutions. *Information Systems Management* 18, 1, 34–46.

Gannon, M.J. 1994. *Understanding Global Cultures: Metaphorical Journey Through 17 Countries.* Thousand Oaks, CA: Sage.

Greenfield, D., and Davis, R.A. 2002. Lost in Cyberspace: The Web @ Work. *CyberPsychology and Behavior* 5, 4, 347–353.

Harris, R., and Davison, R. 1999. Anxiety and involvement: Cultural dimensions of attitudes toward computers in developing societies. *Journal of Global Information Management* 7, 1, 26–38.

Hasan, H., and Ditsa, G. 1999. The impact of culture on the adoption of IT: An interpretive study. *Journal of Global Information Management* 7, 1, 5–15.

Hill, C., Loch, K., and El Sheshai, K. 1998. A qualitative assessment of Arab culture and information technology transfer. *Journal of Global Information Management* 6, 3, 29–38.

Hofstede, G. 1980. *Culture's Consequences: International Differences in Work-related Values.* Beverly Hills, CA: Sage.

———. 1984. *Culture's Consequences: International Differences in Work-related Values.* 2nd ed. Beverly Hills, CA: Sage.

———. 1991. *Cultures and Organizations: Software of the Mind: Intercultural Cooperation and Its Importance for Survival.* New York: McGraw-Hill.

———. 1997. *Cultures and Organizations: Software of the Mind.* New York: McGraw Hill.

Hofstede, G., and Bond, M. 1988. The Confucius connection: From cultural roots to economic growth. *Organizational Dynamics* 16, 4, 4–21.

Hollinger, R.C., and Clark, J.P. 1982. Formal and informal social controls of employee deviance. *Sociological Quarterly* 23, 3, 333–343.

Kandelin, N., Lin, T., and Muntoro, R. 1998. A study of the attitudes of Indonesian managers toward key factors in information system development and implementation. *Journal of Global Information Management* 6, 3, 17–28.

Lim, V.K.G. 2002. The IT way of loafing on the job: Cyberloafing, neutralizing and organizational justice. *Journal of Organizational Behavior* 23, 5, 574–694.

Luna, D., Peracchio, L., and de Juan, M. 2002. Cross-cultural and cognitive aspects of Web site navigation. *Academy of Marketing Science* 30, 4, 397–411.

Martinsons, M., and Westwood, R. 1997. Management information systems in the Chinese business culture: An explanatory theory. *Information and Management* 32, 5, 215–228.

McLeod, R., Kim, C., Saunders, C., Jones, J., Scheel, C., and Estrada, M. 1997. Information management as perceived by CIOs in three Pacific Rim countries. *Journal of Global Information Management* 5, 3, 5–16.

Oravec, J.A. 2002. Constructive approaches to Internet recreation in the workplace. *Communications of the ACM* 45, 1, 60–63.

Rokeach, M. 1973. *Beliefs, Attitudes and Values: A Theory of Organization and Change.* San Francisco: Jossey-Bass.

Rose, G., and Straub, D. 1998. Predicting general IT use: Applying TAM to the Arabic world. *Journal of Global Information Management* 6, 3, 39–46.

Schwartz, S.H. 1992. Universals in the content and structure of values: Theoretical advances and empirical tests in 20 countries. In M.P. Zann (ed.), *Advances in Experimental Social Psychology.* San Diego: Academic Press.

Schwartz, S.H. 1994. Beyond individualism/collectivism. New cultural dimensions of values. In C. Kagitcibasi, C. Triandis, U.H. Kim, S.-C. Choi, and G. Yoon (eds.), *Individualism and Collectivism: Theory, Method, and Applications.* Thousand Oaks, CA: Sage, 85–119.

Simmers, C., and Anandarajan, M. 2004. Convergence or divergence? Web usage in the workplace in Nigeria, Malaysia, and the United States. In C. Simmers and M. Anandarajan (eds.), *Personal Web Usage in the Workplace: A Guide to Effective Human Resources Management.* Hershey, CA: Idea Group, 158–185.

Straub, D. 1994. The effect of culture on IT diffusion: E-mail and FAX in Japan and the U.S. *Information Systems Research* 5, 1, 23–47.

Straub, D., Loch, K., and Hill, C. 2001. Transfer of information technology to the Arab world: A test of cultural influence modeling. *Journal of Global Information Management* 9, 4, 6–28.

Taylor, S., and Todd, P.A. 1995. Understanding information technology usage: A test of competing models. *Information Systems Research* 6, 2, 144–176.

Tian, R., and Emery, C. 2002. Cross-cultural issues in Internet marketing. *Journal of American Academy of Business* 1, 2, 217–225.

EDITORS AND CONTRIBUTORS

Murugan Anandarajan is an associate professor and a distinguished research fellow in the Department of Management at Drexel University. His current research interests include Internet usage and artificial intelligence-based classification. His research has appeared in journals such as *Communications of the ACM, Computers and Operations Research, Decision Sciences, Information and Management, Journal of Management Information Systems, Journal of International Business Studies,* and *Omega-International Journal of Management Science.* He has coedited two books on personal Web usage.

Michael B. Arthur is a professor of management at the Sawyer School of Management, Suffolk University in Boston. He is editor of several works on contemporary career issues, including *The Boundaryless Career* (1996), *Career Frontiers* (2000), and *Career Creativity* (2002). He is also coauthor of *The New Careers* (1999). His recent research emphasizes the links between contemporary careers and the emerging knowledge economy.

Elisabeth E. Bennett is a PhD candidate in adult education/human resources and organizational development at the University of Georgia. Her professional background includes work in corporate financial services, manufacturing, and continuing education. Her interest in intranets began when she managed an intranet for a year. Other research interests include organizational change, organizational culture and knowledge management, technology, and adult creativity.

Constant D. Beugré is an associate professor of management at Delaware State University, School of Management, where he teaches courses in organizational behavior, human resources management at the undergraduate level, and organizational leadership at the graduate level. Prior to joining Delaware State University, he was an assistant professor of management and information systems at Kent State University, Tuscarawas Campus, and was a visiting fellow at Harvard University in 1996. He earned his PhD in management from Rensselaer Polytechnic Institute, Lally School of Management and Technology. His research interests include organizational justice and the organizational impact of information technology. Dr. Beugré has published two books and more than thirty articles.

Scott E. Caplan received his PhD from Purdue University and is an assistant professor of interpersonal communication in the Department of Communication at the University of Delaware. His research focuses on problematic Internet use and other computer-mediated interpersonal communication phenomena. His research on problematic Internet use has been published in *Computers and Human Behavior* and *Communication Research.*

Abraham Carmeli received his PhD from the University of Haifa. He was a visiting assistant professor in the Department of Management at LeBow College of Business at Drexel University and a visiting researcher in the Department of Industrial Economics and Strategy at Copenhagen Business School. He is now a faculty member in the Graduate School of Business Administration and the Department of Political Science (joint appointment) at Bar-Ilan University in Israel. His current research interests include complementarities of intangible resources, managerial skills, top management teams, organizational prestige and image, and individual behaviors at work. His research has appeared in such journals as *Managerial and Decision Economics, Organization Studies, Public Administration,* and *Strategic Management Journal.*

Matthew S. Eastin is an assistant professor in the School of Communication at Ohio State University. He received his PhD in mass media from Michigan State University. His research interests focus on the social and psychological mechanisms that influence the uses and effects of the Internet. Recently he has started to explore how users process peripheral information in online environments, the creation of cognitive scripts through virtual environments, and the relationships among consumer attitudes, self-efficacy, and e-service adoption. His research has appeared in *Media Psychology, Journal of Broadcasting and Electronic Media, Computers in Human Behavior, Social Science Computer Review, Telematics and Informatics,* and *Journal of Computer-Mediated Communication.*

Carroll J. Glynn is professor and director of the School of Communication at Ohio State University. She received her PhD in mass communication from the University of Wisconsin–Madison. Prior to her position at Ohio State, Dr. Glynn was a professor and chair of the Department of Communication at Cornell University, where she taught and conducted research for fourteen years. Her research interests focus on the understanding of public opinion formation and process and the relationship of public opinion to social norms. Dr. Glynn is senior author of *Public Opinion* (now in its second edition), and her works also have appeared in a number of journals, including *Public Opinion Quarterly, Communication Research, Social Science Research,* and *International Journal of Public Opinion Research and Communication Yearbook.*

Veronica M. Godshalk is an associate professor in the Department of Management and Organization at Pennsylvania State University, Great Valley School of Graduate Professional Studies. She earned a PhD from Drexel University in organizational behavior and strategic management, and an MS from the University of Pennsylvania. Her research interests include issues surrounding career management, mentoring, stress, and the intersection of work and nonwork domains. She has published articles in *Journal of Vocational Behavior, Journal of Organizational Behavior, Group and Organization Management,* and *Journal of Management Systems.* In 2000, she published a book, *Career Management,* with coauthors Jeff Greenhaus and Gerry Callanan.

Robert P. Griffiths is a graduate research assistant in the PhD program at Ohio State University. He received his MA in communication from Ohio State University. His research investigates organizational group processes and team norming effects through the utilization of new workplace technologies (e.g., e-mail and instant messaging). Additionally, he is currently investigating transactive memory systems in an organizational team setting.

Gudela Grote is professor of organizational psychology at the Institute for Work Psychology at the Swiss Federal Institute of Technology, Zürich. She earned her doctorate at the Georgia Institute of Technology. Her key core research interests include the interrelation of personality development and occupation; the effects of new technologies on work; complementary task distribution between humans and technology and their implementation in automated production processes; and sociotechnological safety management in high-risk work systems.

Svetlana N. Khapova is a PhD candidate at the School of Business, Public Administration and Technology, University of Twente, the Netherlands. She holds an MBA degree from the University of Portsmouth, United Kingdom, and an MSc (cum laude) in economics and management from North Caucasus State Technical University, the Russian Federation. Her research interests include careers, professional attitudes and behaviors, and effective e-service delivery for career development.

Vivien K.G. Lim is an associate professor in the Department of Management and Organization, National University of Singapore Business School. Her research interests include use and misuse of technology, job insecurity and job loss, workplace deviance and discipline, money ethic, and workplace health issues. She has published more than fifty journal and conference papers. Her works have appeared in internationally refereed journals such as *Communications of the ACM, Human Relations, Journal of Organizational Behavior, Journal of Vocational Behavior, Omega, Journal of Economic Psychology, Personality and Individual Differences,* and *Journal of Behavioral Medicine.* Her research has also been featured in *The Straits Times, Business Times,* and practitioner-oriented outlets such as *Human Resource Review.*

Pruthikrai Mahatanankoon is an assistant professor of information systems at the School of Information Technology at Illinois State University. He holds a BS in computer engineering from King Mongkut's University of Technology, Thonburi, Thailand, an MS in management information systems, and an MS in computer science from Fairleigh Dickinson University, New Jersey. He received a PhD in management information systems from Claremont Graduate University, California. His current research interests focus upon Internet technology abuse in the workplace, mobile commerce, and virtual communities.

Sylvia Manchen-Spörri is a lecturer in organizational psychology at the University of St. Gallen and at the University of Applied Sciences in Lucerne, Switzerland. She earned her doctorate at the University of Konstanz, Germany. Her core research interests include leadership, leadership and gender differences, and the use of new communication technologies in the workplace.

James G. Phillips is a senior lecturer in the Psychology Department of Monash University. He has a BS (Hons) from Adelaide University, Australia, and a PhD from Flinders University, Australia. He has over 100 publications in a variety of areas, the linking theme being human performance and decision making. Apart from studying the psychology of Internet use, he has published papers addressing mobile phone use, gambling behavior, and also basal ganglia disorders.

Christel G. Rutte is professor of organizational psychology at Eindhoven University of Technology, the Netherlands. She is chair of the subdepartment of Human Performance Management. She received her PhD in social psychology at the University of Groningen, the Netherlands. The topic of her dissertation was cooperation in social dilemma situations. Throughout her career, she has continued to study cooperation and competition in teams. Currently her main research interests are team performance management and time management.

Manuel J. Sánchez-Franco, PhD, has been professor of marketing and communication at Seville University (Spain) since 1996. His research efforts focus on Internet marketing strategy and on psychological processes and advertising effects. He has published widely in marketing and management journals. Currently, Professor Sánchez-Franco's research interests include the design and interpretation of models to explain behaviors in online environments. He has designed and run experiments to measure factors that reduce time pressure as a cost for Web users. Specifically, Professor Sánchez-Franco evaluates the mediating role of main intrinsic and extrinsic motives explaining users' Web acceptance and usage.

Claire A. Simmers, PhD, is an associate professor in the Management Department in the Erivan K. Haub School of Business at Saint Joseph's University, Philadelphia. Her research interests are in political and behavioral influences in strategic decision making, work/life issues, and the sociotechnical interface in the digital workplace, focusing on the Internet. Her work has been published in *Behaviour and Information Technology, Journal of Business and Economics Studies, Communications of the ACM, Journal of*

Information Technology, Theory and Application, and *Journal of Organizational Behavior.* She coedited two books with Murugan Anandarajan, *Managing Web Usage in the Workplace: A Social, Ethical and Legal Perspective* and *Personal Web Usage in the Workplace: A Guide to Effective Human Resources Management.*

Lille Springall is a research fellow at the Institute for Work Psychology at the Federal Institute of Technology, Zürich. She earned her doctorate in organizational behavior and theory at Carnegie Mellon University, Pittsburgh, Pennsylvania. In addition to being a work psychologist, she is also a certified professional coach. Her core research interests include leadership, new organizational forms, coaching, interorganizational social networks, and mental models.

Jörgen S. Svensson is an assistant professor in sociology and informatization at the School of Business, Public Administration and Technology, University of Twente, the Netherlands. His work focuses on the use of information and communication technology in the public sector and on new forms of governance in the information age.

Thompson S.H. Teo is information systems area coordinator and associate professor in the Department of Decision Sciences at the National University of Singapore Business School. His research interests include the strategic uses of IT, e-commerce, adoption and diffusion of IT, and strategic IT management and planning. He has published more than eighty papers in international refereed journals such as *Communications of the ACM, Database, Decision Sciences, Decision Support Systems, European Information and Management, International Journal of Electronic Commerce, Journal of Information Systems,* and *Journal of Management Information Systems.* He is also on the editorial board of several information systems journals.

H. Joseph Wen is an associate professor of management information systems and chair of the Department of Accounting and Management Information Systems at Donald L. Harrison College of Business at Southeast Missouri State University. He holds a PhD from Virginia Commonwealth University. He has published over ninety-five articles in academic refereed journals, book chapters, encyclopedias, and national conference proceedings. He has received over $6 million in research grants from various state and federal funding sources. His areas of expertise are Internet research, electronic commerce, transportation information systems, and software development.

Celeste P.M. Wilderom is professor of management and organizational behavior at the School of Business, Public Administration and Technology, University of Twente, the Netherlands. She specializes in leadership, organizational culture, and service management. Currently she is associate editor of *Academy of Management Executive, British Journal of Management,* and *International Journal of Service Industry Management.*

Kimberly S. Young is the executive director of the Center for Online Addiction and associate professor of management science at the School of Business at St. Bonaventure University, New York. An internationally known researcher, author, and speaker on the impact of technology on human behavior, she serves on the editorial boards of *CyberPsychology* and *Behavior and Internet Health.* She has authored numerous articles and two books on Internet addiction, *Caught in the Net* and *Tangled in the Web,* and was the keynote speaker at the first International Congress on Internet Addiction held in Zurich. Her work has been featured in the *Wall Street Journal,* the *New York Times, Newsweek,* and *Time,* and she has appeared on NPR, CNN, CNBC News, Fox News, and ABC's World News Tonight regarding her research.

SERIES EDITOR

Vladimir Zwass is Distinguished Professor of Computer Science and Management Information Systems at Fairleigh Dickinson University. He holds a PhD in computer science from Columbia University. Dr. Zwass is the founding editor-in-chief of the *Journal of Management Information Systems*; one of the three top-ranked journals in the field of information systems, the journal recently celebrated twenty years of publication. He is also the founding editor-in-chief of the *International Journal of Electronic Commerce,* ranked as the top journal in its field. Dr. Zwass is the author of six books and several book chapters, including entries in the *Encyclopaedia Britannica,* as well as a number of papers in various journals and conference proceedings. He has received several grants, consulted for a number of major corporations, and is a frequent speaker to national and international audiences. He is a former member of the professional staff of the International Atomic Energy Agency in Vienna, Austria.

INDEX